The Arab-Israeli Conflict in the Arab Press

Cover headline from *al-Difāʿ*, November 30, 1947: “The decision to partition made in America but will not be carried out in Palestine. And those who would harm us should know that they will be harmed.”

The Arab-Israeli Conflict in the Arab Press: The First Three Decades

William W. Haddad

intellect Bristol, UK / Chicago, USA

First published in the UK in 2018 by
Intellect, The Mill, Parnall Road, Fishponds, Bristol, BS16 3JG, UK

First published in the USA in 2018 by
Intellect, The University of Chicago Press, 1427 E. 60th Street,
Chicago, IL 60637, USA

A catalogue record for this book is available from the British Library.

Copy-editor: MPS Technologies
Cover designer: Aleksandra Szumlas
Production manager: Matthew Floyd, Mareike Wehner
Typesetting: Contentra Technologies

Print ISBN: 978-1-78320-910-1
ePDF ISBN: 978-1-78320-912-5
ePUB ISBN: 978-1-78320-911-8

Printed and bound by Hobbs, UK

This is a peer-reviewed publication.

This monograph is dedicated with all my love to:
Barbara Baker
Wadi' Baker
Katie Shae
and
Princess Quinn Alice

Contents

Acknowledgments

Investigation for the monograph took me to three continents. In Egypt, I researched at the American University in Cairo (AUC). In Damascus, before the outbreak of its civil war, studies were conducted at the Office Arabe de Presse and de Documentation. Most of the research, however, was done in Lebanon at the American University of Beirut (AUB) and to a much lesser extent at the Institute of Palestine Studies. AUB's collection was the largest in terms of the number of different journals, found in hard copies, microfilm and microfiche, and broadest in terms of years covered. Since I teach in southern California, the newspaper collection at the University of California, Los Angeles was accessible and filled in critical gaps in this study. The research was done in pieces over two decades: one full year in Beirut and Damascus, one sabbatical and three summers.

Like others, I am indebted to colleagues who helped along the way. This monograph could not have been written without the aid of many people who provided critical advice and opened doors. I am particularly indebted to Jibran Bikhazi, Mildred Corsette, Linda Sadaka, J.D. Call, Micheline Salhab, Samir A. Darwich, Raymond G. Peterson, Isabel H. George, Tareq Y. Ismael, Amer Haider, Mary Marki, and the three anonymous readers whose critiques allowed me to improve the final product. Most important was Fouad I. Haddad, the retired budget officer at the American University of Beirut. He spent many, many hours reading and improving this manuscript especially making sure the translations were accurate. Though I was trained as a Middle East historian, his knowledge of Middle East history was unsurpassed. And he was a good friend.

Foreword

The Arab-Israeli Crisis in the Arab Press: An Untapped Resource

Mary Marki[1]

When one considers the importance of the Arab-Israeli crisis in contemporary world politics and the vast amount of academic research dedicated to the topic, the absence of scholarship devoted to Arab print media is surprising. Since the Second World War, undoubtedly, no single issue has occupied the Arab mind as the growth of political Zionism and the foundation of the State of Israel. Further, even though Western media outlets regularly quote the Arab press when covering issues concerning the Palestine question, very little is actually written in European languages regarding the origins, biases, and political beliefs of the press in the Middle East regarding the topic, especially in the period surrounding the establishment of Israel.

Although the Arab-Israeli conflict has been analyzed from almost every imagined vantage point, there does not exist a study dedicated exclusively to what Arab journalists and politicians thought about the conflict as expressed in the daily print media during the decades after the 1947 UN partition resolution. While some articles and journals have explored certain minute aspects of the Arab press, they tend to either examine the trials or tribulations of specific newspapers or present short, issue-oriented studies lacking a more comprehensive approach.

The absence of research addressing the relationship of Arab newspaper opinion to the Arab-Israeli conflict was noted three decades ago by Rashid Khalidi when he surveyed one Beirut newspaper, *al-Mufīd*, over a 3-year period. Addressing this void, he urged other scholars to pay more attention to the Arab press as a basic source of knowledge about the contemporary Arab world.[2] Khalidi argued that the press was an untapped yet necessary part of any attempt to trace a mass-based Arab political movement. He went on to decry most scholarly work on the Middle East for not using the Arab press as a major primary source.

Goals of the Manuscript

This monograph attempts to remedy the general lack of information that exists in the West regarding the Arab press by providing a short history of the Arab print media as well as an in-depth study of translated Arab media sources. The manuscript has two different goals. The first is contained in Chapter 1, which begins with a brief historical narrative of Arab newspapers from the 1940s to the mid-1970s, when a free press virtually disappeared. Following this short history of the Arab press during the first three decades of the Arab-Israeli conflict, Haddad explores the historiography of the Arab print media, compiling a valuable collection of available scholarship on the subject. Since censorship was, and is, an ongoing problem in Middle East journalism, Chapter 1 concludes with an introduction to the problem of censorship that began during the Ottoman period, almost simultaneously with the first printed journals.

With this historical background, the reader moves to the second goal, which encompasses the rest of the manuscript beginning with Chapter 2, examining the Arab print media's view of the Arab-Israeli conflict in its first three decades. By giving voice to the Arab political journalists who wrote editorials and opinion pieces, the bulk of the book explores the variety of opinions held in the Arab print media regarding the Arab-Israeli conflict.

Because many of these sources have been unavailable to scholars due to the barriers of language and lack of accessibility, this monograph is an important addition to our knowledge of the Arab-Israeli conflict's early years. Though technically not a primary source, this volume will provide translations of those who had a first-hand view; from the Arab perspective. In providing both a general history of the Arab press and a compiled study of translated sources in one manuscript, this volume helps to bridge the information gap that exists in the West, generally, concerning the Arab press and offers significant new sources for future scholars who examine the first three decades of the Arab-Israeli conflict.

Methodology

In order to explore editorial opinion on the Palestine question, approximately 60 newspapers from five Arab countries were read throughout a 29-year span. The study of editorial opinion is confined to what has historically been called the major Arab confrontation states: Egypt, Syria, Jordan (or Transjordan), Lebanon, and Palestine. The latter was absorbed into the Jordanian press after Israel's occupation of the West Bank in 1967. Each of these countries played a central political and military role in the Arab world in the conflict with Zionism and Israel. They also have borders contiguous with Israel, or in the case of Palestine, claim the land that Israel now holds. Further, these countries have, with the exception of Iraq, the most advanced Arab press. In attempting to interweave a history of the press and the history of Arab press' opinion on the Arab-Israeli conflict, it seems these three factors – leadership, proximity, and an advanced press – were valid reasons for excluding the press of other Arab countries.

Limitations

The sources employed in this monograph have certain limitations. First, certain countries are more robustly represented. For example, more Lebanese, Syrian, and Egyptian newspapers have been read than Jordanian and Palestinian journals. This was not done to bias the study but instead reflects the large number of papers published in Beirut, Damascus, and Cairo and their dearth in Jordan and Palestine.[3]

The reader may note sporadic gaps in the research concerning editorial excerpts regarding the Palestine question. While Haddad's study includes newspapers from Damascus, Beirut, and Cairo, such as *al-Ahrām*, *al-Difā'*, *Filasṭīn*, *al-Nahār*, and *al-Hayāt*, intermittent issues are absent because they were unavailable, no longer extant, or were subjected to forced breaks in a publishing cycle. Copies of several papers used in the study did not appear for a month in one year or a week in another because they were suspended for violating government regulations. In some cases, almost exclusively in Syria, it was common for newspapers to appear and disappear with surprising rapidity due to political circumstances. Other newspapers were forced to merge only to reappear independently at a later date. Therefore, many of the newspapers were simply not issued on a consistent basis, resulting in the gaps in research reflected in this study.

Finally, in dealing with the Arab-Israeli conflict, this book is concerned with opinion. Haddad examines only editorials, or news articles containing editorial opinion. The selection of editorials reflects his reading of a particular point of view on a given topic. This selective process involves the author employing subjective judgment, an unavoidable limitation when attempting to research and capture the mood of the press. In addition, his study does not present nor intends to be a definitive study of Arab opinion toward Palestine and Israel. Instead, only one segment of opinion, albeit important, was studied. Although it was not the purpose of this study, a sampling of political leaders or people in all walks of life may have reflected general opinion toward the Arab-Israeli conflict differently.

Final Comment

This study of Arab print media offers a unique look into Arab opinion concerning the Arab-Israeli conflict. Haddad's sources illustrate how the first three decades after the Second World War saw a variety of perspectives expressed in Arab print media concerning the question of Palestine. It is interesting to note that early reaction of Arab editorials was not one of ubiquitous hatred toward Israel but included expressions of anti-Palestinian opinion. Thus, this study demonstrates how regional and religious factors shaped different views on the conflict and reflects the diversity and complexity of the Arab world.

Overall, this study presents a much needed look into the opinions of the Arab press concerning the Arab-Israeli conflict, and provides the field with a new and valuable source to draw upon in future research.

Notes

1 Mary Marki is a professor of world history at Long Beach City College, California.

2 Rashid I. Khalidi. "The Press as a Source for Modern Arab Political History: 'Abd al-Ghani al-'Uraisi and *al-Mufid*," *Arab Studies Quarterly* 3, no. 1 (Winter 1981): 22–42.

3 For a comparison of the number of newspapers published in the five countries during the period under study see John C. Merrill, *The Foreign Press* (Baton Rouge, Louisiana State University Press 1970), 169–70.

Chapter 1

Introduction to the Manuscript

Notes on Transliteration and Translation

In the transliteration of Arabic into Latin script, I use the US Library of Congress system. This includes the ‘ to represent the Arabic ayn and the ’ to represent the hamza. I have used the Syrian J instead of the Egyptian G.

Arabic places that have a commonly accepted, enduring, and familiar spelling in English are used. Thus, Palestine instead of *Filasṭīn*, Cairo in place of *al-Qāhirah*, Beirut not *Bayrūt*, and so forth. Arab editorialists who wrote for the French or English-language press, largely in Beirut, have their own method of transliterating their names, I have retained their spellings.

One other important characterization of the transliteration system has been the rejection of Western renderings of leaders' names. This has led me to spell, for example, Nasser as 'Abd al-Nāṣir and Abdullah as 'Abd Allāh.

I have attempted to be as accurate as possible in my translations. However, sometimes direct translations from Arabic to English are difficult; for example the second line of the headline on the cover. Therefore I have in some instances translated liberally with the purpose of conveying the meaning if not the exact wording.

The Focus

This manuscript focuses on the Arab-Israeli conflict as seen through opinion pieces and editorials in the Arab print media between 1947 and 1978. It is rare for the defeated in a war to tell their story; this is an attempt to allow the voices of Arab writers to be heard so that we may grasp the perspective of the Arab side in the struggle for Palestine.

The time period was chosen purposefully, from the time of the adoption of the United Nations Partition Resolution until the end of a free press in the countries under examination. As explained in the forward, the papers examined come exclusively from Egypt, Jordan (or Transjordan), Lebanon, Syria, and Palestine.

It is important to emphasize that this study is limited because only one segment of Arab opinion, albeit important, was studied. A further limitation is the issue of literacy: absent subscription and circulation data we cannot be sure how widely disseminated the opinion pieces examined in this study extended. We know that literacy was very low in the Arab states in this study for at least two decades after the Second World War. Nonetheless, I believe the views expressed within newspapers reached the illiterate through oral transmission and informal networks. For example, in my ancestral village of Khirbah Qanafār as well as many other towns, there were literate men who read the newspapers to their communities. More importantly, the newspapers in this study were ordinarily published by political parties, governments, branches of the military and patrons in support of one tendency or another. A reader of a newspaper, for example, *al-'Amal* in Lebanon, which was the spokesman of the Phalangist Party, would receive the party line and presumably act on this knowledge to disseminate the party's platform. Thus, even though circulation might be small, there was a multiplier effect on public opinion.

Approximately 60 newspapers were examined over three decades. I started reading a newspaper beginning in 1947, and thereafter perused every available issue through the 1978 conclusion of the study. I view this monograph as an historical record of the Arab-Israeli conflict as seen by the losing side. Such an account has not previously been available to non-Arabic speakers.

The Historical Context

Just as the end of the Second World War saw the rising Zionist crescendo that would result in the United Nations Partition Plan for Palestine, Resolution 181 of November 1947 and the subsequent establishment of the State of Israel, so too did it mark the nominal end of the British and French occupation of the Levant. The newly independent states also saw the rise of an independent press. This golden period lasted for slightly more than a decade, until 1958, when the press passed from a relatively free era into a time when it was less independent. This was the year of the unification of Egypt and Syria into the United Arab Republic (UAR), initiating a process that would lead to state control of the press in those two countries. One of the first acts of the president of the UAR, Jamāl 'Abd al-Nāṣir, was to ban all political parties in the Syrian province. As a result, the Syrian press lost much of its income from political subsidies. The Syrian press was also subject to competition from Egyptian papers that were flown to Damascus and sold at a cheaper rate. In this manner, many Syrian newspapers declined precipitously. I calculate that of nineteen Damascene dailies in print prior to unification, only four survived. Moreover, the editorial opinion found in those papers that survived was quite sterile. The demise of the Syrian press was formalized in December 1958 with a presidential order banning a large number of Syrian papers. 1958 was also the year of the first Lebanese civil war, during which the Lebanese press was much less interested in Palestine and Israel than with domestic concerns. The Lebanese government was also less inclined to allow its press to operate freely. Thus, 1958 marks the disappearance in Lebanon, even for a short period, of a free press. In Jordan, the political events of 1957 and 1958 destroyed the free press. Beginning as early as the abortive pro-Egyptian Abū Nuwwār coup in April 1957, the Hashimite Kingdom found itself tempted to stifle dissent in whatever form. The subsequent Egyptian campaign to prevent Jordan's joining Iraq and the West, culminating in the landing of British troops in Jordan three days after the July 14 Iraqi coup and the overthrow of the Hashimite monarchy, provided further inducement to muzzle the press. Between 1958 and 1978, freedom of the press in Jordan all but disappeared and editorials in that country reflected a sad sameness.

What was occurring in Syria and to a lesser extent in Lebanon and Jordan was being re-enacted on the Egyptian stage. The revolution of 1952 had promised freedom to that country's press. However, the tradition of party subsidies to newspapers was incompatible with the Egyptian Revolutionary Command Council's (RCC) goal of banning political parties. The steps leading to the demise of the press were similar to those seen in Syria. The government abolished all political parties; the Egyptian press gradually became impoverished and in its death pangs, struck out against the RCC. The regime responded with more controls and eventually nationalized the press.

Thus, for all practical purposes, a free press disappeared in a large part of the Arab World in 1958 or shortly thereafter. This study continues to the late 1970s although editorial opinion generally became more homogeneous within a country as papers reflected the opinions held by their governments. Nonetheless, the journals are worth studying because their editorials reflected national differences. An excellent example of a national agenda and its importance to the Arab discourse is the decade-and-a-half after 1958, which was dominated by Muḥammad Ḥasanayn Haykal. He was the unofficial spokesman of the Egyptian government, even serving as a cabinet member. Under his leadership *Al-Ahrām* (the Pyramids) became the premier Arabic-language publication, and the outspoken proponent of 'Abd al-Nāṣir's Pan-Arabism.

A second phenomenon after 1958 was the gradual emergence of Beirut as the information capital of the Arab world. This was made possible in part due to the results of the suppression of the Arab press elsewhere. Among the city's more notable components were the publications of the Palestinian resistance movement. The Palestinians gained the right to uncensored publication in Lebanon in the 1969 Cairo Agreement. Many Lebanese felt this was an appropriate way to support the anti-Zionist resistance, and because the country prided itself on its free press. In the 1970s, several Arab states purchased newspapers there. Although the civil war, which began in 1975, saw the end of a number of publications, clandestine papers – representing myriad factions – multiplied so that at the height of the war more than 100 publications were in circulation. In October 1976, the Arab League agreed to establish a predominantly Syrian Arab Deterrent Force that was charged with restoring calm. With the Syrian-led occupation, over half a dozen anti-Damascus journals were closed, but Lebanon still had the freest press in the Arab World.[1]

With the exception of Lebanon, a free press ceased to exist in the other confrontation states after 1958. Newspapers were now owned by governments, the military or political parties in one-party nations. It became a truism that there was no censorship in the Arab press, as none was necessary since journalists self-censored or risked losing their jobs and even their lives if they did not adhere to the official line.

Historiography: An Overview of the Research Involving the Evolution of the Arab Press

This historiography is intended to compile what academic scholarship is available concerning the topic of the Arab print media and its relationship to the Arab-Israeli crisis. Considering that the history of the Arab press is a relatively unmined topic in Western research, one must first turn to Arabic sources. We should pay tribute to several books in Arabic from which we have drawn heavily in reconstructing the early history of the Arab press. Especially notable have been Fīlīb dī Ṭarrāzī, *Tārīkh al-Ṣiḥāfah al-'Arabīyah* (History of the Arabic Press) (Beirut, 1913); Adīb Murūwah, *al-Ṣiḥāfah al-'Arabīyah* (the Arabic Press) (Beirut, 1961); Aḥmad K. al-'Aqqād, *al-Ṣiḥāfah al-'Arabīyah fī Filasṭīn* (The Arabic Press in Palestine) (Damascus, 1966); and Yūsuf Q. Khūrī, *al-Ṣiḥāfah al-'Arabīyah fī Filasṭīn: 1876–1948* (The Arabic Press in Palestine: 1876–1948) (Beirut, 1976).

The first and most comprehensive source on the history and evolution of the Arab press has been Ṭarrāzī's *Tārīkh*, a four-volume tome published *in seriatim* between 1913 and 1933 with a second printing in 1948. Scholars generally have looked to Ṭarrāzī's work to learn of the origins of the press in the Middle East, but it does not cover the last hundred years in the evolution of the press, nor does it cover the politics of the era.

More recently, Ami Ayalon, *emeritus professor* at Tel Aviv University and former head of Shin Bet, has published three important books on the print media. *The Press in the Arab Middle East: A History* covers the Middle East from the mid-nineteenth century to the Second World War. He focuses on Egypt and Lebanon, arguing that this is where the press began and spread to the rest of the Arab world. Further limiting the work, it is confined to periodicals dealing with "political reportage." Moreover, the author generally excludes Arab newspapers published in French and English because they were "read by a small sector of society whose needs and outlook were generally different from [...] the Arabic [language] press."[2] Nonetheless, it is an important scholarly addition to our knowledge of the origins of the Arab press and is particularly strong in covering the first half of the twentieth century. In *The Arabic Print Revolution*, Ayalon persuasively shows how at the end of the nineteenth and into the early twentieth century there occurred spectacular changes in Arab society characterized by the appearance of printing presses, publishing houses, a periodical press, and increased literacy. Immortalized by George Antonius as the Arab Awakening, Ayalon takes us on a fascinating trip in cultural transformation. The third monograph, *Reading Palestine: Printing and Literacy, 1900–1948*, further explores the movement of the Palestinians from an oral society into a literate one. The often overlooked side products of this shift were the growth of an education system, libraries, and reading clubs.

Adnan Musallam at Bethlehem University advances our understanding of the establishment of the Palestinian press during the Ottoman period with his excellent article, "Arab press, society and politics at the end of the Ottoman Era."[3] His article illuminates the activities of mostly Christian Arabs and their European Catholic and Orthodox co-religionists in printing activities in the nineteenth century. Musallam continues his narrative about the Palestinian press in "Turbulent times in the life of the Palestinian Arab press: The British Era, 1917–1948."[4]

A welcome addition to our understanding of the Arab press comes from Ghada Talhami's *Palestine in the Egyptian Press* (New York: Lexington Books, 2007). She draws heavily from Egyptian authors who have studied their national press and its relationship to the conflict with Zionism and later Israel. Talhami's monograph is especially useful in relating how Egyptian intellectuals viewed the evolution of their press. As a result of her research, she strongly denounces the notion of the subservience of the Egyptian press to the interests of the state; arguing that competition with the state in the defining of a national discourse more accurately describes the Egyptian press. Talhami argues forcefully that the Western interpretation of freedom of the press and its critique of Egyptian press freedom are parochial and ethnocentric. She chooses, rather, to listen to Egyptian intellectuals who argue that its press confronted "Egypt's rulers and its public over a period of two centuries"[5] and unlike the West has not been subservient to corporate interests or foreign concerns. While it may be true that Egyptian journalists confronted government control and corporate and foreign intrigue, how successful this was is debatable. The Egyptian government and, especially, political parties exerted considerable influence over the printed word. The most important journalist of the period under examination was the previously mentioned Muḥammad Haykal of *al-Ahrām*. For 17 years as editor-in-chief of *al-Ahrām*, he was deeply embedded in the governments of Jamāl 'Abd al-Naṣīr and Anwar al-Sādāt. He was a member of the ruling political party, Minister of Information to both 'Abd al-Naṣīr and al-Sādāt, and 'Abd al-Naṣīr's ghostwriter for which he was chidingly called "his master's voice."

Despite my disagreement with Talhami on influence, she uses her skills as an historian to write a book that is especially useful in interpreting the early origins of the Egyptian press. Unlike previous works, like Ṭarrāzī, which are chronological narratives, Talhami interprets the impetus for the Egyptian press's evolution. Especially useful is her dealing with the birth of a native press during the reign of the Khedive Ismail Pasha (ruled 1863–79). She depends heavily on Egyptian authors so that her monograph is more about interpreting them as primary sources for the times in which they lived and what they had to say about the Palestine question than it is a reading of the press itself as a primary source. She has a remarkable grasp of Egypt and its history, so that intertwining her narrative of that past with others' writings about the press produces a compelling and exhaustive study of Egypt and the Palestine question.

Talhami's work is important for another reason; she introduces us to Egyptian journalists and intellectuals who wrote about the condition of the press in their nation. Most notable, for those who wish to examine the Egyptian press from an indigenous point of view, are the works of Muḥammad Sa'ad Ibrahīm, *Ḥurriȳah al-Ṣihḥafah* (Freedom of the Press), (Cairo: Dār al-Kutub, 1999) and Awātif 'Abd al-Raḥmān, *Humūm al-Ṣihḥafah wa al-Ṣihḥafiyīn fi Miṣr* (Concerns of the Press and Journalists in Egypt), (Cairo: Dār al-Fikr al-'Arabī, 1995). Another piece of scholarship that adds to our knowledge of the Arab press and the Arab-Israeli conflict is Zeki M. Al-Jabir's 1978 doctoral dissertation at the University of Indiana, which dealt with the journals of Lebanon and Egypt between 1966 and 1973 and focused on how those two countries covered the Arab-Israeli conflict.

William A. Rugh has produced numerous works on the field of communication. His earliest contribution, *Arab Perceptions of American Foreign Policy During the October War* (Washington, 1976), examined editorial opinion in Lebanon, Kuwait, Egypt, Saudi Arabia, Iraq, and Syria. Rugh's study is more a defense of US policy in 1973 (the October War) than a critique of Arab perceptions of that policy. He goes to great lengths to try to prove that the United States was even-handed during the war despite considerable evidence to the contrary. Still, if one keeps in mind that Rugh was an employee of the American government, serving as ambassador to Yemen and the United Arab Emirates, his work provides insight into the US government's perception of the Arab press. His most germane work, *The Arab Press* (Syracuse University Press, 1979 and 1987), is a study of the then current Arab media, discussing how media operates within constraints imposed by different governments. A later work, *Arab Mass Media: Newspaper, Radio and Television in Arab Politics* (Greenwood Publishing, 2004), is an update of *The Arab Press* that continues the analysis of political influences and adds a discussion of off-shore pan-Arab media and expanded coverage of radio and television.

The three monographs cited above often deal with the Arab-Israeli conflict but only to provide examples of the political influences of governments or non-state actors on the media. This present work will provide a more focused perspective of the decades' long struggle in the Middle East. In so doing, the reader may note several points of interest. Today, students of the Middle East know that Arab public opinion on the Arab-Israeli conflict is multi-faceted if not divided. They may believe, however, that before Anwar al-Sādāt's November 1977 trip to Jerusalem, editorial opinion was monolithic. In the face of such an assumption, this study will be illuminating. The Arab press has traditionally expressed diverging opinions on the question of Palestine by region, as well as by newspapers within regions. The press also has shown strong cleavages along religious lines, that is, Christian or Muslim, and was often sharply differentiated within the Christian press. This diversity reflects the Arab World itself. The image of all Arabs disliking Israel is proven equally false.

If interest in the Arab-Israeli conflict has waned with the passage of time, studies of the Middle East media have burgeoned. In the last 25 years, with the growth of television, especially satellite TV, and social media through the internet, there has been an exponential growth in studies on the media and communication. An excellent outlet for media scholars has been *Arab Media and Society*, published by the American University in Cairo Press. First begun in 1998 as the *Journal of Transnational Broadcasting Services*, in 2006 it changed its name. Originally focusing on satellite broadcasting, since 2006 it has broadened its coverage to all aspects of the media as its new name indicates. Since this monograph is limited to the Arab-Israeli conflict, there is no need to go into great detail about scholarship in the last 40 years that does not deal explicitly with the conflict or the period under study. Nonetheless, I should mention Miriam Berger who writes extensively about the media in Palestine and Egypt. Readers may want to look at her "Palestine's occupied Fourth Estate: An inside look at the work lives of Palestinian print journalists."[6] Also of interest is *News Media in the Arab World: A Study of 10 Arab and Muslim Countries* (New York: Bloomsbury Press, 2013) edited by Barrie Gunter and Roger Dickinson. Chapter 5, "News consumption and news agendas in Egypt," written by Hamza Mohammed and Barrie Gunter, is an excellent overview of the founding of the Egyptian press. The authors agree with Tarrāzī and Ayalon that 1798 saw the first appearance of an Egyptian newspaper (though they misspell its name). The article covers Arab media since its inception to the fall of Mubarak. In the same volume, Chapter 4, "The development of the Palestinian news media" written by Zaki Hasan Nuseibeh and Roger Dickinson, provides an important overview of the country's media from the nineteenth century to 2012. The authors' critique of the Palestinian press and media seems overly harsh – they argue that it has never been free – while below I will take the position that the journalistic struggle between the Nashāshībīs and the Ḥusaynīs over the future of Palestine was exceptionally free of British mandatory interference.

Nabil Dajani, a prolific writer on the Lebanese media, advances an important viewpoint in his "The myth of media freedom in Lebanon."[7] In this article, he argues that the media are not free because they have not contributed to national development. Rather the large number of media outlets exists because they are controlled by sects, financial structures, and foreign governments. His arguments are undoubtedly persuasive as Lebanon has too small a population to support so many outlets – as many as 110 in 2013. To my reading, however, this does not establish the media as lacking in freedom, but that the media is not civically responsible – which is a different issue.

Two other volumes need to be mentioned: Noha Mellor's *Modern Arab Journalism* (Edinburgh University Press, 2007) and Jabbar Al-Obeidi's *Censorship in the Middle East* (Lewiston, NY: Edwin Mellon Press, 2007). The former is a sociological study of Arab media and seeks answers to questions such as: How is Arab journalism different/similar to journalism in other countries? What defines the tasks of journalists? Who has access to this field? How is power distributed inside the field of Arab journalism? The latter work attempts to answer questions of Middle East censorship and how it is implemented by Middle Eastern states. An uneven work, it is still important for anyone interested in how censorship works and for Al-Obeidi's assertion that it cannot continue in the face of emergent unfettered social media.

* * * *

Ṭarrāzī, Ayalon, Gunter, and Dickinson all agree that the first periodical to appear in an Arabic-speaking country – *Le Courrier d'Egypte* – was published in French by Napoleon Bonaparte's occupation regime in August 1798. *Le Courrier* was not a newspaper as we may understand it today, but rather a government-sponsored publication that contained official announcements. We might call it a government bulletin or gazette, and this form of periodical remained the norm for decades following as there were no privately owned newspapers in the Arab world until the middle of the nineteenth century. How Napoleon controlled the press is sometimes blamed for the lack of press freedom in the Arab nations today. The Chair of the Middle East News Agency has claimed that one of the first things Napoleon did was to issue an order severely limiting what the bulletins could publish while at the same time placing all periodicals under the control of French officers who functioned as censors. This served as the model for future generations of Arab politicians, who saw the press not as a source of information, but as an outlet for governmental propaganda.[8] If *Le Courrier* is recognized as the first newspaper, the answer as to the first published in Arabic remains unclear as no extant copies of any of the claimants are in existence. Ṭarrāzī says it was *al-Ḥawādith al-Yawmīyah* (Daily Events), published in Cairo in 1801, which he calls the "mother of all Arabic newspapers."[9]

While these fitful starts were occurring in Egypt, the Ottoman state was quick to grasp the importance of periodicals, seeking to control their publication in areas under their sovereignty. Anticipating that so powerful a tool would not long remain the exclusive domain of governments, the Ottomans passed the first Press Law in 1857. It established two principles for state control: the licensing of publishers and prior censorship of publications. The law was modified in 1865 to say that a publishing license would only be granted to a male over 30, who would be known as the Responsible Director (*al-mudīr al-mas'ūl*). According to the 1865 law, the Director was liable in all civil or criminal actions brought against the periodical.[10]

Several months after the passage of the 1857 Ottoman Law, Khalīl al-Khūrī founded Syria's first newspaper, *Ḥadīqah al-Akhbār* (the News Garden). Tarrāzī has a comprehensive list of all of the papers founded in geographic Syria, as well as those in Iraq, beginning in January 1858.[11] The press literally exploded in Syria after the Ottoman revolt of 1908 as in the twelve months that followed some 35 papers were founded, with an additional 60 more between 1908 and 1914.[12] Ayalon argues that this was largely led by Lebanese Christians who established large numbers of privately owned journals. In Cairo, both *al-Ahrām*, to this day still the most widely read Egyptian newspaper, and *al-Muqaṭṭam* (Mount Muqattam) were among the earliest private newspapers – both established by Lebanese Christian expatriates. The Egyptian press, however, had flourished even before gaining nominal independence from Great Britain in March 1923. Prior to that date, Ṭarrāzī enumerates 418, while following independence an additional 125 were founded through 1929 as the country was acquiring a monarchy, a constitution, and a parliament.

A 1937 survey identified over 250 Arabic and 65 foreign-language papers in circulation throughout the Middle East.[13] Ayalon believes Lebanese Christians were in the forefront of this new and revolutionary mode of communication due to their tradition of resourcefulness and creativity. Added to this was the presence of Protestant missionaries, who arrived in 1821, increasing the competition between Christian sects as well as the fact that Christian Lebanese had no qualms about borrowing from the West.[14] In this way, a second center of the Arab press emerged in Beirut, establishing the city as a center of media production that would last until the 1990s. One might note that the Lebanese Maronites who entered the publishing business tended to produce periodicals in French. Largely educated at the University of Saint Joseph in Beirut, with religious ties to France, the Maronites were often more comfortable in French than in English or even in Arabic. Two of the more important dailies for the Maronite community were Emile Ede's *L'Orient* established in 1923 and Bishārah al-Khūrī's *Le Jour* founded in 1934.

Outside of Egypt and Lebanon, the period also witnessed a surge of new publications across the whole of geographic Syria. Lacking in population, reader and subscriber demand was scarce – a continuous problem for many Syrian periodicals not subsidized by patron or party. The most popular papers in the 1930s, Ayalon reports, probably sold no more than 3000 copies. Lesser journals probably had runs of perhaps 1000.[15] To respond to the inability to make a profit, owners per force aligned themselves with political parties or foreign interests and governments and received subventions in return for hewing to the subsidizers' political perspectives.

The revival of the privately owned press in the Middle East after the First World War saw the sector on the verge of a new era. Many publications could only afford to appear once or twice a week, but as they struggled to maintain their financial viability, many of these papers began to publish daily by the 1930s. As the Levantine countries emerged from the mandate system following the Second World War, one American writer noted that the press there reminded him of the press after the American Revolution: "numerous, tiny enterprise, highly partisan, political party press." Tom McFadden felt this held great promise because the American experience showed that there might evolve an Arab press of greater substance and higher standards.[16]

The Palestinian press, as an instrument of Palestinian nationalism, did not emerge until well after the First World War. What journals had existed previously were shuttered or at least quieted during the war, with a resurgence following the end of hostilities. In 1919, *Al-Surīyā al-Janūbīyah* (Southern Syria) was the first newspaper to reappear, published in Jaffa. Its name speaks volumes about the political consciousness of the Palestinians of the time. *Al-Surīyā al-Janūbīyah* was followed by *al-Karmil* ((Mount) Carmel) in 1920. *Filasṭīn* (Palestine), which had been founded in 1914, ceased publication during the First World War, resuming publication in Jaffa in 1921. After the *Nakba* and Israeli independence, *Filasṭīn* moved to Jerusalem, which was now under Jordanian control, where it remained even after Israel captured the city and the West Bank in 1967.

The Issue of Censorship

Censorship of the press was pervasive from the establishment of privately owned newspapers across all the localities in this study. Perhaps the best definition of censorship remains that of the *New York Times*, which wrote in an editorial that it is the attempt of a government to conceal what is happening, "The more rigorous the censorship the more justified we are in believing that the Governments responsible are deceiving and defrauding their people."[17]

The discussion of censorship, which as it pertains to modern Arab media began in the early nineteenth century, augurs caution in any assumption that such behavior is unique to the Middle East. We should recall that the English press was censored until the 1860s, while Russians – with the exception of the short interregnum following the dissolution of the Soviet Union – have never known a period in which the state did not possess pre- and post-publication censorship. As noted earlier, the first Ottoman Press law was passed in 1857 and with it came the *maktūbjī*. The first important Official Censor was Khalīl al-Khūrī who took over the Ottoman office of censor in 1880. This institution was the first to formalize the process of censorship. Donald J. Cioeta provides us with an interesting insight into the Ottoman censorship process: Al-Khūrī would receive two proof copies of each newspaper shortly before noon. The *maktūbjī* would read the proofs, deleting and changing words, with one of the corrected proofs then returned to *al-mudīr al-mas'ul*. Corrections and additions were made and a new set of proofs returned to the censor where they were read once again. This process continued until all of the daily's articles had passed inspection.[18]

Though sanctioning censorship at home, European observers of the Middle East could not refrain from criticizing it when conducted by authorities in the Ottoman Empire. Often cited by European observers as evidence of the *maktūbjī*'s absurdness was forbidding the sentence, "O you foolish Galatians" from Paul's third letter to the Galations. The *maktūbjī* removed the sentence because it slandered the people of the Galata district in Istanbul! Still, Cioeta argues that Ottoman censorship was not that harsh, rather identifying it as more foolish and capricious. He asks that the *maktūbjī*'s actions be compared with the populist mob actions against newspapers in the United States and the threat of imprisonment present in today's Russia, "[...] and at its worst it was certainly not the harshest censorship regime in Europe."[19] Censorship during the Ottoman period was inextricably tied to the *maktubji* – what will he pass and what will he cut? What can be slipped past him, and what will he discover? The *maktubjis* who followed al-Khūrī were often not journalists and many knew no Arabic. Thus began a cat-and-mouse game of trying to bypass the *maktubji* or to try and anticipate what topics, word, or phrases he might censor. Ottoman officials often banned words like: king, prince, sultan, and caliph. Once the Pope was denied the title of successor to Peter (*Khalīfah Buṭrus*) because it contained the word caliph. As the First World War approached, words considered subversive were cut, though not uniformly: for example, revolution (*thawrah*), movement (*ḥarikah*), disturbance (*ikhtilāl*), republic (*jumhūrrīyah*), freedom (*ḥurrīyah*), homeland (*waṭan*), union (*ittiḥād*), and Turk.[20]

After the fall of the Ottomans, continued and pervasive censorship remained the norm in the twentieth century under the Republic of Turkey as well as the majority-Arab Ottoman successor states. An excellent example was the French mandates over Syria and Lebanon. The standard, and often used, reason for deleting material was *considerés comme de nature à troubler l'ordre public.*[21] Post-mandate, different means were used to achieve the same goal of protecting the state. Most notable was the Arab governments' establishment of ministries of information. The most notorious examples of this new government arm were in Syria, Libya, Ṣaddām Ḥusayn's Iraq, and the Sudan. As a result of their Soviet-style blind allegiance to those in power, censors were often the butt of jokes. In this context, in which the periodicals reflect the bidding of the government's information machine, Arab journalism has often been characterized as "receive and send-off" reporting. Such media reports focused on who the leader had seen on a given day and who he had seen off since the previous news cycle.

Other disparaging comments about the information bureaucracy included references to them as "ministries of denial and praise" – e.g. deny the news and praise the ruler.[22]

In Baʿthist Iraq, the Ministry of Information required that every typewriter, photocopier, tape recorder, and short wave radio be registered with its offices. In Egypt, following the ascension of Ḥusnī Mubārak in 1981, there was slightly more freedom than under Anwar al-Sādāt. This trend has been reversed with the ascension of al-Sīsī in 2014. Ministerial control of the news was most strenuous in Syria prior to its civil war (2011–). Censorship from Damascus began with the first military coup in 1949 and with each successive coup it became worse. When the Baʿth Party came to power in 1963, disputes stopped being settled in courts – journalists were simply arrested.[23] In order to remove any vestige of freedom of the press, the ruling party established its own journal *al-Baʿth* and the Ministry of Information began publishing *al-Thawrah* (the Revolution). After the 1971 coup, which brought Ḥāfiẓ al-'Asad to power, all remaining independent publications were nationalized and journalists became state employees. In order to make sure that compliance with the dictates of the state were universally followed, a 1973 decree stated that all publications had to be distributed by the Ministry of Information. The message was that journalists could publish what they wished, but that all distribution would be controlled by the state. Thus, since the early 1970s, and continuing into the twenty-first century, traditional journalism has ceased to exist in Syria. As state employees, reporters compete to show who can please the regime the most. Thus, laws in Syria used to control news content are unnecessary – editors and journalists are hired precisely because they are ready to please, often being close friends of the rulers. In return, they are given many perks – housing allowances, for example, with the privilege of buying homes at a fraction of their nominal market cost.[24] One is reminded of the adage that freedom of the press belongs to those who own one.

Taking the issue of censorship to the present, little has changed in the period after that under examination in this study. Since the press serves as an arm of the state, censorship is unnecessary. It is "[...] pointless to talk about censorship of the press, because the press was created by the state. Nothing that offends the system will appear. So censorship is unnecessary."[25] If one violates the unwritten code, a job or a life can disappear. Mona Eltahawy, a weekly columnist for *al-Sharq al-Awṣaṭ* (the Middle East), a Saudi-owned newspaper based in London, was terminated in 2006 for describing the anti-democratic aspects of the Mubārak government.[26] When the Palestinian Authority regained control of the Gaza and parts of the West Bank in the 1990s, this did not usher in an independent press despite previous calls for a democratic Palestine by the PNA, successor to the PLO. Yāsir ʿArafāt's government did not permit criticism of his Presidency, or of his family, while also off limits were any discussion of cronyism, favoritism, or corruption among senior Palestinian officials. In 1996, Māhir al-ʿAlamī, an editor of *al-Quds* (Jerusalem), was abducted by Palestinian security agents in Jericho. He was interrogated because he had the audacity to publish a story of ʿArafāt's Christmas visit to Bethlehem on an inside page.[27] One writer has gone so far as to assert that the Palestinian Ministry of Information is draconian and as a result, Palestinian journalists currently have less freedom in the West Bank and Gaza than they had possessed under Israeli occupation.[28]

One should conclude by noting that the information ministries' job is also to introduce legislation, allegedly to protect the country, but in reality to protect the politicians. The ministries are known for their insipidness and fawning coverage of the various regimes.[29] The ministries also disseminate information, which is then published in all the newspapers in the country, resulting in a stultifying sameness. Only in Lebanon was this pattern different. We have noted that the press was a Western invention successfully imported into Lebanon and even greater Syria by Christian Lebanese. Added to this was the traditionally weak central government and its sectarian society, all of which encouraged a free press to flourish in Beirut during the period covered in this monograph. There were some notable exceptions, for example in 1949 when the *Parti Populaire Syrienne* attempted a coup and its leader was caught and executed, two editors of *L'Orient* were arrested for abusing the government. Ghassān Twaynī, the editor and publisher of *al-Nahār*, was arrested for criticizing the speed with which the government sentenced and executed the rebel.

Perhaps the most important limit on the independence of the press in Lebanon has been pressure from other Arab governments. When the Lebanese press' tradition of freedom was brought together with an influx of refugees and the subsequent rise of Palestinian nationalism after 1948, with the call for a democratic state in all of Palestine (also known as the one-state solution), the result was the emergence of a radical press calling for the spread of democracy. This was anathema to the other Arab regimes, none of which were democratic nor allowed popular opinion to be expressed or for popular input into governance through elections. Thus, the free-wheeling Lebanese press was often brought to task for advancing these radical notions in newspapers that circulated the entire region. When Israel bombed and besieged Beirut and occupied half of Lebanon in 1982, many Arab regimes were relieved at the diminution of freedom in Beirut. Amman saw itself as a potential new banking center, Cairo imagined that it would re-emerge as the center of intellectual activity, and the Gulf states expected to become the focus of holiday travelers. An Egyptian journalist wrote of the Israeli attacks of 1982, "Most Arab rulers enjoy watching this because the sight of an Arab woman reading an uncensored book, printed in Beirut, would upset them far more than the sight of phosphorus-burnt children in a Beirut hospital."[30]

With the exception of Beirut, and it was largely brought to heal in 1990 when Syria occupied the country to halt the civil war, self-censorship cemented its hold as the norm across the Arab world, though glimpses of self-assertiveness did appear in the Lebanese press even under Syrian tutelage. Taking advantage of the limited freedom under Ḥāfiẓ al-'Asad, the press enjoyed making fun of the occupation. For example, publishing the word for condom, *ḥāfiẓ al-'āir* (protector of the penis) can also be translated as "Ḥāfiẓ is the prick." Nonetheless, describing today's Arab press is not quite so funny. Prior to the Syrian occupation of Lebanon, Beirut had over 40 publishing houses and 71 newspapers and other periodicals. It was in many ways a secure location for intellectuals to publish their ideas. But there was also a violent side to this, especially if one seriously offended power and privilege.

Kāmil Mruwwah, who founded and edited *al-Ḥayāt* from 1946, was assassinated in his Beirut office in 1966. During the Lebanese civil war, it stopped publishing in 1976, before moving its offices to London where it resumed publication in 1988. Further, in 2005, two anti-Syrian journalists were killed in separate car bombs. Jibrān Twaynī, son of Ghassān, the editor-in-chief of *al-Nahār*, was killed in December and one of its columnists, Samīr Kassir, died in June. The most notorious of the killings occurred in March 1980. Salīm al-Lawzī was the editor of *al-Ḥawādith* (the Events) who had moved his operation to London from Beirut after the 1973 Arab-Israeli war where it continued to criticize the Syrian government. When he came to Lebanon for his mother's funeral, he was kidnapped with the story being that before he was killed, his captors asked which hand he wrote with before dipping it into boiling water.[31]

In its first annual report in 2002, the Paris-based Reporters without Borders wrote that "no Arab country is among the top 50 [in press freedom]. Lebanon only makes 56th place and the press freedom situation in the region is not encouraging [...] [I]n Syria (126th), the state uses every means to control the media and stifle any dissenting voice." The 2005 annual report labeled the Middle East and North Africa as the most dangerous region in the world for journalists. Much of that was attributed to the war in Iraq where 40% of the worldwide deaths of journalists occurred, leading to the migration of journalists from the Middle East to, most notably, London and Paris. "The deadliest country for journalists in 2012 was Syria where journalists and netizens are the victims of an information war waged by both the 'Asad regime, which stops at nothing in order to crack down and impose a news blackout, and by opposition factions that are increasingly intolerant of dissent." By 2015, Reporters without Borders said that no Middle Eastern country was in the top 100 in press freedom.[32]

There have been some sputtering attempts to establish new print journals in Kuwait. More successful has been social media and satellite television. In the latter area, surprisingly, the government-owned Qatari satellite channels, al-Jazeera in Arabic and English, have been the most successful. Al-Jazeera has a larger following than the BBC Arabic service, London's Arab News Network, or the Saudi-sponsored Middle East Broadcasting Centre. In spite of the presence of al-Jazeera, Qatar was ranked 110th in press freedom in 2013.

Notes

1 David Hirst, *International Herald Tribune*, November 21, 1977.
2 p. xii.
3 http://bethlehem-holy-land.net/Adnan/publications/EndofTheOttomanEra.htm. Published in 2013.
4 http://bethlehem-holy-land.net/Adnan/publications/Turbulent_Times.htm. Published in 2013.
5 Talhami, *Palestine in the Egyptian Press*, p. 22.

6 *Arab Media and Society* (Issue 17, Winter 2013). Besides describing the hardships of contemporary Palestinian journalists, she writes about Yasser Arafat's meeting with the Greek Orthodox Patriarch who compared him to the second caliph, Umar. She goes on to write that the "Crusade-era Patriarch" conferred control of Jerusalem to Umar!

7 *Arab Media and Society* (Issue 18, Summer 2013).

8 Mohamed Abdel Gawad, the chair of MENA, went on: After the Arabs won their independence, "[…] the gratuitous foreign advice was that they should free their mass information media from government tutelage […]. [Yet,] Reuters, for instance, played an open role in the service of British propaganda during World War I; Sir Roderick Jones was at the same time manager of the agency and director of propaganda in the British Ministry of Information" (from Abdel Gawad's article, "Attempts of the Arab World to Participate in Balancing the Flow of Information," in *The Third World and Press Freedom*, ed. Philip C. Horton (New York: Praeger Publishers, 1978): 174.

9 Ṭarrāzī, vol. I, p. 49. However, the *Encyclopedia of Islam*, New Edition, 1965, Volume II, 465, under the entry "djarida," maintains that the first Arabic language newspaper, *al-Tanbih*, was printed in 1800 under the direction of Jacques-François de Menou, one of Napoleon's generals in Egypt.

10 Donald J. Cioeta, "Ottoman Censorship in Lebanon and Syria, 1876–1908." *International Journal of Middle East Studies* 10 (1979): 168.

11 Ṭarrāzī, volume 3, 4–149.

12 Ibid., 9; Khalidi, 23.

13 Ayalon, 75.

14 Ibid., 29.

15 Ibid., 84.

16 Tom McFadden, *Daily Journalism in the Arab States* (Columbus: Ohio State University Press, 1953), 36–37.

17 *New York Times*, July 2, 1951. The counterargument is that sometimes the press itself deceives and therefore needs to have checks put on it: "If in fact people in large numbers are being deceived, injured or degraded by the manner in which others are using their freedom to speak or print or show pictures […] the public authority cannot retreat behind […] *inaction*" (William Ernest Hocking, *Freedom of the Press* [Chicago: University of Chicago Press, Second Impression, 1948], 117).

18 Cioeta, 174–176.

19 Ibid., 181.

20 Ibid., 174–176. The process continues today – in the Israeli occupied West Bank, the word *'awdah* (return) is not permitted.

21 Ayalon, 85.

22 Jihad Khazen, "Censorship and State Control of the Press in the Arab World," *Harvard Journal of Press Politics* 4, no. 3 (1999): 87. Also as a corollary, "Never believe the news till it is officially denied."

23 Barbara Koeppel, "The Press in the Middle East: Constraint, Consensus, Censorship," *MERIP Special Report*, (December 1988): No pagination. Page 6 of text if it were numbered.

24 Ibid., 8–9.

25 Ibid., 1.

26 *International Herald Tribune*, June 20, 2006.

27 Khalid Amayreh, “Self-Censorship – The New Ghoul Haunting Palestinian Journalists,” *Palestinian Human Rights Monitor*, (January 1997), no pagination.

28 Amayreh, op. cit.

29 Faisal al-Kasim, “Crossfire: The Arab Version,” *Harvard International Journal of Press Politics* 4, no. 3 (1999): 93–97.

30 Trevor Mostyn, *Censorship in Islamic Societies* (London: Saqi Books, 2002), 65.

31 Barbara Koeppel, “The Press in the Middle East: Constraint, Consensus, Censorship,” *MERIP Special Report*, December (1988): 1.

32 Reporters without Borders with annual reports as current as 2018 can be accessed at http://en.rsf.org. Accessed May 25, 2018.

Chapter 2

Editorial Opinion on May 1948

There are parallel stories occurring as we begin the study of Arab editorial opinion toward Palestine. There is the Zionist discourse that had begun in the nineteenth century and had not changed as 1948 approached. Political Zionism adhered strictly to five basic principles: concentrate the Jews in Palestine, be a majority there, be productive ("the conquest of labor"), and the renaissance of Hebrew culture.[1] The fifth goal was "[...] to confront the great powers and international organizations with an established Jewish presence in areas susceptible to possible negotiations."[2] There were arguments amongst Zionists as how best to achieve these goals, but the goals themselves never varied. Some Zionists, like the Jerusalem born Eliyahu Saphir, wanted to integrate with the Arabs. These Altruistic Integrationists argued that the Arabs were a great people, and integration would be the best way to achieve the aims of Zionism. Others, for example Ze'ev Jabotinsky, wanted separation based on superiority and domination.

The achievement of the five goals would lead to what became the founding myths of the Jewish state: the 2000-year exile was an anomaly in Jewish history, Jews were returning to the Land of Israel since the 2000-year Diaspora was temporary, and once having reestablished themselves on their land, the Jewish people would participate once again in the history of civilized people.[3]

The other discourse involves the Arab response to the Zionist enterprise. Rashid Khalidi has intimated that he was surprised by the large number of articles that he discovered in reading *al-Mufīd* during a 3-year period beginning in 1908. He counted 53 articles on Zionism in less than an eight-month period.[4] Further, he asserts that the ideas of Zionist thinkers were published regularly in *al-Mufīd* and other Arabic journals of the time. Their readers knew of the basic aims of Zionism, knew of Herzl's *Der Judenstaat*, and were familiar with the Basle Congress of 1897.

Neville Mandel comes to the same conclusion. Though relying heavily on Zionist archives and the Hebrew language press in Palestine, he nonetheless concludes that Arab intellectuals and journalists, principally in Cairo, Beirut, and Damascus, were opposed to Zionism much earlier than previously thought.[5]

This study comes to a somewhat different observation regarding the period leading up to 1948. In the dailies that I examined in the 1930s and early 1940s, one can find very little written about the issue of Zionism and a Jewish state. Only in the Palestinian press was the question one of constant recurrence; but, even there, British censorship limited free expression of opinion. Quite naturally the volume of editorial opinion on the question of Palestine increased in the Arab press as the perceived danger increased. When the Arab revolt began in Palestine in 1936, the British imposed censorship to stop statements like those that appeared in *al-Difāʿ* in December 1936 that called Zionism the last chapter in imperialism. With the end of the Second World War and as the European powers began to remove themselves from the Arab world, editorial opinion became more open and a discussion of Palestine more acceptable. At least up to the adoption of the partition resolution of the United Nations in November 1947, Arab editorial opinion was what one might imagine it to have been. In Arab newspapers, generally, discussion prior to November 1947 centered on intellectual arguments, essentially non-military, concerning the rights of both the Arabs and the Jews.

Such editorial opinion as did appear prior to November 1947 wondered about the defensibility of the Jewish position. It refused to accept the right of the Jews in Europe to come to Palestine. And it argued that the coming to Palestine of a large Jewish population would severely upset Arab life.

> One of the least defensible Jewish political positions was searching for a second nationality, even though all the countries where they live offered them one. Was not being English, French, American, Dutch, Swiss, or Danish sufficient? And sufficiently honorable…?
>
> How is it possible that Jews from Eastern Europe can be transported to Palestine, by the thousands and hundreds of thousands without upsetting the Arabs of Palestine and their neighbors? [...] [A]nd how can peace result from such an audacious adventure, so full of perils?[6]

The last sentence of this editorial, however, shows that by 1945 there was an awareness on the part of a number of writers that a military conflict of some sort might develop out of the influx of Jews and the results "may become the most bloody and terrible."

Faced before 1947 with obvious facts before them, the Arabs more and more, in their editorial opinion, began to formulate a position of solid opposition to partition – a position that they articulated from several perspectives. When the UN General Assembly passed Resolution 181 (the Partition Resolution) in November 1947, the response was immediate and angry.

First, the Arabs felt that inordinate pressure from a few big powers, acting through the United Nations, had forced the partition of Palestine upon the rest of the world. Second, with this realization and the placing of the blame, there was an affirmation of their own unity. And third, there was almost unanimous agreement to refuse partition of Palestine because it was unjust. There was not in these positions a hint of difference between the respective Arab writers, no matter the country in which they wrote. Perhaps this can be attributed to their feeling of confidence. When one believes he is going to win, there is no need to search for areas of disaccord. Since the Arab press recognized the unity of Palestine and its Arab character, the discussions and resolutions being worked out in the United Nations were viewed with considerable suspicion. Of those delegations involved with Palestine, that of the United States came under the heaviest fire. The American delegation was, throughout the

Arab world, viewed as having Jewish pressure put upon it. The approaches which editorialists took, however, toward this pressure were sometimes pity for, and other times castigation of, the American-supported partition resolution. Many editorialists wondered if the emergence of the United States as a world power in the twentieth century was not a debit for other nations. Another point, galling to the Arab journalists, besides the role of the United States, was the fact that it was largely western hemisphere and western European nations that had voted for partition and therefore against the interests of an Asian nation.

> How could the United States stick to a resolution [181] that was adopted under pressure and bribery, where countries like Paraguay and Uruguay were the deciding factors, while countries like Pakistan, India and Turkey refused the resolution, in addition to all of the Arab people, who are about seventy million living in the east on the coast of the Mediterranean.[7]

> We have seen that all of the Oriental states voted against partition or abstained while the Occidental states – with the exception of a few noble nations – have supported Zionism. So the partition of Palestine is an indication that right and justice are composed of different things in the East and in the West. And Rudyard Kipling was right when he said, "East is East and West is West and never the twain shall meet."[8]

Clearly Arab writers were dismayed by what they felt were transgressions committed against Palestine. This feeling, however, is doubly interesting when it is placed in juxtaposition to what was felt in the West at the same period. Often the Westerner did not see the question as being whether it was right or not to give Palestine to the immigrating Europeans, but felt the question was over how the game of politics was played in the United Nations. For some Western writers and diplomats what had happened in the United Nations during the partition vote was what gnawed at their consciences. Thus, James V. Forrestal could agonize over the way the United States had forced nations to change their votes to favor partition and write that the "methods that had been used [...] to bring coercion and duress on other nations in the general assembly bordered closely unto scandal."[9] But for the Arab writer, the Western dilemma over the moral question of coercing nations to vote favorably or unfavorably in the United Nations was largely irrelevant. To reduce the morality of partition in Palestine to a vote in the United Nations was incomprehensible for him. His view was smaller and more parochial and he saw Palestine, often no farther away than 20 or 30 kilometers, being torn asunder. It was here that morality came into play. The question was not what the great nations might decide to do. The question was how to keep the Arab country of Palestine intact, and to prevent it from being turned into a Jewish nation.

> The attitude of the Arab states toward Palestine leaves no room for equivocating. Directly or indirectly, Palestine will be defended against Zionism. By every means, the Jewish state will be fought. The Arabs consider themselves to be in a state of legitimate defense and no informed and just person will say that they are not right. No one will consent to admit

> that, with the Jews having for thirty years settled themselves in so great number on the land of Palestine, the hospitable welcome of Palestine may paradoxically end up in the exercise of Jewish sovereignty over the soil.[10]

Thus, having rejected the moral right of the United Nations to vote on partition, Arab editorialists were practically unanimous in rejecting partition. What comes to mind is the now famous statement allegedly made by an Arab diplomat calling the partition plan, which divided Palestine into seven areas, "death by a thousand strokes." The editorialists, with great foresight, warned that any attempt to apply the partition resolution would result in a general conflagration in Palestine, would spread to the Arab countries, and perhaps to the rest of the world.[11] Further, there was a belief that the introduction of a Jewish state in Palestine would eventually threaten the existence of the Arab countries – Egypt, Syria, Lebanon, and Jordan that would have contiguous borders with the new state. This menace that Israel would pose was physical and economic. Very few people in November 1947 realized that the trickle of Palestinians fleeing from their country would soon become a flood, and that another threat to several Arab regimes would be the presence of a group of angry, dispossessed peoples as refugees within their borders.

Having dismissed the partition resolution as an act perpetrated by the morally bankrupt, and having unanimously agreed to reject it, the Arab editorialists began to turn to a third aspect, the affirmation of Arab unity in the face of a hostile world and the determination to oppose partition by whatever means necessary, including the use of force. It is well to note that Arab opinion at this stage in the Palestine problem, that is to say in November and December 1947, showed surprising unity, at least a unity of editorial opinion. Much has been said of the differences that led to the disastrous results for the Arabs in 1948, but these differences did not manifest themselves in editorial opinion until reverses in Palestine stunned the Arab world. In fact, when one compares the most ardent pro-Palestinian, pro-Mufti Ḥājj Amīn al-Ḥūsaynī paper, *Filasṭīn*, with the most conservative Maronite papers, *L'Orient* and *al-'Amal*, one discovers that editorial opinion was very similar. *L'Orient* wrote, "Our fierce attachment to the independence and sovereignty of Lebanon has never prevented us and will never prevent us from practicing, in the future, the most fruitful collaboration with our neighbors, and to accept, when need be, the defense of their interests."[12]

Many observers have wondered about this rare display of Arab editorial unity at the end of 1947 – unity that began to crumble as May 1948 drew closer and continues to today. Unity of this type should not be a surprise except in the case of elements in the Arab press that represented Lebanese Christian opinion. The aid that Israel has given the Maronites, ever since the second Lebanese civil war of 1975–76 and the ferocity with which Christians attacked the Palestinian camps of Tal al-Zaʿtar, Sabra and Shatila, lend credence to one's suspicion of Maronite Lebanese feelings toward the Palestinians. Thus for various reasons, often valid, we think of the Maronite population of Lebanon as having been historically more amenable to the establishment of a Jewish state, almost certainly because some

Christians felt that the establishment of a Jewish state in Palestine would protect and aid the Christians of Lebanon.

Undoubtedly, there have been many Arab Christians who have felt threatened by the sea of Muslims that surrounded them. But with one exception, this segment of Christian Arab belief did not appear in the newspapers covered in this study. This one exception was the publication in 1947 in Lebanese newspapers of a statement by the Maronite Archbishop of Beirut, Ighnatiyius Mubārak. Archbishop Mubārak said, "Major reasons – social, humane, and religious – demand that there be created [...] a Christian home in Lebanon as there has always been; a Jewish home in Palestine [...] The Lebanon demands liberty and independence."[13] The publication of this statement by the Archbishop gave rise to a tremendous storm of indignant protest from Lebanese Christians. The parliament adopted a resolution sponsored by Christian members denouncing Mubārak and assuring the world that he did not speak for any large group. Likewise, Mubārak's statement did not give rise to favorable editorial comment in the Christian Arab newspapers. Also appalled were Rome and the Maronite Patriarch who restricted him to a monastery and exiled him from his diocese until his death. Thus, the editorial ranks chose temporarily to maintain unity in their determination to prosecute a war in Palestine when the British mandate ended.

United in their opposition to Zionism, the Arab editorialists began to demand the neutrality of the world, especially Britain, in Palestine. They also wanted the Arab nations to unite, and finally they called upon the Arabs to forcefully resist the Zionists in Palestine. While later attacks against foreigners would be aimed particularly at the United States, at this stage Britain, as the mandatory country in Palestine, was singled out for what was believed to be a lack of impartiality in taking arms away from the Arabs while not disarming the Zionists.[14] If the great powers would leave the Middle East alone, there was little doubt in the newspapers about who would win since the Arabs were "more systematic, more devoted, and stronger than their enemies."[15] Left to their own devices, the only problem that possibly could prevent a victory, in which the Arabs were to engage the Zionists in a war without mercy, "on land, sea, and in the air,"[16] would be not a lack of heroism on the part of those who are fighting, but in the lack of unity on the political front.

Often when a Westerner conjures up images of the Arabs, one description almost certainly in the forefront is that of lack of unity, even violent disagreement, among themselves. And this foreign conception was also a self-perception held by the Arabs. Writers felt the Arabs were far superior as long as their politicians filled their roles correctly. But there was a sense of uneasiness in editorials as 1947 drew to a close. Some newspapers tried to make propaganda out of reported fissures within the Arab front by claiming that stories of internal differences were largely fabricated and exaggerated. They characterized the rumor that there was a lack of unity on the Arab political front as being "political bankruptcy to which the desperate resort."[17]

Despite this attempt to whitewash supposed Arab leadership differences, many Arab newspapers wrote that these differences were more than just fabrications. There was a feeling pervading a good number of the newspapers that the Arab politicians were just playing for headlines and pictures and that they did not realize that what was being enacted in Palestine was, in fact, a matter of life and death. There was also frustration at the slowness with which the politicians were acting:

> While the Arabs of Palestine are being burned by Jewish bombs and their houses destroyed, we look and see here in Damascus nothing but speeches, demonstrations, and figures about volunteers. At the same time we see in Cairo, where Arab foreign ministers are meeting, nothing but photographs of parties, feasts, and speeches threatening the Zionists and the countries which support them. All this does not help the Arabs of Palestine.[18]

Nevertheless, the impression left by the Arab newspapers was that in spite of possible shortcomings, especially from the political segment, the Arab nation as a whole might reasonably hope for a victory against the Zionists in Palestine. This hope was based upon the large numerical advantage that the Arabs had and was predicated also on the belief that if only the world would maintain its neutrality, the Arabs would be the victors in any military engagement. Although there were signs to show that among some segments of the Arab people there was a belief that war would not come, this belief came from optimism on the part of the Arabs that the Jews in Palestine, faced with overwhelming Arab superiority, would capitulate to the Arabs before fighting. The opinion expressed in the newspapers called, therefore, for military action in Palestine and perhaps in the back of some editorialists' minds, although rarely expressed in the papers, was the belief that as May 15, 1948 approached, the Zionists would surrender and military action on the part of the Arab armies would be unnecessary.[19]

With the coming of the New Year, Arab writers began to look at what they thought were the reasons for the impending crisis of May 15, 1948. They viewed the causes for the Palestinian problem as being almost exclusively non-Arab.[20] The year 1948 was also an American presidential-election year and this fact did not escape Arab editorialists. Many felt that President Harry Truman, in a bid to become re-elected, had sacrificed morality and principles of humanity in Palestine. The belief was that for Jewish-American money and votes, Truman was willing to give Zionists a country in Palestine. Still other editorial comment placed the blame on the United Nations for voting partition in Palestine. And others, like the forceful Najīb al-Rayyis, painted the impending struggle in religious colors:

> If it were only a question of a war between Arabs and Jews, it would mean the Arabs would only defend themselves and their patrimony. But a localized war over a small, restricted space has been transformed into a Crusader War against the Arabs [...] led by the Christian states.[21]

The general feeling, then, of the editorialists was that Zionism was being aided by Western nations (or sometimes vice versa) and was attempting to establish a type of colonial state in Palestine. This belief gave rise to comparing the twentieth-century Haganah to the eleventh-century Crusaders. Once again, the Arab East was to be invaded by the West and there was little doubt that the result would be the same as it had been many centuries earlier.

The result of this conviction, that Zionism was a subversive element within the Middle East and the belief also that Zionism and Judaism were the same things, was the appearance of a degree of anti-Jewish sentiment in the press. Usually this feeling manifested itself in editorials which claimed that Jews in the Diaspora held loyalties to other Jews and therefore, whether Zionists or not, were happy to see the establishment of a Zionist state in Palestine. Jews were also given characteristics that included meanness and barbarism for their methods in killing Arabs in Palestine.[22] This anti-Jewish feeling expressed in the Arab press undoubtedly led to overt action on the part of certain communities, for example, the attack on the Jewish quarter in Aleppo in December 1947. There seems little doubt, also, that this kind of inflammatory writing resulted in the flight of Jews from their ancient homes throughout the Arab world. The usual accusation against the Jewish Arabs was that no matter how they might voice their support for anti-Zionism, this was not a true expression of their feelings.

> When some papers published telegrams supporting Arab Palestine from some Syrian Jews or their societies or their spiritual leaders, people wonder whether the government or the papers trust the signers of these telegrams. Would it not be stupid to believe any Jew in the world dislikes the establishment of a Jewish state or feels sorry for the cruel and barbarian acts which the Jews are committing in Palestine?[23]

Arab feeling toward the Jews, however, was not entirely negative. A Lebanese editorialist was not only able to make a differentiation between Zionism and Judaism, but he also was able to project a purely Lebanese belief in writing that Lebanon was a home for minority groups. Kesrouan Labaki felt that if Jews were not allowed their freedom in Lebanon then the *raison d'être* of the Lebanon would be lost. Therefore, he pleaded, "Leave the Jews of Beirut in peace."[24] An Egyptian writer, however, approached the problem not from an exclusively nationalistic point of view but from a pan-Arab viewpoint.

> We do not need to ascertain that the Arabs, whether they are Palestinians or not, hold no prejudice against the Jews. The Arab east has always been known for its hospitality and generosity and the Jews, being a small minority, lived among their Muslim and Christian brothers in peace and unity. And they were not persecuted as they were in Europe.[25]

Of course this last sentence is still debated in the Middle East. A whole historiographic argument has developed since the events of 1948 with each side arguing the pros and cons of whether or not the Arabs are anti-Semites and how Jews were treated in the realm of Islam. Those who support the need for a Jewish state argue that Arabs always have been prejudiced against Jews, while the supporters of the Palestinians take the opposite position. The path of justifying present excesses by the past is quite rocky.

The topics involved in the immediately preceding paragraphs cover only a small portion of the overall range of editorial opinion. By far the greatest percentage centered on the future of Palestine and the patriotic call to the defense of Arab Palestine. The future of Palestine and the demands of the Arab editorialists in this regard may be neatly summarized as follows: "Abandonment of partition; expulsion of [Zionist] terrorists; stopping of Jewish immigration; dissolution of the Haganah; end of the British mandate; immediate proclamation of the independence of Palestine; the creation, in Palestine, of a Judeo-Arab state in which all the inhabitants would enjoy the same rights and would have the same obligations."[26] To achieve their plan for Palestine, the Arabs were exhorted to defend Palestine and defeat Zionism.

As the date for the termination of the British mandate drew closer, Arab editorialists were unanimous in their call for a military solution. The headline in Syria's *al-Qabas* of May 16, 1948 that said "writing and speaking have ended and courage and blood have begun," accurately reflected Arab editorial opinion.

Here we might look more closely at how each of the four countries viewed the impending struggle in Palestine. Generally, Syrian editorialists, no matter their faction or party, were emotional in their appeal to their readers. For the Syrians, recalling the glories of Ṣalāḥ al-Dīn was part of the attempt to get the Syrian people prepared for war.[27] They were anxious to begin the battle and seemed reluctant to await the final withdrawal of British troops scheduled for the middle of May. In fact several of the Syrian newspapers advocated "cutting off the viper's head before it grows larger."[28] This attitude was reinforced by the belief that "force has been, and does not cease to be, for all eternity, the only practical argument which asserts its rights in this world."[29] Thus the Syrian reader was urged by the editorials in his country to fight the Zionists in Palestine and to recognize, in this world, Might conquers Right. If he and his friends did not do so, in the future they would "cry like women over a homeland you were not able to save like men."[30] Along with this exhortation was a warning that the road ahead might be difficult since the enemy was powerful, disciplined, and supported by important external forces.

For the Lebanese, there was a realization that they were militarily the weakest of the four nations touching the borders of Palestine. Thus, their editorials, while no less patriotic in their call to liberate Palestine from the Zionists, were aware of the implications for a vulnerable Lebanon if a strong, militant Israel was established on its southern border:

> Israel at our gates obliges us to consider every aspect and every consequence of its closeness. It is no game when a small country tries to guess the weight, on its frontier, of such a peril. [...] The hymn of David, which the Hebrews chant, resounds throughout the Orient. And the weight of Israel, weight which is numerous and powerful, appears heavy and full of dangers for those nations who have, in all fields, but limited resources.[31]

In contrast to the narrow, even parochial, attitude of the Lebanese press, Egyptian editorials were more worldly in their outlook. They viewed what was going on in Palestine as not reflecting so much a limited battle between a group of Arabs and a group of Zionists, but as a battle on a larger scale that involved the Arab nation and its renaissance against the Western World and the remnants of colonialism. This attitude may have come in part from the relatively great distance between Cairo and Tel Aviv when compared with the distance of Amman, Damascus, and Beirut from Tel Aviv. But an added reason for Egypt's more distant approach to the problem was its preoccupation with the British occupation.

One consequence of this was the blending together of the causes of its occupation with the causes of the emergence of Zionism in Palestine. There was a call in the Egyptian press to fight the Zionists in Palestine, but it was mild and tended to see the Palestinian problem in the light of the British occupation of Egypt. From this hypothesis, the Egyptian press then drew a parallel between Palestine and Egypt and felt that any fight that might result in Palestine, although certainly important, was nothing more than a prelude to a much greater test, that of fighting colonialism everywhere. "The fighting going on in Palestine is the smaller struggle and may the Arab nation return from the field stronger and more capable of the greater struggle."[32]

The Palestinian press was not offered the luxury of distance from the battleground. The writers for *al-Difāʿ* and *Filasṭīn* were well aware of the action that surrounded them. They exhorted their readers to defend those portions of Palestine held or promised to the Zionists.

> We are convinced that this struggle we are involved in is for the protection of our country's unity and for the attainment of our rights and liberties.
>
> We are convinced that our enemies are fighting a losing battle and that the odds are not on their side.
>
> We are also convinced that the solution will be here not in New York or London.
>
> At the same time we know that we will face difficult situations and we will suffer sacrifices and losses. And the state of affairs will ebb and flow for some time.
>
> Even though our destiny is assured, we avoid being overoptimistic and always call for preparation and alertness, for more organization and putting time to better value.[33]

It has often been repeated that one cause for Arab flight from Palestine, in late 1947 and in 1948, was Arab leaders' calls through the media for the Palestinians to leave their homes in 1947 and 1948. Erskine Childers in his examination of monitored radio broadcasts[34] has shown this myth to be false. Insofar as it is concerned with the Arab press, it too may be laid to rest. Quite the opposite in fact occurred. Numerous papers reported that the borders with Palestine were closed to males of fighting age and all of the papers urged the Palestinians and Arabs to stay and fight. Of particular interest, where this question of flight is concerned, is the reaction of the Palestinian papers, themselves, to the impending war in Palestine. There is an overwhelming amount of evidence to show *al-Difāʿ* and *Filasṭīn* never urged their readers to abandon their homes. To the contrary, Palestinian editorials argued:

> [...] the Palestinians have to make the greatest sacrifice and be an example for others. Who will sacrifice for us if we do not sacrifice for ourselves first?[35]

Recent scholarship on the issue of whose fault the refugee problem was has shed even more light. The so-called "New Historians," authors like Benny Morris, Ilan Pappe, and Gabriel Piterberg, have investigated the fate suffered by the Palestinians during the 1940s when hundreds of thousands became refugees. Their findings, based on declassified Israeli military archives, cabinet meeting minutes, and memoirs of key Israeli participants should put an end to one of the most enduring claims of the Zionists: that the Arabs urged the Palestinians to leave. They have found quite the opposite. For example, on March 10, 1948 a group of Zionist leaders met and dispatched to Jewish forces an order to prepare for the systematic expulsion of the Palestinians, code named Plan Dalet. In Pappe's words, Israeli historiography subsequently concocted the story of a voluntary exodus by the Palestinians.[36] Pappe then quotes from an Israeli operational plan to show the inaccuracy of the voluntary exodus myth:

> These operations [of ethnic cleansing] can be carried out in the following manner: either by destroying villages (by setting fire to them, by blowing them up, and by planting mines in their debris) and especially of those population centers which are difficult to control continuously; or by mounting combing and control operations according to the following guidelines: encirclement of the villages, conducting a search inside them. In case of resistance, the armed forces must be wiped out and the population expelled outside the borders of the state.[37]

Benny Morris discovered that in November 1947 there were 219 Palestinian villages and four towns earmarked for the Jewish state in the Partition Resolution. They had a total population of 342,000. By June 1, 1948, 180 of the villages and towns had been evacuated with 239,000 Palestinians fleeing. Another 152,000 in the villages and towns around Jaffa, Jenin, and Acre, areas designated for the Palestinian state but under Israeli control, became stateless. Thus by late 1947, the Arab exodus had begun and was accelerated by the Irgun's massacre at Dayr Yāsīn in April 1948. This well-publicized event spread panic among the Palestinians. To quote the Israeli intelligence analysis, the disappearance of the Palestinians marked the "final chapter" in the struggle for Palestine and "the end of the job."[38]

Although the Arab editorialists sought to instill within the Arab peoples a feeling of unity before the Zionists, these editorialists were not blind to what they saw of a negative nature in the handling of the war for Palestine, and the stream of refugees well before the partition resolution was to be implemented in May 1948.

Before the entrance of the regular Arab armies into Palestine in May 1948, the newspaper writers brought to the attention of their readers many faults being perpetrated by the Arab side. There was editorial criticism of the training of the armies, use of volunteers, lack of coordination among the Arab states, the tendency of politicians to talk instead of work, the absence of Palestinians defending their country, and the greed of some Arabs in wanting to pursue regional self-interest above Arab self-interest. Although the official government-produced news during April and May 1948 left the impression that the Arab volunteers were winning a great victory in Palestine, editorial opinion did not reflect the optimism found in the news stories. The sense left by the lack of editorial support for the news stories and government news releases was that the news was an attempt to increase circulation and raise morale, but the editorialists took it with a grain of salt.

The two largest volunteer Arab groups fighting in Palestine prior to May 15 were those headed by 'Abd al-Qādir al-Ḥusaynī and Fawzī al-Qāwuqjī. Al-Ḥusaynī took his orders from the Arab Higher Committee (*al-Hay'ah al-'Arabīyah al-'Ulyā*), which was headed by his cousin the Mufti of Jerusalem, al-Ḥājj Amīn al-Ḥusaynī. The Higher Committee was established in 1936 to loosely coordinate the Arab revolt in Palestine, and its supporters were called *al-majlassīyīn* (supporters of the Supreme Muslim Council under Ḥusaynī's leadership). It also served as the political organization for the Mufti. Though it was the most widely recognized political group, it did not have the support of the entire Palestinian community which for years had been split in support of several notables. The largest Palestinian opposition to the Ḥusaynī family came from the Nashāshībīs who were loyal to King 'Abd Allāh of Transjordan. This polarizing rivalry between the two clans led to a political rift amongst the Palestinians, and also to a religious rift since Christians tended to favor the Nashāshībīs. The Christian-founded *Filasṭīn* saw its readership decline because of its identification with the Nashāshībīs. Both families, along with a third power, the Ḥawrānīs, began to flee by 1947 so that when warfare broke out, the Palestinian people were not only divided but leaderless.

Al-Qāwuqjī, on the other hand, owed his position to the Arab League operating out of Cairo. Of the two Troops of Liberation (*Jaysh al-Inqādh*), as they were commonly known, the forces of al-Ḥusaynī were, because of their leader's ability, the more effective group.[39] Unfortunately for the Arabs, 'Abd al-Qādir al-Ḥusaynī was killed in Palestine in the first week of April 1948. It is debatable whether the Palestinian liberation armies could have influenced the outcome of the 1948 war even if al-Ḥusaynī had not been killed in action. The *Jaysh al-Inqādh* were hastily put together, they were not well trained; and with the prospect of a quick and easy victory appearing before many Arabs, politicians in great numbers rushed to join the volunteer forces. "Against an adversary who has been armed and organized for a long time, the first Arab group contained only ill-matched elements, hastily introduced, insufficiently trained, and lacking any heavy armaments."[40]

Added to this realization, on the part of some editorialists, of the paltriness of the volunteer forces which entered Palestine, was a recognition of the lack of armed Palestinians able to defend their own country. The complaint against the Palestinians, while limited, was centered largely in Syria. Several newspapers noted with sarcasm the movement of the Arab Higher Committee from Jerusalem to Damascus at the beginning of 1948. Many of the editorial writers may well have wondered why the Committee had moved to the Syrian capital instead of remaining in Jerusalem. The Syrian papers reiterated their determination to fight to free the Palestinians, but were angered by the lack of effort on the part of the Palestinian leaders to help themselves. One editorial chastised Palestine's leaders for "surveying" the military operations and "conducting the battles" from luxurious drawing rooms, from comfortable arm chairs, and for using binoculars, because they were too far away from the battles to use their naked eyes.[41]

The amount of criticism of the Palestinians and of the volunteer armies was minimal, both in space given to berating them and in the newspapers that broached the two topics. Perhaps this lack of editorial treatment by the newspapers accurately reflected the lack of importance of these two factors in the overall picture. The role of the regular armies and the role of the Arab politicians were more important for the final disposition of Palestine. It is not strange to discover, then, that more editorial opinion was paid to the Arab politicians and to the problems involved with the approaching intervention by the regular Arab armies.

More will be said in the following chapter about the role of the regular armies in the war of the spring of 1948. Here it is sufficient to say that the editorials dealing with the role of the Arab armies gave the impression that the troops were sufficiently strong to deal with the Zionists in Palestine. There was no doubt about the strength or the will of these armies. Where questions did arise about the regular forces, it was over the coordination between the armies of the Arab countries involved. And here, also, the general impression was that the details of collaboration for the liberation of Palestine were completed and the governments were in full agreement.[42] But even in this, there were negative notes made in some of the newspapers. One newspaper put the matter quite succinctly:

> Within forty-eight hours the Palestinian bill must be paid and the Lebanese are held in almost total ignorance or Arab preparation [...]
>
> Where are we?
>
> And where will we be tomorrow?
>
> Has agreement been reached between Amman and Riyad?
>
> Has King ʿAbd Allāh received *carte blanche* to intervene in the Holy Land?
>
> The Arab Legion currently stationed in Palestine, will it alone operate against the Haganah?
>
> Will the governmental and administrative authority be exercised, after 15 May, in the name of King ʿAbd Allāh or the Arab League?
>
> All of these questions which are pre-occupying the Lebanese to a great extent have not, up to now, received any response [...]
>
> Will our soldiers enter into Palestine?
>
> Will they be engaged in fighting the Haganah?
>
> We are ignorant of all this.[43]

If the military situation was not fully comprehended by Arab editorialists prior to May 1948, the political situation and the private ambitions of the political leaders were better recognized.

As we will show in subsequent chapters, political hindsight would be a major characteristic of the editorialists. But foresight was also evident, especially in the Syrian press. Of particular interest to the Syrian papers were the thinly veiled attempts by King ʻAbd Allāh, to annex the portions of Palestine which, according to United Nations resolutions, were to become the Arab Palestinian state. The Syrian papers, especially those hostile to the Hashemites, the unity of geographic Syria, and the British who supported both – like *Baradā* – felt that the announced intention of Transjordan to annex Palestine was really the annexation of Palestine by John Glubb Pasha, the British commander of the Jordanian Arab Legion. The fact that Jordan was tied both through treaty and by having her army officered and paid for by the British did not escape the Syrian editorialists. Another paper called the Jordanian plans an "occupation of slaves" because Jordan was so tied to the British.[44]

The other major figure in Palestine, the Mufti of Palestine, al-Ḥājj Amīn al-Ḥusaynī, also came in for sharp attack. Already writers had frowned on his moving his organization from Jerusalem to Damascus. Still other editorials questioned his leadership abilities and the way he was spending the money allotted to him for his Palestinian campaign against the Zionists. One newspaper commented that the Mufti had been given 250,000 Egyptian pounds, and he spent 100,000 pounds on "organization," another 100,000 on "propaganda," and only the remainder was spent on war materials.[45]

Criticism was not limited to ʻAbd Allāh and al-Ḥusaynī. With Arab reverses in Jaffa and Haifa and with the events that occurred in Dayr Yāsīn, Arab editorialists began to attack a larger circle of political leaders. One could list literally scores of newspapers that wrote, "We have had enough words and communiqués."[46] The warning was quite clear. Responsibility for the future of Palestine would rest on the Arab politicians. If they were successful they could bask in glory. If they failed they would be held accountable. To save themselves, the Arab editorialists urged political leaders to take the initiative in the field of battle, to listen to public opinion which was angry over the postponement of action until May 15, the date the mandate was to end, and to enter Palestine with their armed forces as quickly as possible.[47]

However, with official military statements being issued announcing victories in the field, the few notes of warning published by editorialists appear to have gone largely unheeded. The Arab reader was left with the overall impression that victory after May 15 would be complete and quick. But the warning was there and on the day the mandate ended Kesrouan Labaki of *L'Orient* summed it up concisely when he wrote, "The past died at midnight. It is not necessary to revive it. Errors – grave errors – have been committed. Among the Arab leaders, some have failed in their mission [...]."[48]

In reviewing Arab editorial opinion up to the end of the British mandate in Palestine, one can discover distinct patterns in the editorials written for the Arab newspapers.

Prior to 1947, the arguments in the newspapers displayed a rather distant and almost disinterested viewpoint. This distance allowed them to view the problem non-militarily. But as 1947 came to an end and May 1948 approached, there seemed to be a correlation between the approach of the end of the mandate and the end of the coolness that distance had provided in the past. The result, especially after the United Nations' adoption of the partition resolution, was a change in editorial opinion. This change affected what the writers saw and what they predicted would be the consequences of what they had seen.

What they began to perceive was outside influence, particularly on the part of the British, of the Zionists in the United States, and of the United Nations. The consequence that they foresaw from these causes was possible violence in the Holy Land. Seeing a battle ahead, the editorialists did not shirk from it but instead believed that a war in Palestine might forever end the Zionists' dream and provide the Arabs with a way of preserving the Arab character of Palestine. Therefore, they encouraged military intervention, believing this was a way to gain their rights, and they felt that it would be successful.

However, the unity of opinion that we have observed also carried with it two undercurrents of disunity. There continued to be calls for unity within editorials and there was still a pervading belief in victory, perhaps due largely to the optimism of the official reports coming from the unofficial war. Censorship of an extreme sort severely handicapped the Arab press in reporting events. Skeptical questioning of governmental news releases was viewed almost as treason. Despite the death of ʻAbd al-Qādir al-Ḥusaynī; the absence of political leaders from Palestine; the small number of Palestinian fighters in the field; the failure of the Palestinian community to recover from their revolt of 1936–39; and in spite of the losses of Dayr Yāsīn, Tiberias, Haifa, Jaffa, Safad, and Acre to the Zionists even before the British mandate ended, the Arab masses were led to believe that victory was certain.

Still the Arab writers were sometimes incredulous. And as the war approached, the editorialists began to look around and view the war from a limited, nationalistic viewpoint. The impending war and the fear of defeat began to bring a hint of a breakup of the editorial unity that had characterized the writing before 1948. Syria and its writers felt that it was making the greatest sacrifices and urged concerted military effort. Syria was especially hostile toward the Jordanians and the Palestinians for their military weaknesses and therefore urged total Arab military commitment. The Lebanese were often editorially aware of their own military weaknesses and seemed to fear war though supporting it. The Egyptians seemed more interested in the British and viewed the Palestine problem as part of the overall problem of the British presence in the Middle East. The Palestinian papers reflected their proximity to the fight, and their newspapers urged a battle till death.

This first sense of a fracturing of Arab unity also manifested itself on a level other than national. Thus, there was a growing belief that perhaps Arab volunteers, the regular armies, and the political leaders were not prepared for the events ahead. As the official war began, there was a willingness on the part of the Arab writers to forgive and forget, possibly because of a belief that the Arab armies would be victorious. But there was a definite warning that if the Arabs were not successful in combat, the politicians would be held responsible. When defeat resulted and the political leaders were called to answer the charges of neglect, a far-reaching movement to do away with the old order infected the Arab world, especially in the countries that comprised geographic Syria. Violent revolution and coups of one variety or another touched every nation that was involved in the unsuccessful effort of 1947–48.

Notes

1 Yosef Gorny, "Attitudes to Arab-Jewish Confrontation as Reflected in the Hebrew Press, 1900–1918." *Arab Studies Quarterly* 1, no. 1 (1979): 47–48.
2 John Ruedy, "Dynamics of Land Acquisition," in *The Transformation of Palestine: Essays on the Origin and Development of the Arab-Israeli Conflict*, ed. Ibrahim Abu-Lughod (Evanston, AAUG Press, 1971), 129.
3 For a more complete exposition of this paragraph, see Gabriel Piterberg, "Erasures," *New Left Review*, no. 10 (July–August 2001): 31–46.
4 Rashid Khalidi, "The Press as a Source for Modern Arab Political History: 'Abd al-Ghani al-Uraisi and *al-Mufid*," *Arab Studies Quarterly* 3, no. 1 (Winter 1981): 34.
5 Neville Mandel, *The Arabs and Zionism Before World War I* (Berkeley, University of California Press, 1976).
6 Michel Chiha, *Le Jour*, April 19, 1945.
7 Najīb al-Rayyas, *al-Qabas*, December 3, 1947.
8 Kāmil Murūwah, *al-Ḥayāt*, December 3, 1947.
9 James V. Forrestal, *The Forrestal Diaries* (New York, Viking Press, 1951), 363.
10 Michel Chiha, *Le Jour*, December 18, 1947.
11 See for example Muhyī al-Dīn al-Nuṣūlī, *Bayrūt*, November 15, 1947; *al-Ḥayāt*, November 28, 1947; and *al-Manār*, September 4, 1947.
12 Kesrouan Labaki, *L'Orient*, December 2, 1947.
13 For the full text of Mubārak's statement see *al-Diyār*, September 27, 1947.
14 *Al-Difā'*, December 24 and 26, 1947; *Filasṭīn*, December 28, 1947.
15 Muhyī al-Dīn al-Nuṣūlī, *Bayrūt*, December 10, 1947.
16 Ibid., December 17, 1947.
17 *Al-Difā'*, November 11, 1947.
18 *Al-Qabas*, December 16, 1947.
19 George Kirk, *The Middle East 1945–1950* (London, Oxford University Press, 1954), 270. Kirk is of the belief that there were some Arabs, including the Secretary General of the Arab League, 'Abd al-Raḥmān 'Azzam, who felt the Arab states would not fight in Palestine.
20 One can argue whose fault the Palestine problem was. Undoubtedly, however, the vast majority of Arabs felt it was not originally of their own making.
21 *Al-Qabas*, May 13, 1948.
22 *Filasṭīn*, January 6, 1948.
23 Najīb al-Rayyis, *al-Qabas*, May 21, 1948. For another aspect see Gordon H. Torrey, *Syrian Politics and the Military* (Columbus, Ohio State University Press, 1964), 104.
24 *L'Orient*, January 13, 1948. Also see his editorial in *L'Orient* of May 18, 1948, which says of the Jewish Lebanese "[...] they have done more for Palestine than the Christians and Muslims combined."
25 *Al-Ahrām*, April 25, 1948. Although the study has covered several months, up to this point, Egyptian newspapers, and especially *al-Ahrām*, were largely void of any type of editorial comment on Palestine from November 1947 to the beginning of March 1948. This may have

been due to censorship. Another factor involved was the Egyptian preoccupation with the British at the expense of the events occurring in Palestine.

26 Kesrouan Labaki, *L'Orient*, March 23, 1948.

27 *Al-Qabas*, March 20, 1948.

28 *Al-'Ilm*, March 26, 1948.

29 *Baradā*, March 11, 1948.

30 *Al-Qabas*, May 9, 1948.

31 Michel Chiha, *Le Jour*, May 28, 1948.

32 Fu'ād Sarrūf, *al-Ahrām*, May 18, 1948. A corroborating argument, that Egypt was a reluctant participant, is made by Jon and David Kimche, *Both Sides of the Hill* (London, Secker and Warburg, 1960), 48–49.

33 *Al-Difā'*, February 1, 1948.

34 Erskine Childers, "The Other Exodus," *The Spectator* 206, no. 6933 (May 12, 1961): 672–675.

35 *Filasṭīn*, November 19, 1947. This writer found no evidence of any official or unofficial call for the Arabs to leave Palestine published in any Arab newspaper.

36 Ilan Pappe, *The Ethnic Cleansing of Palestine* (Oxford, Oneworld Publications, 2006), xv.

37 Ibid., 39. Quoting Ben Gurion on the subject: "If we will receive in time the arms we have already purchased [...] we will be able not only to defend [ourselves] but also to inflict death blows on the Syrians in their country – and take over Palestine as a whole. I am in no doubt of this. We can face all the Arab forces. This is not a mystical belief but a cold and rational calculation based on practical examination" (Ibid., 46). Michael Palumbo wrote the *Palestinian Catastrophe* (London, Quartet Books, 1987), which further validated the Palestinian view of events using oral history and UN documents.

38 Benny Morris, "The Causes and Character of the Arab Exodus from Palestine: The Israel Defense Forces Intelligence Branch Analysis of June 1948," *Middle East Studies* 22, no. 1 (1986): 5–19. The analysis reported by Morris goes on to say that at least 70% of the exodus was caused by "our [Haganah/Israel Defense Forces] operations and by their influence [...] [and by irregular forces like the Irgun and Lohamei Herut Yisrael] who directly [caused] 15 per cent [...] of the emigration" (Ibid., 9). Nowhere in the report is there a mention of an Arab order to evacuate. In fact the report goes out of its way to stress that the exodus was contrary to the political-strategic desires of the Arab Higher Committee and the neighboring Arab states.

39 Actually neither of the two groups was very effective. However, al-Qāwuqjī "did his side great harm. He aroused extravagant hopes by his boasting amongst the Palestinian Arab villagers, whose morale was undermined by disappointment when the supreme test came of resisting the advance of the Jewish forces." Sir Alec Kirkbride, *A Crackle of Thorns* (London, Murray Press, 1956), 158–159.

40 *L'Orient*, April 26, 1948.

41 *Al-Qabas*, April 22, 1948.

42 *Al-Kifāḥ*, May 13, 1948.

43 Kesrouan Labaki, *L'Orient*, May 13, 1948.

44 *Al-Manār*, April 9, 1948.

45 *Baradā*, May 12, 1948. If there is a correlation between the number of soldiers the Palestinians themselves were able to put in the field and the amount of money spent for this purpose by the Mufti, then the allegations by *Barada* appear to be true. Aqil H. H. Abidi, *Jordan: A Political Study* (London, Asia Publishing House, 1965), 42, puts the number of soldiers the Palestinians were able to muster at only a little over two thousand.

46 *Al-Niḍāl*, quoted in *L'Orient*, April 15, 1948.

47 See for example Kāmil Murūwah, *al-Ḥayāt*, April 17, 1948, and *Baradā*, April 24, 1948. For an opposing view that waiting until the end of the British mandate would not seriously hinder Arab efforts in fighting Zionism see *al-Ahrām*, May 6, 1948.

48 *L'Orient*, May 15, 1948.

Chapter 3

From the Palestine War to the Assassination of King ‘Abd Allāh

As the war for Palestine began officially on May 15, 1948, the place of editorial opinion was not the most dominant feature of the dailies. Commentary devoted to the events unfolding in Jaffa, Haifa, the Negev, and Jerusalem was extensive, but it was just one part of any given newspaper, and the papers were largely filled with descriptions, not opinions, of the events in Palestine. Earlier, an editorial might have been the greatest portion of the day's print devoted to Palestine. In April and May 1948 this was not the case.

However, we should not minimize the role of the editorialists. They exhorted their readers to defense, pleaded for more patriotism, provided their own ideas on how a successful fight might be waged, and warned of consequences if the Arabs lost. To the statement that "Palestine was the one subject on which the rulers and governments of the Arab states were more or less united in opinion"[1] might be added that editorial opinion also was united as the war began.

Censorship, however, limited the topics freely discussed and, in the case of the Lebanese and Syrian papers, made some articles difficult to comprehend. Still, with few exceptions, as for example the shock surrounding the fall of Haifa toward the end of April, the articles were optimistic, although often lacking originality in their content.

As events became more important than any comment upon them, the headlines of the daily press often reflected editorial opinion since they interpreted the content of the story that followed. If the headlines in the newspapers from differing nations are compared, one generalization can be made. There is a striking correlation between what has been stated in the preceding chapter about national interests in Palestine and the headlines from each country.

Filasṭīn, as a Palestinian paper, devoted all of its main headlines from the first of April to the end of May to the events within the country. *Al-Qabas*, as a Syrian representative and perhaps the most emotionally involved, had the second highest percentage of headlines devoted to Palestine. Lebanon's *Le Jour* had what might be termed the most balanced and factual while *al-Ahrām* of Egypt, when compared with the other papers, seemed almost detached from the Palestine problem. *Al-Ahrām*'s attitude appears extraordinary, especially in April when its lead headline for five days dealt with the Italian elections. The day after Haifa fell, April 23, *al-Ahrām* only noted that there was an "Important Military Conference in Amman."

Reading the headlines alone, one would come away with the impression that the fighting that lasted from May 15 until June 11, 1948, resulted in the Arabs having the upper hand, and a general feeling of confidence. Examples of headlines, in Syria's *al-Qabas*: "Planes attack

Tel Aviv and destroy its quarters and the Jewish colonies surrender to the freedom fighters" (May 16), "100,000 Jews in Jerusalem surrender and give their arms unconditionally to the Arabs," and "Victories of the Arab armies yesterday and today in the North, Middle, and South and the threatening of Tel Aviv" (May 20); and in *al-Ahrām*: "Egyptian troops advance in the South of Palestine" (May 16), "The Egyptian army occupies Hebron," and "The push of the Iraqi army toward the sea" (May 31).

But if the Arab newspapers gave the impression of victory, Why was there a cease-fire? If the Arabs had the upper hand during the fighting, Why did it not end in military victory for the Arabs? The Arabs were not defeated but neither did they win. And Israel had been born. Why had the promised quick victory become illusive? Editorials had several answers. A common Syrian reply was that the people, especially the wealthy, were not sacrificing enough. "We wonder where our wealthy people are and where is their generosity?"[2]

Though this tendency to criticize the Arab peoples themselves will increase when the full scope of the debacle became clearer, one Lebanese writer felt that, even as early as May 1948, his country had sacrificed sufficiently:

> Lebanon has been the only one of the member-states of the Arab League to apply, without hesitation and without reservation, the boycott of Zionist industry. Lebanon has been, also, the only one to suffer from this boycott. The Jews, who had bought our fruits and skied in the Cedars, have renounced our cherries and stopped skiing. The Arab countries have not even offered us symbolic compensation. Egypt buys her apples from California, the Aghas of Iraq do not ski and the Pashas of Cairo take their vacations along the Côte d'Azur.[3]

Another reason advanced to answer the general disappointment was that "[...] the firm solidarity between the Jews was stronger than the modest unity amongst the Arabs [remainder censored]."[4] A third conjecture held that the military fighting was only part of the story that was unfolding. The Arab armies were handling themselves well but there was also a political battle to be fought. World sympathy for the justness of the Arab cause was felt to be necessary to insure the military victory because "the time when things were done by orders of ministers and politicians is gone and we have entered an age where we cannot deny the power of public opinion and its influence on governments."[5]

Finally, Arab editorialists placed the blame for the lack of success on the world's Great Powers, especially the Soviet Union and the United States. The United Nations, up to the first truce, escaped chastisement to a great extent, as did Great Britain. What rankled the Arabs was the quickness of the recognition of the new State of Israel by the Soviet Union and the United States. The forthcoming presidential election in the United States was viewed as a likely reason for the action of President Truman.

> [...] in precipitously recognizing the Jewish state, they have encouraged, in decisive fashion, the Israeli war. These great countries have thus sought war and not peace.

> Undoubtedly their reasons were not the same; but the brutal fact is there. And history will register against the United States that, for reasons of internal policy, for reasons of electoral subterfuge, even though it was six or seven thousand kilometers away, it, a country of Christian civilization, deliberately sacrificed the Holy Land.[6]

The comments offered by the Arab writers and their analysis of what was happening at this time in Palestine appear to be, in retrospect, rather naive. The benefit of time and the declassification of documents provide a clearer idea of what occurred. Thus, many of the major causes for the poor Arab showing in the first Palestinian campaign were not remarked upon in the newspapers and were probably unknown to the commentators. One example was the lack of preparedness on the part of the Arab armies, with the exceptions of the British-officered Arab Legion and the Iraqi army. The Lebanese army's lack of offensive capability was so universally recognized as to require no comment. The Syrian army's weaknesses were apparent within ten days of the Arab intervention in May.[7]

However, the Egyptian army's performance has been termed "humiliating."[8] There was, as mentioned earlier, a sense in Cairo that war could be avoided, and preparations for it were unnecessary. King Farūq played a pitiful role in the decision to enter the fray. From his point-of-view, the war was to last only several days and would be essentially a victorious march to Tel Aviv. Convinced of Egypt's imminent victory, after he decided to support military action, Farūq busied himself with more important issues such as the sizes of the victory flags, the victory palace to be built in Gaza, and the great avenue to be constructed from Heliopolis to Cairo for the march of the triumphant armies on their return home.[9] Echoing this delusion, during the first round of fighting, the Egyptian press wrote of their army being "at the gates of Jerusalem" and the Syrian journals told of "a chain of glorious victories" for their army and those of the other Arab states.[10]

Censorship was universal for Arab (and Israeli) publications. The only area from which foreign correspondents were free to report was Amman. As a result of domestic Arab censorship, the populace was misled and the newspapers did not mention, at the time of the war, the scandals that were being perpetrated. In particular, there was the case of the Egyptians boarding a ship carrying ammunition bound for Jordan. The ship was unloaded by the Egyptians and the ammunition never reached the Jordanian army. There was also the case of Captain Fu'ād Mardam, the nephew of the Syrian prime minister, Jamīl Mardam, who was on an arms-purchasing mission in Italy. After he had purchased the arms, the Israelis pirated the loaded vessel as it was heading for Syria. It is still not known whether the act was perpetrated with or without the prior knowledge of Captain Mardam. The incident is reminiscent of the disappearance of five men-of-war from France in 1969 that turned up in Israel, much to the embarrassment of the Paris government.

There was also no mention in May and June 1948 of the secret meetings that had occurred between King 'Abd Allāh and Zionist leaders. These meetings, and subsequent ones, will come to the surface at a later period. The contacts between the nominal Arab military leader and his enemies over the prospects of a secret peace appear now to be incongruous.

However, this lack of information in certain areas did not prevent the editorialists from passing judgment on the unfolding events. But their conclusions were limited by the incomplete facts that were available. Censorship in time of war thus became an important factor preventing a larger discussion of the events in the Middle East. When the war ended, this unwillingness on the part of the Arab governments to trust the maturity of their own people led inevitably to violent upheaval aimed at those in power who had betrayed their trust.

Count Folke Bernadotte, the United Nations' mediator, was able to negotiate a four-week truce beginning on June 11. The reasons for the Arab acceptance of the first truce are debated even today, and were asked in 1948, though there is considerable evidence to support exhaustion. Several commentators felt that the Arabs had consented to the truce in order to show their good will and their willingness to enter into negotiations.

> The acceptance of the Arab countries to stop the fighting does not mean weakness but it means that the Arab countries are giving another chance to the Security Council and by this move the Arab countries give evidence of their sincere desire to cooperate with the United Nations to reach a solution.[11]

Other writers believed that perhaps Western coercion had been applied to the Arabs to make them accept the truce. And here the implication was that the British, having special relations with Egypt, Iraq, and Jordan, had applied pressure for acceptance. "It is because they could not do otherwise that the Arabs have accepted the truce."[12]

Though the first truce saw some benefits for the Arabs, especially the Arab Legion controlling the Old City of Jerusalem and Count Bernadotte's submission of a peace plan to both sides that permanently recognized that annexation in contravention of United Nations' resolutions, the Arab newspapers were not happy. The right of the world body to dispose of Palestine was always rejected in 1948, and the journals called on the Arab governments to take action against what it considered an illegal state. The acceptance of the first truce was thus viewed as giving Israel extra time to live and reorganize. The general feeling, correct or incorrect, was that the Arabs had been on the offensive and the acceptance of the truce threatened the momentum that was propelling them toward an eventual, if slower, victory. "Poor Arabs – what good hearts you have"[13] was a commonly expressed belief among the editorialists.

Besides allowing the Arabs to lose their momentum, the truce also was viewed as a means by which the Israelis would be able to increase their provisions and to complete their military preparations; this, while the Arab armies were at the gates of Tel Aviv.

> Each day that passes, each hour that passes is a day and an hour gained by the Jews. The State of Israel will live, starting tomorrow, its first four weeks of peace. It will dress its wounds and get organized with a view toward the eventual resumption of hostilities. The same respite is given to the Arabs. But the Arabs had been, till today, on the offensive. It must be hoped that they can keep it for a month.[14]

While the truce was in force, the Arabs and the Israelis did tend to their respective wounds and prepared for the coming battle when the truce would expire on July 9. But the two adversaries were not the only ones busy at work in Palestine. Count Bernadotte was occupied traveling between the belligerents and eventually proposed a plan to settle the Palestine problem. To the proposals already enumerated was added the merger of the Arab portion of the Palestinian partition with Transjordan. The inclusion of all of Jerusalem in this Arab state would presumably be under the scepter of the Hashimites. Another of Bernadotte's proposals was unlimited Jewish immigration into the State of Israel for two years. Also the Arabs were to be given the Negev region in exchange for the Galilee.[15]

The Bernadotte proposal was a boon for King ʿAbd Allāh who was anxious to make peace with the Israelis. His reasons were many, including the realization that Transjordan was not a viable kingdom unless its territories were increased and it had access to the Mediterranean Sea. However, the other Arab states were reluctant to allow ʿAbd Allāh to increase the size of his country and the extent of his power. Arab editorials outside Transjordan were almost one voice in rejecting the proposals of Count Bernadotte, although a fear of Transjordanian pre-eminence was not voiced. The main reason given for dismissing the mediator's proposals was that in accepting them, the Arab states would be guilty of *de facto* recognition of a Jewish state established on Arab land. There is no reason to doubt that, along with a fear of Transjordanian expansion, another factor, and perhaps *the* major factor, was a fear of what the future would bring to the Middle East if a Zionist state were established there.

"No government can approve the propositions of Count Bernadotte. How could it be otherwise as long as the Arabs know that the establishment of a Jewish state would be a fatal blow to their aspirations and would constitute a permanent danger to their national future?"[16] As long as the Zionists were felt to be using the truce period to consolidate and strengthen the State of Israel, Arab editorials were against the prolongation of the truce. They called for the Arabs to fight the "Jewish Crusaders"[17] because "the question is very simple, Palestine is an Arab land and must forever belong to its legitimate sons."[18] The Arab editorials were outspoken in their call for a resumption of the hostilities. They warned the mediator and the Zionists that the Arabs would meet next in Tel Aviv. They therefore called upon the Arab armies to pursue the fight until victory was obtained.[19]

The fighting resumed with the end of the first truce on July 9, 1948. The result of the ten-day war which followed was the rout of the Arab forces. In the north, Israeli troops captured the western Galilee and crossed the Lebanese border where they occupied a dozen or more villages. In the central portion of Palestine, they captured, among other towns, Nazareth, Lydda, and Ramlah, and widened the corridor that led from the coast to the New City of Jerusalem. In the south, Israeli forces probed into the Negev.

Thus defeated, the Arab leaders were willing to agree to a second truce. The popular reaction to the second truce, however, was one of opposition. This response was quite natural since the Arab masses were kept largely in the dark about the terrible showing of their forces in the field and the resulting setbacks. King ʿAbd Allāh had to unexpectedly confront an angry crowd of demonstrators in which he and his truce were roundly denounced. In reflecting popular opinion the Arab newspapers also expressed disappointment, and the Syrian papers were in the forefront of those who condemned the truce. The word emanating from a good number of these papers was that the people wanted combat, not a truce. Even Syria's *al-Ayyām*, a supporter of the National Party then in power under President Shukrī al-Quwatlī, felt that the cease-fire ought not be adhered to and called the Security Council, which had been in the lead in calling for a truce, the "Injustice Council."[20] That these statements came from a journal supporting the regime can only lead us to conjecture what opposition newspapers might have printed about their leadership had they been allowed. It is no conjecture, however, to state that the future of the Arab leaders who allowed 1948 to occur was in jeopardy.

The press of Egypt and Lebanon was more willing to accept the necessity for a cease-fire, perhaps because they did not see the Palestinian struggle as primarily theirs. For the Egyptian papers, the second truce was just a stop in the long struggle that lay ahead. In the end, the Arab people could rightfully expect to be victorious. On the other hand, the Lebanese papers were more pessimistic. "Our dreams vanished on the evening of 18 July. [...] Beloved Palestine was nailed to the cross as if those who crucified Christ wanted also to crucify the land where He was born."[21]

Despite the attempts at bravado by the official spokesmen for the various Arab governments, it was obvious, as the second truce began, that the victory that the Arab people had been promised was nowhere in sight. Twice within two months, the Arabs were disappointed to find the State of Israel still existed. This condition caused the Arab editorialists to reflect upon what had happened and why they were not victorious. Many reasons were put forward for the lack of victory. They included blaming the Western nations for their aid of Israel. The Arab League came under fire. The role of Transjordan was questioned, and Arab leaders found themselves chastised in the press.

Coming under special scrutiny by the Arab press was the role of the British. The English were damned since the Arabs felt they had been wronged more than a quarter of a century earlier when the English agreed with the French to split the Middle East into spheres of influence. And they felt that the British had wronged the Arabs again in 1948 by helping the Zionists. Along with the British, the role of the United States was questioned.

> On this occasion, we would like to direct our speech to Britain and America. The Arabs believe that the Zionists alone cannot attain any of their ambitions. And if it were not for the support of the Great Powers and their assistance, they [the Israelis] could not have done what they did in Palestine.[22]

However, criticism of outside countries for their role in creating the Palestine problem was minimal compared to the castigation heaped on allegedly false and ineffective leaders within. The feeling pervading the editorials was that it was well and good to assert that Israel had been established by foreign powers, but why were the Arabs not able to destroy a country that was so small, so young, and so weak?

The Arab League, as a focus for Arab anger, came under heavy fire. The fact that the League and its Secretary-General, ʿAbd al-Raḥmān ʿAzzām, acted as lightning rods was due in part to the fact that for the previous three months, Arab League headquarters, in Cairo, had been acting as a paper mill. It distributed literally hundreds of memos and announcements which implied great Arab victories in the field. When the victories failed to materialize, the wrath of the Arab writers fell on those who had been misleading them. *Al-Nahār*, under the headline "What have you done?," wrote:

> The Political Committee [of the Arab League] has affirmed that our forces will remain in the Holy Land until "peace returns to the Land of Peace."
>
> Does the Political Committee believe that those forces which will stay in Palestine will guarantee its [i.e., the Arab League's] rights if the truce negotiations fail? If this is so, why don't these forces continue the battle which was started and get these rights, since the Political Committee is convinced that force is the only solution and the truce is nothing but deceit [...]?
>
> We ourselves believe that the only thing the Political Committee of the League will do is submit to the *fait accompli* while trying to save face. And if we have anything to say to it [...] it is that its policy has failed and fools no one.[23]

Other comment on the role of the Arab League and its Secretary-General was biting in its sarcasm:

> Let us confess [...] that in the East, the ridiculous never kills. If ridiculousness killed, Mr. ʿAbd al-Raḥmān ʿAzzām, Secretary-General of the League, would have already died 107 times.
>
> Mr. ʿAbd al-Raḥmān ʿAzzām would have been a dead man every time that he, through his effusive verbiage, annihilated Israel; every time he expressed his optimism regarding the developments of the Palestine affair at the United Nations; every time he announced to the world the secret resolutions and mysterious decisions of the Council of the League and of the Committee [...].
>
> Mr. ʿAbd al-Raḥmān ʿAzzām and the pontiffs of the Arab League have not visibly learned anything.
>
> They have not learned, in any case, that their victory [!!] in Palestine was not due solely to foreign factors but also – and to a large extent – to the incoherence of their foreign policy.[24]

The bitterness felt resulted in the call, in some newspapers, for the abolition of the Arab League. Since it had practiced a policy that was not within its means, several papers, including Egyptian ones which ordinarily would support the Egyptian-dominated League, felt that it should be buried so that future Arab generations would not know how weak the League had been.[25]

By far the largest amount of editorial criticism was directed not at the Arab League, nor at foreign influence, but at the responsibility of the Arab leaders for the disaster. The editorialists blamed them for having two major faults. The first was that the Arab leaders had disregarded the people and did not realize that war could no longer be won unless the people were informed of what was going on about them. The leaders had to solicit popular support in order to win and this had not been done. Second, the editorialists felt that their leaders were not organized and had limited objectives in mind in Palestine. They thus felt that their leaders were more interested in personal aggrandizement rather than having in mind the welfare of the Palestinians or the Arab peoples.[26]

There is the implication in almost all of the editorials that if only there had been a real, unified military command, if only there had not been treachery on the part of some leaders, if only there had been no foreigners aiding Israel, if only the Arab League had functioned as it was designed, then undoubtedly the Arabs would have been successful.

This "only if" syndrome, while touching on valid points, does not really answer the question of why the Arabs were defeated. The Arab editorialists seemed to be afflicted with the same illusion that was rampant in China during the nineteenth century. The feeling in China then, and in the Arab Middle East in the twentieth century, was that there could be a merger of modern technology with Eastern ethics. However, the Chinese soon learned, much to their chagrin in the Sino-Japanese War of 1895, that it does no good to have a modern machine in the hands of someone with no technological understanding.

There has to be modernization not only in technology but modernization of the minds that will run the machines, be they political or physical. Nowhere did an Arab editorialist write, "The reason for this [Israeli] victory is that the roots of Zionism are grounded in modern Western life while we for the most part are distant from this life and hostile to it."[27] And by missing this point, Arab editorialists overlooked what was perhaps the greatest reason for the defeat of the Arabs in 1948. They also overlooked an opportunity not only to help their people to understand the reasons for the disaster but also to show how subsequent ones could be avoided.

The passage of time did not always ameliorate the negative attitudes of the Arab editorialists. The feeling of Arab unity that had characterized the pre-1948 period evaporated like an aura before the Israeli victory; and, like a mirage, it was as elusive as ever in 1950. "We are still shouting at each other."[28] There remained the feeling that Arab leaders were doing nothing but "meeting, deciding, exchanging greetings, and filling the world with promises."[29]

But the role of the newspaper editorials did not continue in an exclusively negative vein after the fighting stopped in July 1948. As time passed, the writers began to pick up what pieces remained and tried to lead public opinion once again. One of the concerns was with the fate of the more than 700,000 refugees who had fled Palestine. The editorialists called for those with wealth to aid their less fortunate brothers. Several editorials wondered whether the Arab refugees were going to form a new Diaspora in place of the in-gathered Jews in Palestine. But with the seeming possibility in late 1948 that negotiations might result in the repatriation of the Palestinians, editorialists did not spend a great deal of time on the refugee issue. The disconnect between Israel and the Arabs is nowhere more apparent than in the issue of the refugees. The Arabs depended on General Assembly Resolution 194, which called for their return to their homes, while the Israelis made sure this eventuality was not possible. From its inception, a Jewish state was fundamental to Zionist principles. There could be no binational state since this would compromise the Jewish character of Israel. The Jews return to Israel, the Palestinians do not. In the Israeli narrative, the refugee problem was caused by others and the only solution, therefore, was their resettlement elsewhere. Concomitant with this narrative was the destruction and erasure of Palestinian villages and neighborhoods, and the systematic seizure of land and property owned by Palestinians. To quote one of the New Israeli historians, Benny Morris, "A Jewish state would not have come into being without the uprooting of 700,000 Palestinians. Therefore it was necessary to uproot them. There was no choice but to expel that population. It was necessary to cleanse the villages." Morris goes on to point out that Yitzhak Rabin signed the expulsion order for the city of Lod. And that David Ben-Gurion was a "transferist." "Ben Gurion was right. If he had not done what he did, a state would not have come into being. That has to be clear. It is impossible to evade it. Without the uprooting of the Palestinians, a Jewish state would not have arisen here."[30]

If the problem of the refugees escaped close scrutiny, the actions of King ʿAbd Allāh did not. As early as October 1948 there began to appear hostile criticism of his role in managing the Transjordanian sector of the war. In particular, there was criticism of his demand, as early as 1947, that no government be formed in Palestine since the king wanted to annex Arab Palestine to Transjordan.

> If there had been a government in Palestine in mid-May, the least that could be said is that the unhappiness of the refugees would have been less great and that other miseries would have been avoided. In refusing a government for Palestine at that moment, there was tragically, in the place of a country which could defend itself, a country occupied. [...] All this has happened because intentions were not innocent. Palestine was coveted, at least in part, by the very ones who claimed to save it.[31]

The editorial campaign against ʿAbd Allāh, begun in the last quarter of 1948, was a reflection of the anger felt toward the annexation of the West Bank of the Jordan River to the Kingdom of Transjordan. There had been for years a suspicion on the part of other Arab countries directly involved in the Palestinian problem that ʿAbd Allāh wished to unify all of the Near East under the Hashimite crown, a fulfillment of the Ḥusayn-McMahon Correspondences. In order to forestall Transjordanian expansion, the Arab countries having borders contiguous with Transjordan had begun encouraging the Palestinians in 1948 to form their own government with its temporary capital in Gaza. Egypt, as the principal opponent to the Hashimites for Arab leadership, was in the forefront of those supporting the All-Palestine Government. This government was formed on September 20, 1948 and had as its prime minister Aḥmad Ḥilmī ʿAbd al-Bāqī.[32]

The All-Palestine Government's National Assembly, meeting in Gaza, elected the Mufti of Jerusalem, al-Ḥājj Amīn al-Ḥusaynī, as its president. At the end of September, the Mufti arrived in Gaza with the blessing of his Egyptian supporters – his first appearance in Palestine in eleven years.

King 'Abd Allāh termed the whole process "strange," vowed to keep the new Palestinian government out of his "security area," and began the process of retaliation by preparing for the overt annexation of the West Bank. The tenor of the ensuing confrontation between the contending sides was signaled when the king appointed a scion of a prominent Palestinian family long in opposition to the Ḥusaynīs. Raghīb al-Nashāshībī, as the military governor of the West Bank. More ominous, perhaps, was the gathering on the same day as the formation of the All-Palestine government in Gaza of several thousand Palestinian notables in Amman. It called for 'Abd Allāh to act as the protector of the Palestinian people. This was followed two months later, on December 1, by a meeting of Palestinian leaders, headed by the Mayor of Hebron, Muḥammad 'Alī al-Jabrī, in the city of Jericho. The Jericho Congress passed seven resolutions, the most important of which called for the union of Palestine and Transjordan into one kingdom and for 'Abd Allāh to accept the title King of Palestine. The acceptance in Transjordan of this point of view was a foregone conclusion. Within a week, the Amman government agreed to allow 'Abd Allāh to accept the title.

The reaction in the remainder of the Arab world was quick and unanimous. Lebanon, Syria, and Egypt all denounced the Jericho Congress and the actions of the Transjordanian government. King Farūq sent a telegram to all of the Arab governments, except Transjordan, denouncing the Jericho resolutions. The Syrian press thought the actions of 'Abd Allāh had sown discord in the League of Arab States and resulted in the destruction of the Arab cause against the Zionists in Palestine. The Arab League as well as the Palestinian Government in Gaza also denounced the events occurring in the West Bank and in Amman. Even the religious leaders of the Arab world were called in to give their opinions. The Grand Ulamā' of al-Azhar University denounced the Transjordanian king for his "nefarious interference" in the affairs of Palestine and said that his actions were a threat to Palestine, Arabism, and a violation of previous pledges to God.

Egypt, Syria, Lebanon, and even Iraq quickly recognized the All-Palestine government in Gaza and warned the Transjordanian leader not to attempt to annex the West Bank. The governments' demands were strongly echoed in the press of their respective countries. The Lebanese press was the most restrained in its condemnation of the actions of 'Abd Allāh, a result of the imposition in July 1948 of a law forbidding the publication of intra-Arab squabbles. However, Egyptian and Syrian editorials lashed out at the policies of the Hashimite king.

The Egyptian papers warned that the attempt to annex Palestine would "serve as a means of division and conflict between" the heretofore solid Arabs facing the Zionists in Palestine.[33] To this extent, the Egyptian editorialists were correct in their assessment. Prior to the annexation of Palestine to Transjordan, the Arabs, at least on the surface, were united in their opposition to the Zionists. But with the aggrandizement of Transjordan, a new chapter was opened in the Palestinian question. This was the question of inter-Arab rivalries for supremacy within the Near East. Henceforth, where there had been restraint on the part of the editorial writers in attacking leaders of the various Arab nations (perhaps enforced by their respective governments), there was no such restraint following the announced intentions of King ʿAbd Allāh. If one may judge from the amount of editorial opinion devoted to both, the role of the Arab leaders in the Palestine war did not upset the writers as much as ʿAbd Allāh's actions in annexation. One might then draw the conclusion that for Syria, Egypt, and Lebanon, the loss of Palestine to Israel was less bitter than the loss of the West Bank to ʿAbd Allāh. One could rationally explain the former but was hard-pressed to understand the latter.

Jordan's action initiated a period in which papers of one nation denounced the leaders of other nations. The Syrian journal, *al-Manār*, summed it up well when it wrote that ʿAbd Allāh's annexation of a portion of Palestine to Transjordan had sown discord in the Arab League and in the Arab cause for the sole benefit of individuals, not peoples.[34]

Almost simultaneously with the developing friction over the formation of an All-Palestinian government, the United Nations received the second report of Count Folke Bernadotte on September 16. Its most controversial parts called for the Negev, which had been part of the Jewish state in partition, to be given to the Arabs, and the Galilee, assigned to the Arabs, should be Israeli. To the Israelis, the report was anathema since they wanted both territories. Viewed as a threat to the Zionist cause, Bernadotte was assassinated on September 17 by members of the Stern Gang under the leadership of Yitzhak Shamir. The second report was also rejected by Arab editorialists. The newspapers were still unwilling to accept partition. "The mediator brings nothing new. And it is unquestionably true, the rights of the Arabs in Palestine cannot be the object of negotiations."[35]

Although the Arabs rejected the proposals of Count Bernadotte, they were forceful in condemning his assassination. They even rationalized his death, saying that it was for such terrorist activities, perpetrated by the Zionists, that the states of the Arab League had come to the aid of Palestine on May 15.[36]

As the events of the first half of 1948 drew more distant in time, the Arab writers began to formulate ideas about the results of the fighting. There began to develop in Arab editorials a premonition of the long and difficult struggle ahead.

> On the eve of 15 May, the Arab declarations permitted the belief that our armies in Palestine would carry out a military pleasure trip. Today there is no question of a pleasure trip.[37]

Editorialists wrote that the long battle against the forces of Zionism could be speeded toward a successful conclusion if only the Arabs would unite. "The first lesson we learned from Palestine, and one we should always remember, is that our unity gives us strength."[38]

Others, however, saw in any prolonged struggle, whether or not the Arabs were united, the victory of the Israelis. The belief was that every second Israel lived was a period of time in which it would consolidate itself and increase both its numbers and its arms. The call from these editorialists was for an immediate resumption of combat.[39]

For two Christian Lebanese editorialists, the danger to the Arabs lay in the international character of Zionism. The fact that Jews from throughout the world were supporting Israel rankled these writers. And being Christians, they focused on the city of Jerusalem.

Kesrouan Labaki wrote that for Zionists, "[...] the Jewish state without Jerusalem would be a body with no soul." But he pleaded that Jerusalem no longer belonged exclusively to the Jews but also belonged to Muslims and Christians.[40] Echoing this belief, Michel Chiha wrote, "There is no Zionism without Zion and there is no State of Israel which will indefinitely do without Jerusalem."[41]

Editorial opinion continued in a pessimistic tone when fighting erupted in the Negev region during the last quarter of 1948. It seems clear that Israel benefited from the dispute between Egypt and Transjordan by pressing its military advantage. Egypt was defeated by the Israelis. The Arab world was in shambles. In Egypt, the attempt to stifle dissent led the ruling Sa'dist Party to attack the Muslim Brotherhood and its organ, *al-Ikhwān al-Muslimūn*, which had published reports of official ineptness during the fighting. As the latter's views became more widely known, hatred for the incumbent government spread, and Muḥmūd Fahmī al-Naqrāshī, the Sa'dist prime minister was assassinated on December 28 in an act of vengeance. It was clear the Egyptians had lost the war. Less than two months later, the head of the Muslim Brotherhood, Ḥasan al-Bannā, was murdered in retaliation.

In Syria, demonstrations marking the first anniversary of the voting of the partition resolution by the United Nations turned into violent attacks on the government, forcing the resignation of the government of Jamīl Mardam on December 1 and presaging the coup of Colonel Ḥusnī al-Za'īm. A few months earlier, the Lebanese government of Riyāḍ al-Ṣulḥ had resigned. At this crucial time in the history of the Arab world, everything seemed in disarray. Economies were on the verge of collapse, politicians were without honor, and many Arab armies felt betrayed by scheming politicians. Frustrated and yet unable to continue the war against Israel, the Arabs were on the verge of a period of severe domestic unrest and change.

Perhaps as a result of its inability to continue the war, Egypt accepted the invitation of the acting UN Mediator, Ralph Bunche, and went to the island of Rhodes to negotiate the first armistice. The Egyptian delegation arrived in January 1949, and this demarche caused an editorialist to remark that with the journey of the Egyptians to Rhodes the game was over for the other Arab states. They would all fall in line and "play dead, just as they always have, and accept disgrace and the *fait accompli*."[42]

Transjordan followed Egypt to Rhodes in February 1949. Lebanon began negotiations in March while Syria and the Israelis signed a truce agreement in July 1949.

Egyptian editorials attempted to be understanding of the causes that had brought Egypt to the negotiating table:

> The truce in Palestine is considered an important stage because it opens the way for a permanent solution of the Palestine problem. [...] As for Egypt [...] it can review its

> situation with pride since it has done its duty and did what it promised and was faithful to the Arab cause.[43]

The Syrian press was uniformly opposed to the Egyptian action in going to Rhodes although adverse comment was not permitted later when the delegation from Syria went there.[44] This surprising turn of events, the almost eager entry of Syria into talks with the Israelis after the al-Zaʿīm coup on March 30, 1949, led to horror amongst some Syrian politicians and military men. Al-Zaʿīm had come to power, at least in part, as a reaction to the corruption that the military viewed as rampant amongst the civilian politicians, and thus the real cause of defeat in 1948. But once having gained power, he began suggesting a meeting with the Israeli prime minister, David Ben-Gurion. The haughty air and independent disposition of al-Zaʿīm and his too quick agreement to a truce at Rhodes were largely responsible for his overthrow after only four-and-one-half months in power.

The editorial comment on the refugee question, the proposals of Count Bernadotte, the fate of Jerusalem, and the events at Rhodes seem less important when compared with the continuing drama between Transjordan, on the one hand, and the other Arab states, led by Egypt, on the other hand. The muffled protest and lack of outraged commentary concerning the former events were not characteristic of the writing on the topic of the fate of ʿAbd Allāh-held Palestine.

The announced annexation scheme of Transjordan brought inter-Arab friction into the open. One may hypothesize that there was genuine worry on the part of the Arab countries that Transjordan was subordinating the interests of the Palestinians to dynastic considerations. A more accurate analysis is that there was an Arab fear of Transjordanian growth, especially on the part of Egypt, which viewed itself as the leader of the Arab world. But it was not Egypt alone that opposed Transjordan. The diplomatic recognition of the All-Palestine government in Gaza by the Hashimites of Iraq can only be explained in terms of Iraqi fear of their cousin ʿAbd Allāh's ambitions. The Saudis were afraid of a too-strong Hashimite ruler who might decide to try to recapture his family's old hegemony in the Arabian Peninsula. Syria often feared ʿAbd Allāh might try to take Damascus (as his brother had done) as part of a Greater Syria plan. The opposition of a Christian Lebanon to any movement dominated by Muslims that might lead to a Greater Syria needs no explanation.

It is in the light of Transjordanian-Arab rivalry that the question of Palestine must be seen. The feeling of the Arab writers toward the Palestinian refugees was in part humanitarian, but it also provided an opportunity to advance political ideas. Consequently, when the negotiations over the return of the refugees failed because of Israel's refusal to allow return, attention refocused on their plight. For reasons largely attached to politics, Transjordan and the other Arab countries, respectively, came up with two diverging opinions over how the refugee question could be solved.

Egypt, in opposing the union of the West Bank with Transjordan, naturally opposed any plan for the refugees that would further that merger. Therefore, it opposed the settlement of the refugees in Transjordan. Egyptian editorials did not, however, voice any fear of

Transjordanian aggrandizement. Rather, Egypt said it was only being just in demanding that the refugees return to that portion of Palestine the United Nations had originally assigned to the Zionists. In this manner, it refused to further Transjordanian aims by declining to cooperate with the United Nations in its attempts to provide an economic settlement of the problem of the refugees.

This attitude first appeared in the autumn of 1949 when the United Nations dispatched an economic commission to study the possibility of providing jobs for the refugees. Egypt viewed this as a step toward an economic settlement of a problem that it saw as being military and political.

> It is obvious from the [United Nations'] Committee's assignment that it is trying to make a connection between the refugees' destiny and the economic plans which help their settlement, as if it is already decided that the [Arab] countries of the Middle East should settle the refugees. But it is known that the Arab countries adhere to the principle that the refugees must go back to the country from which they were evicted and any other solution is unjust.[45]

The Transjordanians, however, viewed the problem differently. King 'Abd Allāh was, in 1949 and 1950, still anxious to find common ground on which to base a settlement with the Israelis and was more prone, therefore, to accept a settlement that did not require the return of the Palestinians to their former homes. *Filasṭīn*, which had become after 1948 the outspoken leader of the pro-'Abd Allāh newspapers, felt that "the inevitable, practical solution is that the refugees settle in Jordan alone, as Jordan can make available for them work and shelter."[46] Thus, *Filasṭīn* asked the United Nations to provide for a just economic settlement by beginning development projects in Jordan. In this way, the refugees might begin once again to depend on themselves to earn a living, thus regaining their lost dignity.

Where the refugees were to be settled was often only a topic on which the growing Arab-Transjordan dispute could focus. This was also true of the friction that resulted over Transjordan's annexation plans. When on December 27, 1949 King 'Abd Allāh announced that the Transjordanian parliament had been dissolved and that new elections were to be held the following April on both sides of the Jordan River, it was obvious that 'Abd Allāh was finally going to finish what had begun in 1948 with the call for the unification of the two banks of the Jordan River.

The pro-'Abd Allāh papers in Transjordan busied themselves with editorials describing the reasons for the necessity of the annexation of the West Bank. They stated that all the Arab countries, except Transjordan, had sold out the Palestinians and that the only country capable of preserving a measure of dignity for them was his Hashimite Majesty's. Not only were the other Arab countries not capable of regaining the rights of the Palestinian Arabs, they had washed their hand of the Palestine question and "followed the motto that the annihilation of the Arabs of Palestine is a solution for the Palestine question."[47]

On the other side, the anti-ʿAbd Allāh forces viewed the impending annexation of Arab Palestine as a betrayal of the Arab cause. Some newspapers called Israel and Transjordan "allies" because the two had split the Holy Land between themselves like old friends. They declared that as a result of this insidious behavior, "Palestine has disappeared."[48]

The anti-ʿAbd Allāh campaign increased in tempo until it reached its zenith on March 4, 1950, with the publication in the Egyptian newspaper, *Akhbār al-Yawm*, of an exposé of the secret meetings between ʿAbd Allāh and the Zionists.[49] This attack was continued two weeks later when on March 18, *Akhbār al-Yawm* produced photo copies of letters said to have been written by ʿAbd Allāh. The letters graphically pointed out the attempts by the king to make peace with the Israelis. One letter was singled out for special scorn because it addressed Moshe Shertok as "My Dear."

This Egyptian campaign against the Transjordanian monarch had wide repercussions throughout the Arab world. Many newspapers reprinted the damning evidence against ʿAbd Allāh and broadened the charges. Interviews were given by those opposed to the king, thus furthering anti-ʿAbd Allāh feeling. Newspaper readers were reminded that British circles, three years earlier, had stated they would not oppose absorption of parts of Palestine to Transjordan.[50] Some papers even assured their subscribers that a peace treaty already had been concluded between Transjordan and Israel and would be announced at an opportune time.[51] There resulted a call to drive Transjordan from the Arab League for having "betrayed Islam, Arab unity, and the Arab cause." The next sentence in the same editorial, often quoted, reads, "The time has come to sever this decayed member from the body of the Arab world and to bury it and heap dung on it."[52] *Filasṭīn* was not long in responding. An editorial of May 9, 1950, accused a former Egyptian Foreign Minister, Aḥmad Luṭfī al-Sayyid, of calling for peace between Arabs and Zionists.[53] The pro-ʿAbd Allāh press also stated in no uncertain terms that the other Arab countries had forfeited their right to speak for the Palestinians as a result of their pitiful showing in the recent war. It was now up to the Palestinians to speak for themselves and they said they desired union with Transjordan.

"If the Arab League does not want to understand that the Palestinian Arabs themselves asked for unity with their brothers, the Jordanians, it is because the League has bad intentions against this portion of the Arab world and it wants to make it a prey for Israel."[54] The Egyptian-led campaign against Transjordan was unsuccessful. A parliament composed of Palestinians and Transjordanians met in Amman in April 1950 and there ratified the unification of the two banks of the Jordan River. The name of the unified state had earlier become the Hashemite Kingdom of Jordan. Despite periodic threats, Jordan was not expelled from the Arab League and its new borders were *de facto* accepted by the Arab states.

No sooner had the Jordanian affair quieted down when a new Arab irritant entered the Middle East. This was the proclamation of the French, British, and American Tripartite Declaration of May 25, 1950. This Declaration is best remembered for its guaranteeing the integrity of the borders of all countries in the Middle East.[55]

Jordanian editorial opinion was not outspoken on the respective merits or demerits of the Tripartite Declaration. One can assume that ʿAbd Allāh was not adverse to having international guarantees for his newly enlarged nation. One may also assume there was anti-Tripartite feeling, but this was not permitted to become manifest in the Jordanian newspapers. The Lebanese journals left the impression, at least when the Declaration first appeared, that they were not opposed to having their southern border guaranteed against Israeli designs. This Lebanese support was reinforced by the government's issuance of a statement that supported the Tripartite Declaration.[56]

What can be assumed to have been Lebanese and Jordanian passive acceptance of the Declaration was not reflected in the newspapers of Syria and Egypt. Each of these countries opposed the ideas incorporated in the Three Power statement. Their editorials reflected three reasons for opposing it. First and most important, they felt the Declaration protected the State of Israel and guaranteed its borders, thus finalizing the *status quo*. Second, they viewed the Great Powers' declaration as a means of intervening in the affairs of the Middle East. Finally, they saw it as a means for the three nations to reaffirm old influence in the Arab countries under the guise of providing peace and stability. Although the latter two points were sometimes hazy in their exposition, the general feeling in the papers of Egypt and Syria was that the Tripartite Declaration was nothing more than another species of the Balfour Declaration. It would provide for the definitive establishment of Israel's borders and thus was an attempt to liquidate, through subterfuge, the Palestinian affair.[57]

Frustration and bitterness toward the Western Powers and their policies in the Middle East were also reflected in the Arab attitude toward the Korean conflict. There was a feeling that the United States and its Western allies were menacing, through the exportation of colonialist and imperialist ideas, the peace of the world.

Other opinion was equally biting in its comment and chastised the United Nations for its lack of aid in the Middle East. Why was the United Nations aiding the South Koreans against their enemies but not the Arabs? The blame for lack of Middle Eastern action on the part of the world organization was placed on President Truman and his government.

> [...] One can speak of the weakness of the United Nations in Palestine. For Korea, this language cannot be used. But in order to be just, a bitter remark must be made: in Korea, Interest and Justice were on the same side; while in Palestine, Interest played against Justice. These things must be said because the truth must be told.[58]

If the Jordanian newspapers were silent on the UN intervention in Korea, they were not as silent in discussing the role of the United Nations in settling the plight of the refugees. Whereas in early 1950 the pro-'Abd Allāh paper, *Filasṭīn*, had supported the settlement of the refugees in Jordan, by the end of 1950, this position had changed. Now *Filasṭīn* and *al-Difā'*, perhaps out of anti-'Abd Allāh pressure, out of the desire of 'Abd Allāh to placate his Egyptian-aroused opponents, or out of a desire to delay a new UN resolution on the refugees, had begun to call for the unqualified return of the refugees to their former homes.

The call for the settlement of the refugees in Jordan was now substituted with, "The refugee accepts nothing less than return to his home. His return should not be the subject of discussion and bargaining."[59] And to facilitate this return, the Palestinian-Jordanian newspapers called for positive action on the part of the United Nations and its Relief and Works Administration.

The discussion in the Jordanian papers around the refugee problem corresponded in time to a debate going on at the United Nations over a revision of the UN resolution of December 1948[60] for a return of the refugees to their homes. An Israeli offensive at the United Nations in late 1950 culminated in a new resolution, which affirmed that the refugees could either return home or be compensated. However, this second resolution placed emphasis on compensation rather than return.[61] The Israeli position, as voiced by UN Delegate Abba Eban, was that Israel was not to blame for the flight of the refugees. To this argument came the editorial reply:

> It may seem to the reader that the Arab situation with respect to refugees is sound and just but Mr. Eban, the Jewish delegate to the United Nations, has a different opinion. He spoke before the [UN] Political Committee and pretended that his government was innocent in the refugee crisis. He tried to make the entrance of the Arab armies into Palestine the scapegoat.
>
> We wonder whether Eban believed what he said yesterday. He has overlooked what happened in Palestine and that is the refugee problem reached its climax before the end of the Mandate and before the entrance of the Arab armies into Palestine. Did he forget that about half a million Arabs were forced to evacuate their homes by force of arms? Do we have to remind him of Dayr Yāsīn which was the main reason for the entrance of the Arab armies into Palestine? Eban knows these facts but ignored them. [...]
>
> The refugees' tragedy is a result of the devilish and deadly plan devised by world Zionism to uproot the Palestinian Arabs and settle foreigners in their place.[62]

This type of editorial did not alter the adoption of the resolution calling for either repatriation or compensation. The Palestinian press in Jordan was unanimous in condemning this alteration of a previous resolution. By making the return of refugees less positive, it was felt that Israel would only have to say return was impossible and the refugees would be forced to take compensation.[63] The impression given by editorials was that once again the United Nations had been forced to bow before Zionist pressure. As a result, the prestige of the already damaged United Nations sank even lower. The world body was once again seeking the easy way out of a dilemma without giving full recompense to the injuries done to the Palestinians.

The scope of this chapter, from the entrance of the Arab armies into Palestine to the assassination of King ʿAbd Allāh in July 1951 has dealt largely with topical problems. The Arab press, as a generalization, can be said to have played a reacting role rather than a leading role in the events that surrounded the Palestine question. Editorialists tended to see problems already manifest and then react to them, proposing suggestions to ameliorate them. Rare was the editorial that foresaw problems and wished to inform its readers of possible dangers and the methods to be taken to avoid them.

However, the Arab press was not universally backward-looking. There was a perceptible segment of editorial opinion that commented not only upon what Israel had done or was doing but upon what Israel might do. This portion of the press tried to draw a larger picture of the implications, for the Arabs, of Israel on their borders. There was, then, a segment of the press that not only looked *back* but also looked *forward* to discover the meaning of Israel for the Middle East. This type of editorial treatment was usually confined to a limited number of negative observations. There was a feeling that the State of Israel was racist and confessional in nature while the nations of the world were moving toward separation of Church and State and were condemning racially established nations. Arab editorial opinion felt that Israel was a new colonial adventure when, in contrast, the world was moving away from colonial states. The writers also agreed that perhaps because of the tragedies that had befallen the Jews in Europe under Hitler, Israel was now receiving favored treatment from other countries. And finally, there was a universal Arab editorial belief that Israel wanted territorial expansion in the future. This last point was most ominous since the only place the Arabs could see Israeli expansion was into the land of the Arabs.

To support their claims that Israel was a racist-confessional state, editorials dealing with this felt the Arab refugees had been expelled from Palestine for religious reasons. It was felt to be a step backward in the development of modern nation-states since the nations of the world had declared themselves for tolerance, protection of minorities, and civil equality. Israel was alleged to be against all of these rights. The question was then asked, if Israel was permitted to practice racial and confessional discrimination, why was it being encouraged by others? The implied answer was that because Jews had been forced to suffer so greatly, the Western nations were trying to salve their consciences by permitting the Israelis to do as they pleased.[64]

A corollary to this belief was the idea that Israel was a colony of the West. But here the interpretation that Britain was responsible for the creation of Israel was not given. Also not iterated were the commonly held Western beliefs that Britain had helped establish Israel in order to maintain a strong power, friendly to the West, on the Suez Canal; that Israel would keep in check the influence of the French.

Rather, the Arab editorialists felt that Israel's colonial status came as the result of Jewish pressure, largely in Britain and the United States, to form a Jewish-Western state in the Arab East. Jewish money and votes in the United States were particularly suspect. The general feeling was that Jewish-American votes in the New York elections and in the presidential election were enough to cause politicians to do everything in their power to gain this believed bloc of votes. The wealth of the Jewish community in the United States was also identified, and it was implied that this community could secure favors as a result of its wealth.[65]

To expound upon how the Arabs felt the Israelis were being favored would be to reiterate what has come before and what follows in this study. Throughout is the Arab belief that Justice was on the side of the Arabs and for many reasons – economic, political, as well as those reasons engendered by the Second World War – Justice was not important except in Arab eyes. This frustration over believed favoritism was often more implicit than explicit.

Two instances where this feeling became explicit were the diplomatic recognition of Israel and its admittance to the United Nations. There were genuine feelings of editorial shock over the rapidity with which the United States and Russia recognized Israel.[66]

The second incident was the seeming haste with which Israel was admitted to the world body:

> Before the fate of Jerusalem and Nazareth is decided, and before the question, for example of Italy and Spain [being admitted into membership], the Security Council, almost unanimously, is recommending the admission of Israel into the United Nations Organization. The country of Dante and that of Charles V can languish in waiting; but Israel cannot wait; and nations are seen seized with a feverish zeal as soon as it is a question of Israel.[67]

Finally, there was the fear of Israeli expansion and its implications for the Arabs in the future. There were many editorials on this topic in almost all of the Arab journals. They voiced a fear of believed Zionist intentions to expand. However, the greatest number of editorials on this particular subject, and often the best handled, came from the pen of the Lebanese writer Michel Chiha. Chiha's editorials must be read with caution, however, since he was sometimes unable or unwilling to make a differentiation between Zionism and Judaism.[68]

The feeling that Israel was and would be an expansionist state grew out of the thesis, adhered to by the editorialists, that with the establishment of Israel, world-wide Jewry had in one stroke discovered a home for itself. Comment was made of the fact that henceforth Israelis could gain benefits not normally accruing to others by their ability to hold two passports. But more important than this was the establishment in a small area of a country which claimed a potential population of fifteen or sixteen million people dispersed throughout the world.

At a time when the Arabs neither knew of the wealth of their own resources nor dreamed of controlling the vast oil riches in their lands, they felt that these scattered millions of Jews possessed greater wealth and knowledge than the Arabs. It was felt, then, that the first steps, prior to physical expansion, would be economic expansion followed by political and military expansion.

> [...] The Jewish state, conceived according to the partition plan of the United Nations is, we have written it ten times, a bridgehead, a departure point, a commencement. It is the means of arriving at the possession of Palestine entirely, of vast territories on the other side of the Jordan [River], of other [territories] in Syria, which belonged to the Twelve Tribes, and later, when circumstances will permit it, of territories which were of old the Kingdom of Israel, and, yet further, that which was the patrimony of Abraham.[69]

> [...] It is not the business of Israel to produce cereals and sugar beets. [...] Israel is made for power, for the management of money and what comes with it, for the final revolution which will establish its prevalence.[70]

> For Israel, all the universe could perish provided the Kingdom of David would emerge triumphant. That, for Israel, is a congenital concept of all policy and a fearful concept.
>
> The good men who think that Israel can represent, through this, a power for security and order have given themselves over to illusions.[71]

Editorialists felt that tragically the Palestinians would replace the Jews in a new Diaspora. Thus once again, as at the time prior to May 1948, the Arab editorialists were militant in their call for arms to settle their grievances. This call was not heeded, to any large degree, by the Arab governments. This was probably due to a recognition on the part of the Arab leaders that military victory was not possible. It may also have been unheeded because of official hope that some arrangement could be made between the Arabs, led by King ʿAbd Allāh, and the Israelis.

The slim chance for an early *modus vivendi* ended with the assassination of King ʿAbd Allāh as he was entering the Aqsa Mosque in July 1951. Of the ten people implicated in the murder, three were from the Ḥusayni family. It has been widely speculated that one of the causes for the assassination was the resentment felt toward ʿAbd Allāh as a result of the press campaign against the king. Particularly damaging to him were the disclosures in *Akhbār al-Yawm* which, as have been mentioned, were widely reported and expanded. Not surprisingly, Arab editorials outside of Jordan used only minimal space in extolling the virtues of the late Hashimite ruler. *Al-Ahrām*, for example, was devastating with its faint praise on July 22 when it wrote, "Undoubtedly the situation in Jordan will change after his assassination for many reasons, particularly since Ṭalāl [ʿAbd Allāh's son] is inclined to follow an effective Arab policy" Clearly there existed a militant press, more in tune with the Arab people than with their rulers, which still identified the dead king with peace with the Zionists and the annexation of Palestine.

Editorial opinion expressed in the Arab world from the beginning of the Palestine war was markedly different from the opinion written at the time of the assassination of ʿAbd Allāh. Early in 1948, although there was a hint of future strife, editorials were united against the Zionists. This is probably not unusual for any press and may be explained as national unity in the face of an enemy. Whatever differences were observed between the newspapers were in tone (the degree of devotional fervor) and in the amount of space given to the events in Palestine. It is not unexpected that those papers most closely associated, geographically and emotionally, with Palestine spent the largest amount of editorial and other space on that country's tribulations.

With the first truce, the Arab newspapers were generally one voice in condemning it. And after the second truce, there began to appear sustained dissent in the editorials. This dissent centered on the reasons for the lack of Arab victories. Since differing reasons were given for the defeat, there developed a movement away from the unified optimism, prior to the war, to fractured pessimism, after the war. Pessimism often not so much over Arab defeats but over how these defeats occurred. As a result, the Arab League became a prime target for adverse opinion. The West, too, was blamed for the ability of the Israelis to withstand the Arabs. More than this, the Arab leaders would be called upon to answer for their role in the disaster of Palestine.

The loss of Palestine thus resulted in a verbal war waged amongst the newspapers of the Arab countries over who was at fault. The effect of this "war" was to put on the one side the supporters of ʿAbd Allāh and on the other the supporters of the various Arab rulers. The feeling of anger toward the role of Transjordan in the Palestine war was heightened by the annexation of the West Bank to Transjordan in 1950. As a consequence, any proposed solution to the Palestine problem was inevitably opposed by one of the two feuding sides. The formation of the All-Palestine government in Gaza, under the leadership of the Mufti of Jerusalem, was denounced by those papers supporting the king of Transjordan. On the other side, the attempts to find a peaceful solution, as advanced twice by Count Bernadotte, and an economic solution, as put forward by the United Nations, were invariably condemned by the other Arab states, with Egypt in the forefront.

Each side accused the other side of betrayal. To a certain extent, both sides were correct. Anti-Egyptian editorials pointed out that it was Egypt that first went to the conference table with Israel. Anti-ʿAbd Allāh editorials declared that it was ʿAbd Allāh who had hoped, from the very beginning, to arrange a mutually acceptable settlement with the Zionists. One of the results of these editorial campaigns may well have been the assassination of ʿAbd Allāh in 1951.

Despite this bulk of editorial condemnation on both sides, there was a different leitmotif observable throughout the period covered in this chapter. This theme was the fear that the establishment of the State of Israel would be a disaster for the Arab nations. The editorialists who wrote on this subject felt that a Zionist state, by its nature, would have to be expansionist since it claimed a citizenship of at least fifteen million and the space it was given could hold only a fraction of that number. From this fear developed a belief that the Arabs might form a new Diaspora. To prevent this from occurring, the Arab writers called for a return to arms. This editorial appeal was not heeded by the Arab governments probably because of a lack of Arab ability to wage a successful war and perhaps a hope that the United Nations could arrange a settlement. There was also another reason for not resorting to arms. This was the possibility that permanent peace might be made between the Arabs and Israel, with Jordan in the lead. This marginal hope was ended with the death of the Hashimite ruler.

Notes

1 John Marlowe, *Anglo-Egyptian Relations, 1800–1953* (London, The Cresset Press, 1954), 323.
2 Najīb al-Rayyis, *al-Qabas*, June 3, 1948. See *al-Manār*, July 14, 1948, for a similar call to sacrifice.
3 Kesrouan Labaki, *L'Orient*, April 28, 1948.
4 Kāmil Murūwah, *al-Ḥayāt*, July 8, 1948.

5 *Al-Ahrām*, May 27, 1948. See also the same paper of June 1, 1948.
6 Michel Chiha, *Le Jour*, July 7, 1948. See also the same writer, ibid., June 11, 1948.
7 Patrick Seale, *The Struggle for Syria* (London, Oxford University Press, 1965), 33.
8 Sir Reader Bullard, *The Middle East* (London, Oxford University Press, 1961), 188.
9 Thomas Mayer, "Egypt's 1948 Invasion of Palestine," *Middle Eastern Studies*, 22, no. 1 (January 1986): 20–36. Much of the material Mayer uses in his article comes from Hugh McLeave, *The Last Pharaoh* (London, Tower Publications, 1969), 169 and *passim*.
10 Respectively, *al-Ahrām*, May 24, 1948, and *al-Qabas*, May 19, 1948.
11 *Al-Ahrām*, June 3, 1948. See also Muḥyī al-Dīn al-Nuṣūlī, *Bayrūt*, June 3, 1948.
12 Kesrouan Labaki, *L'Orient*, June 11, 1948.
13 *Al-Ayyām*, June 20, 1948.
14 Kesrouan Labaki, *L'Orient*, June 11, 1948.
15 The text of Count Bernadotte's proposal was published in the *New York Times*, July 5, 1948. A largely accurate version of the proposal appeared in *al-Miṣrī*, July 1, 1948, which was three days prior to the official release of the document.
16 Ḥannā Ghusun, *al-Diyār*, July 4, 1948.
17 Najīb al-Rayyis, *al-Qabas*, June 7, 1948. See also Fu'ād Sarrūf in *al-Ahrām*, June 22, 1948.
18 Ḥannā Ghusun, *al-Diyār*, June 12, 1948. See also Muḥyī al-Dīn al-Nuṣūlī in *Bayrūt*, June 16, 1948.
19 See for example *al-Balad*, July 7, 1948; *al-Kifāḥ*, July 10, 1948; and *al-Ayyām*, July 14, 1948.
20 July 18, 1948.
21 Ḥannā Ghusun, *al-Diyār*, July 22, 1948. See also Kāmil Murūwah in *al-Ḥayāt*, June 19, 1948.
22 *Al-Ahrām*, November 22, 1948.
23 July 20, 1948.
24 Kesrouan Labaki, *L'Orient*, December 1, 1948. For a corroborating view, see Fayez Sayegh, *Arab Unity: Hope and Fulfillment* (New York, Devin-Adair Co., 1958), 144.
25 See for example *al-Zamān* (of Egypt), January 10, 1949.
26 For representative editorials see Kāmil Murūwah, *al-Ḥayāt*, July 20, 1948, or *al-Manār*, July 29, 1948. See also a poem written by Muḥammad al-Asmar in *al-Ahrām*, October 3, 1948, with apologies for the translation, which reads in part:

> I do not fault the Jews
> Our allies are to blame
> They desired our friendship
> But their actions refuted their claim.

For a more detailed discussion of the role of the Arab leaders and their betrayal of the Palestine cause, see Mūsā al-ʿAlamī, *ʿIbrat Filasṭīn* (*The Lesson of Palestine*), (Beirut, Dār al-Kashshāf, 1949), 23–30.
27 Constantine K. Zurayk, *The Meaning of the Disaster* (Beirut, Khayats, 1956), 34.
28 Yūsuf Ḥannā, *al-Difāʿ*, May 15, 1950.
29 Ibid., April 21, 1950.

30 Interview with Benny Morris, *New Left Review*, no. 26 (March–April, 2004). In this context Gabriel Piterberg writes in "Erasures", *New Left Review*, no. 10 (July–August, 2001): 31–46, about the disappearance of the village of Shaykh Mu'nis that was destroyed by the Israelis though it had cooperated with the Zionists. The village land became part of Tel Aviv that took the name Ramat Aviv. In the 1990s, the University of Tel Aviv built a VIP club called the Green House on the hill where the Shaykh Mu'nis headman's home once stood. "The information of the site's past, and who owned it, may be found in the menu of the Green House" (ibid., 39).

31 Michel Chiha, *Le Jour*, October 27, 1948. Although some of the Arab newspapers noted that ʿAbd Allāh's actions in the Palestine war were not exactly what was expected, there was no hint at this time of the king's meetings and agreements with, among others, Golda Meir and Moshe Shertok. These were made public only in late 1949 and early 1950. The details of the meetings may be found in volume one of ʿAbd Allāh al-Tal, *Kārithat Filasṭīn* (*The Catastrophe of Palestine*) (Cairo, Maṭbaʿat Miṣr, 1959). A detailed analysis of the meetings may be seen in *Jordan: A Political Study* (New York, Asia Publishing House, 1962), 25–38.

32 For a complete listing of the cabinet members in the All-Palestine Government and their portfolios see `Arif al-`Arif, *Al-Nakbah* (*The Calamity*), 3 (Sidon, al-Ṭabʿah al-ʿAṣrīyah 1956), 704–705.

33 *Al-Ahrām*, December 9, 10, and 12, 1948.

34 December 9, 1948. See also *Alif Bā'*, September 29, 1948; and a*l-Balad*, October 9, 1948.

35 *Al-Fayḥā'*, September 16, 1948. See also *al-Ahrām*, September 22 and 23, 1948. These editorials cast some doubt on the accuracy of A. H. H. Abidi's statement that "Bernadotte's posthumous report, on the whole, was well received by the Arabs" (*Jordan: A Political Study* [New York, Asia Publishing House, 1962], 49). The Arab writers were, however, wrong in saying that Bernadotte's second proposal brought "nothing new." The Port of Haifa and the airport at Lydda were taken from Israel and declared "free".

36 *L'Orient*, September 18, 1948; *al-Kifāḥ*, September 18, 1948; and *al-Qabas*, November 2, 1948.

37 Kesrouan Labaki, *L'Orient*, September 8, 1948.

38 *Al-Ahrām*, July 25, 1948.

39 *Al-Balad*, October 30, 1948. See *al-Ahrām*, October 26, 1948. The latter editorial recognized the danger, for the Arabs, of Israel's ability to strengthen itself. The editorial said that a quick solution would be the best. But then it did not say what it would like to see in any quick solution.

40 *L'Orient*, September 21, 1948.

41 *Le Jour*, September 4, 1948.

42 Muḥyī al-Dīn al-Nuṣūlī, *Bayrūt*, January 17, 1949.

43 *Al-Ahrām*, February 25, 1949.

44 See for example *al-Fayḥā'*, February 9, 1949; *Baradā*, February 19, 1949; and *al-Manār*, February 21, 1949. The editorial comment in the last newspaper was especially bitter toward the Egyptian government. This may be explained, in part, by the fact that *al-Manār* was the spokesman in Syria for the Muslim Brotherhood. The Brotherhood's leader, Ḥasan al-Bannā, was assassinated on February 12, 1949, and *al-Manār* held the Egyptian government responsible.

45 *Al-Ahrām*, September 14, 1949.

46 January 12, 1950.
47 *Filasṭīn*, January 15, 1950. Also see the same paper on January 11, 1950.
48 *Al-Sūrī al-Jadīd*, December 21, 1949. See the same newspaper of December 25, 1949 as well as *al-Naṣr*, October 21, 1949.
49 That the meetings between ʿAbd Allāh and the Zionists are really more than an "allegation" have been confirmed by Walter Eytan, *The First Ten Years* (London, Weidenfeld and Nicolson, 1958), 42–43; John Glubb, *A Soldier with the Arabs* (New York, Hodder, and Stoughton, 1958), 258, 340–341; James G. McDonald, *My Mission in Israel* (London, Victor Gollancz, 1951), 194; and ʿAbd Allāh al-Tal, *Kārithat Filasṭīn*, Volume I (Cairo, Maṭbaʿat Miṣr, 1959).
50 *Al-Ahrām*, May 9, 1950. This editorial is undoubtedly based on a statement by British Foreign Secretary Ernest Bevin. See Parliamentary Debates House of Commons, vol. 451, columns 999–1000, June 4, 1948.
51 *Baradā*, March 19, 1950. See also *al-Ahrām*, May 11, 1950.
52 *Al-Miṣrī*, March 19, 1950.
53 Confirming that the first overt call for peace with Israel came from the Egyptians, see Benjamin Shwadran, *Jordan: A State of Tension* (New York, Middle Eastern Affairs Press, 1959), 272.
54 *Filasṭīn*, May 17, 1950. See also the same newspaper on June 3, 1950.
55 The Tripartite Declaration is published in the US Department of State *Bulletin* 52, no. 570 (June 5, 1950): 886.
56 Published in *L'Orient*, May 27, 1950.
57 Representative opinion may be seen in *Alif Bā'*, June 9, 1950; *al-Ahrām*, May 30, 1950; and *al-Inshā'*, May 11, 1951.
58 Michel Chiha, *Le Jour*, December 27, 1950. See also *al-Qabas*, May 27, 1951.
59 *Filasṭīn*, November 19, 1950.
60 U.N. Resolution No. 194 (III) of December 11, 1948.
61 U.N. Resolution No. 394 (V) of December 14, 1950.
62 *Al-Difāʿ*, November 10, 1950. Also see the same paper on November 12, 1950.
63 *Filasṭīn*, December 8 and 9, 1950, and January 25, 1951.
64 See for example Michel Chiha, *Le Jour*, October 25, 1948; *al-Difāʿ*, April 17, 1950; and *al-Ahrām*, October 3, 1950.
65 Representative editorials may be seen in Michel Chiha, *Le Jour*, January 6, 1949; *al-Ahrām*, June 13, 1949; and *al-Difāʿ*, August 30, 1950; and *al-Qabas*, April 9, 1951.
66 See note 6 of this chapter.
67 Michel Chiha, *Le Jour*, March 6, 1949. See also *al-Ahrām*, May 13, 1949.
68 For more on Michel Chiha's writings on Palestine, see "The Christian Arab Press and the Palestine Conflict: A Case Study of Michel Chiha of Beirut's *Le Jour*," *Muslim World*, 64, no. 2 (May, 1975): 119–131.
69 Michel Chiha, *Le Jour*, September 4, 1948.
70 Ibid., March 25, 1949.
71 Ibid., July 29, 1950. See also *al-Ahrām*, March 25, 1949.

Chapter 4

The Decline of Western Influence from the Death of ʻAbd Allāh to the 1956 Suez Crisis

Certainly the death of King ʿAbd Allāh was a major event in the history of the Palestine question. It marked the end of a period where a peaceful settlement, commonly arranged and commonly acceptable, might have been made between Arabs and Israelis. King ʿAbd Allāh, for all his faults and his desire to settle with Israel at the expense of the Palestinians, was a strong man, who, had he been able to conclude peace, might have been able to make the peace succeed. This was undoubtedly not the case with his successor and son, Ṭalāl, nor was it true in 1952 when his grandson, Ḥusayn, ascended the throne at 17 years of age. If one searches the Arab world at that period, it is clear that no other ruler was capable of doing what ʿAbd Allāh had desired to do.

Particularly tragic for the Arab world was the mental illness of King Ṭalāl, which led to his deposition thirteen months after the death of his father. While Ṭalāl ruled, censorship was eased, especially on foreign dispatches, and a liberal constitution was promulgated for the peoples of Jordan. For these and other acts, he was widely loved. Increasingly prolonged absences from his country, necessitated by recurring illness, finally forced Jordan's parliament to act.

The Arab world, after ʿAbd Allāh and Ṭalāl, turned to other areas to find a solution to the question of Palestine. Editorial opinion reflected this change.

One possible solution, briefly mentioned in the previous chapter, was settlement through the permanent maintenance of the status quo, guaranteed by the Tripartite Declaration. Arab editorial opinion, as already noted, did not put a great amount of faith in the Declaration and what support did accrue to it had been passive in nature, centering largely in Jordan and Lebanon. The passive attitude of the Lebanese writers became more positive in 1953 and after. Such a stance arose out of the growing fear that Israel had intentions toward south Lebanon and especially that portion of the Litani River that flows westward from the Biqāʿ valley toward the Mediterranean. Newspapers called for the Powers who had issued the Declaration of May 1950 to "not forget that it is not only in their interest, but their primary duty and obligation, to take seriously their responsibilities to execute and enforce the commitments they have assumed."[1] That Israel viewed the southern portion of Lebanon with special interest has often been affirmed. After the June 1967 war, Moshe Dayan maintained that Israel's new borders were all satisfactory except those with Lebanon. In the Lebanese Civil War of 1975–76, the Israelis warned Syria to stay out of the south of Lebanon and subsequently literally annexed the area through free-moving patrols, road construction, an open-border policy, and arming a Lebanese militia friendly to them. The Israeli invasions of 1978 and 1982 reaffirmed Israel's determination to, at least, control events in the south.

For the Jordanians, the problem in the early 1950s was more acute because of Israeli pressure, most notably around Jerusalem. So its papers, too, called for Western intervention to guarantee the borders. Jordan's government was even asked by its editorial writers to invoke the Anglo-Jordanian Treaty of March 1948, which provided for mutual military assistance in the event one or the other nation was attacked.[2]

The two nations that had earlier opposed the Tripartite Declaration, that is Egypt and Syria, did not change their attitude. They felt that any Western intervention in Palestine, under the pretext of attempting to preserve the existing borders, would continue to be a conspiracy directed against the Arabs for reasons already mentioned.[3] In spite of the eventual pleas of the Lebanese and Jordanians for a firm stand on the part of those who had offered guarantees, by 1954, only 4 years after its inception, the Declaration for all practical purposes had become a dead letter. Other factors were pushing it into the background, including a fear of Western intervention. Moreover, Arab editorial hostility to the Declaration had aided in putting an end to the Tripartite Declaration.

If the Tripartite Declaration was pushed quickly aside, an older problem, that of the refugees, did not disappear with the passage of time. The same forcefulness that characterized Arab editorials in the summer of 1948 was visible throughout this later period. With surprising unanimity, the Arab papers viewed the problem, above all, as being political. When the Jordanian papers ceased calling for the refugees to be resettled in Jordan, all of the Arab countries were unanimous in their desire for return of the refugees to their former homes. The papers felt that if the Zionists could return after 2000 years certainly the claim of the refugees was just as valid.[4] To even suggest that it might be two millennia before the Palestinians could return represents a more pessimistic view of the refugee situation than was apparent in 1948. When the first war erupted, the disposition of the Palestinians was often viewed as a temporary inconvenience. By the early 1950s, it was finally realized that the Palestinians might never be allowed to return.

The same transition occurred in Israeli popular perception. In 1948, there seemed to be no overt policy on the return of those who had left. Within a few years, however, Israeli public policy was firmly aligned with what had been Israel's clandestine policy as early as 1947. Perhaps a small number of refugees would be allowed back into historic Palestine, but the refugee question was to be solved by their settlement in the Arab countries. As early as 1950, Israel had enacted the infamous "Absentee Property Law." Under this law, a Palestinian who had never left what became the state of Israel, but during the fighting had moved perhaps for safety only a few feet away from his property was classified as an "absentee." "A Custodian of Absentee Property was charged with supervising or 'selling' this property to Jews." A Development Authority, set up specifically to acquire "absentee" property, purchased 2.37 million dunums (approximately four to the acre) and it in turn sold it to the Jewish National Fund, which then sold or leased it exclusively to Jews.[5] These subterfuges, the creation of government entities, were designed to make it look as though nothing illegal was occurring. The Office of Custodian and the Development Authority were attempts to avoid international condemnation for the violation of Article 47 of the Fourth

Geneva Convention that proscribes the annexation of occupied territory, and Article 49 which prohibits the forcible transfer or deportation of residents from an occupied area.

Arab writers were fully aware of the Israeli desire to have an exclusively Jewish state, but they also discerned another reason why the Israelis did not permit the refugees to return: repatriation would end a source of tension in the Arab states that was preventing Arab modernization and self-strengthening.[6]

The Arab writers were generally just as intransigent as the Israelis on the problem of the refugees. To this end, they refused to accept any solution other than repatriation since they felt that if another solution were agreed upon, for instance compensation and resettlement, the whole question of Palestine and its disposition would disappear. As long as the refugees existed, the Arab peoples would have world public opinion on their side and a future repatriation could be hoped for.[7]

If editorialists were hostile toward the concept of dispersion of the Palestinians, they were even more antagonistic to plans that would achieve the same ends under a different guise, for example through economics. This negative attitude toward an economic solution to the refugee problem was magnified, in the editorials, by the attitude of the United Nations Relief and Works Agency for Palestine Refugees in the Near East (UNRWA). This agency was created in December 1949 to aid Palestinians who had fled their homes. In attempting to assist, the directors had encouraged refugee resettlement and training to make them self-sufficient. The reasons for these plans were largely economic – the refugees would be less of a financial burden on the world if they could support themselves. However, Arab editorialists, practically to a writer, rejected UNRWA's scheme of resettlement and employment of the refugees, using American Point IV aid[8] and other monies, as nothing but a means of making firm the status quo for Israel's benefit. The thought was widely published that UNRWA was nothing more than an organization serving Israeli interests because UNRWA's plan was no more than the Israelis had asked. Israelis wanted the Palestinians dispersed amongst the Arab countries, and the plan for small communities and resettlement in the various Arab states would do this. The Israelis wanted the Palestinians to be engaged only in agricultural work. It seemed that what was being advocated by UNRWA would insure that the majority of the refugees would be farming the land.[9] The wariness of Arab editorialists was not lessened by the speech of the American Secretary of State, John Foster Dulles, upon his return from a trip to the Middle East in 1953. "Some of these refugees could be settled in the area presently controlled by Israel. Most, however, could be more readily integrated into the lives of the neighboring countries. This, however, awaits irrigation projects which will permit more soil to be cultivated."[10]

Opposition to the plans of UNRWA to alleviate the condition of the refugees by temporarily resettling them and training them with money provided by the West had cumulative results. In retrospect, it is fairly easy to see the snowballing effect that opposition to resettlement had on relations between the Arabs and those who were proposing any solution other than repatriation.

If resettlement and training projects gave the Arab writers the feeling that the refugees and their grievances were being pushed aside and liquidated, then anything that aided the fulfillment of these ideas was reviled. A case to illustrate this feeling was editorial opinion toward American Point IV aid to underdeveloped nations.

Editorialists wrote that since UNRWA's ideas were condemnable, so was Point IV that was thought in part to be used for implementing UNRWA's projects. The Western nations said they wanted to aid the Arabs but only gave them a very small portion of the total amount of funds allocated, while giving Israel larger sums. Further, they continued, although the avowed purpose of the aid was to help the refugees, how could the diversion of the Litani River to the south, for example, help the refugees? The only people who would benefit from such enterprises would be the Israelis.[11]

Editorial opinion noted that the Israelis, with aid received from America, were to build armaments and factories while the same aid to the Arabs was to provide for the dispersion of the refugees and their employment in agricultural production that would continually make them economically subservient to the more advanced Israelis.

> Behind these financial contributions – contributions which from dollars are translated at a later date into shells, guns, and military equipment – lies the real cause of this prevalent state of unrest throughout the Arab World. And naively, America feeds the Jews with dollars and wonders why its Middle Eastern policy has failed to meet with success. Very candidly, they wonder why their every move finds no response and why the Arabs consider them responsible for the present state of affairs.[12]

The attacks on Point IV were widened not only to question the motivation behind the giving of the aid, but to include the idea that there were more sinister reasons. A number of editorials intimated that Point IV had Jewish-Americans working for it and why should anyone be involved in studying the exclusively Lebanese Litani River unless the motivation of Point IV was not honorable? The result was a cry that Point IV had as its true mission espionage and obtaining military secrets.[13]

The lack of confidence in Point IV, in UNRWA, and in similar projects emanating from the world-at-large, forced many editorial writers to wonder about the ability or lack of ability of the United Nations. In this respect, there was a significant change in the attitudes of the Arab editorialist toward the question of the United Nations and its resolutions. Earlier, before the death of King 'Abd Allāh, the papers of Egypt, Syria, Palestine, and Lebanon had opposed the UN resolution concerning the partition of Palestine. Jordan, although not overtly accepting the resolution, was known to have accepted it in principle.

However, these attitudes changed with the passage of time. The transition was slow in Egypt, Syria, and Lebanon. The reversal of Jordanian opinion was more pronounced because of the relative freedom of opinion that was permitted after 'Abd Allāh's death. At any rate, the Jordanian papers, after the summer of 1951, called for a rejection of partition.

On the other hand, the newspapers of the other Arab countries, especially those of Lebanon, had accepted in principle the existence of Israel if it would implement the three resolutions involving repatriation of refugees (GA Resolution 194), internationalization of Jerusalem (GA Resolution 303), and the partition of Palestine (GA Resolution 181).[14] Some newspapers called for the sending of United Nations' troops to the Middle East to enforce its resolutions while others said that since the United Nations would not enforce its resolutions, the Arab countries should withdraw from the world organization.[15]

Hostile criticism of the United Nations and its inactivity was not limited to what has been described in the preceding paragraphs. Criticism of the United Nations also included condemnation of that organization for lack of action in handling the fate of Jerusalem. When the fighting had stopped in 1948, the city of Jerusalem had been in effect partitioned between the two belligerents. The Old City was in Jordanian hands while the New City, comprising at least 75% of the total, was in Israeli hands. Arab consternation centered on the belief that Israel would at some future date attempt to conquer the Old City. This fear of Israeli intentions was heightened in 1952 when word began to appear in Arab papers that Israel was moving its Foreign Office to the New City from Tel Aviv. There was also a fear in April 1953 when sporadic fighting between Jordan and Israel broke out in Jerusalem.

But Arab concern did not limit itself to expressions that Israel was going to make Jerusalem its capital. The fear was expressed that the Jews of Israel had, in fact, a special desire for the area known to Muslims as the Noble Sanctuary (with the Dome of the Rock and the Mosque of al-Aqsa) and to Jews as the Temple Mount. The rock under the Dome is, in Islam, the place from which Muḥammad ascended to Heaven to talk with God and thus has been revered for thirteen centuries. In Judaism, somewhere in the same area was the location of the first and second Temples. In the Arab view, Israel wanted to destroy the Muslims' buildings and then rebuild Solomon's Temple on its original site.[16]

Once again, however, as was the case with partition, the Arab states were divided with Egypt, Syria, and Lebanon facing Jordan. The Jordanians had opposed putting Jerusalem under the care of the United Nations. As a result, there were no editorials in the Jordanian papers that called for internationalization. To the contrary, the newspapers of Jordan repeatedly called for conquering the New City. They also said the Israeli plan to move its seat of government to Jerusalem should be countered by a Jordanian move of the same nature.[17]

Editorial opinion, excluding Jordanian, found itself in the unenviable position of attacking the Israelis and the Jordanian Hashimites. Thus, Michel Chiha, for one, was forced to write in editorials approximately one year apart that the Israelis and the Jordanians were both at fault in their attitudes.

> For Israel, the hill of Zion is the justification for Zionism (with the obsession for Jerusalem); but for Christianity and for all of Islam, Jerusalem is a Holy Place which cannot be permitted to be placed, no matter what the promises, under the political authority of Israel.[18]

> Israel is the master of three-fourths of the Holy City; and what it wants, first of all, is the other fourth, that is above all, the site of the Temple. [...]
>
> In order to possess a fragment of Jerusalem, Jordan exposes the entire city and all of the neighboring area. In the Palestinian affair, Jordan, since the beginning, carries heavy responsibilities. [...]
>
> Feeble Jordan opposes that which could make it secure. It is to its own safety that it is opposed. [...]
>
> The Jordanian pretension does not honor the Hashimites, does not make them greater in the Arab World; it shows them to be subordinate to a vain and false glory[...].[19]

The problem was how to reconcile Jordanian desires and Zionist plans. The practically unanimous answer from those opposed to both Jordan and Israel was the internationalization of Jerusalem. Once again General Assembly Resolution 303 was recalled, and the editorial writers pleaded with the world organization to implement what it had agreed upon.[20]

One can surmise the thoughts that permeated the minds of the various editorial writers. To think of the refugees in the camps, the division of a country that they believed could have been whole, and the Israeli push to occupy what remained of Arab Jerusalem appeared to be a nightmare being enacted before their eyes. Their tendency was to look about to discover the causes of the dilemmas they faced. The attempts at finding fault and the editorial remedies have been mentioned previously. But another reason for apprehension that developed rapidly in the 1950s was a fear of Jewish immigration. Perhaps it would be best to say that this was a re-emerging fright. Before the establishment of the State of Israel there had been consternation voiced about Jewish immigration and what it would do to the Arab population in Palestine. The most famous of these alarms was expressed by George Antonius when he wrote, "The logic is inexorable. It shows that no room can be made in Palestine for a second nation except by dislodging or exterminating the nation in possession."[21] But during the period 1948–51, criticism of the events in Palestine did not include a significant amount of comment on Jewish immigration. Nor did the writers spend a great deal of space discussing the ramifications of continued immigration, largely because the writers were more concerned with other events.

However, as opinion turned to the attempts at settling the refugees outside of Palestine and to the drama unfolding in Jerusalem, there arose a small cry against continued Jewish immigration into Israel. The Arab writers felt that the problems the Second World War had created for world Jewry had ended. In 1951 and after, one could not speak of Jewish refugees. Therefore, the writers felt that the incessant calls of the Israelis for more and more immigrants was just a means of denying the Arabs their right to return and a way to gain manpower so as to be able to "expand its area into the Arab countries such as taking south Lebanon, part of Syria, the Sinai peninsula, and northern Saudi Arabia."[22]

Meanwhile, the chain of events since the State of Israel came into being – the fact of Israel's existence, the resulting tensions and upheavals among the Arabs, the notion that Israel would be the home of the Jews of the whole world, and the favoritism shown to Jewish immigrants over Arab refugees could not fail to influence editorial opinion toward Jewish Arabs. Signs of anti-Jewish feeling in the Arab press, described in a previous chapter, became much more prevalent in the 1950s, although still not widespread. It is not the purpose of this book to discuss the treatment of Jewish Arabs by Muslim and Christian Arabs, nor for that matter of Arab Israelis by Jewish Israelis. It is sufficient to say that many newspapers, particularly those of Syria, were willing to draw an unfortunate connection between what was occurring and what had occurred in Palestine and to their own populations.

There was a Syrian campaign that aimed at those countries which were attempting to be judicious in the care of their Jewish citizens. In particular, several Syrian newspapers wondered about Lebanese treatment of its Jews. The American University of Beirut was mentioned since it had several Jewish faculty members.[23] More important than this was the Syrian disclosure that there were Jewish officers in the Lebanese army. Editorialists asked how Lebanon could claim to be an Arab nation when it had within its officer corps those who were hostile to Arab aims. Lebanon was accused of being a weak link among the Arab states.[24] Unfortunately, there were seemingly no voices raised in support of the Jewish Arabs. This was in sharp contrast to what has been discussed earlier. In fact, Lebanese comment, when it did appear, was sympathetic to Syrian demands that the Lebanese army be purged.[25]

Even General Muḥammad Najīb, the popular front man of the Egyptian Revolutionary Command Council, did not escape chastisement. When he made courtesy calls on the Shaykh of al-Azhar, the Coptic Patriarch, and the Chief Rabbi of Egypt, comment was hostile. "We know the good intentions of General Najīb. But we wish him and every other Arab to realize that a Jew has no specific country and has no loyalty except to Judaism."[26]

Up to this point in this chapter events that had antecedents in preceding chapters have been considered. Jerusalem, the refugees, the United Nations, its resolutions and its organs, the Tripartite Declaration, and anti-Jewish feeling were all discussed in previous chapters and were mentioned again since they reappeared during the period we are presently examining. We can now turn our attention to new topics that first gained prominence during the period from the assassination of ʿAbd Allāh to the 1956 Suez War.

The first of these was the controversy over the diversion of the Jordan River south of Lake Hulah and the Johnston Plan for regional exploitation of water resources in the Jordan Valley.

One can understand that once it had established itself as a nation, Israel would seek to improve the use of available resources. One of the first attempts was a water-diversion canal from the Jordan River south of Lake Hulah near the Bridge of Jacob's Daughters. The main purposes of this diversion scheme were to produce hydro-electric power and to use the fresh water of the Jordan for irrigation purposes.

Problems arose because the Israeli diversion project took place on land, on both sides of the Jordan River south of the lake that was in dispute. The area had originally been awarded to the Jewish state in the 1947 partition resolution. However, during the fighting in 1948, the area was occupied by the Syrians. In the 1949 armistice agreement between Israel and Syria, in order to break the deadlock over who had the rights to the land, it was decided to make the area a demilitarized zone. Article 12 of the armistice agreement stated that neither side would do anything within the zone that would upset the strategic balance between the two countries.

The Israelis, in defending their project, maintained there was no question of ownership of the land since it had been given to the Jewish state at partition. They also argued that their work in the zone was not upsetting the strategic balance.

The Arab view of the problem was quite different. The Syrians and their allies felt that by diverting the waters of the Jordan, several debits would befall Syria. First, there was a fear that if the Jordan were diverted, a natural boundary separating the belligerents would be erased and Israel's claim to the disputed area strengthened. Editorial opinion also expressed a fear that the water level of the Jordan would fall, thus causing a hardship to many Arab farmers who used it for irrigation. There was also the belief that removing the waters of the Jordan from its own valley to irrigate previously arid portions of Israel in the Negev and the coastal plain would work a dual hardship. It would, by increasing arable land in Israel, enable the Jewish state to accommodate more immigrants while at the same time take water from the more than half-million refugees in Jordan who desperately needed it. Editorialists wrote that the new project, though presented as another example of the Israeli genius for making the desert bloom, really constituted a threat to the safety of the Arab countries because it would give Israel strategic and economic advantages that it previously had not been allowed.[27]

Syrian editorial opinion was split over what action its government should take in the face of Israeli attempts to divert the Jordan. Several newspapers felt the best action Syria could take would be to act with Lebanon to divert the two streams, the Ḥaṣbānī and the Bānyās, which join to form the Jordan.[28] Other Syrian papers were pessimistic about what could be done in the face of Israeli intransigence. These papers felt that Syria would not fight for its rights. Once again the Arabs would be confronted with a *fait accompli* while they themselves were engaged in a never-ending campaign of speeches and declarations.[29]

The Syrian papers were temporarily wrong in their estimation of what might happen. The Syrians and Lebanese did not divert the sources of the Jordan nor did the Israelis, at this time, put their canal to use. The United States on October 20, 1953 stopped giving Israel economic aid. When, as a result of this pressure, the Israelis agreed to forego diversion, America promptly resumed its aid, nine days later. After this brief setback, the Israelis were back at work in the demilitarized zone, and be February 1956 David Ben-Gurion announced that Israel had completed the diversionary project and would soon thereafter take water from the Jordan to the south.

The problem involved in the Jordan River diversion plan and what was to be done with the development of the other waters, including the previously mentioned Litani River, was finally brought to a climax with the project commonly known as the Johnston Plan. This far-reaching development plan for the water resources in and around the Jordan Valley was named after Eric Johnston, the special representative of President Dwight Eisenhower. The development project was introduced to the Arabs in the autumn of 1953. Full details of this plan need not be included here, but there were certain key provisions that should be mentioned in order to have a better understanding of editorial opinion.

First, the Johnston Plan was a regional proposal for the systematic exploitation of the water resources of the entire Jordan Valley. This meant the development of the Bānyās, Ḥāṣbānī, Yarmūk, Dān, Līṭanī, and Jordan Rivers. Second, Johnston argued that one of the purposes of the project was to economically aid the Palestinian refugees, though it was based on a Zionist-backed book written with the aid of a number of engineers who had never been to the Middle East, i.e., James B. Hays' *T.V.A. on the Jordan, Proposals for Irrigation and Hydro-Electric Development in Palestine* (Washington: Public Affairs Press, 1948). And Hays' book was a revision of an earlier Zionist plan proposed by W. C. Lowdermilk in the 1930s. Thus, one finds in the introduction to Hays' book, "The Jewish state was awarded an area embracing the upper reaches of the Jordan in the north [...] thereby the opportunity was given for carrying out the basic conception of the Lowdermilk-Hays project." Finally, and most importantly, the project did not take into consideration political boundaries, since the plan was regional.

A worse political time could not have been chosen to gain Arab support for the Johnston Plan. One only has to recall that it was in early September 1953 that the diversion of the Jordan River between Lakes Hulah and Tiberias had been started by the Israelis, and had caused considerable consternation in the Arab camp. One must also remember that Ben-Gurion was at the time not only prime minister but minister of defense. This was an ominous sign that resulted in the Israeli attack on Qabīyah (October 14) in which over 60 civilians were killed.[30] Following immediately upon Qabīyah was the announcement of the Eric Johnston Mission (October 16) while the Arabs were in a condition of extreme stress.

The Johnston Plan, rightly or wrongly, was identified with the Israeli attempt to divert the Jordan River, with Ben-Gurion's being in power, and with the killings at Qabīyah. The Arab writers felt that Johnston appeared as the agent of Israel and would gain concessions from the Arabs because of their trauma and the knowledge that they were no military match for the Israelis. The implication was that the Arabs could reject the plan only at their own risk. From the American point of view, the plan was brought forward to provide an equitable solution to the existing problem of riparian rights, without a political settlement. If the Arabs rejected the plan, then they would have only themselves to blame for whatever Israel might do. "Johnston's mission, if looked at objectively, appears to be one which aims at making peace between the Arab states and Israel through economic projects."[31]

The Johnston Plan was positive in that it sought to bring some development projects to an area badly in need of such plans. But in doing so, and this exception was widely voiced in Arab editorials, political boundaries had been disregarded and thus the political aspects of any cooperation between the belligerents were not taken into account. This only served to reinforce the feeling that, first and foremost, the problems surrounding Palestine were largely political. Any solution that did not take into account political considerations was doomed to failure.

"The Arab-Israeli problem is firstly a political problem. It is a political problem above all. If there has ever been a political problem, this is it. To say that economics alone can solve such a problem is to make a great error."[32] Other Arab editorialists took an opposite stand to reach the same conclusion. There were those who felt that, indeed, the problem of the refugees was political but that the problem could be solved by economic means. The belief among these writers was that by starting projects that would employ refugee workers and by irrigating land in the Jordan Valley where Palestinians could then be settled, the political aspects of the Palestine problem would disappear with the disappearance of the refugee camps. "Johnston, as well as any other man who knows the true basis of the conflict between the Arabs and Israel, knows that if the conflict between the Arabs and Israel should ever be wiped out, it would be on the basis of economics."[33]

The one conclusion of these two diverging opinions was that the Johnston Plan should be turned down because a political settlement to the problems of the area was preferable to an economic settlement – an economic solution whose greatest beneficiary would be Israel.

> We warn our American friends that we do not hate progress or construction, but we are simply trying to imitate them when they preferred destruction to construction and spent their money and energy turning cities into deserts. We have to compare our negative attitude toward the development of schemes beneficial to Israel to America's positive attitude when it sent its huge bombers to enemy cities and towns to destroy their factories and hinder their industrial production.
>
> Do Americans think that their fight against the Nazis and their allies was more justified than our struggle against the Zionists and their allies? The reasons which the Americans had for destroying the countries of their enemies are the same reasons which we have for refusing to develop the country of our enemies.[34]

Johnston's tour throughout the Arab countries did not result in acceptance of the project bearing his name. However, a small segment of Lebanese opinion was in favor of adopting the plan. This opinion argued that if some modified form of the plan was not adopted for the joint development of water resources, then Israel, using its superior military force, would unilaterally use the waters around it as it had shown it could at Lake Hulah. The Arabs would thus lose whatever water rights they might have gained had they adopted the American plan.[35] This feeling was apparently reflected in some Arab governmental circles since the Johnston Plan was not completely rejected.

The Arabs, as well as the Israelis, offered counter-proposals. Slowly, however, the question of what was to be done with the waters receded into the background. Then in early 1955, Johnston announced his imminent return to the Middle East with a compromise proposal, combining the best of all three plans: Johnston, Hays, and Lowdermilk. This was in February 1955. He warned the Arabs that they should act upon the proposals to be set forth or else they risked losing American aid as well as their own natural resources. This attack by Johnston corresponded to the return to power of Ben-Gurion as Minister of Defense. To one editorial writer, René Aggiouri, the events unfolding before him in early 1955 recalled the events of the autumn of 1953. He wrote that in the autumn of 1953, while Ben-Gurion was in power, the water diversion project south of Lake Hulah was begun. Arab political circles were upset by this and their fear increased with the Israeli attack on the village of Qabīyah. It was at this precise moment, when "the fifty-four bodies of Qabīyah were still warm," that Johnston had produced, as if by magic, his plan. And now, said the writer, Ben-Gurion has returned to power and Johnston has announced his approaching return to the Middle East. One could almost expect another Qabīyah: there was no question in Aggiouri's mind that there was a plot to take advantage of Arab military weakness to force them to agree to the Johnston Plan and forever put an end to the political problems by resolving them in an economic settlement.[36] As though in response to Aggiouri's premonitions, the Israelis launched an attack into Gaza on February 28, killing 38 Egyptian soldiers. The repercussions from this act, which will be discussed later in this chapter, led it to be called by a contemporary "one of the most fateful" in Middle East history.[37]

The fact that the Arabs were weak and unable to resist was usually not argued in editorials. But with the opening of a new economic offensive by the Israelis, symbolized by the Johnston Plan, many Arab writers thought that this thrust could be handled by the Arabs through diplomatic channels. But even this battle was in danger of being lost because full attention was not being paid to the problem. There was editorial questioning of who was and who was not sharing the burden imposed by Israel. Needless to say, the writers of each country usually felt that their nation was doing the utmost. However, editorial opinion, in attacking one possible cause of Arab failure, felt that the Egyptian regime that had overthrown King Farūq in 1952 had not subsequently fulfilled its Arab responsibilities. That the Revolutionary Command Council (RCC) and General Muḥammad Najīb were extremely popular at home was no surprise. What may be surprising was that the RCC was not welcomed as enthusiastically throughout the remainder of the Arab world. One of the reasons for the lack of acceptance was the gentle policy Egypt adopted toward Israel after July 23, 1952.

Arab papers, excluding Egypt, carried news stories and editorials alleging that Egypt was going to make peace with Israel. General Najīb was quoted in one paper, when asked if Egypt was going to attack Israel, as saying that Egypt sought to establish amicable relations with all nations.[38]

Evidently Egypt realized it would not be able to conclude peace with Israel but felt that it could not fight it, either. Egyptian editorials emphasized that Egypt could only engage one enemy at a time. The British were still controlling the Suez Canal and RCC policy gave priority to forcing the British to leave and then worrying about Palestine. This Egyptian policy was presented by Major Ṣalāḥ Sālim, prominent RCC member and Egyptian Minister of National Guidance, when he spoke before the Lebanese Chamber of Deputies in July 1954. In that speech, the "Dancing Major" said that the Suez question was the foremost Arab problem because with the British in Egypt over half the Arab world was paralyzed.[39]

But prior to this statement, the Arab countries that had to face the Israeli danger as they saw it wondered whether Egypt's preoccupation with the Suez Canal was not detrimental to Arab interests in general.

> [...] is the central problem of the Arab World that of the [Suez] Canal or that of Israel? By getting bogged down in the Canal, surely a mistake has been committed; and however fraternal may be our sentiments for Egypt, we must tell it this.
>
> The Israeli affair has a character distinctly permanent and crucial. It menaces the Arab World differently than a [British] presence on the Canal, which for whatever irritant it may appear to be, is at least in the end for Egypt itself, a guarantee in the face of more grave dangers. [...]
>
> Cannot Cairo be shown that the time is short, that Israel is growing roots and that its chances increase?[40]

That Egypt in 1952 placed the "British question" and putting its own house in order as having priority over the Palestine issue is indisputable. Perhaps, one might argue, this was not so much an act of volition but a recognition of the paralysis that was affecting Egyptian life in the hectic months surrounding the overthrow of the last Albanian-Turkish monarch. The presence of the British since 1882 had grown to be a festering sore on Egyptian national sentiment by the time of the Second World War. Many Egyptians blamed the British for the latter's role in the establishment of Israel. This attitude, combined with a desire to be rid of a colonial power, led the Egyptians to begin a series of clashes which led to "Black Saturday" in Cairo in January 1952.[41] Actually, major clashes had begun over two months earlier when British soldiers kidnapped an Egyptian officer who was taking pictures of Egyptians working for the British. In any event, the rioting that lasted into February resulted in the resignation of the Wafdist government, the reintroduction of press censorship, and the closing of that country's universities and schools. The government was not willing to take the blame for the state of affairs and so through its journals intimated that the military was at fault.[42]

Within a few months, the monarchy was overthrown and the military became dominant. The nominal head of the new government, Muḥammad Najīb, virtually unknown to his countrymen, however, was locked in a struggle for power within the RCC. This clash over the leadership of the new regime, combined with the presence of the British, foreclosed any chance that the Egyptians could possibly take an active role in Palestine until the two former issues were resolved. The denouement took almost two years and presaged the end of a free Egyptian press.

The question within the RCC was whom to follow, the more democratic Najīb or the more militant Jamāl 'Abd al-Nāṣir. For the press and politicians of the country, there was no doubt – Najīb promised a return to civilian control of the government. A curious assortment of Left and Right thus began to attack the 'Abd al-Nāṣir bloc and were bellicose in their demands, which regularly appeared in the Wafdist journals.

Between February 21 and 25, 1954 the RCC held three chaotic meetings. The first of them was headed by Najīb, but the last two were chaired by a seemingly victorious 'Abd al-Nāṣir. Pressure, however, from the Muslim Brotherhood, a section of the military loyal to Khālid Muḥyī al-Dīn, and the parties and their newspapers forced 'Abd al-Nāṣir to reinstate Najīb within a few days. Thus as March began, the press, especially the Wafdist, began an extremely vitriolic attack on ʿAbd al-Nāṣir. The Egyptian Press Syndicate, with its president Ḥusayn Abū al-Fatḥ in the lead, daily issued pro-Najīb declarations.

But ʿAbd al-Nāṣir was not to be denied. Najīb made a fateful error by forcefully advocating a return of Egypt to party control. ʿAbd al-Nāṣir was able to make it appear that Najīb was trying to subvert the goals of the 1952 revolution by returning the country to its old corrupt hands. Demonstrations against the return to civil rule were led by an organization loyal to ʿAbd al-Nāṣir, the Liberation Rally, which had since its inception in January 1953 successfully infiltrated the trade unions. By the end of March 1954, Muḥammad Najīb had slipped from power and by the end of the year he was under house arrest. Now it was time for ʿAbd al-Nāṣir to suppress those who had opposed him. Within a short time, the powerful pro-Wafdist journalists, the Abū al-Fatḥ brothers, were under arrest, the Wafdist organ *al-Miṣrī* had lost its license to publish, the Egyptian Press Syndicate was reorganized under governmental control, and no journalist could write in Egypt without being a member of the syndicate. The process of the destruction of a free press in Egypt had begun.

The changes that had begun in Egypt were reflective of the Arab world in general. The year 1952 was particularly volatile. In Lebanon, corruption on the part of the Bishārah al-Khūrī administration had led to journalistic calls for the government's resignation and in response a speedy governmental suspension of the offending journals. When the country shut down and 27 newspapers went on strike, President al-Khūrī was forced to resign. Jordan during the same year deposed its king. A month before the start of 1952, Adīb al-Shīshaklī had overthrown the government of Syria and within a few months oversaw a shake-up called euphemistically the "Syrian Press Reform."

In 1952, the greater part of the Arab world was engrossed in its own domestic problems and not Palestine. This was particularly true for Egypt, which was undergoing revolutionary change while under foreign occupation. That this made less imperative the question of Palestine was not lost on many of the Arab commentators. Though the struggle for power was never alluded to in the editorials of non-Egyptian countries as the possible reason for Egypt's distraction, when the power struggle had ended and the triumphant leadership decided to be rid of the British before turning its attention to foreign affairs, the RCC was once again castigated. We have mentioned Chiha's views on this, but his words were relatively kind when compared to others. Several editorialists felt that the Egyptians, in advocating a Suez-first policy, were myopic in their vision and really did not care about the Palestinian people. Attempts were made, editorially, to link the negotiations over Suez with Palestine and concluded that Egypt might make a settlement over the Canal to the detriment of Palestine.[43]

The adverse comments against the RCC, and eventually against Jamāl ʿAbd al-Nāṣir, culminated in a report that stated that the Egyptian opposition was closing its ranks against ʿAbd al-Nāṣir and there would result a second Egyptian revolution. One Syrian paper went so far as to intimate that ʿAbd al-Nāṣir was so depressed over his imminent fall that he would soon commit suicide.[44]

It is noteworthy that one of the accusations leveled against Egypt and ʿAbd al-Nāṣir was similar in tone to that which had appeared in various newspapers attacking King ʿAbd Allāh.

The intimation that one of the Arab countries was soon to make peace with Israel was a powerful weapon during the 1950s that one Arab faction could use against another. In this campaign of innuendo, the leader was the Syrian journal, *al-Manār*, spokesman for the RCC-repressed Muslim Brotherhood.[45]

Despite the recourse, on the part of some newspapers, to resort to name calling, the events of 1951 and 1952 brought to the foreground the fact that Israel was in the Middle East to stay for some time. "Israel is here, beyond all question."[46] Once having recognized this fact, however bitter, the question was what was to be done about its existence. For the first time, there began a serious discussion, in Arab newspapers, of the prospects of peace with Israel. Speculation about the reasons for this desire for peace, however small, is intriguing. Certainly, the pressures being placed upon Jordan's frontiers, world pressure on all the Arabs, the absence of Egypt from the battlefield while it was engaged with England, and Arab military weakness all contributed to the discussion.

The first comments about a cessation of hostilities stated that the Israelis would like nothing better than a peace that they would impose as the victors of 1948. The feeling was that the Israelis would wish to make permanent the *fait accompli* consisting of the following:

> – that half of Palestine has become a Jewish state, organized, armed, and supported by the Great Powers;
> – that this State which receives close to 15,000 immigrants per month, gathered from every corner of the earth, no longer has any place for the 970,000 refugees chased from their homes;
> – that Jerusalem, the Holy City of the three greatest religions of humanity, is split between Israel and Jordan.
>
> There is the *fait*, the *fait juif accompli* in front of which the United Nations, with its Charter and its Universal Declaration of Human Rights bows; and in front of which the Arab states are invited to become realists.[47]

To counter the believed Israeli desire to make peace on the basis of the borders after 1948 and the non-repatriation of the refugees, the Arab writers offered positive alternatives. Although they rejected the Israeli conditions, they did not reject peace. "We take the existence of Israel as a fact and there is no question of pushing the Israelis into the sea. We have said for a long time that the question of Israel is less a question of presence than a question of power."[48] The conditions, almost universally accepted by those writers who were willing to write of peace, were three: the internationalization of Jerusalem, the repatriation of those refugees who wished to go home, and a return to the partition as envisioned in General Assembly Resolution 181 of November 1947.[49]

This willingness on the part of Arab writers to recognize the existence of the Zionist state may not seem to be a great step forward. But if one compares the Arab attitude prior to May 15, 1948 when only a few Christian Arabs were willing to accept a Jewish state, the editorials of the 1950s were quite revolutionary. One should say, however, that the basic reason for even invoking the UN resolutions was the Arab defeat in 1948.

Of course there was also the thought that even with the Arab concession to abide by the resolutions, peace was not possible. This type of editorial expressed the feeling that Israel no longer recognized the validity of the resolutions, especially the one which called for repatriation. There is no question that Arab and Israeli positions seemed irreconcilable. The Israelis accepted partition prior to May 1948 and rejected it after the Palestine war. The Arab position was exactly opposite. In this respect, it seems as though the Israeli position was often one war ahead while the Arabs were always one war behind.

Closely connected with the idea of accepting peace negotiations was the topic of direct negotiations with Israel. The Arab feeling, generally, was that although they might be interested in a peace with Israel based upon UN resolutions, they were not interested in direct negotiations that might lead to a normalization of relations. At this period, perhaps, direct negotiations did not have the implication of recognition that they do today. However, the feeling then was that direct negotiations were capitulation. One sees continuously the statement that the United Nations had already passed resolutions upon which an honorable peace could be established. If this were the case, why, went the argument, should negotiation be necessary? There was nothing to negotiate since a blueprint for peace had already been drawn. The Arab feeling was that if the UN resolutions were negotiated, the only losers would be the Arabs.[50]

In the complete rejection of the idea of direct negotiation, perhaps the real feelings of Arab editorialists toward Israel were revealed. Many of the newspapers called for peace. And yet the writers were unwilling to enter into direct negotiations. This seemed to be a mild contradiction. It revealed a belief, sometimes below the surface, that peace was the only alternative open to the Arabs. The feeling that emerged from the editorials of both those who accepted and rejected peace was that the Arabs were slowly being trapped by the Middle East problem. Those who rejected warfare did so reluctantly, not out of any great pacifism. Nowhere did a peace advocate plead strongly to the Arab governments for peace. Rather, the plea appeared to be the cry of a man who had been forced into a corner and saw no alternative that was less fearful. Had an alternative that they could accept been presented to those who called for peace, it would most surely have been adopted quickly. One possible option did present itself in the form of ʿAbd al-Nāṣir and several newspapers looked to him as the savior of the Middle East.

A more likely ally for the Arabs, other than the emergence of a strong Arab leader, was the Soviet Union. In 1948, it was virtually unthinkable that the Soviet Union would be able to strengthen its influence in the Arab East, since Russia had quickly recognized the State of Israel and had been one of its strong supporters. There were other good reasons for believing that communism would be unpalatable in the Middle East. Primary among them was Arab antipathy to the atheism which Marxism advocated. A common reference to this was "Communism does not fit our country."[51]

However, the desperate situation into which the Arab countries had been forced caused their writers to look for new alternatives. Here the attitude of the West was certainly to blame, as far as editorial opinion was concerned. The West was more preoccupied with communism, for instance in Korea and in the McCarthy hearings. As a result the West, especially the United States, tended to see everything in a communist or anti-communist light. The Arab countries and their newspapers continually criticized the West for failing to realize "the desperate position into which we have been forced by them. [...] [And, therefore,] we find it imperative to take steps we have never considered before."[52]

There were Arab editorials that voiced the opinion that there was a special relationship between Israel and the United States resulting from the large number of Jewish citizens in America. Many of the editorials suggested that, as a result, Israel had become a client-state of the Americans and a just policy for the Middle East was no longer possible. When this belief was added to the attempts, on the part of the United States and the United Nations, to involve the Arabs in direct talks with Israel, one can better understand the dilemma faced by Arab writers as they tried to evaluate the forces moving around them. The constant rumors that aid was to be cut off to the refugees and that the Arabs would not receive help in the face of Israeli expansion did not assuage their uncertainty. This is not to intimate that there were not those who realized that the Soviet Union was only following a policy of *realpolitik*. There were many editorials explaining that Moscow, in becoming the ally of the Arabs, was only following its own self-interest and was, perhaps, only filling the vacuum left when the West moved to Israel.[53]

There were papers that cared neither for Western aid nor for Eastern friendship. These papers, although few, called for a "plague on both houses" since neither side was interested in the Arabs as people and their lost rights.[54] But an increasing number of papers began to openly endorse a policy of friendship with the Eastern Bloc.

Still, the advance of Russia to the Middle East was slow until 1955. One can point to the rise of the Ba'th Party in Syria to argue that the march to the left was speedy. However, there was no great feeling of affection between the Ba'th and the communists. One of the reasons for the union of Egypt and Syria in 1958 was the Ba'th fear of a communist take-over in Syria. It is more realistic to say that at best Soviet influence in the Middle East was marginal until late 1954 or early 1955. At that time, it was well-established that the West would arm the Arabs to a lesser degree than it armed Israel. Arab weakness was vividly shown on February 28, 1955 when Israel attacked Egyptian held Gaza, killed a number of Egyptian soldiers, and humiliated 'Abd al-Nāṣir. Immediately, the pro-Western papers, centered largely in Beirut, began to cry loudly that the West was committing suicide by supporting Israel.[55]

The countermove to the Israeli attack on Gaza occurred some six months later when 'Abd al-Nāṣir announced his arms agreement with the Soviet Bloc, known as the Czech arms deal. Even those papers that had in the past decried Russian influence in the Middle East were forced to give grudging admiration to 'Abd al-Nāṣir's political coup. Almost every paper wrote that the West did not realize that for the Arabs there were other enemies than communism.

> We are not unaware of the objectives behind the Russian generosity in arming us. We are also aware of the objectives that lie behind the refusal of the Anglo-Saxons to arm us. But we cannot forget that we have interests which must be safeguarded.[56]

There can be little doubt that with the announcement of the Soviet arms deal, the influence of the communists increased within editorials. Many newspapers were jubilant with what they called Soviet Point IV, and urged the Arabs to negotiate with Moscow and prepare for war.[57]

> The Great Power that respects our revolution and does not impede the popular gains in our country is the Soviet Union! So far the Soviet Union has not stood in our way; it has not attacked Egypt in its press and radio and it has not accused Jamāl ʿAbd al-Nāṣir of being a dictator.[58]

The Soviet arms agreement was not the only event occurring that tended to polarize East-West feelings in the Middle East. We should also mention the English and American attempts to implement a defense pact against Russia. Commonly known as the Baghdad Pact, the alliance was originally between Turkey and Iraq. However, many Arab newspapers, when the pact was announced in January 1955, felt that this was still another attempt to make a peace settlement with Israel. The feeling was that Turkey was nothing but an agent of the West since it had established diplomatic relations with Israel. Because of a realization in America and western Europe that the Arab countries would not ally with the West because of Israel, the West was trying to forge an alliance between Muslim countries with the same purpose – peace with Israel.[59]

The attack on the Baghdad Pact, or Turko-Iraqi Pact, was led by Egypt. Its papers insinuated that if other Arab states joined the pact, Palestine would be lost since one of the alliance's purposes was to bring peace between Arab and Israeli. Many non-Egyptian newspapers felt that the purpose of the Baghdad Pact was not related to Palestine but that for purposes of Arab leadership, Egypt and Iraq were using it to focus on Palestine to champion their separate national leadership causes. In the battle for popular opinion and Arab leadership, one Egyptian newspaper, *al-Jumhūrīyah*, even intimated that the Gaza attack of February 1955 resulted from the Baghdad Pact.[60]

The Baghdad Alliance and the Czech arms agreement, as sensational as they were, were only preludes to other events. Apparently angered by Egyptian opposition to the Baghdad Pact, the buying of arms from the Soviet Bloc, and the recognition by Egypt of the Peoples' Republic of China (PRC), the American Secretary of State on July 19, 1956 withdrew the American offer to financially support the building of the High Dam at Aswan. The British withdrew their offer the following day. This was an unmistakable slap in the face of Egypt which was felt, editorially, to be an attempt to embarrass ʿAbd al-Nāṣir. In retaliation one week later, the Egyptian president nationalized the Suez Canal Company. If ʿAbd al-Nāṣir had taken on superhuman characteristics with his Soviet arms agreement, he now became almost god-like with his nationalization of the company that controlled and collected fees on the Canal. There were no voices raised in the newspapers against the action of nationalization.[61]

While events were marching forward in Egypt, one Arab commentator sounded an ominous note to an otherwise inconspicuous event. The same author, René Aggiouri, who had anticipated the Israeli raid on Gaza, noted another change of personnel in the Israeli cabinet. To this editorialist, writing prior to the American cancellation of the Aswan Dam aid and the nationalization of the Suez Canal, the Czech arms agreement and the British departure from Suez were dangerous for the Arabs when mixed with the cabinet change in Israel.

> If one had the slightest doubt about the meaning of Mr. Sharett's leaving Ben-Gurion's cabinet, the first declarations of Mrs. Myerson [Meir], who succeeds him as [Minister of] Foreign Affairs, and the commentary of Radio Israel, cited by A.F.P. [*Agence France Presse*], proves the necessity of getting rid [of any doubts about the meaning of the change].
>
> Mrs. Myerson says that her first objective is the Suez blockade. She will apply herself to making the Great Powers understand "the necessity for Israel to defend herself and to have free access."
>
> "The necessity to defend herself" is the necessity to procure arms for herself. And "free access" is the Suez again which Mr. Hammarskjoeld has not succeeded in unblocking.
>
> The commentary of Radio Israel again is very precise: "Mr. Sharett," it said, "represents a policy which seeks to resolve all problems by negotiation." And adds: "Our country needs a less supple policy [...]. It is not in accepting concessions that one gains an audience with the Great Powers."
>
> This is what the American "experts" in the State Department call the "contrast between the moderate views of Mr. Sharett and the more positive ones of Mr. Ben-Gurion."
>
> Everyone knows now what the "positive views" of Mr. Ben-Gurion signify: placing the world before *faits accomplis*; provoking frontier incidents; gaining the intervention of the Powers; driving the Arabs into negotiation.[62]

The nationalization of the Suez by the Egyptians could only serve to add to the unquiet in Tel Aviv. And Mr. Aggiouri proved once again to be an accurate prognosticator.[63]

During this period between the assassination of King 'Abd Allāh and the nationalization of Suez, Arab editorials reflected the gradual and then accelerated deterioration of Western influence in the Middle East. They disclosed the mood of the Arab writers as they viewed with disdain the Western attempts to solve the problems caused by the Zionist state in the Arab world.

Each attempt by the West to find a solution to the "Zionist cancer" only served to make the Arab patient more ill. In editorial eyes, the Zionist danger had to be eradicated finally, but this expunction was something the West was unwilling to do. Instead, the West attempted to placate the Arabs with aid such as UNRWA and Point IV. However, these palliative measures only served to increase editorial anger since they were thought to be only measures to prolong Israel's existence in the hope that the Arabs would become unmindful of the Zionists.

Editorials were particularly bitter at these international moves, in the form of aid, when the United Nations had passed three resolutions on which peace could be established. This turnabout on the part of the Arabs in accepting the U.N. resolutions, especially the partition, was one of the major editorial changes during the period covered in this chapter. However, the act of accepting the resolutions of the world body was not without its contradictions since Jordan, along with Israel, refused to accept the resolution that called for the internationalization of Jerusalem. Thus, the journalists of Egypt, Lebanon, and Syria found themselves criticizing Jordan as well as Israel for their position on Jerusalem.

The question of Jerusalem, however, was a minor one when compared with the implications of the Johnston Plan. This project, introduced by Washington, confirmed the worst fears of the Arab writers. Here was a plan which in its inception did not even take into consideration political boundaries, thereby giving credence to Arab apprehensions that Israel's boundaries were not yet extensive enough. The writers felt that the Arabs were being blackmailed. They could either accept regional exploitation of the area's natural resources or face the Israeli consequences. Not only this, but the Johnston Plan implied that the refugees would not be repatriated but would be put to work as agriculturalists in newly irrigated Arab lands. Once again, the Americans had failed to understand the desires of the Arab peoples. Or worse still, they understood but did not care.

In the battle to stave off an economic settlement, many writers felt that Egypt was not doing its share for the Arab cause since it was preoccupied with the British in Suez. Thus, abandoned by the strongest Arab state, and for other pressing considerations, many Arab editorialists began to talk of peace for the first time. Once having recognized the validity of the three UN resolutions, the next step to peace might not be a difficult one to take. But once again the Arab writers called for a peace based on justice, not on victory in battle. And for the most part, the writers rejected a peace based on face-to-face negotiations with the Israelis. In this respect, the writers seemed less married to the idea of peace than to a recognition of the apparent hopelessness of their cause. The net impression was that had the writers found a way to avoid making peace with Israel, they would have accepted it, however reluctantly.

Events moved quickly in 1955 and after. There was, first of all, the Israeli attack on Gaza followed by the Czech arms agreement, Egypt's recognition of the PRC, withdrawal of the High Dam offer, and the nationalization of the Suez Canal Company. Each step seemed somehow to lead inexorably to the next until Western influence had been greatly eroded. Arab editorialists were saddened by the blunders they felt the West was committing. Certainly most of the editorialists in the Arab world up to 1956 were pro-West. But they felt the West did not understand the problems of the Arabs and that the Arabs would willingly ally with anyone who would help them gain their desired goals.

Notes

1 Bāsil Daqqāq, *Daily Star*, September 9, 1954; see also the same author in *al-Ḥayāt*, March 17, 1954; Naṣrī al-Maʿluf, *al-Jarīdah*, September 30, 1953; and *L'Orient*, May 1, 1954.
2 *Al-Difāʿ*, December 15, 1953.
3 See for example *al-Yawm*, June 5, 1953.
4 *Daily Star*, June 8, 1952; and René Aggiouri, *L'Orient*, October 15, 1954.
5 Janet Abu-Lughod, "Israeli Settlement in Occupied Arab Lands: Conquest to Colony," *Journal of Palestine Studies* 11, no. 2 (Winter 1982): 22.
6 *Filasṭīn*, December 19, 1952.
7 See for example *al-Jumhūrīyah*, January 26, 1954. Editorial opinion may appear to be lacking in feeling for the conditions under which the refugees were living. Yet there is ample evidence to support the belief that the refugees themselves refused resettlement and demanded a return to their homes. See, as an illustration, the resolution adopted by a convention of Palestine refugees which said in part, "Nothing can change our desire to return." The full text may be seen in *al-Jīl al-Jadīd*, October 2, 1951. See also the statements made by the first two UNRWA directors, Howard Kennedy and John Blandford, Jr: U.N. Document A/1451/ Rev. 1, *General Assembly, Fifth Session Supplement No. 19*; and U.N. Document A/1905, *General Assembly, Sixth Session Supplement No. 16*. One segment of Arab opinion, the nationalistic Christian Lebanese, did not voice the usual reasons for refusing resettlement. This segment, with *al-ʿAmal* as the leading spokesman, refused resettlement out of a fear that some of the refugees would be resettled in Lebanon. With the vast majority of the refugees professing Islam, their becoming Lebanese citizens was considered to be a threat to Christian predominance.
8 Point IV was a technical assistance program for "developing nations" and was part of the larger Cold War goal of stopping the expansion of communism. Point IV was named after President Truman's inaugural address in 1949 where it was the fourth point mentioned of his foreign policy objectives.
9 *Al-Difāʿ*, 'July 2, 1952. See also *Bayrūt al-Masāʾ*, June 28, 1952; and *al-Fayḥāʾ*, October 22, 1953.
10 "Report on the Near and Middle East by Secretary of State John Foster Dulles," *Department of State Bulletin* 28 (June 15, 1953): 835.
11 *Al-Fayḥāʾ*, May 15, 1951.
12 Kāmil Murūwah, *al-Ḥayāt*, April 17, 1954. See also *Filasṭīn*, December 13, 1951.
13 See for example *al-Hadaf* and *al-Sharq*, both of December 8, 1953 and *al-Difāʿ*, March 10, 1954. The attacks on Point IV caused a minor government crisis in Lebanon in 1953. In accepting Point IV the government was accused of being in the service of Zionism. The Beirut newspapers of early December 1953 are replete with descriptions of the crisis. Debate on Point IV was not without its lighter moments, for instance when it was revealed that some Lebanese parliament deputies had accepted prize bulls as gifts, while criticizing the aid.
14 Partition of Palestine, UN General Assembly Resolution 181, November 1947; Repatriation of Palestinian Refugees, UN General Assembly Resolution 194, December 1948; Internationalization of Jerusalem: UN General Assembly Resolution 303, December 1949.

15 For various negative expressions, see for example René Aggiouri, *L'Orient*, November 28, 1952; *Le Jour*, November 15, 1955; and *al-Manār*, November 17, 1955.

16 *Al-Ahrām*, July 25, 1952; Bāsil Daqqāq, *al-Ḥayāt*, November 14, 1954; and Michel Chiha, *Le Jour*, December 15, 1954.

17 See for example *al-Difā'*, December 3, 1953; and *Filasṭīn*, November 14, 1954. The Jordanian and Hashimite desire for Jerusalem was no great secret. "The demand for the internationalization of Jerusalem was the strangest and most unbalanced of the [Arab] national aims. It was one that disregarded the Arab rights and interests by handing the Holy Places over to international control and wrenching Jerusalem from the possession of the Arabs. It was my duty to stand resolutely and firmly in the defense of the Arab character of the Holy City and resist internationalization in all its aspects" (Abdallah, King of Jordan, *My Memoirs Completed* [Washington, American Council of Learned Societies, 1954], 13).

18 *Le Jour*, December 30, 1953.

19 Ibid., December 15, 1954.

20 Representative editorials may be seen in *Baradā*, May 16, 1952; and *L'Orient*, May 5, 1954.

21 *The Arab Awakening* (Philadelphia, J.P. Lippincott, 1939), 142.

22 *Al-Ahrām*, May 19, 1952. See also *Filasṭīn*, March 18, 1952; and *Daily Star*, July 15, 1952.

23 *Al-Fayḥā'*, October 29, 1951.

24 *Al-Naṣr*, April 20, 1952. See also *Baradā*, March 30, 1952; and *Al-Fayḥā'*, April 21, 1952.

25 *Bayrūt al-Masā'*, June 6, 1952.

26 *Al-Difā'*, October 6, 1952.

27 See for example *al-Miṣrī*, September 28 and 29, 1953.

28 See for example *al-Fayḥā'*, September 26, 1953.

29 *Al-Zamān*, September 27, 1953. See also *al-Yawm*, October 14, 1953.

30 On the evening of October 12, 1953, a group of infiltrators crossed from Jordan controlled territory into Israel and killed three people. On the evening of October 14, an Israeli commando unit led by Ariel Sharon retaliated by attacking the village of Qabīyah. Its soldiers blew up 45 homes and killed 60 villagers, mostly women and children. In order to hide the fact that it was an IDF operation, Ben-Gurion went on the radio on October 19 and lied; saying that enraged Israeli settlers had attacked the town. Benny Morris states that in this episode, "the press functioned as the servant of the state[...]." Jordan was swept with demonstrations demanding that John Glubb resign, along with 70 other British officers in the Arab Legion, for nonintervention (Benny Morris, "The Israeli Press and the Qibya Operation, 1953," *Journal of Palestine Studies* 25, no. 4 [Summer 1996]: 40–52).

31 *Al-Akhbār*, October 30, 1953.

32 Michel Chiha, *Le Jour*, October 21, 1953.

33 Ghassān Twaynī, *al-Nahār*, October 25, 1953.

34 Naṣrī al-Ma'lūf, *al-Jarīdah*, October 25, 1953.

35 The leading proponent of the Johnston Plan was Bāsil Daqqāq. See his editorials in *al-Ḥayāt*, June 23, 1954 and January 11, 1955.

36 René Aggiouri, *L'Orient*, February 22, 1955.

37 Guy Wint, *Middle East Crisis* (London, Penguin Books, 1957), 57–58.
38 *Al-Anbā'*, August 28, 1952. See also *al-Nāṣr*, October 2, 1952.
39 *Al-Jarīdah*, July 2, 1954, among others.
40 Michel Chiha, *Le Jour*, May 28, 1953.
41 Black Saturday began after British troops killed 50 Egyptian policemen in the city of Ismā'ilīyah. Anti-British protests erupted and large sectors of Cairo were burned and ransacked.
42 *Al-Miṣrī* was suspended on February 12 for one day for blaming the military for the burning of Cairo.
43 *Al-Nahār*, July 2, 1954; *al-Binā'*, July 4, 1954; and *L'Orient*, October 25, 1954.
44 *Al-Manār*, October 11, 1954.
45 See for example ibid., May 18, 1954 and June 21, 1955. The charges of collusion with the enemy were not without their more bizarre moments. The Lebanese paper, *al-Hadaf*, is quoted in *al-Zamān*, August 30, 1953, as saying that a feudal lord of south Lebanon, Aḥmad al-As'ad, proposed that a buffer state between Israel and Lebanon be created. Al-As'ad, of course, suggested himself as the prince of the new nation. *Al-Hadaf*'s report may be viewed with some skepticism since its publisher belonged to the Usayran family, a Shi'ah family from south Lebanon and traditional rival of the As'ad family. However, the plan may not be as far-fetched as it would first appear since it was widely believed that Aḥmad al-As'ad had sought a *modus vivendi* with the Israelis and had sold them extensive amounts of land in the Hulah region.
46 *Daily Star*, November 1, 1952.
47 René Aggiouri, *L'Orient*, September 18, 1951.
48 Michel Chiha, *Le Jour*, December 10, 1952.
49 Representative opinion may be seen in *al-Ahrām*, September 12, 1951 and November 27, 1952; *al-Sha'b*, September 28, 1951; *al-Binā'*, December 2, 1952; and René Aggiouri, *L'Orient*, May 22, 1955.
50 *Al-Ahrām*, July 25, 1952; *al-Yawm*, December 2, 1952; and *Daily Star*, December 13, 1952.
51 *Al-Miṣrī*, December 10, 1953.
52 *Al-Qāhirah*, December 30, 1953. "The Arab-Israeli conflict is just as dangerous for the Arabs as a world-wide conflict [with communism], something still not comprehended in Washington" (Michel Chiha, *Le Jour*, May 14, 1953).
53 See for example Bāsil Daqqāq in *al-Ḥayāt*, February 13, 1953, who called the Russian move a "master stroke."
54 *Filasṭīn*, January 13, 1952; and *al-Tilighrāf*, May 17, 1954.
55 See the following Lebanese journals: *Bayrūt*, June 10, 1955; Kāmil Murūwah, *al-Ḥayāt*, October 1, 1955; René Aggiouri, *L'Orient*, February 28, 1956; and *Sadā Lubnān*, April 5, 1956.
56 Kāmil Murūwah in *al-Ḥayāt*, September 29, 1955. Major Ṣalāh Sālim said that in fact the Czechoslovakian arms shipments had begun as early as July 1955. See his interview in *The Struggle for Syria*, 235–236. It seems that 'Abd al-Nāṣir may have decided to postpone the announcement of the arms agreement until an advantageous moment. 'Abd al-Nāṣir had abolished the religious courts of Egypt on September 22, 1955, and this was known to have generated considerable opposition. The announcement of the arms deal shortly thereafter may have been designed to rally support for his regime.

57 *Al-Ra'y al-ʿĀmm,* February 13, 1956.

58 Anwar al-Sādāt writing in *al-Jumhūrīyah* (Egypt), April 9, 1956. Compare this with the *New York Times*, July 23, 1956, which wrote: "To make himself mighty he has mortgaged Egypt's economic future to get, not bread for his people, but arms in the hope of becoming the leader of a pan-Arab empire that would stretch from the Atlantic to the Persian Gulf and would wipe out Israel." *Al-Ḥayāt*, which was usually pro-Western, replied to the *New York Times* that the Egyptian action was most worthy of Arab praise, July 25, 1956.

59 *Al-Jumhūrīyah*, January 18 and February 2, 1955; *Filasṭīn*, January 20, 1955; and *L'Orient*, February 13, 1955.

60 March 2, 1955.

61 Arab feeling about American action in the Middle East was neatly summed up by Richard Nolte and William Polk, "Toward a Policy for the Middle East," *Foreign Affairs*, 36, no. 4 (July 1958): 656: "The inference drawn by the Arabs from these episodes was that an American promise about arms or a dam was not necessarily a promise when it was made to an Arab; that failure to secure arms from the United States did not give Arabs a right to try elsewhere; that in American eyes the only people who counted in the Middle East (apart from the Israelis) were the Russians; that the United States had no genuine interest in Arab economic development as such. [...] In short the Arabs concluded that Americans did not look on them as being on the same level as other peoples or nations. By contrast, the actions of the Soviet Union seemed to shine with a pure white light."

62 *L'Orient*, June 21, 1956.

63 He was not the only clairvoyant. See *Le Jour*, July 11, 1956. This paper, however, felt that besides wanting to start a war, Israel was willing to begin a world war. Israel, the paper wrote, was also rumored to have an atomic bomb.

Chapter 5

From Sinai to the End of a Free Press in the UAR, 1956-58

In retrospect, it appears that the Czech arms agreement, the recognition of the Peoples' Republic of China, the withdrawal of British troops from Egypt, and the nationalization of the Suez Canal Company were more than Britain, France, and Israel were willing to accept in the period of one year. For these reasons the worst Arab fears were to be fulfilled.

Even before the Egyptian action taken on the Suez Canal, Israel had been pressing for the recognition of free passage for its ships through that waterway (and the Strait of Tiran). Israel felt that with the withdrawal of the British, its rights had to be established immediately. It therefore began an offensive in the United Nations and elsewhere to have its right of passage firmly established. This was something that the Egyptian Government did not favor, and it may be here that the most immediate reasons for the 1956 Suez War should be sought.[1]

In attempting to discover the reasons for Britain's and France's joining this military adventure, it should not be overlooked that Britain wished to maintain a friendly force on the Suez. Oil shipped through the canal supplied over half of Europe's needs. The British were also upset by the nationalization of the Universal Suez Canal Company and the loss of its revenue. The Algerian Revolution against the French and the moral and substantive aid that Cairo was giving the rebels were sufficient stimuli for French participation. There was also the hope that, faced with a military defeat at the hands of the allies, the regime of President 'Abd al-Nāṣir would fall and one more amenable to the desires of the three would be forthcoming.

The Israeli, British, and French design against Egypt and the Suez Canal was not unknown to the Arabs. One can frequently see in their newspapers references to a planned invasion of Egypt. One Lebanese newspaper mentioned that it had from a "usually reliable source" that the originator of the invasion plan was Israel. The plan had been submitted to and supported by the French and was, at the date of publication of the newspaper, being studied by the English.[2]

Climaxing what was often seen as an inevitability was the Israeli invasion of the Sinai Peninsula on October 29, 1956. The invasion took place at two points north of the Gulf of Aqaba. The Arab press, especially the Lebanese, was not fooled into believing the invasion would continue unilaterally. Many editorials reflected that in spite of Israel's apparent solitary action, it "cannot proceed without foreign intervention."[3]

To the Arab editorialists, it was only a matter of time until the West found an excuse to aid Israel. There was some writing which said that perhaps the excuse used to legitimize intervention would be the Tripartite Declaration of 1950.[4] When Britain and France threatened to occupy the Canal if the two belligerents did not withdraw from that waterway, this was immediately viewed by the editorialists as confirmation of their belief that the West would invade as Israel's ally. There was no possibility of believing the French and British assertion that they were entering as disinterested parties and their only aim was to restore peace to the area.[5] The comment on the role of Israel, Britain, and France, prior to and during their action against Egypt in Sinai and Port Sa'īd, viewed the goals of the three nations as being both short-term and long-term. The short-term aims, as the editorialists viewed them, were largely Israel's. As the short-term benefactor, Israel was felt to gain, maximally, an imposed peace between Arabs and Israelis and, minimally, modern British and French weapons.[6]

The long-term benefactors of the war with Egypt would be primarily Britain and France, but not completely excluding Israel. The object of the Western invasion of Egypt was not simply to overthrow 'Abd al-Nāṣir but to restore Western influence throughout the Arab world which the Egyptian revolution of 1952 had eroded.

> It is not a limited war against the person of 'Abd al-Nāṣir [...]. It is a colonial war against the whole Arab nation.
>
> The formation of this unholy alliance between Britain, France, and Israel affirms the fact that this expedition is against the whole Arab nation.[7]

No matter the political shade of the newspaper, the editorialists felt that the attack was nothing more than colonial, imperialistic aggression. The Great Powers saw their former influence dwindling in the Arab East and North Africa. The writers felt that what was being enacted was the last desperate effort of the protagonists of a dying ideology to preserve their former positions.[8] Anti-English feeling was especially strong in Jordan, which traditionally had close ties with Britain. *Filasṭīn*[9] demanded that the Anglo-Jordanian Treaty of 1948 be abrogated, an act which the Hashimites unilaterally took in March 1957. Thus for England the invasion of Egypt resulted in a significant loss of power in Jordan. Furthermore, the elections in Jordan in October 1956 brought the National Socialist Party (NSP) of Sulaymān al-Nābulsī to power. Certainly as a result of the tripartite aggression, al-Nābulsī's declared support for a union with Syria and Egypt was widely applauded. In reaction to this drift toward a pan-Arab policy centering in Cairo and the anti-Western stance it implied, King Ḥusayn was forced to warn his prime minister to be on the lookout for subversives, usually in communist clothing! The star of Jamāl 'Abd al-Nāṣir was so far in the ascendant, however, by 1956 that one could only take him on with great trepidation. The king's Bedouin-based army was called from its barracks in April 1957 to stand behind the king's deposition of the NSP government and to quell 'Alī Abū Nuwwār's attempt to overthrow the monarchy and attach Jordan to Egypt. This having been forestalled, the monarchy began to move against dissidents; it banned all political parties, muzzled the press by instituting strict domestic censorship, and put out of business papers that had shown themselves to be supporters of the NSP or the attempted coup.

Likewise, the French attack on Egypt presented difficult problems for the Maronite-dominated government of Lebanon. President Kamīl Sham'ūn refused to break relations with the West, arguing later that 'Abd al-Nāṣir had asked him not to, in order to serve as a possible negotiator with the West. This reason was apparently unknown to the Lebanese prime minister, 'Abd Allāh al-Yāfī, who resigned in protest. Many Arab editorialists, usually non-Lebanese, wondered when Lebanon was going to be even passively in harmony with Arab policy.[10] Two years later when the 1958 Lebanese civil war erupted, it seems quite likely that those opposed to Sham'ūn remembered how he had acted in 1956. The failure of Sham'ūn to break relations with countries at war with an Arab state and subsequently his adherence to the Eisenhower Doctrine were major factors that led to the outbreak of rebellion in the first Lebanese civil war.

One of the unforeseen results of the 1956 war was the rise in stature of the Soviet Union and the United States in Arab editorials. The papers of early November 1956 are full of praise of the Soviet Union for its role in the war against Egypt. It was Russia that had proposed a joint Soviet-American force to restore peace to the area. The Russians had also severed relations with Israel. And it was generally believed that the Soviets' firm stance led to the ceasefire resolution adopted by the United Nations on November 2.

There were writers, however, who warned the Arabs not to be carried away with euphoria by the Soviet stand.

> [...] beyond the questions of personal prestige and of national pride, permanent interests and centuries-old bonds must be safeguarded. One should not build a policy upon friendships accepted in a moment of despair.[11]

An extension of this warning, that Russia was a friend today and might in the future be an enemy, and vice versa for the Western nations, was an admonition for the Arabs not to become too involved with the problem of the role of the West. This argument said that the position of the East and the West was peripheral to the real problem. For these writers, the true enemy was Israel, and it would serve whoever agreed with its views.

> In the last year, Israel was used by the English and French colonialists to hurt us and thus it was ascertained that Israel is at the disposal of any enemy that wants to hurt us. Times may change and enemies may change but Israel will remain a weapon against us.[12]

The role of the United States was widely praised in the Arab states immediately after the invasion of Sinai. Encouraged by President Eisenhower's statement that there were not two "codes of international conduct" by which the world was ruled, one for allies and one for enemies,[13] Arab editorials commented positively on America's role. The writers felt that the strong position of the United States in condemning France, Britain, and Israel might be the basis on which a new American policy could be established in the Middle East. There were comparisons of the pro-Zionist policy of President Truman with the more moderate views emanating from the Republican-controlled White House. For a short period, the papers were willing to forget the Aswan High Dam debacle and to be forgiving of the United States.

Some editorials reviewed American foreign policy and saw it as having been originally positive. The United States was praised for having fought two world wars without territorial ambitions. Editorials would then continue by saying that the Americans had made at least two mistakes in the Middle East after the Second World War. One was supporting the State of Israel and the second was the withdrawal of the High Dam at Aswan offer. But the papers said that the recent action of the United States, in response to the aggression aimed at Egypt, had redeemed some of the injustice the American government had caused the Arab people to suffer.[14]

The Arab honeymoon with the United States did not continue for an extended period of time. The Arab hopes for a new American policy in the Middle East were largely unfounded. The statement that the United States did not support territorial aggrandizement, whether by friend or foe, did not change America's basic support for the right of the State of Israel to exist. It did not take a protracted time for America's support of Israel to resurface. And this reassertion resulted in a return to negative comment on the United States in Arab editorials. The re-emergence of this attitude toward the United States was aided by events related to the Sinai invasion.

The British and French, within a matter of weeks, had withdrawn from Egyptian territory. However, Israel refused to withdraw from the Gaza Strip and Sharm al-Shaykh, an area controlling the entrance to the Gulf of Aqaba at the Strait of Tiran.

> Britain and France accepted the United Nations' resolution and withdrew from Egypt in a few days. Although the withdrawal of the Israeli forces would not take more than a day, we see Israel delaying withdrawal and trying to impose some conditions that do not exist in the United Nations' resolution.[15]

The withdrawal of France and Britain and the diplomatic isolation of Israel allowed the Arab editorialists to become more belligerent in their stand.

> Had the matter been limited to Arab states and Israel, the Arabs would have taught this trifling state a lesson which it never would have forgotten. But Arab states, led by Egypt, have pledged themselves to respect the United Nations Charter.[16]
>
> We will wait until the United Nations proves it is unable to carry out its resolutions, and then we will destroy the idea that Israel can get what it likes through aggression.[17]

Israel continued to maintain itself on Egyptian territory as the year 1957 began. However, it was clear that the earlier editorial opinion on the reasons for Israeli participation in the attack on Egypt were incorrect. There seemed to be no diplomatic offensive to impose a peace between Arabs and Israelis. Nor had Israel obtained an untoward amount of military equipment from the West. Clearly there were other reasons for Israel's actions. The most obvious was territorial aggrandizement. Equally likely, however, and a situation that did not escape editorial perusal, was the maintenance of Israeli forces in the south of Sinai and in Gaza. The changing view now held that the Israelis either wanted to increase their territory or to use the continued occupation as a bargaining point to gain the right of free passage in and out of the Gulf of Aqaba.

It was also widely believed that Israel was suffering economically from its isolation at the hands of the Arab boycott. An extension of this belief led to editorials that said Israel entered the Sinai campaign with the purpose of gaining egress from the Gulf of Aqaba in order to find new markets in East Asia.[18]

To counter this attempt of Israel to escape from the boycott several writers suggested that the Arab states respond by tightening it. A plea was made to stop the clearance of the Suez Canal, which had been blocked during the war. This was felt to be a way to hurt the West economically. Also the flow of Arab oil to the West should be stopped and a boycott of the products emanating from countries that supported Israel should be introduced.[19]

It soon became apparent that the good will of Russia was not enough to force Israel from the territory it occupied. Britain and France stood behind their recent ally. The only power left was the United States. Despite the earlier flamboyant articles in the Arab press, there was no real question of Egypt's forcing Israel from the Sinai Peninsula. So the United States became the butt of Arab frustration because Israel refused to withdraw from the areas it had conquered.

> Not Egypt alone, or the Arab states alone, or the Middle East alone but millions [throughout the world] [...] have their eyes set on the United States president to see if he will force the snake back into its pit. Today, President Eisenhower stands face to face with Zionism. [...] Will he be able defeat it and thus prove to the world that he is a man of principle and that he is a believer in the principles of the United Nations?[20]

The implication was clear. Either Israel would withdraw under the prodding of the United States or it would remain with America's blessing. As January 1957 passed and so too the first few weeks of February, with no sign of an Israeli withdrawal, editorial comment condemned the United States for not forcing its ally to withdraw.[21]

The United Nations on February 19 reiterated its call for Israel to quit the Sinai and Gaza within five days. When this period passed without results, vituperative comments against the United States increased. All the advantages that had accrued to the United States in the Arab press, as a result of its stand on the Sinai invasion, had disappeared by February 1957. And when the Israelis finally announced their willingness to withdraw in March 1957, the comment was not generally favorable toward the United States. "America forced Israel to withdraw from Gaza but it did not win the confidence of the Middle Eastern countries."[22]

The Arab editorialists were angry with the United States because it was attempting to fulfill their worst fears. One problem was that in forcing Israel to withdraw from Gaza and

Sharm al-Shaykh, the United States wanted to substitute one foreign power for another: that is, substituting a United Nations Emergency Force (UNEF) for the Israeli army.

> The latest U.N. debates have shown that the majority of members of the Organization, with the U.S. at the head, want to maintain some international forces at Gaza and Sharm al-Shaykh in order to stop a repeat of the hostilities on the Negev front and to assure the freedom of navigation in the Gulf of Aqaba.
>
> But to accept that would be for Egypt the recognition that the aggression of October 29 was not a total failure for the aggressor. ʻAbd al-Nāṣir is not ready to accord the enemy such an advantage. It is on this point that he intends to put American friendship to the test.[23]

The point, as the editorialists saw it, was that the Israelis were attempting to reap some benefit from their attack of October 1956. They were to gain the right of passage through the Strait of Tiran into the Gulf of Aqaba. The Strait was considered by the Arabs to be within their territorial waters and the rights of belligerency should allow them to close the waterway to their enemy, as they had done prior to October 1956.

> [Any] modification of the *status quo ante* would signify a result for Israel, this is to say a success, however precarious it might be, of the operation of October 29. And it is a question for the Arabs of imposing on Israel the proof of the principle: Aggression does not pay.[24]

The Arabs were unable to prove to the Israelis that aggression did not pay. Israel gained the right of egress from and ingress to the Gulf of Aqaba. This right was viewed by the editorialists as being achieved largely by the position of the United States, which held that the Strait of Tiran was an international waterway. This American position was condemned editorially. Anti-American feeling increased when the first ship to test the new freedom through Tiran was an American oil tanker.[25]

At least one Arab writer did not fault America as much as he blamed the Arabs for Israeli gains:

> It would probably be impolite on our part to ask the Arab states to give an opinion on this subject since the Palestine case is good for bellowing and for popular consumption only. And no one has the courage to face Arab opinion with the bitter truths which have afflicted the Palestine case since the aggression at the Canal. [...]
>
> So Arab quarters are now quiet about something as grave as the opening of the Aqaba Straits to the enemy and are concealing the news with the same care as Israel. As if the important thing was not the passage incident, but the concealing of the news from the sight of the Arab peoples.[26]

It was in the middle of the crisis over Suez and the Sinai, on January 5, 1957, that President Eisenhower announced his Doctrine for the Middle East. Apparently motivated by a fear that there was imminent danger from the Soviet Union, as a result of the vacuum caused by the French and British fiasco, the American president sought to step into the breach. But the Doctrine only served to antagonize a majority of the Arab writers. Editorials felt it was ludicrous that, at a time when the Western pawn, Israel, was still occupying Arab lands and the West had only recently attacked the Arabs, one of the Western nations should propose a defense pact aimed at communism.

The "pure white light" of the Soviet Union had only increased in brilliance during the Suez crisis. How could one speak of a fear of Soviet aggression when anger over Gaza, Port Saʿīd, and Sharm al-Shaykh was still fresh in Arab minds? *Al-Jumhūrīyah* added that though the American plan talked dramatically about the future and the dangers lying ahead, it was strangely silent regarding the present.[27]

> With one eye open, the United States saw the far away threat which endangers the Arab world, namely the communist danger. But with the closed eye, the United States [...] wants the Arabs not to think about the Anglo-French attack on Port Saʿīd and to forget Palestine.[28]

It appeared to the Arab writers that the United States simply could not understand the Arabs. Americans were bogged down in their own conception of the world and could not comprehend that, for the Arabs, communism was not as great an enemy as the Israelis. Once again, similar to the cold reception given to the Johnston Plan, Arab editorials did not warmly receive the Eisenhower Doctrine. They viewed it as another attempt to avoid the real problem of the Middle East. Some papers felt that had the US president tried to make the Israelis respect the resolutions adopted by the United Nations, he could have served his cause better.[29]

Those governments which did accept the Eisenhower Doctrine, notably Saudi Arabia, Iraq, Jordan, and Lebanon, were subjected to vilification in the press of Egypt, Syria, and opposition papers in Lebanon. In these attacks, the focus was often on the refugees. It was alleged, by those who were opposed to the Doctrine, that those who had accepted it had done so with the understanding that the Palestine refugees would be resettled. The opinion voiced was that the United States was behind these attempts and one billion dollars had already been set aside for this purpose. The United States, with its allies, was meeting secretly with the Israelis, another adherent to the Eisenhower Doctrine, with the intent of liquidating the refugee problem.[30]

The campaign against those allied with the West reached a low when a Syrian paper openly vilified King Ḥusayn calling him "ʿAbd Allāh the Little." This editorial said that his crimes against the Arab nation were unsurpassed since he had agreed to make peace with Israel.[31]

The counterattack against the campaign led by Egypt was confined to those newspapers sympathetic to the West or supporting those governments aligned with the West. Many such papers refuted the Egyptian-led campaign of vilification of King Ḥusayn. *Filasṭīn* commented favorably on the expressions of loyalty coming from the refugees and others in Jordan for their king. The paper was happy to report demonstrations throughout Jordan in support of the Hashimites.[32]

As 1958 approached, the Arab world became polarized into two camps: one that looked to ʿAbd al-Nāṣir as its leader and the other comprised of those who followed Iraq, the Hashimites, and the West. What resulted was that those editorials dealing with the Palestine question were used by one contending side to attack the other. This disintegration of the Palestine question resulted in a rise in emotional invective fired from side-to-side.

Egypt and Syria merged into the UAR on February 1, 1958. A union of Iraq and Jordan was announced on February 14, 1958 as the Arab Federated State (AFS). The papers of the UAR attacked those of the AFS, and vice versa. The Lebanese journals took sides according to whether they supported the opposition or the government in their presidential election year.

The Egyptian-led bloc attacked the Hashimite monarchies in an attempt to rally support to its cause. In doing so the bloc used Palestine as a point on which to pin failure on its opponents.

> [...] It is time the Arab nation rid itself of the Hashimite Kingdom [...].
>
> It was because of the Hashimites' participation in the Palestine War [of 1948] that we lost that war. It was they who handed over to the Jews the lands on which Israel emerged; these lands which the Arabs of Palestine had put as a trust in their hands.[33]

The Jordanian rulers were also accused of selling lands to Israel and of not taking adequate care of Jerusalem. Worse still, the AFS was indicted for being in an alliance with Israel, since both had joined in supporting the Eisenhower Doctrine. One Damascus paper alleged that there was an agreement whereby Israel would attack the UAR, and while this was occurring, the Arab Federated State would invade and conquer the Syrian region.[34] And there was the repeated accusations that the Hashimites had concluded or were on the verge of concluding peace with Israel.[35]

The newspapers favorable to the West and to the AFS were not reluctant to strike back at ʿAbd al-Nāṣir, although in general their attacks were not as strong. Usually they did not accuse the UAR president of laxity in the past. But when in 1958 civil strife erupted in Lebanon and ʿAbd al-Nāṣir sided with the insurgents, his largely Maronite opponents accused him of agreeing to settle with Israel in return for a free hand in Lebanon. "He sold Palestine to purchase Lebanon, and absolute leadership in the Arab East [...]."[36] That the opposition to ʿAbd al-Nāṣir in Lebanon were predominantly Maronites should not hide the firm support which the secular *Partie Populaire Syrienne* (PPS) gave them. By 1958, the PPS was militantly resisting ʿAbd al-Nāṣir's growing influence in Lebanon and amongst the Palestinians.

The Palestine problem became not so much a vital issue as an object to be hurled by contending sides in the battle for Arab supremacy. There was the polarization of political fortunes in the Middle East with the Egyptians leading one contingent and the Iraqis and Hashimites leading the other. In this setting, the Palestine question often became only a weapon to be discharged at one's enemy. The deterioration of the Arab press was perceptible when it became the primary soldier in this battle. Its role of questioning, probing, and attempting to solve the Palestine problem came to an end.

There were other factors that ended its semi-independent commenting on Palestine. The unification of Egypt and Syria into the United Arab Republic hurt the newspapers of the new nation in at least two respects. First, political parties were disbanded early in 1958, shortly after the birth of the UAR. This disbanding of political organizations meant the end of monetary subsidies to the newspapers.

> The press's honorable struggle in various political battles [...] is not denied by anyone [...]. But the great union between Egypt and Syria meant prosperity for all citizens save newsmen. [...] With the dissolution of political parties and organizations in our country, many sources of press income ceased to exist.[37]

Second, the regime of 'Abd al-Nāṣir had become increasingly hostile to a free press in Egypt, and later in the UAR. This hostility was manifested in Egypt by the ending of the publication of many newspapers. The greatest signal, though certainly not the first, of the termination of a free press was the government's takeover of *al-Ahrām* in 1957. The emergence of government-owned papers, such as *al-Jumhūrīyah* and *al-Sha'b*, should also be noted. This policy of a controlled press also exerted itself in the Syrian region of the UAR. Although the papers were badly injured by the ban on political parties, the *coup de grâce* was administered in September 1958 when the government urged all newspapers to accept monetary compensation in return for agreeing to stop printing. Most newspapers agreed to cease publication,[38] their positions increasingly untenable because of a loss of financial support from the banned political parties and the damaging competition from the regime's newspapers flown in from Cairo and sold at cheaper prices. By the end of the year, only four papers in Damascus were locally published. Latakia, Homs, and Allepo had one paper each.

In Jordan, the assassination of King Fayṣal of Iraq and his cousin, 'Abd al-Ilāh, in the middle of July 1958 signified even greater control of a press already severely hobbled in 1956 by the Jordanian monarch who feared for his throne. The result in Syria, Egypt, and Jordan was the cessation of varied comments on the problem of Palestine. Now the papers of each country did no more than follow their respective governments' lines.

In Lebanon, although censorship in 1958 was not instituted for editorial opinion on Palestine, the outbreak of hostilities amongst the Lebanese meant that editorials were not greatly concerned with Palestine. The survival or non-survival of the nation occupied all minds.

What has been discussed in this chapter has been the Palestine question after the Czech arms deal and the nationalization of the Suez Canal Company. What the newspapers saw was often not pleasant, especially when viewed by a Westerner. They wrote that the French, British, and Israeli action against Egypt was unlawful and motivated by base aims of territorial aggrandizement, forced recognition of Israel, economic benefit, or worse, colonial superiority of one people over another. In their denunciations, the Lebanese press corps, often French-educated and French-bred, were the least vociferous in their condemnation, reflecting a governmental reluctance to break all ties with the West.

Out of the Sinai War of 1956, the United States and Russia emerged unscathed in their positions with the Arabs. One may even say that the American position was enhanced by its condemnation of the invasion of Egypt. But this advantage was lost under the deluge of subsequent events. The souring of Arab-American relations has been mentioned in the previous chapter. The Sinai campaign tended to put this Arab hostility below the surface. But it did not end it.

There was editorial suspicion that even though the United States did not overtly support the three allies, there was still no doubt of overall American friendship for the nations involved, especially Israel.

Arab editorial suspicion was confirmed when Israel refused to withdraw from the territories that it had conquered. Rightly or wrongly, it identified this Israeli attitude as being backed by the United States. Both were partners in desiring some benefit from the action of October and November 1956. How else could the writers explain the American ship that subsequently sailed through the Strait of Tiran?

It is in the light of the gradual re-emergence of anti-American sentiment, while Israeli troops still occupied Sharm al-Shaykh and Gaza, that each writer's reaction to the Eisenhower Doctrine must be seen. There could be no question of its rejection by the Egyptians. They could not possibly ally with a Western nation while its client occupied Egyptian territory. The same was true of Egypt's allies as was demonstrated in Syria and in certain Lebanese political and journalistic circles.

More accurately, however, the anti-American sentiment, the Eisenhower Doctrine, and even the question of Palestine must be viewed within the context of the fight in 1958 for supremacy within the Arab world: the battle between the progressive socialism and positive neutrality of ʿAbd al-Nāṣir and the more traditional, Western-oriented philosophy represented by the Hashimites.

Plans, developments, accusations, and countercharges might take the form of a debate on Palestine or the merits of one alliance or another, but underlying all was the question of which way the Arabs would move and who would lead them. The effect on Arab newspapers was marked. As the governments were polarized, so too were the papers. As governments adopted dogmatic positions or accused their enemies of deviating from stands amenable to Arab goals, so too did the newspapers. The precarious freedom that many of the newspapers had enjoyed came to a halt, as they became mere spokesmen for their respective governments. When the political situation began to accelerate more and more (union of

Syria and Egypt, attempted overthrow of the Hashimites in Jordan, union of Jordan and Iraq, civil war in Lebanon, overthrow of the Iraqi monarchy) and the governments became more harsh toward any dissent, several papers ceased publication. Others were taken over by government, and censorship was imposed. Thus, Palestine declined as a question that could be objectively probed and constructively criticized. Arab editorial opinion became less a function of the newsman and more a function of what a government wanted published. In this sense, the history of the Arab press becomes different after 1958 from what it was before. The press after 1958 is in general a reflection of governments. When Arab papers are quoted in the West, the quotes are often preceded by "the semi-official *al-Ahrām* wrote" or "the authoritative *al-Ba'th* said." The editorials are less diverse; reading one journal is enough to predict what all the other papers in the same country will say.

Though less diverse, they are no less interesting. They also provide valuable information as to what was the official position. It is to a study of this new direction in the press that we turn our attention in the next chapter.

Notes

1 See for example *al-Sha'b*, October 1, 1956. For the official Egyptian statement concerning the reasons behind the Israeli invasion, see *al-Ahrām*, October 30, 1956.
2 *Al-Diyār*, September 13, 1956.
3 René Aggiouri, *L'Orient*, October 30, 1956.
4 See for example *al-Naṣr*, October 30, 1956; and *al-Jarīdah*, October 31, 1956.
5 See the two-day commentary by Kāmil Murūwah in *al-Ḥayāt*, October 30 and 31, 1956.
6 *Bayrūt*, October 30, 1956.
7 Kāmil Murūwah, *al-Ḥayāt*, November 1, 1956.
8 Representative editorials may be seen in *al-Ayyām*, October 31, 1956; Renê Aggiouri, *L'Orient*, November 2, 1956; and *Bayrūt al-Masā'*, November 5, 1956.
9 November 28, 1956.
10 See for example *al-Ra'y al-'Āmm*, November 7, 1956.
11 *L'Orient*, November 9, 1956.
12 Kāmil Murūwah, *al-Ḥayāt*, May 15, 1957.
13 Text in the *New York Times*, November 1, 1956.
14 Representative editorials may be seen in *al-Ayyām*, December 3, 1956; *Bayrūt*, December 7, 1956; and *al-Siyāsah*, December 17, 1956. The Arab press was not uniformly enamored with America. At least one newspaper warned editorially that the American policy of support for Israel had not changed. *Le Jour*, December 10, 1956.
15 Kāmil Murūwah, *al-Ḥayāt*, December 27, 1956.
16 *Al-Ahrām*, January 8, 1957.
17 *Al-Jumhūrīyah*, January 16, 1957. See also the same newspaper on January 21, 1957.
18 See for example Kāmil Murūwah in *al-Ḥayāt*, January 5 and February 16, 1957 and *al-Ahrām*, February 14, 1957.

19 Representative editorials may be seen in *al-Ra'y al-ʿĀmm*, January 3, 1957; and *al-Difāʿ*, January 28, 1957.
20 *Al-Ahrām*, February 12, 1957.
21 See, among others, *al-Jumhūrīyah*, February 6, 1957; *al-Siyāsah*, February 10, 1957; and *al-Naṣr*, February 12, 1957.
22 *Al-Jarīdah*, March 3, 1957.
23 René Aggouri, *L'Orient*, January 24, 1957.
24 Ibid., February 3, 1957.
25 See for example *al-Tilighrāf*, April 8, 1957; and *al-Jumhūrīyah*, May 16, 1957.
26 *Al-Ḥayāt*, May 22, 1957.
27 *Al-Jumhūrīyah*, January 8, 1957.
28 *Filasṭīn*, January 16, 1957. Western scholars have agreed that the Eisenhower Doctrine was an answer to American fears not an attempt to fulfill Arab needs. "[...] fear of Soviet aggression [...] was fundamentally a Western fear." Among others, J.C. Hurewitz, *Middle East Dilemmas* (New York, Harper, 1953), 251.
29 *Al-Fayḥā'*, January 16, 1957. Compare the Arab orientation with the *New York Times*, August 6, 1957; "The [Eisenhower] Doctrine has aligned most of the Middle Eastern states on the side of the West and has thereby checked President Nasser's Soviet-backed Arabic and ultimately pan-Islamic empire [...]."
30 Representative editorials may be seen in *al-Ahrām*, August 12, August 14, and November 18, 1957; ʿAbd Allāh al-Yāfī in *al-Siyāsah* (of Lebanon), July 18, 1957; and *Ra'y al-ʿĀmm*, July 17 and November 4, 1957. See also *al-Shaʿb* (of Egypt), November 3, 1957, which published a news story alleging that a meeting on the ministerial level had been held in Nablus between the Jordanians and the Israelis. Peace between the two nations was the topic of the meeting.
31 *Alif Bā'*, November 12, 1957. The same writer called the Jordanian monarch, Ḥusayn Ibn Zayn. This was a great insult – calling an Arab by his mother's name, as though his father was unknown.
32 *Filasṭīn*, November 11 and 13, 1957. One of the strongest attacks against the Egyptians was broadcast on Amman Radio by an official Jordanian spokesman on November 4, 1957:

> Arab public opinion knows that those who fabricate and disseminate such lies and fabrications are the first to be accused of them, and are more deserving of shame and disgrace and to be called traitors and plotters because of the Arab rights and interest which they lost. They are the ones responsible for all the setbacks which the Palestine question, the foremost problem of the Arabs, [has] suffered at their criminal hands. They are the ones who handed over the Gaza sector, first to the military occupation of the Jews and then the UNEF.
>
> They are the ones responsible for opening the Suez Canal to Israeli ships, which are now sailing through its waters before their very eyes. They are the ones who agreed to the occupation of the Sinai Peninsula, Sharm al-Shaykh, and the Egyptian coastline along the Gulf of Aqaba by the UNEF in order that this force could insure the passage of Israeli and foreign convoys and ships to the Israeli harbor of Elath [...].

In view of this condition prevailing in their territories and their peaceful attitude toward Israel as we have mentioned, responsible Egyptian officials and the hired Egyptian press, as well as the government of the Egyptian dictator, should be the last to accuse the noble patriots among responsible Jordanian officials of seeking pacification with Israel and paving the way for peace and the settlement of the Palestine question. They should be the last because of the secret contacts, plots, and treason that Egyptian rulers committed, proof of which can be found in a large number of documents and information that we possess. We have been reluctant until now to publish these documents and information in order to preserve the reputation of these rulers and hired men.

33 *Al-Naṣr* (Syria), March 14, 1958.

34 *Al-Ra'y al-'Āmm*, April 2, 1958.

35 See, among others, *al-Naṣr*, April 15, 1958; and *al-Ahrām*, June 17, 1958.

36 *Al-'Amal*, May 20, 1958. See also *al-Bayraq* (Lebanon), June 16, 1958.

37 *Al-Shām*, April 2, 1958.

38 Included were *Alif Bā'*, *Baradā*, *al-Haḍārah*, *al-Manār*, *al-Qabas*, and *al-Ra'y al-'Āmm*.

Chapter 6

The Period Dominated by ʻAbd al-Nāṣir: 1958-70

The period between 1958 and 1961, when Egypt and Syria were united in the UAR, was probably the most sterile time in the Arab press' discussion of the Arab-Israeli conflict. This was in part a result of the uniformity of treatment of a given topic in the UAR due to the emasculation of the press there. Even so the press of the area was not focused on the Arab-Israeli question but other intra-regional conflicts, for example, the often-intense ideological and political struggle for Arab hegemony between 'Abd al-Nāṣir and 'Abd al-Karīm Qāsim of Iraq.

Insofar as editorial opinion did deal with Israel, there appeared to be no overriding issue or theme on which the press concentrated. Topics might be mentioned in one column in one journal and not be repeated in the same paper or raised in any other. If one were forced, however, to look for topics, probably the relationship between the Soviet Union and the Arab world was one that was as frequently written about as any. The period immediately after 1958 saw the Soviet Union generally praised for its support of the Arabs, especially the UAR. But even then, though the UAR became a close ally of the Soviet Union, there was at least one subject that threatened this friendship. This was the issue of Jewish immigrants from the USSR finding their way to Israel. The question was taken up with vehemence in February 1959. Such was the nature of the press in Egypt and Syria that, when directed to do so, the papers marched in unison. The greatest peril to Arab nationalism, they declared, was the immigration of East European Jews to Israel.[1] Once stated, the theme was repeated daily in the northern and southern regions of the UAR with only slight differences. Commentaries and stories urged the Soviet Union and the East European countries to ban the flight of Jews.[2] Even in Beirut, the pro-'Abd al-Nāṣir press noted ironically that the United States supplied Israel with money while East Europe supplied it with immigrants.[3] Hard pressed to defend this onslaught, the only communist daily in the Arab world, Beirut's *al-Nidā'*, replied that the story of huge Jewish immigration into Israel was a Western propaganda scheme. The Arabs knew that "this was not the first time that American and British intelligence services have transported millions of Jews from Moscow to Israel on large ships made of the newsprint of certain newspapers [...]."[4]

If the supporters of the Soviet Union in the Arab world were sometimes dismayed with their ally, those newspapers that traditionally supported the United States and the West were also discomfited. They argued that while the Soviet Union made steady progress in gaining allies amongst the Arabs, the United States, since the Tripartite Declaration and the Eisenhower Doctrine, had acted thoughtlessly and to its own detriment. In fact it seemed, said *al-Nahār*, that all allies of the United States were doomed.[5] Another pro-Western journal added:

> The biggest defect in America's policy is its reluctance to solve the greatest problem that has ever faced the Arab states in their history which is the problem of Palestine and the refugees. Their presence in small countries with limited resources, like Lebanon and Jordan, threatens the political, economic, and social balance and threatens to produce a catastrophe of unforeseen consequences.[6]

Support for at least one American came from an unexpected source, *al-Ahrām*, when it wrote a eulogy on the death of John Foster Dulles in May 1959. "Though his strong determination often led him to err, Dulles went ahead with his job with the zeal of a Crusader. Dulles was also a courageous foe."[7]

Perhaps praise of Dulles only attests to the paucity of new topics that journalists had to deal with on the Arab-Israeli conflict. As if to wake the Arab writers from their lethargy, Israel announced in early December 1959 that it was about to finish the first portion of the Jordan River diversion designed to bring fresh water from the north of Israel to the more arid regions of the south. The project already had taken four years to reach this stage and 160 kilometers of pipe had been laid in this unilateral effort following the failure of the Arabs and Israelis to agree to the United States' Johnston Plan. The Israeli announcement came as a shock to the press which found it difficult to believe that such an audacious operation could have been going on for so long and only now publicly noted by the Arab governments. Cynical editorials suggested that over the past 4 years nothing had been done because the Arabs were too busy insulting one another.[8] Though there was some writing of going to war,[9] nothing in fact was done and the Arab press recognized that their people had, in a sense, suffered still one more defeat.

The malaise in the Arab world, vis-à-vis the Arab-Israeli conflict, was also reflected in questions about the leadership of the Palestinian community. Though living in Beirut, al-Ḥājj Amīn al-Ḥusaynī, through his religious position and as head of the Arab Higher Committee, continued to claim leadership of the Palestinian people. But his leadership had been an open question since 1948 as a result of the Palestinian and Arab defeats, for which he was held in part responsible. The press loyal to ʿAbd al-Nāṣir began, in the summer of 1959, to raise questions about the ability of al-Ḥusaynī to lead. One Syrian paper revived an old complaint against the mufti of Jerusalem, that of corruption. Unlike 1948 when the Syrian press charged that money intended for arms was spent by al-Ḥusayni on himself, this time the accusation was made that money intended for ameliorating the conditions of the refugees was being siphoned away by the Arab Higher Committee.[10] The hint of scandal was accompanied by a demand that the next generation of leaders be divorced from the men of the previous one. Times had changed, it was the era of ʿAbd al-Nāṣir, and it was time to do away with those who, by their quarrels and plots, had lost Palestine.[11] There was another Palestinian leadership alternative, the moribund Government of All

Palestine in the Gaza Strip. Aḥmad Ḥilmī, its head, never attracted much support and when he died in June 1963; ʿAbd al-Nāṣir used his death as an opportunity to do away with this vestigial organ.

If the call for a new generation of leaders meant also the arming of the Palestinians, the pro-Hashimite press would have none of it. "The creation of Palestinian armed units is redundant since the mission [of regaining Palestine] is assigned to the Arab armies."[12] Perhaps anticipating the consequences for Jordan a decade later of the arming of the Palestinians, the Hashimites were wary of giving the population under its control weapons for fear that they might be turned against the regime. The Hashimite government had, in principle, no objection to Palestinians joining the Jordanian army and, in order to hasten the integration of the Palestinian population, in February 1960, Jordan extended its citizenship to all Palestinians who desired it, no matter where they were living. The previous law required 4 years residence in Jordan before the acquisition of citizenship. ʿAbd al-Nāṣir was known to oppose the offering of citizenship to the Palestinians, because it suggested their integration into an aggrandized Jordan. Further, he thought of Ḥusayn as a fifth columnist in the Arab world who stood in the way of the liberation of Palestine. Certainly he considered the Jordanian annexation of the West Bank as illegal. Thus, though the new citizenship law was lauded in the Jordanian press, the journals of the UAR condemned it:

> What Israel and the forces that support it want is the liquidation of the Palestine problem and the liquidation of the refugee problem. What the Jordanian government is doing is in complete agreement with what Israel desires. The integration of refugees in Jordan and the granting to them of Jordanian citizenship means the liquidation of the Palestine problem.[13]

That editorial debates of this type were printed during the 1960s does not mean that the Palestine question was the major issue covered in Arab editorials. It was not. After a coup in September 1961, the Syrian province of the UAR withdrew from the union, though Egypt continued to call itself the UAR until 1971. With the break-up, the Arab-Israeli conflict took on even more limited space in the newspapers. There was a great deal written about the failure of the UAR and what was said involved mutual recriminations. There was also a large amount of editorial comment on the war for Algerian independence and the subsequent border disputes between Algeria and Morocco. Also of interest was the struggle for power in Syria. Would the Baʿth Party be able to re-assert itself after September 28? What was the meaning of the Syrian army move against the conservative government six months later on March 28, 1962? Then there was the coup in Iraq in February 1963 against ʿAbd al-Karīm Qāsim. Arab editorialists wondered about its implications for the region. Other issues of interest were the civil war in Yemen, the desire of ʿAbd al-Nāṣir to dominate the Arab world, the question of whether or not Fuʾād Shihāb would seek a second term as president of Lebanon, and the verbal fighting between the Syrian Baʿth Party and Egypt's unofficial spokesman, Muḥammad Ḥasanayn Haykal. This latter battle was part of the war of words over who was at fault for the failure of the union. The Syrian press may have won at least one argument amongst its readers when it reproduced the front page of the *Jewish Observer and Middle East Review* which had, on January 4, 1963, proclaimed Haykal its "Man of the Year."[14] In all of these distractions, there was little space to write about the Palestinians or the Arab-Israeli conflict.

By the end of 1963, the Israelis were nearing the final stage of their diversion of sweet water from the north toward the Negev. Once more the Arab press sounded the alarm, calling the Israeli project robbery.[15] The Syrian press led the way in demanding action to stop the diversionary project. "History condemned the rulers who misused their national trust in 1948 and our Arab people punished them severely. Today, the Arab nation is again watching […]"[16] Clearly, this was a challenge to Egypt to join in a concerted effort to stop the diversion, which some Arabs argued would allow another two million Jews to find a home in Israel. President 'Abd al-Nāṣir responded by calling for an Arab summit of kings and presidents to discuss the diversionary scheme. The Egyptian press and those papers in Beirut who supported the Egyptian leader were cautious, perhaps reflecting 'Abd al-Nāṣir's opinion that eventually triumphed at the summit held in January 1964. The Egyptian press theme was that lacking Arab unity, Egypt would not go to war over the Jordan River diversion and thus be stabbed in the back by Syria which was "unstable," Saudi Arabia which was "isolationist," and Jordan which was "unfriendly."[17] A relatively new writer, Palestinian Ghassān Kanafānī, who was later to become an unofficial voice of the Palestinian people, supported the Egyptian president.

> There is one primary reality, which is also basic and important, and that is that the battle around the diversion of the Jordan River, strategically, is a battle of the Syrian front and the Jordanian front [and] will never be […] a conflict on the southern [Egyptian] front.
>
> If the goal of the Jordan [River] conflict is to stop the practical diversion of the river […] then this merely requires destroying the instruments of diversion and pumping which are primarily on the Syrian front and to a lesser extent on the Jordanian front.[18]

The Syrian press rejected this kind of argument stating that "the fight with Israel is not just stopping the diversion of the Jordan River." Syria was not going to take on Israel by itself and so its press requested that the upcoming summit conference not limit itself to just the question of the diversion of the Jordan, but to the entire Arab-Israeli conflict.[19] The state controlled presses of Egypt and Syria were in open opposition to each other and in this they were reflecting the official view of their respective countries. Yet, in their opposition they agreed; the Arabs, jointly or unilaterally, were not prepared to confront Israel. Haykal, in analyzing this state of unpreparedness, came out with what was then a startling conclusion. The Arabs were not using all of their power. First, he wrote, they confined the battle to those countries with borders on the Zionist state but in any future war "its dimensions must exceed the borders of the Negev desert." Once the idea of a broadened war was accepted, he then put forward the striking opinion, "Arab oil, in the area extending from the [Persian] Gulf to the [Atlantic] Ocean, is the only moving force for life in the

West."[20] This was one of the earliest important calls for the use of economics in the war with Israel. For the next several months in a number of his weekly columns, he continued to elaborate and develop this theme. Haykal's basic tenet centered on the fact that Israel had spent millions of dollars in building the water project, which it viewed as crucial to its life. Therefore, if the Arabs attempted to stop the project, Israel would not stand idly by and war would ensue. If war broke out, the West would intervene to protect Israel with consequences for the Arabs as yet unforeseen. To avoid this eventuality, the Arabs must plan ahead and attempt to neutralize Western interference; to make the West realize that it would pay heavily for intervening and so decide not to support Israel. In addition the Arabs, from the Euphrates to the Nile, had to mobilize all of their human and material resources particularly oil.[21]

> The battle against the entire Israeli presence in Palestine and its complication, such as the problem [of the diversion] of the waters of the Jordan River, is a fierce battle encompassing the economic, political, and military fields [...].
>
> What I am saying is that petroleum is the strongest Arab force. When the battles of destiny get to the decisive moment of life and death, every force must be thrown on the side of the fight for life.[22]

Haykal's analysis was ahead of its time. The already concluded Arab summit of January 1964 decided, for all practical purposes, to do nothing to stop the Israeli diversion of water to the Negev region. When the Israelis made their announcement on May 5 that all was completed and that tests would be carried out for a few weeks before serious pumping began, the Arab press was virtually silent. An Arab editorialist lamented:

> Should we expect the Arab forces to attack the Israeli pumping stations or should we wait until the committees of Arab engineers have completed their blueprints for the diversion of the Banyas and Hasbani Rivers? [...] Or shall we wait till the enemy attacks us so that we may "defend" ourselves?
>
> We do not want to embarrass anyone [...].
>
> But [we would like to make] one last observation. Yesterday passed without our hearing in the Arab world any popular response to the [Israeli] event [...]. What has happened to the Arabs...?[23]

If the Arab summit of January 1964 took no action on Israel's diversion plan, it did approve what was then a little noted project to revitalize the moribund Palestinian community through the creation of some kind of Palestinian entity, an idea first broached by the Arab League in 1959. Aḥmad al-Shuqayrī, the Palestinian representative to the Arab League, was charged with carrying out this new decision that was aimed, at least in part, at bypassing the traditional Palestinian leadership. Al-Shuqayrī quickly set about preparing a Palestine National Charter and the convening of the Palestine National Council. To a press, wary of yet another group that would fill the air with talk and not much else, comment was minimal and reserved. One Syrian paper warned that:

> Any project on the Palestinian entity that does not manifest an organizational structure containing popular struggle will not win the support of the displaced masses.... The entity that the Palestinians have been demanding for years is that entity capable of mobilizing their resources [...] and capable of liberating the homeland now in captivity.[24]

With the preliminaries out of the way, the Palestine National Council met in Jerusalem on May 28, 1964. One of its first acts was the proclamation of the Palestine Liberation Organization (PLO) with Aḥmad al-Shuqayrī as its head. Ironically, King Ḥusayn was present at the opening session of the congress and later hailed the formation of the PLO. Al-Shuqayrī was popular with the Palestinian people, but was handicapped by being closely connected to ʿAbd al-Nāṣir and the Arab League, and not having been chosen by the people he was supposed to lead or supported by any legitimate Palestinian institution, since there was none.

As 1964 drew to a close, another body was meeting in Europe that seemed at the time to be of more interest to the Arab press than the Palestine National Council and that was the second Roman Catholic Ecumenical Council, also known as Vatican II. What interested the Middle Eastern journalists about the conclave was the debate over a resolution to absolve Jews of responsibility for the death of Jesus. Almost uniformly the Arab press opposed the lifting of guilt.[25] That largely Muslim Arab papers should become upset is ironic, since Muslims do not believe that Jesus was crucified, as *Surah* iv, 154, attests. But the Arab press did not view the debate in Rome as religious but as political and it was on that basis that they opposed it. When the resolution was adopted on October 15, 1965 by a vote of 1793 to 250, continued editorial comment emphasized the political victory that the adoption was for Israel and that "Jews will not hesitate to use the ... document to try to justify their illegal usurpation of the land of Christ."[26] But at least one commentator saw a positive outcome for the Arabs of the Ecumenical Council decision that the death of Jesus, as the resolution states, "cannot be imputed to all the Jews [...]."

> It is obvious that present Jewish immigration is based, from the Zionist point of view, on two factors: anti-Semitism, or the persecution of Jews in areas where they form an important minority [...] and stability in Israel [...]. In so far as concerns the document on the Jews [adopted by Vatican II], it certainly is in Arab interests that Jews should not be persecuted [...] because such persecution may result in further waves of immigration which is desired by the Zionist movement.[27]

The question of guilt of the Jewish people to an event that occurred 2000 years ago was not crucial to the struggle for Palestine but was largely a psychological fight. More important were concrete proposals for peace. When the Afro-Asian countries met in Bandung in 1955, one of the resolutions they adopted called for a peaceful solution to the conflict in the

Middle East by the implementation of United Nations' resolutions on Palestine. Though these resolutions did not call for direct talks between the belligerents, they did carry with them an implicit recognition of Israel since the primary resolution dealing with the Arab-Israeli conflict was that of November 1947 that called for the formation of a Jewish and an Arab state in Palestine. As the tenth anniversary of the Asian-African Conference approached, it was with some surprise that a Beirut journal quoted from an interview President 'Abd al-Nāṣir gave to the Tunisian *Jeune Afrique*. In it the Egyptian leader said that the Arab states concurred with the resolutions adopted at Bandung that called for a peaceful solution to the conflict.[28] There was no comment on the Beirut story but one week later, on April 21, 1965, President Habib Bourguiba called for a negotiated settlement between the Arabs and Israel. In his speech, he became the first Arab head-of-state to call openly for the Arabs to negotiate with Israel. The interesting conjunction of the call for negotiations by Bourguiba with 'Abd al-Nāṣir's support for the Bandung resolutions was noted by an editorialist writing under the *nom de plume*, "A Veteran Arab Politician":

> The two presidents, of Tunisia and Egypt, are agreed that their goal is implementing United Nations' resolutions on Palestine and not the destruction of the state of Israel. This is why President 'Abd al-Nāṣir, if the *Jeune Afrique* magazine report is true, [called] for the implementation of United Nations' resolutions, not the liberation of all of Palestine.[29]

It was one of the characteristics of those times that 'Abd al-Nāṣir could agree to a negotiated peace, a radical idea in 1965, without being attacked but when another head of state called for the same, he was violently assailed in the Arab press. "Throw Tunisia out of the [Arab] League" wrote a Beirut journal[30] and several other papers echoed that sentiment, including those of the Egyptian press. One Cairo paper went so far as to declare that President Bourguiba's statement was prompted by financial exigencies. His country was in such dire straits that he had been forced to make a deal with the European Rothschilds whereby, in return for financial help for his country, he would call for an end to Arab belligerency toward the Jewish state.[31]

Whatever the reasons, the print media was not willing to consider a negotiated settlement and the comments in the Arab press subsided when no more of the two presidents' proposals were pursued. Rather, as the 1960s progressed, the Arab press was still overwhelmingly in favor of a military solution. One of the signs that the papers were interested in a victory of arms was the curious and hopeful attention they paid to the rise of the mysterious new commando groups, about which we will shortly have more to say. But the road to a military settlement, advantageous to the Arabs, was blocked by the actions of Israel's allies, most notably the United States. The Johnson Administration, as perceived by the Arab press, seemed to be committed to two major goals in the Middle East. The first was the maintenance of "a balance" in the area, which Arabs interpreted to mean that Israel should be as strong as or stronger than the military capability of all the Arab states combined. The second was that though America had adopted a policy of no longer intervening directly in the Middle East, as it did in 1958, it would strengthen its Jewish surrogate through arms supply thus enabling Israel to act "as a base of aggression that could maneuver somewhat independently of the Sixth Fleet [...]."[32] This latter change in attitude, from direct to indirect intervention, was conceded to have come about as a result of the increasingly difficult time the United States was having in Vietnam.

> All the arguments that American and Zionist propaganda offer to justify arming Israel do not hide the aggressive intentions [America has] against the citadels of liberation in the Arab world and the [United States'] threat to overthrow the nationalist regimes which are strengthening their own positions and [gaining] support throughout the Arab World.[33]
>
> America by its latest sales [of arms to Israel] deviated from its alleged neutrality in the Arab-Israeli conflict to open partiality [...]. It is still deceiving world public opinion by claiming the arms are tactical and defensive rather than offensive [...].[34]
>
> Tell me who arms you, and I will tell you who you are.[35]

To counter increasing American aid to Israel, several proposals were put forward by the Arab press. Barely noticed at that time was the call in the Syrian press for the Arabs to play their oil card. Middle East oil production in 1966 was almost exclusively in non-Arab hands, so the demand, though muted, was for the "liberation" of Arab petroleum. "Either the Arab people should rise to support this struggle [to nationalize oil] so as to benefit from this wealth and the importance the industrialized would place on it [...] or else continue living in slavery [...]."[36]

The Syrian press had switched alliances immediately after the February 23, 1966 coup that had overthrown the Pan-Arab Command within the Ba'th Party in favor of the National, sometimes called the Regional or even the Syrian, Command of the Party led by Ṣalāḥ Jadīd. After that change in government, the Syrian press became increasingly polemical and anti-capitalist. At the same time that it called for the nationalization of foreign oil companies, it also called for the abolition of monarchies in the Arab world, holding that those conservative regimes had created an informal alliance with America and Zionism that hindered Arab liberation of its oil. But the United States and its allies could be defeated, witness the problems America was having in Vietnam. The trend of the war in Asia was a herald of future setbacks for "reactionaries" throughout the world.[37]

The focus on American tribulations in Vietnam often mesmerized the Arab press. Though the press, which we might call leftist or progressive, was obviously gleeful over American difficulties, even the press on the right could find nothing to applaud in Southeast Asia. The question that editorials asked rhetorically was: Cannot the Arab world have a north Vietnam? By this they meant a country that would be willing to sacrifice itself to achieve the liberation of its neighbor from foreign, in this case Israeli, occupation.[38]

> [...] why do we [Arabs] not, for example, add to the exhaustion of the United States by opening a new front that would be difficult for the United States to face? [...] In addition to the front in Cuba [...] in south Vietnam [...] in the Dominican [Republic] [...] north Vietnam [...] and in occupied south Yemen, we should open our front with Israel so we

> may exhaust the Washington government and realize the aspirations of the Arab nation [...] And why do we not call this front a popular war of liberation [which is a slogan] which frightens the United States [...]?
>
> Let us further exhaust the invaders while they are feeling weak.[39]

As though anticipating the question, Ghassān Kanafānī wrote:

> The largest portion of the Palestinian people live in Jordan [...]. Therefore it is only logical that the largest number of Palestinian warriors be mobilized [...] in Jordan. But this cannot be achieved without a radical change in the Jordanian system, a change that would place this entity, which is basically a Palestinian entity [...] on a level requisite for war [...].
>
> A Palestinian liberation war above all requires a north Vietnam that could sustain, perhaps for years, devastation, raids, and death without complaints [...]. Of all the Arab states surrounding Israel, only Jordan can play the role of a north Vietnam. As to who shall play the role of Vietcong – since we have used the Vietnamese example – this can only be played by Palestinians.[40]

That there was going to be an Arab equivalent to the Vietcong began to be widely speculated about in the Arab press in 1965. Though there is some debate about when the first organized commando operation inside Israel occurred, a newly-created, clandestine, and anonymous organization named *al-ʿĀṣifah* (the Storm) claimed credit for a raid on the night of December31–January 1, 1965. In its first military communiqué *al-ʿĀṣifah* said it engaged Israeli forces and inflicted "heavy damages" on its enemy.[41] There is some doubt that the raid actually occurred.[42]

But the debate is only of interest to historians. The real importance of the announcement was that some Palestinians were attempting to take their destiny in their own hands. By so doing, they were removing a burden from the other Arab governments that the latter reluctantly accepted. The traditional governments had failed to gain the goals that the Palestinians, awakened in the last part of the 1960s, demanded. Now it was the turn of the Palestinians. There was widespread press speculation about the identity of the *ʿĀṣifah* group in January 1965. While still remaining anonymous, it did produce in Damascus its own magazine, *Ṣawt al-ʿĀṣifah*. The cloak of secrecy that wrapped the commando organization was partially lifted when a Beirut journal, *al-Sayyad*, printed an exposé in August 1965 in which it disclosed that *al-ʿĀṣifah* was actually the military wing of the National Movement for the Liberation of Palestine, *Fatḥ*. The pro-Egyptian journal correctly pointed out that *Fatḥ*'s leader was Yāsir ʿArafāt but claimed that he was a former Muslim Brother whom Egypt had deported and that he was now working for Baʿthist Syria. It went on to say that the group was not to be taken too seriously and most of their "operations" inside Israel were fictitious.

At the same time that commando operations were being given often romantic coverage by the press, the PLO was negotiating, under the mandate given to it at the Arab summit of 1964, to form the Palestine Liberation Army (PLA), a regular military force of the PLO.

An agreement was eventually reached whereby the Jordanian government agreed to allow the PLO to train units outside of the framework of the Jordanian army. There were rumors that this did not sit well with the Jordanian military.[43] It certainly did not appeal to the United States which asked that any Palestinian receiving military training be removed from the roles of UNRWA. American policy, remarked one Jordanian paper, had become so enmeshed in Zionist influence that it attempted to protect the Jewish state from things that did not yet exist.[44]

If the PLA was still in its formative stage, not so the commandos and their operations, both of which, by 1966, were beginning to irritate Israel. The Jewish state threatened retaliation against the commandos' host countries, which were then only Jordan and Syria. Each of the countries responded in a different way. Jordan began to crack down on operations from its territory, and Damascus charged Jordanian forces with attacking and killing the commandos.[45] Syria, at least overtly through its controlled press, lauded and encouraged the Palestinian commandos, praising *Fatḥ* as the nucleus of a "war of liberation."[46] The press brushed aside Israeli complaints saying they were simply an excuse for more aggression against Syria.

Though the trend in the Arab world was rising esteem for the commandos, they were not without their detractors. The Jordanian army, as we have noted, was hostile to extra-legal operations from Jordanian territory and King Ḥusayn was known to fear the rise of a Palestinian force that would identify him with his grandfather, ʿAbd Allāh. It was in this tense Jordanian atmosphere, kept alive by commando raids into Israel, that a vicious editorial campaign began amongst the Arab states. Syrian and Egyptian papers maintained that the Jordanian regime was more interested in protecting itself than in fighting the Israeli enemy. Allegations were made that the Jordanian government had pulled its forces out of the West Bank in order to defend the throne of the king in Amman.[47] Worse still was the Hashemite unwillingness to allow the West Bankers to even defend themselves by being armed, though Aḥmad al-Shuqayrī had asked the king for this. Editorials in Egypt and Syria bemoaned the fact that the Palestinians were left defenseless by the Hashimites and that the West Bankers were taking to the hills not to fight Israel but the "traitors" ruling in the East Bank.[48]

When Israel attacked the West Bank, south of Hebron, on November 13, 1966, Arab press reaction was predictable. The Jordanian papers angrily wondered where the Arab armies were. It was not enough to send cables of support to Amman after every Israeli raid on the Hashimite kingdom.[49] But Syria and Egypt in their press reacted against the Jordanian regime. Papers proclaimed King Ḥusayn guilty of "treason" for not arming the Palestinian people. They accused him of being able to repel the Israeli incursions but having no interest in doing so and in fact encouraging attacks on Palestinians. "The Arab masses, which are aware of colonial tactics and maneuvers, easily discovered the new game and expressed their anger and desire to destroy the royal throne as it insolently celebrates over the corpses that fell in the criminal attack."[50] The fear was expressed that the Israeli raid, besides being done in collusion with Jordan, might also give the Hashimites the excuse to destroy the fledgling commando movement. The thought seems to have crossed some minds in the United States as well. But American fear was not that the commandos might be crushed by Jordanian forces but the opposite, leading to the fall of the pro-American monarchy. American Senator Jacob Javits sent a telegram to then Secretary of State Dean Rusk asserting that the fall of King Ḥusayn would not be in the interests of Israel. Commenting on that letter, Egypt's *al-Jumhūrīyah* wrote,

> [a]nd who asks for support of the throne [of Ḥusayn]? A Zionist senator in the American Senate seeks help for Ḥusayn from the government in Washington. Another shaykh [this is a play on words since the English "senator" is translated into Arabic as "shaykh"], Saudi Arabia's King Fayṣal, is also trying to assist King Ḥusayn. [...] There is no doubt that the position of these two shaykhs represents the truth about the alliance between [Arab] Reaction and Imperialism, an alliance now using the throne of King Ḥusayn as an outpost, just like Israel, to combat Arab liberation movements.[51]

While it was Jordan that received the brunt of the verbal attack from the Arab press, it was Syria that received the severest military blows from Israel. The escalation of the fighting can perhaps be dated to have begun on July 14, 1966, when Israeli planes hit Syrian work on a project to divert the headwaters of the Jordan River. The attack was meant to stop the work and was successful. A month later, on August 15, the Syrians claimed a victory over Israeli forces when they said they destroyed twelve gun-boats on the Sea of Galilee. This was viewed as a "smashing victory" and heralded the Syrian move from the defensive to the offensive.[52]

> Israel attaches great importance to the psychological aspect of its battle with the Arabs. But if Damascus, now forced by the present political and strategic facts can, even gradually, destroy the Israeli myth [that it is able] to take punitive action against the Arabs without fear of punishment, Israel would then have lost half its battle.[53]

The fighting escalated one more step when, on January 11, 1967, Syrian and Israeli forces clashed as Syria attempted to stop armed Israeli tractors from farming the demilitarized zone (DMZ) established between the two countries in 1949. Syria argued the Israeli action was aimed at annexation of a disputed territory and that if Israel was allowed to farm the area, including Arab-owned land, it would claim *de facto* rights there. As a result of the fighting, Israel was able to establish itself in the area. Consequently, Israel argued that a ceasefire should be imposed under the new conditions prevailing in the DMZ.

Syria maintained that this was a violation of the 1949 armistice agreement. When the Israelis refused to remove themselves, the Syrians resumed the shelling of the DMZ from the Golan Heights. Tension increased on both sides to such an extent that on April 7, Israeli planes flew over Damascus for the first time since 1948 with the resulting air clashes being the heaviest since 1956. In this threatening mood, the Arab press began to analyze the motives behind the growing military activity. For the Egyptian press the answer was clear: Israel and its Western friends were using psychological warfare against Syria, using as an excuse the DMZ and the commandos. The enemy's real aim was "to threaten Damascus and bring down the present [Syrian] government." This would be accompanied by the capture of the Golan Heights so it could not be used to threaten Israel.[54] That the aim of Israel and the West was to topple the Damascus government was also supported by the Syrian press.[55] Even the conservative Christian press in Lebanon denounced Israel's motives. "We are in the forefront of those who wish to see the Marxist-atheistic regime in Damascus collapse. But if bringing it down is to be done at Israel's hands, then we wish to see it become immortal."[56]

Israeli military pressure on Syria forced Egypt to react in support of the ally with whom it had signed a mutual defense treaty seven months earlier. The UAR did so by asking for the United Nations Emergency Force in Sinai, established after the 1956 war, to be removed. United Nations Secretary-General U Thant agreed on May 18, 1967. Four days later 'Abd al-Nāṣir closed the Gulf of Aqaba to all ships flying the Israeli flag and to those carrying strategic materials to Israel. He did this by mining the Straits of Tiran.

The psychological and political battle intensified when Lyndon Johnson argued on May 23 that the closing of the Gulf of Aqaba was illegal since this was an international body of water. To judge the Arab press response to this statement, perhaps it would be best to quote from that section of the press, in 1967 almost exclusively in Lebanon that was the traditional supporter of the United States.

> As for the government in Washington saying that it considers the Gulf of Aqaba international waters, this does not find support in history, in international law, or in tradition. Washington claims this to give Israel a permanent right of passage in the Gulf. [...] Anyone with a little knowledge of navigational laws can tell that a strait, not wider than 400 meters, cannot be international.[57]
>
> The mind is at a loss to find even one reason how it [the U.S.], can benefit from this stand – unless the Marxists are right in saying the United States has created Israel to use it to fulfill [American] political and economic colonial motives.[58]
>
> Have the Straits of Tiran been closed to American trade?
>
> No.
>
> Does Egypt's closing of the Straits of Tiran to Israeli ships and to strategic materials going to Israel threaten America's security and safety?
>
> No.
>
> Does closure of the Straits of Tiran to Israel and to its strategic materials tip the scale in favor of the Soviet Union against the United States in the world?
>
> No.
>
> Does the closure of the Straits of Tiran [...] threaten American oil interests in the area?
>
> No.
>
> Does the closure of the Straits of Tiran to Israeli shipping lead to a victory for worldwide communism?
>
> No.

> Therefore, there is not one single "American reason" that can justify, in the eyes of American public opinion or the whole world, any American military action against Egypt and the Arabs and in favor of Israel.[59]

> The United States appears today as "the original enemy" while Israel is "only a copy". It pains the friends of the great American nation in the Arab world that this situation has been reached in Arab-American relations. …
>
> If it cannot support the Arab fight in Palestine, it should at least take a neutral position between the Arab states and Israel.[60]

Needless to say, the comments of the press usually opposed to America were even more scathing. Papers noted that President Johnson's position may have been dictated by growing disenchantment with Vietnam and was, therefore, a diversion. There was also space devoted to the fact that an election year was approaching and that a tough line with the Arabs was always a good way to get votes.[61]

And thus the Middle East lurched toward war. Though we have mentioned the defense treaty between Egypt and Syria, when viewed in its entirety, the Arab world, in its ability to face Israel, was in a shambles. The relationship between Jordan and her principal allies in war, Syria and Egypt, had deteriorated to such an extent that Cairo's "Voice of the Arabs" took great joy in playing the Jordanian national anthem followed by the reading of King Ḥusayn's death warrant. Furthermore, there was tension on both banks of the Jordan between Jordanians and Palestinians and a fear that the Hashimites would not defend the West Bank if attacked. Tens of thousands of Egyptian troops were fighting in Yemen in an expensive and militarily draining war. In Syria, there were reports of a campaign of dismissals of officers from the Syrian army for reasons of personal vengeance between Ṣalāḥ Jadīd and his main adversary for power, Foreign Minister and head of the Air Force, Ḥāfiz al-ʾAsad. As a result, the Syrian army was in tatters, not only from these purges but also from the repeated military coups which found those ousted from power, with their supporters, also removed from the armed services.

Probably more energy has been expended analyzing, writing about, and talking about the Six-Day War than was used fighting it. We regret adding to the seemingly endless number of words, but can find no other alternative than to describe, perhaps briefly, Arab press responses to the war. The events of the first day, June 5, began too late to be reported by the press and so news of the war was obtained largely by radio. Emphasis was placed on the fact that it was the Israelis who attacked first. The following day the press featured headlines such as "The Arab forces have entered enemy territory," "The Egyptian army has penetrated into the Negev," "Egypt moves to the offensive today," and so forth.[62] Press comments were generally positive though the radio reports, because they were more current, were less optimistic. Amman Radio reported on June 6 that Israeli air activity far exceeded its capabilities and that three non-Israeli aircraft carriers in the Mediterranean were being used to launch planes attacking the Arabs. The implication was clear and the same evening the United Arab Republic broke diplomatic relations with the United States. As each day proceeded in the war, the Arab press became more and more pessimistic as the extent of the losses became known, despite governmental attempts to hide the magnitude of the defeat suffered and the growing awareness that the press had been lied to in the first hours of the war. As a result of the newly emerging truth, the analysis and blaming began. Defending the Egyptian break with the United States, *al-Ahrām* argued on June 7 that America and Great Britain were providing an aerial umbrella over Israeli territory using their pilots thus leaving Israeli pilots free to attack Arab land. In this way, the West could hide its activity since no Western pilots would be shot down over Arab territory. The paper also said that the West was supplying Israel with pilots disguised as volunteers. That the journalists were on the right track in accusing the United States of aiding Israel has been subsequently affirmed most notably in Stephen Green's *Taking Sides*.

By June 8 and 9, the enormity of the Arab loss was generally known and papers began to encourage their readers to take heart. Editorialists wrote that high morale was important to victory. The psychological battle at home was as important as the fighting elsewhere. Citizens were urged not to listen to rumors and lies and to be brave.[63]

> […] [T]here may be setbacks and retreats but we shall not permit despair to infiltrate our hearts. […] We shall raise our heads high above the ruins and we shall not look back except to profit from our mistakes […].[64]

On June 9, President 'Abd al-Nāṣir accepted responsibility for the defeat and offered to resign. Arab editorial response, reflecting Egyptian popular response, was universally negative.

> There is no doubt that the Egyptians and the Arabs refuse to have their leaders resign under foreign pressure let alone because of Israeli aggression. The Egyptians and the Arabs did not agree to 'Abd al-Nāṣir's resignation because if they did agree it would have meant they have changed their position concerning the basic question for which they had chosen 'Abd al-Nāṣir for leadership. This is [also] their stand with regards to King Ḥusayn and the Syrian government […].[65]

But for the third time the Arabs had been tested and for the third time they had been found wanting. Perhaps of all the Arab defeats this was the most difficult one to accept. Certainly if one examines the literature of the Arab world, especially that of the Palestinians, between June 1967 and October 1973, nothing similar can be found in the writings that followed the 1948 and 1956 wars. It is a literature of anguish. To a great extent the press, too, despaired but since it was largely state-controlled it had to serve another function, that of rebuilding and providing hope for the future.

> Time now is not for blaming or defining who is responsible […]. But this must be the time for talking frankly – the time for self-criticism. […] Now is the time for listening to

> logic not to emotion – the logic that would lead us to wisdom instead of the emotion that has led us to where we are now. [...] The time now is for calculations, not for illusions. The time now is for depending on planning and we must ask ourselves: Who are we? What have we? What have we fulfilled so far? Where have we failed and where have we succeeded [...]? We are all responsible for the setback [...].[66]

In analyzing the defeat at Israeli hands, it is probably well once again to examine each nation's response to its latest loss while paying special attention to the extensive analysis by Muḥammad Haykal of *al-Ahrām*. The Lebanese press, to begin, reflected variety in its opinion. This was so because of the diverse character of the population, the expanding usage of Beirut as the propaganda center for the growing Palestinian national movement, and because, besides being the Arab world's largest free press, it was also for hire. One of the earliest Christian responses came from *al-ʿAmal* which called for the "neutralization" of Lebanon, a call for the Lebanese to get off the sinking Arab ship.[67] This was immediately retorted to by two Christina papers who decried Pierre Gemayel and *al-ʿAmal's* "mercantile thinking." Printed the Maronite *al-Jarīdah*:

> The Western World which dazzles us with its civilization and its industrial and scientific progress is but a toy in the hands of international Zionism. This West has mortgaged its conscience, heart, and mind to the banks and companies owned or financed by international Zionism.
>
> The duty of the Arabs today – and particularly the duty of Lebanon – is not only to regain Arab rights in Palestine and defend their national sovereignty and right to live, but also to liberate the mind and heart of the West from Zionist domination [...].
>
> The Arab states, with Lebanon in the lead, have only one course: the course of mobilization, preparation, construction, and sacrifice so that the Arab peoples may surpass the enemy [...].
>
> This may take great effort and sacrifice, more than human beings can bear, and may take one or two generations. But that is alright since it is the right and dignified course.[68]

Added the Greek Orthodox-owned *al-Anwār*:

> And you, Oh, kings of Christianity [...] and princes of the Church in the East and West, what has happened to you? Why do you not this time declare a real Crusade against those who yesterday crucified the Messiah and are today desecrating His church and crib and crucifying His people in Palestine?[69]

The editorials published in the Lebanese Muslim papers and the emerging pro-Palestinian press reflected more of a pan-Arab feeling. While the Lebanese Christians might begin to say out loud that they were actually Phoenicians, and therefore not a part of the Arab failure, the Arab nationalist press never denied its roots. *Al-Muḥarrir*, for example, proudly said it was

Arab. In an editorial on June 26, it asserted that though others, like the racists in Britain, might put up signs saying dogs, Blacks, and Arabs were not allowed in, Arab civilization had nothing of which to be ashamed. One could also see analogies drawn to the Chinese experience of repeated setbacks before success under Mao Tse-tung.[70] After 1967, *Al-Muḥarrir* and *al-Anwār* became more and more prominent. Writers such as Shafīq al-Ḥūt and Ghassān Kanafānī established themselves as the leading spokesmen for points of view which supported 'Abd al-Nāṣir, Arab socialism, the Palestinian commando movement, and closer ties with the Soviet Union. Though they had divergent interests, for example after 'Abd al-Nāṣir accepted the concept of a negotiated settlement and thereby ran afoul of the commando movement, the result of the 1967 war for the Lebanese press was to bring into being a clearly defined group of newspapers that called themselves progressive or leftist. They tried to gloss over contradictions between supporting sometimes divergent interests by emphasizing several thing held in common. One was to eliminate what 'Abd al-Nāṣir called "the traces of aggression." Another was a vague support of socialism over capitalism, an idea that manifested itself largely in support for nationalization of Arab oil and distrust of the motives of the West.

For the Jordanian press, the war was viewed as being particularly disastrous for the Hashimite kingdom. There was the flight of refugees from the West Bank to the East. This was compounded by the loss of valuable touristic and farming property, thus increasing Jordan's economic problems. Two of Jordan's three papers were destroyed or captured in the war leaving only *al-Dustūr* to write of the consequences.[71] Even arch-enemy 'Abd al-Nāṣir had recognized the gallantry of the Jordanian king and his army in the Egyptian's resignation speech of June 9. So, on at least the Jordanian front the press and other supporters of King Ḥusayn could speak with some pride. When racial riots broke out in the United States, *al-Dustūr* could write about them in terms of its own experience; the loss of Palestinian, then Jordanian, territory.

> We, the Arabs, have suffered much from the policy of partition that was invented by Britain and implemented by America within the framework of a contemptuous Zionist-imperialist conspiracy [...]. We hate to see any country suffer from the same thing, even if that country is the United States. We know that Negroes are deprived of many rights as a result of the contempt and shortsightedness of the whites. But partition of the United States would be a disaster [...].[72]

The leading supporter of the Hashimites in Lebanon, *al-Ḥayāt*, defended the Jordanian monarchy against the rising tide of anti-monarchical feeling that argued that Arab kings were too tied to the conservative West to be interested in anything more than keeping their respective thrones intact:

> In 1948 the Arab states, which were not liberal, were able to inflict on the enemy, through regular and irregular wars, many more losses in lives and property than they did after twenty years preparation and spending billions [...].

> In spite of the fact that the recent setback was more a failure of a regime [i.e., Syria] than of a nation or of a people, the immediate concern of the revolutionary rulers was over [the protection of] their own regime rather than the outcome of the conflict with Israel [...].
>
> The glorious defense put up by the brave Jordanian army in Jerusalem and on all the other fronts in the West Bank clearly showed that gallantry and heroism are not the monopoly of the revolutionaries.[73]

The implied criticism of the Syrian performance in the war is based on the Syrian regime's decision to defend itself rather than make a stand against the Israelis on the Golan Heights where the Syrians had built their own Maginot Line.[74] Needless to say, the papers of Syria expressed no criticism of the regime nor of the performance of the Syrian armed forces. Rather, the papers ignored the lack of resistance on the Syrian front and examined the war as a single entity. In a series of articles in *al-Baʿth* and *al-Thawrah*, the papers defined the faults of the Arabs as a whole and in doing so proposed new measures to insure that in the next round a similar catastrophe might not be inflicted on them. First, the newspapers tended to decry the lack of military coordination between Jordan, Egypt, and Syria. Huge numbers of forces were concentrated in the Sinai when, in the Syrian view, the main attack of the enemy would be against the West Bank. Therefore, the Syrian and Egyptian fronts should have been used to harass the enemy while the greatest concentration of forces should have been in Jordan. As a coordinating body, the League of Arab States had utterly failed, was obsolete, and had produced in 20 years nothing but hot air.

A second lesson learned from the war, continued the Syrian press, was that along with regular forces, popular forces were needed. It was necessary to arm the population and to make sure they received the proper technical and ideological information to enable them to face the enemy resolutely and be able to use their arms with accuracy. The Arab world should be turned into another Vietnam.

Further, the people had learned who their friends were and who their enemies were. Naturally Israel was one of the enemy, but it was not alone. The enemy was in fact a collective that included Britain and the United States. These three countries had rained bombs and bullets on the Arab people. In order to punish the West for its alliance with Israel, all vestiges of Western imperialistic influence had to be destroyed in the Middle East. The Arabs must be rid of Western military bases on their territories, nationalize Arab oil in Western hands, and withdraw Arab funds and investments from the West.

Finally, ties should be strengthened with the world's socialistic countries, especially the Soviet Union. The Syrian press lashed out at those who said that Russia was just as guilty of aggression against the Arabs as was the West because the Soviet Union did not help its allies the way the West helped its. Syrian editorials argued that the Arabs did not want Russia to fight its battles. Russia had given military and political support to the Arab cause. Where it might be faulted is in not neutralizing Anglo-American support for Israel. But that was only one negative aspect in an otherwise positive picture of the socialist camp. The Arabs had no choice but to embrace it more closely.[75]

In Egypt the analysis of the June war took several aspects. There was undoubtedly an attempt in the press between June and September 1967 to place the blame on the military and not on the political leaders. This campaign of exposure and vilification focused on deposed Marshal 'Abd al-Ḥakīm 'Āmir, holding him and several dozen other officers responsible for the defeat. As a result of his deposition and the subsequent allegation that he was involved in a plot to overthrow 'Abd al-Nāṣir, he allegedly committed suicide on September 14, 1967.[76] Elsewhere in the Egyptian press analysis of the causes of the spectacular setback focused on the faults of the military as a whole and on the Egyptians' aping of Western ways. There was a call to liquidate "imperialist culture" from the schools and the press.[77] Still others focused on the Egyptian way of life:

> We must strengthen ourselves and defeat the desire for luxury [...].
>
> We must look among ourselves for the reasons for our failure and our backwardness and we must be frank with ourselves – perhaps every one of us may have been a link in the setback.[78]

At best, this type of editorializing was superficial. But one writer, Muḥammad Haykal, editor of *al-Ahrām*, did write a series of articles over a one-year period that analyzed the reasons for the Arab defeat, especially Egypt's failures. In his first article diagnosing the war, he began the series by making three broad generalizations that he viewed as indisputable. The Israelis received extraordinary assistance and they used that assistance extraordinarily well. Secondly, the Israelis used their abilities, which were not little, with astonishing skill. Finally, the Arabs used their abilities, which were not little, with devastating inefficiency. The result was that Israel achieved "a victory greater than it merited while we suffered a defeat greater than we deserved."[79]

Once having given that summation, Haykal then proceeded to divide the war into three periods and spent numerous columns discussing Egyptian failures in each of the periods. To paraphrase the editor, the first period was a number of years prior to May 14, 1967, the date the Arabs discovered that Israel intended to attack Syria.[80] The second period covered some 20 days, from May 15 till the outbreak of the war. The third period covered the six days of the war in June.

As to the first period, covering several years before the 1967 war, Haykal felt that Egypt and the Arabs suffered during that period from at least three deficiencies. The first was unrealistic planning. Arabs operated in "an atmosphere of fulfilling an unlimited goal [presumably the destruction of the state of Israel] at a time when no one is allowed to fulfill an unlimited goal [...]." Haykal drew his readers' attention to the fact that this was the United States' problem in Vietnam. How much more unreasonable were Arab desires when even the strongest power on Earth could not have its unlimited goals satisfied?[81]

Further, in the years prior to 1967 Egypt suffered from the quality of its officers in the armed services.[82] Many of these men had made no progress in the military sciences for perhaps 15 years while Israeli officers were continuously keeping abreast of the latest developments in modern warfare. And finally, Egypt as a whole was not preparing itself for combat with the enemy because of its preoccupation elsewhere as a result of almost constant upheaval in the area. First there was the tripartite attack on Egypt in 1956, then the military coup in Iraq in 1958, followed the same year by the union of Egypt and Syria and its consequent rupture in 1961. Then there was the fighting in Yemen in which Egypt became involved beginning in October 1962, one month after the war's eruption. The fighting might have provided some beneficial military training except for the fact that the experience the armed forces received on Yemeni terrain was of little benefit in fighting in the Sinai.[83]

Not a deficiency but a setback in the first period was the defection in 1966 of an Iraqi Air Force pilot to Israel with his MIG-21. The Israelis were naturally interested in getting this piece of equipment since they were able to study it and detect its weak points as well as its strengths to better prepare themselves for war.[84] None of the results, then, of the first period were positive and Haykal believed that the resulting general malaise was undoubtedly felt by the military and therefore adversely affected the way they were led and the way they fought.

The second period, in Haykal's continuing analysis, was from May 15 until June 5. The period began with the discovery of Israel's plan to attack Syria and ended with the first day of the attack. Egypt's goal in that period was to persuade the Israelis not to attack Syria by moving Egyptian forces into the Sinai, forcing Israel to move its troops southward, thus relieving pressure on Syria. This strategy was successful and Israeli troops were forced to move south. But it was at this point, wrote Haykal, that several crucial errors were made. The first was not signaling Israel that Egypt had no desire to start a war "due to the massive repercussions that would have occurred at the international level."[85] This was not done and so when the war broke out huge numbers of Egypt's forces were sacrificed unnecessarily. This movement of large numbers of troops to the Sinai front was also not done properly. The military command sought to create what it called "pre-war clouds"; that is to move troops around constantly in order to fool the enemy as to one's real intentions. The Egyptian command did this in such an exaggerated manner in terms of the amount of time taken in developing these "clouds" and the distances troops were moved that when the war began, Egypt's forces in the Sinai were exhausted. At any rate the creating of "pre-war clouds" was superfluous since, when the object of relieving pressure on the Syrian front had been achieved, Egypt's forces should have been drastically reduced in the Sinai to show Israel that Egypt had no intention of striking.[86]

Another mistake made in the twenty-day period prior to the Israeli invasion was again laid at the feet of the military leaders, especially those of the air force. According to faulty intelligence reports provided by the armed forces, Egyptian military power was put far too high while Israeli forces were greatly underestimated. This was particularly crucial in the making of judgments about relative air strength. It was estimated that Egypt's air force outnumbered the enemy by three to one. But if one took such important facts as airworthiness of the machines and the number of qualified pilots to fly them, the ratio was exactly opposite. As Haykal had pointed out when writing about the Sinai infantry forces, modern warfare had changed. The goal was no longer to have huge numbers of people or machines, but to destroy the forces of the enemy. To count planes was not realistic; the question was how many of them could be flown by competent pilots. But these kinds of questions were not asked.[87] Further, the military command and its intelligence arm were to be trusted, not interrogated. When an unnamed country [India] informed the Egyptian government that an Israeli plane had flown undetected near Cairo on May 31, 1967, the information was conveyed to the command of the air force. The veracity of the information was denied with the implication that it was not good to cast aspersions on those charged with the defense of the UAR.[88]

Finally, during this period Israeli propaganda and political dominance was supreme. They made it appear as though the Israelis were being attacked and used diplomatic maneuvers to hide their aggressive designs. Prime Minister Levi Eshkol, as part of his creating "pre-War clouds," even asked to be invited to the Soviet Union one week before the war began.[89]

Haykal then moved to the Six-Day War or, as he might have called it, the third stage of his analysis of the Arab failure of 1967. He wrote that the beginning of the June war was not a surprise. The Egyptians knew that a war was coming and that the first blow would be aimed at the air force since control of the skies was the crucial element. When the Israelis did attack, "It was not so much the surprise that decided the war in the first few hours as much as the failure to avoid it. The blow itself was expected in the manner it came and on the same day it happened. But the failure to avert it was astounding."[90]

Still, continued Haykal, credit should be given to Israeli intelligence, which operated superbly in at least two crucial areas in the first hours of the battle. First was the decision not to attack in the traditional method, at the end of day or at dawn. Rather it was decided to strike between 8:30 and 9:00 a.m. when the soldiers would be thinking that an attack would no longer be coming since the early hours when the onset might have come had passed. When the attack commenced, Egyptian military men were thus caught in the middle of their morning chores. Or to use Haykal's words, the Egyptian military was caught "eating breakfast."[91]

At the moment the air offensive began, Marshal 'Abd al-Ḥakīm 'Āmir was flying over the Sinai. Israeli intelligence, argued Haykal, must have known this. For Egypt, the result of this knowledge was disasterous. The Israelis knew that when 'Āmir landed in Sinai, on his inspection tour, some military commanders would be there to greet him and others would be present to accompany him on his inspection tour. The Sinai was thus practically leaderless at the time Israel began the war. Israeli intelligence also apparently knew the exact time that 'Amir would be in the air over Sinai and used that knowledge to determine when to begin their assault. The Egyptian military, while 'Āmir was airborne, was under orders not to fire at any plane for fear they might accidentally hit 'Āmir and his entourage.[92] Thus, Israeli intelligence provided crucial information that allowed its side to win a virtually unimaginable victory. Egyptian intelligence, on the other hand, was more interested in gaining domestic power than in finding out about the enemy.[93]

The actual carrying out of the war was equally well done and, according to Haykal, did not differ that much from the invasion plan used in the 1956 war. The Israelis knew that they could not afford to allow the war to be fought on their own territory and so their basic objective was to strike quickly and move the battle to their opponents' territories. To this end, they emphasized speed and agility and used weaponry compatible with their goals. Haykal further argued that their success also was due to the complete silence imposed on their troops facing the Sinai. Jeeps and helicopters alone were used to carry messages and radio silence was only broken fifteen minutes before the attack commenced. The battle was fought on the Israeli side by a soldier of much higher quality than his Egyptian counterpart. Since military training was obligatory in Israel, its armed forces included all kinds of professionals like doctors, engineers, and professors.[94]

When the first strike came, the Egyptian High Command became hysterical and this virtually paralyzed its ability to analyze. The military leaders thought in terms of the 1956 experience, and this was why accusations against the United States were issued by the command. When the extent of the damage that was done by the Israeli air force was discerned, the military commanders tried for several hours to suppress the news, thus giving false information to those who had a right to know in order to make judgments about the course of the battle. The failure of the UAR High Command not only affected the ability of its political superiors to make proper decisions, but the nervousness of the top officers also influenced the fighting ability of their subordinates. When the High Command lost all hope for victory, the forces in the Sinai lost heart. With this tremendous advantage, the Israelis were emboldened to take chances that they previously had not dreamed possible.[95]

Even with all these setbacks, something could have been saved from the deteriorating situation had it not been for one last fatal mistake, the military decision to retreat to the west bank of the Suez. Even though air superiority was lost, the Egyptian forces could have fought on, and Haykal cited the Fourth Armored Brigade as an example of a unit that did not retreat but fought on even terms with Israel even though two-thirds of its armor had been destroyed. While Egyptian and Israeli forces were close together in combat, Israeli air strikes were difficult. Haykal noted that in the first three days of the war, Egyptian forces only suffered 250 casualties. It was only when they began to retreat that they suffered heavy casualties.[96]

Thus summarized was Haykal's extensive commentary and analysis of the Six-Day War. In all of it there was only one positive comment and that concerned the fact that Egyptian planes were destroyed on the ground rather than in the air. Haykal argued that even if the Egyptians had started the war, the chances for victory were slim because of the desperate circumstances in the Arab world. Thus, Israel's destruction of Egypt's planes on the ground was in some ways a blessing since the pilots' lives were saved. He argued that the planes were replaced in months but that to retrain a new generation of pilots would have taken a decade. "But I say [...] real honor is to live to fight. To commit suicide in a desperate battle is not real honor, regardless of noble feelings and love of sacrifice [...]."[97]

Those who recall or have studied the Six-Day War can attest to the euphoria amongst those who supported Israel and its incredible victory. Haykal noted that those who supported Egypt had a different reaction.

> The Soviets were surprised by the outcome of the battles which began on June 5. Regardless of what they had seen of inefficiency, the magnitude of the defeat was to them incredible. In the end they accepted it – they had no choice – as if it were a natural disaster, like hurricanes or earthquakes [...].[98]

Few would deny that the 1967 war was till then the most disastrous event in the contemporary history of the Arab world – the loss of the Sinai, Gaza, the West Bank, East Jerusalem, and the Golan Heights.[99] This was so at least in part because there was no question of a 1956-type pullback in 1967. International interests simply saw no benefit in forcing it. In 1956, the United States could do so because its authority was virtually unchallenged in the area and America saw both sides as allies. Since that time, the Soviet Union had penetrated the area, polarizing views. More importantly, Zionist influence essentially controlled the US Congress so that the American government saw no advantage in forcing Israel to withdraw. Lacking that pressure, the Jewish state was not going to unilaterally give up occupied territory. In reading the Arab press, we saw only one editorial that urged America to make Israel give up its conquests.[100] Everyone else recognized that this was not going to happen.

In a state of disarray after the June War, the Arab world looked for consolation and succor. One of the few signs of support in the West came in January 1969 when France banned all military equipment and spare parts to Israel. This came after the Israeli raid the previous month on Beirut's international airport in which over a dozen civil aircraft were destroyed or damaged. It was one of the few victories the Arabs achieved in the West and was widely hailed in their papers. France continued to hold a special place in the Arab heart even after Georges Pompidou succeeded Charles DeGaulle as president. At his first press conference after his June 1969 election, Pompidou reaffirmed the arms embargo of Israel and a Lebanese headline the next day gratefully editorialized it as "a wise decision."[101]

However helpful France might be to the Arab world, it was generally recognized in the Arab press, and elsewhere, that it was the Soviet Union and the United States who were the keys to producing an end to the Arab-Israeli conflict that the belligerents could accept. Despite the aid America gave to Israel, there was still a press call after the war ended for forging a closer relationship with the United States. Leading this bid was Haykal who noted that the Arab tendency was to be concerned with other nations only in times of duress. Furthermore, if the Arab world was to maintain a balance in its international relations then openings should be made to both East and West. By so doing, the Arabs could minimally neutralize the United States. Maximally, the Arabs would be like the bullfighter who defeats his stronger adversary not through direct clashes but through maneuvers.[102] Though the Phalangist *al-'Amal* responded on July 2, 1967 that this was what it had called for all along, other responses to Haykal's suggestion were almost universally condemnatory. The Syrian press called it "strange" and if it were followed would result in a policy of capitulation that would allow the "flag of imperialism to fly over the entire world." There were other similar Syrian statements, such as the United States offering the Middle East a "peace stained with napalm."[103] When North Korea seized the *U.S.S. Pueblo* in January 1968, the Damascene *al-Thawrah* alluded sarcastically to Haykal's bull column; "Regardless of everything, another people has confronted the bull [...]. North Korea has confronted the American bull without bothering to philosophize on the nature of its horns and strength."[104]

Anti-American sentiment amongst the Arabs was extremely high after the 1967 war. The Arab defeat was a major cause of this feeling but it can also be attributed to the Vietnamese war, continuing military support to Israel, and the fact that a presidential election campaign soon ensued, none of which were popular in the Arab press. The north Vietnamese and Vietcong cause had large support in the Arab press because of the comparisons that could be made between it and the Arab conflict with the United States. When, in April 1968, President Johnson agreed to stop bombing a large part of north Vietnam in the hope of getting peace talks started, Israeli Foreign Minister Abba Eban called on the Arabs to also begin negotiations.

> The United States backing down on the logic of the use of force with north Vietnam has deprived Israel of the logic of the use of force with the Arab states.
>
> However, rather than surrender to a position similar to America, namely stop using force with the Arabs, Israel has insisted, through Abba Eban, on inviting the Arab states to follow north Vietnam and accept negotiation. This, purely and simply, is ignoring what happened in Vietnam [...]
>
> North Vietnam refused to yield to force and the United States capitulated. Only after American capitulation did Hanoi agree to negotiate.
>
> [...] America only backed down [...] after north Vietnam continued its war of liberation. And this is what the Arab side needs [to learn] [...].[105]

In part to gain support for the presidential campaign of Hubert Humphrey, Johnson, besides the halt in bombing of Vietnam, also ordered the sending of Phantom jets to Israel. There was no doubt that this was done solely, in the opinion of the Arab press, to gain votes for the Democratic candidate. To deal thus with Arab lives was termed "an act of madness" and the alliance between the Israeli government and that of the United States was arranged by the devil.[106]

With the election of Richard Nixon as president there seemed to be a willingness to give the new president a chance though it was recognized that "in the final analysis, President Nixon is the president of the United States. Egypt and the Arabs have no right to expect him to be more or less than that. In return, however, it is the right of Egypt and the Arabs to expect that the new American president will not act as though he is the president of Israel [...]."[107] Nixon did get off to a good start in his Arab critics' eyes when he sent former Pennsylvania governor, William Scranton, on a fact-finding tour of the area to ascertain what the new administration's policies toward the Middle East might be. When he announced that it should be "evenhanded," one editorialist argued that the Arabs should pursue this apparent breakthrough by sending Arab intellectuals to the United States to explain why even-handedness was sound.[108] But other writers wondered if the new president could act free from pressure groups like "the financial monopolists or the arms industry monopolists [...]?"[109]

Editorial comments toward Nixon soured when he was blamed for a series of American policies that followed the Republican's coming to power. The first was the decision to allow Americans to hold dual citizenship and to serve in the armed forces of foreign countries. Press reaction was hostile, despite State Department reassurances that the American government did not encourage Americans to become dual nationals or to serve in the armed forces of other nations. Editorials said the decision would have two negative effects on the Arabs. The first was obvious; it would allow Israel to recruit men with impunity in the United States. The second would be to encourage immigration to Israel since a person who did immigrate would not be deprived of his original citizenship.[110] Comments on this turn of events became more bitter when President Nixon sent a letter on January 25, 1970 to Jewish leaders meeting in New York that he was sending more arms to Israel. Despite the hopeful first steps linked to Scranton's mission, editorialists were quickly disillusioned with the new American administration which had no new policy toward the Middle East.[111] To reaffirm with a new administration the old relationship between Israel and America, Golda Meir made a trip to Washington soon after Nixon came to power. One Arab editorialist wrote that she came to ask for more money since "[t]he mercenaries are demanding an increase in pay."[112] A cartoonist showed the two leaders staring longingly at each other on a love seat, the conversation going: Meir: "Oh, Phantom of my life." Nixon: "Oh, napalm of my heart."[113]

The question of more Phantoms for Israel undoubtedly led to worsening ties between the Arabs and the United States. Egypt, particularly during 1970 when the "War of Attrition" was going on along the cease-fire line on the Suez, was vulnerable to Israeli raids by these planes. On February 12, 1970, an Israeli attack destroyed an Egyptian metal factory in the village of Abū Z'abal, north of Cairo, in which seventy workers were killed.

> The president of the United States, who has given himself one month [...] to decide on the Israeli request for additional Phantoms knows very well that the planes and arms he will send to Israel are not for defense and not for hitting military targets only [...].
>
> Pictures of the Israeli raid on Egyptian civilians should by now have reached his office [...].
>
> American arms will not ensure the security of Israel or even Middle East peace [...] but more war and more fighting [...] and will only contribute to making the American image in the Arab world uglier.[114]

The Nixon decision in March 1970 was not to supply more Phantoms at that time to Israel. However, within four months he did agree to send more planes after Egypt successfully stationed SAM-3s along the Suez front, providing an effective deterrent to Israeli raids west of the Suez. The introduction of SAM-3s was decried by Israel "[...] as if Israel, which occupies part of Egyptian territory, has the right to attack what remains of [Egyptian] territory while Egypt does not have the right to defend it."[115] Thus on the eve of 'Abd al-Nāṣir's death, one of the two super powers seemed in Arab eyes not only to be continuing its traditional support for Israel but to be increasing it. By supplying the Jewish state with Phantoms, the United

States was allowing Israel to continue its occupation of Arab territory and to bomb the cities of the Arab country with the largest population. Editorialists noted that in this, two things seemed to remain constant; American foreign policy and Israeli aggression supported by US arms. Writers lamented that US diplomacy in the area had three main goals: to get the USSR out of the region without resorting to war, keep the Arabs, especially Egypt, weak so it would be easier to maintain American interests, and keep Israel strong to protect US interests.[116] It was as though Israel had become one of the United States.[117]

Arab press reaction to the other super power, Russia, we would describe as being more enigmatic when compared to that written about the United States. Editorials dealing with the Soviet Union produced neither as much love nor as much hate, from its supporters and detractors, as did articles dealing with the American position vis-à-vis the Arabs. One is not hard pressed to discover reasons for the lack of polarization when discussing the Soviet Union that a similar discussion of the United States would induce. Journals that gave editorial support to the socialist countries were largely Muslim. They were products of their own society, which, no matter how hard they might try to escape its influence, was a religious one. Atheistic communism did not sit well with the average Arab, no matter how secular he had become. Up to 1969, when Lebanese Interior Minister Kamāl Junblāṭ sanctioned the Lebanese branch, there was no legal communist party in the Arab world. The Russian was also less well understood than his counterpart in the West. Centuries of Western domination, not only militarily but educationally and linguistically, had left an impression on even those who hated the West the most. If one were to ask a Zionist in the 1960s and 1970s who were Israel's staunchest foes, any list would contain the names of George Ḥabash and Wadīʿ Ḥaddād. Both advocated Marxism. And both were graduates of the American University of Beirut.

On the other hand, the press that criticized the Soviet Union, largely the Christian and the conservative Muslim press, had to give grudging recognition to the fact that Russia did support the Arab position more than the West that they admired. Thus their opposition to the USSR was less biting than their ideological opponents' criticisms of the West and the United States. The Six-day War, however, had put the Soviet Union in a difficult position in the Arab world. As the main supporter and trainer of the Arab military, the Soviets could be held partly responsible for the defeat. The Arab press, when the course of the war became clear, began to criticize the Soviet Union, not as an enemy but as "that certain Big Power that was supposed to be our friend" but had failed to avert the Arab loss of June 1967.[118] Criticism was so intense that the communist organ, *al-Nidā'*, which ordinarily did not publish on Mondays came out with a special edition on June 12, 1967 defending the Russian role.

The Soviet Union acted quickly after the fighting to mend its fences when President Nikolai Podgorny arrived in Cairo on June 21, 1967. The press which supported friendship with the USSR, and this was practically the entire press of the countries included in this study except for a very few recalcitrant Christian journals in Lebanon, welcomed the visit and whatever criticism there had been of Soviet actions during the course of the war came to an end.

> [...] the policy of the Soviet Union is based on principles. It is a policy it has pursued since its birth. [...] The Soviet Union is now the principal deterring force in the face of American imperialism [...].[119]

> As for the Soviet Union, it is not only not a party in the [Israeli] aggression, but its political efforts put an end to the aggression and we used its weapons in defending ourselves and its friendship supports us in all fields.[120]

The Soviet Union was the strongest power supporting the Arab world after 1967. But what was the type of support was the USSR willing to give the Arabs? They did receive unlimited diplomatic support and help in rebuilding their destroyed military. But was the Soviet Union willing to support the Arabs to gain a military victory, as the United States had done for Israel? This was a question that the Arab editorialists often asked and the answer they deduced, and upon which they elucidated, often did not please them. As early as November 1967, with the passage, with Russian support, of UN Security Council Resolution 242, the outlines of Soviet foreign policy in the Middle East were clear. The Soviet Union favored a political, not a military, settlement to the Arab-Israeli conflict.

The negotiations over an acceptable United Nations resolution following the June 1967 war had taken over five months. When it was passed on November 22, a new element entered the conflict. Security Council Resolution 242 called for Israeli withdrawal from territories occupied during the war, the territorial integrity and political independence of all countries of the area, a just solution to the refugee problem, and an ending to the state of belligerency in the Middle East. Israel was not a warm supporter of the document since it dealt with the Palestinians, avoided the question of direct negotiations, said nothing about the legitimacy of Israel, and called for Israeli withdrawal. Syria, too, was opposed to 242 because it did not call for Israeli withdrawal from all territory occupied and because it implicitly recognized Israel's right to exist. Before the resolution was adopted, the Syrian press waged a strong campaign against Arab acceptance of any political solution. It wrote that though Arab governments might succumb, the Arab masses led by Syria would make sure no capitulationist plan was implemented. Several editorials said that many Arab regimes were openly hoping someone would impose a solution on them to save them from the embarrassment of their losses.[121]

A little over a year after 242 had passed and little progress had been made toward its implementation, the Soviet Union took the initiative by suggesting a series of steps to be followed to reach a political settlement. The text of the proposals was published in Beirut's *al-Anwār* on January 10, 1969 and commented upon the same day in *al-Ahrām* by Haykal. Basically the Russian plan called for five stages in reaching a settlement. The first would be the withdrawal of Israel from territory occupied in the 1967 war. After the withdrawal was completed, there would be a joint declaration of non-belligerency. This would be followed by United Nations' efforts to solve the problems of the Palestinian "refugees," the term used in 242, and then the question of navigation through the Suez Canal and the Straits of Tiran would be faced. Finally the United Nations' Security Council would guarantee the negotiated borders of the region and if necessary send UN forces to the area to implement its resolutions. Haykal suggested that the Soviet initiative was begun as a result of 'Abd al-Nāṣir's trip to the Soviet Union the previous July. Haykal supported the initiative suggesting that it might be the last chance for a political solution.

One week later, Haykal was more pessimistic. No matter Moscow's good intentions, a political settlement was not possible. The success of the Soviet initiative depended on the willingness of Israel to accept it. But the Israelis were so arrogant from their military successes that they were acting like "Greek gods." He quoted one Israeli who said that his country was willing to take on Russia itself if it dared to try to impose withdrawal from territories captured in 1967. Haykal went on to say that though the Arabs might like a political settlement, the United States encouraged the Israeli stance, and as a result it would continue to occupy Arab territory.[122]

On the issue of a political settlement, whether that put forward by the Soviet Union or Resolution 242, about which we shall have more to say, it is interesting to note that the strongest defenders of the Israelis and the most belligerent of the Arabs both rejected this approach. They did so because a political settlement required compromise, something both extremes refused. In response to the Soviet initiative, Ghassān Kanafānī responded that the USSR's peace plan gave Israel too much. It implicitly recognized the Israeli right to exist and also gave the Jewish state sovereignty, territorial integrity, and independence.[123]

One of the last acts of the Johnson Administration was to respond to the Soviet proposals. The United States said that the USSR was causing tension in the area by supplying the Arabs with arms and that it did not feel that the Israelis had to withdraw to the borders of June 4, 1967. Further, the United States' response criticized the Soviet initiative for failing to call for direct negotiations between the belligerents and termed the growing Palestinian commando movement as "Arab terrorism."[124] This rebuttal caused an uproar in the editorials of the Arab press. *Al-Ahrām* said that the US response condoned Israeli expansion and that the United States was no more than the spokesman for Israel.[125]

Despite this editorial hostility, the problem remained; how to get Israel out of the territory occupied in 1967 when both the United States and the Soviet Union opposed further military action? From the Arab perspective it was clear that the Soviet initiative, no matter its good intent, was doomed because, as Haykal had noted, it was no longer a question of the Arabs acting but Israel. If the positions were reversed and the Arabs had occupied Israeli territory, then the Soviet peace initiative would have had some effect because the Russians had leverage in the Arab world. The Soviet Union did not even have diplomatic relations with Israel, let alone the ability to pressure the Jewish state.

Journalists wrote that there were several options open to the Arabs. One was to rebuild their armies and prepare for another war. Another was to increase support to the Palestinian commando movement, using the successful Vietcong as a model. A third alternative was to bring pressure on the United States to put pressure on Israel to accept 242 thereby "removing the traces of aggression" of which 'Abd al-Nāṣir had spoken.

But the press of Jordan, Lebanon, and Egypt, recognizing the futility of pressing for a military solution, generally backed the diplomatic efforts which they said had borne fruit in the form of 242.[126]

> Those with ill intentions describe the diplomatic dialogue now going on between the United Arab Republic, on the one hand, and the United States and the United Kingdom, on the other, as backing down by Nāṣirism. [...] [They] are ignorant of Nāṣirism [...] Nāṣirism knows no malice and believes in positive neutrality [...]. Any settlement that guarantees the elimination of the traces of aggression, the spread of peace and the support of justice is acceptable to the Arabs in general and to Nāṣirism in particular.[127]

The Syrian press once again hit out at regimes who agreed to a political settlement, not a military one. The Syrian press even noted that Israel did not accept the resolution even though the document "blessed aggression" and went against the wishes of the Arab masses.[128]

Haykal responded to Arab opposition by defending the resolution and by putting in writing the same arguments for its acceptance that the government of Egypt would use in the future. He stated that the resolution demanded that Israel withdraw from occupied Arab territory. It was only after that occurred that the Arabs would be required to negotiate over "secure and recognized" borders, to use the phrase found in the resolution. Presumably the Israelis, once they had withdrawn, would then claim that those should be its borders, demanding recognition of them. "What stops us from saying in this case that secure and recognized borders are, in our opinion, one Jewish synagogue in Tel Aviv, with ten meters on a side?"[129] Perhaps in part because of this kind of editorial, Israel refused to execute 242. When it did agree on the last day of July 1970 to negotiate a peace settlement, 242 was to be only the basis for negotiation and not to be implemented first then followed by negotiations – a subtle but important difference in the Israeli perspective.

As a result of the passage of 242, several Arab countries, with Egypt in the lead, had officially committed themselves to a political settlement. The editor-publisher of *al-Anwār*, Sa'īd Frayḥah, saw that this presented a new dilemma for the Arab world. Once having accepted 242, the Arabs had a moral commitment to pursue a political course. The Arabs' closest friends, with the Soviet Union in the forefront, were urging this kind of solution. But there were obstacles. Most likely in the course of negotiations, some of Israel's plans for territorial aggrandizement would be realized. This would make, wrote Frayḥah, acceptance difficult for the Arabs. How could leaders go to the masses, increasingly led by Palestinians opposed to a political settlement, with a solution that would involve territorial concessions and which would thus appear to be imposed as a result of military defeat? Further, the idea of a fighting Palestinian commando had fired the imagination of the Arabs. In the aftermath of the defeat of 1967, the Palestinian cause had emerged untainted by the war. The press argued that it would be difficult to deny this group a chance to succeed where the Arabs had failed. Thus, Frayḥah wrote, the choice for the Arab world was a difficult one. Ultimately the decision would be made by ʿAbd al-Nāṣir, and he was, after all, before he was a president, a leader of a revolutionary movement.[130]

Certainly Frayḥah's commentaries captured the mood of the Arabs. In the stupendous defeat suffered by their governments and regular armies in 1967, attention switched to the increasing, and successful when compared to other Arab action, activity of the Palestinian commandos, with *Fatḥ* in the lead. There was some attempt, especially by Haykal, to point out the limitations of a popular war as led by the Palestinians and the futility of putting all of one's hopes in their abilities. Though the pro-Palestinian press in Syria and Lebanon continued to call for the arming of all citizens and the waging of a Vietnamese-type war, Haykal pointed out the difficulties involved in such action, especially for Egypt.

> The example of the Vietnamese war is good and achieved miracles in its place, but is not, by nature, particularly applicable to the Egyptian front.
>
> This is because the land occupied by the enemy in Sinai has a population of not more than 20,000, most of whom are nomadic tribes in the desert. The largest concentration of population in all of Sinai is in the city of al-ʿArīsh where the population is not more than 5,000.
>
> Popular war is not possible without people in addition to the fact that [where it would be fought] is open desert.

In the same article, he further argued that had the Israelis crossed the Suez Canal and occupied Egypt's cities, then a popular war would have been the right choice of action.[131] But as it stood now, the course for the Arabs was to have a regular army to face that of the enemy, an air force to fight their air force and the same for the navy.[132] The Syrian press responded by saying that a popular war was not necessarily a jungle war and that Haykal's analysis missed the point in not recognizing the need to arm the people, especially the Palestinians.[133] Haykal replied:

> I am not belittling the value of commando activity inside Palestine. But I do not place on it the entire burden. Those on the Arab side who believe that the main burden of the problem can be solved through commando activity are, simply and indolently, trying to escape [their] responsibility. Commando activity will not be able to get Israel out of the West Bank, the Syrian Heights, or the Sinai Desert.
>
> Commando activity must continue as an element of anxiety for Israel and to keep the issue [of Palestinian claims] alive.[134]

But the activity of the commandos had caught the imagination of the Arab world. Strikes against Israel, like that in Jerusalem on September 19, 1967, further bolstered the Palestinian armed struggle so that by the end of the year *Fatḥ* had become more important than the PLO. As if to signify this new development, Aḥmad al-Shuqayrī resigned as the head of the latter to be replaced by a Palestinian lawyer, Yaḥyā Ḥāmmudah. This turn of events obviously irritated the Israelis and they showed their displeasure on February 15, 1968 in the largest Israeli action since the June war. Attacking through the air and with tanks and field artillery, they said the assault into Jordan was aimed at destroying "Arab terrorist" bases, eschewing the use of the words Palestinian or commando, and at the same time holding the Hashimites responsible for the attacks. Arab writers noted the Israeli reluctance to blame the former inhabitants of Palestine and felt this was part of an Israeli strategy. If the Israelis acted otherwise, it would be reviving the Palestinian "that it has tried for twenty years ... to wipe out."[135]

Israeli assaults continued intermittently for six weeks till the early morning of March 21, 1968 when they attacked near the small town of al-Karāmah, five kilometers east of the Jordan River where a large Palestinian camp was located. The Palestinians and Jordanians were apparently aware of the coming attack and for the first time fought in coordination. The Israelis withdrew after fifteen hours of fighting, apparently with some difficulty. Thus was born in the Palestinian psyche the legendary "Battle of al-Karāmah." Celebrated in song and word as a great Arab, essentially Palestinian, victory, King Ḥusayn proclaimed, in words now reminiscent of President Kennedy's speech in West Berlin, "We are all fedayeen." Even the Egyptian press was impressed:

> There is no doubt that the new [Israeli] aggression against Jordan shows how important and effective popular resistance is as a cornerstone in the liberation of usurped Arab land. We should, therefore, support the [commando] forces that have shaken and frightened Israel.[136]

1968 was the year of the commando. At the end of March, Yāsir ʿArafāt gave his first interview to an Arab newspaper. This was followed on April 15 with the announcement that he was the official spokesman of *Fatḥ* thus putting an end, as one editorial put it, to attempts by "enemies of the Arabs" to say that *Fatḥ* was a sabotage and terrorist organization run by non-Palestinians.[137]

"The Voice of al-ʿĀṣifah" began broadcasting in May from Cairo. There were more commando activities inside Israel and then on July 23, Palestinians hijacked an El Al airplane from Rome diverting it to Algeria. Euphoria reigned in the Arab press. The result of these actions, as one editorialist put it, was to end the Israeli hope that twenty years would go by and an Arab generation would grow up that would neither know Palestine nor fight for it.[138] When Israeli prime minister Levi Eshkol stated he could not understand how Algeria, a member of the United Nations, could harbor the commandos who hijacked the Israeli plane, editorial response was one of derision.

> He cannot understand? Is the aggression of Israel since its creation not a huge robbery, perhaps the biggest in history? The gradual hijacking of Palestine, the hijacking of Sinai, the West Bank, and the Golan Heights are understandable to Eshkol but the hijacking of an airplane is incomprehensible.[139]

The Palestinians continued their attacks: in Jerusalem, Tel Aviv, and in Athens. A Palestinian assassinated American presidential candidate Robert Kennedy. Editorial opinion about this latter act was overwhelmingly condemnatory. But one writer, though not condoning it, still thought there was a lesson to be learned.

> [...] [R]egardless of everything, [Sirḥān] Sirḥān's bloody bullets have carried Palestine into every American home [...] the price may be high, it may be illegal and unethical. But American deafness [to the Palestinian cause] is also illegal, unethical, and truly high priced [...].[140]

The whole world seemed vulnerable to the Palestinian. No one any longer could deny he existed. The ultimate recognition of this was Yāsir ʿArafāt's picture on the December 13, 1968 cover of *Time* magazine.

The next year, 1969, witnessed the takeover of the PLO by the commandos. Yāsir ʿArafāt became the leader of the organization recognized and created by the Arab League. No longer were they refugees or commandos but a people with their own quasi-legal government. Editorial opinion hailed the election and the comparison to the Vietnamese experience was inevitable. The United States refused to recognize the Vietcong while the Israelis refused to recognize the Palestinians and the PLO. The Americans bombed the north for years blaming Hanoi for sending terrorists south but ultimately recognized the Vietcong as a separate entity. So, too, did Israel bomb and attack the neighboring Arab states, but it too would have to eventually bow to reality, a Palestinian reality.[141]

The commando movement produced its own heroes, including Laylā Khālid. She and a male accomplice in August 1969 hijacked a Trans World Airline plane and named their action after Che Guevara.

> They flew in the skies of southern Europe and the eastern Mediterranean conveying the voice of the Palestinian to the peoples of the area [...]. They chose the name "Che Guevara" in order to tell the world revolutionaries that the rebel who was killed by United States intelligence agents in Bolivia has been resurrected here.[142]

American Secretary of State William Rogers called the perpetrators "pirates" and said the Middle East was explosive. Do not be so defensive, responded the Arab press. Pirates were mercenaries, the commandos worked for love of their country. And of course the situation was explosive. If the commandos had not been so active, the situation would be calm, thus consecrating Israeli aggression and the continued occupation of Arab territory. As for hijacking itself, Rogers was asked to look at his own country first before condemning others. American plane hijackings to Cuba were so common that US-Havana was now considered a domestic flight.[143]

The apparent initial success of the revolution was not without darker sides that did not bode well for the future of the commando movement. One of the more obvious was the proliferation of commando groups. Only a few months after the commandos took over the PLO, estimates of the number of guerrilla groups ran as high as 30 with *Fatḥ* being the largest. Ideological considerations as well as support from various Arab regimes were the major factors in the increase in the number of commando organizations.

'Alyā' al-Ṣulḥ, daughter of former Lebanese prime minister Rashīd al-Ṣulḥ, warned in a commentary in 1968 that the road of revolution was not easy nor paved with victories as the "professional revolutionaries" portrayed it. These confidence men exploit the revolution for their own ends. They never start a revolution but only join when it is appealing. They assert themselves through ideological discussions, publication of articles, and constant talk. But when thing get rough, they are not around. "I am concerned over the Palestine revolution. I am not afraid of its enemies [...]. I am concerned about the revolution because of some of its friends."[144]

The most spectacular creation of a new organization occurred in February 1969 when the second largest commando group, the Popular Front for the Liberation of Palestine, under the leadership of pediatrician George Ḥabash, gave revolutionary birth to two new groups, the Popular Democratic Front for the Liberation of Palestine (PDFLP), under Nāyif Ḥawātmah, and the Popular Front for the Liberation of Palestine-General Command (PFLP-GC), under a former Syrian army officer, Captain Aḥmad Jabrīl. Other important guerrilla groups included the pro-Iraqi Arab Liberation Front (ALF) and the pro-Syrian *al-Ṣā'iqah* (the Thunderbolt). Egypt had its own commando group, the Arab Liberation Organization but it was composed of Egyptians. The PLO also had its own regular army, the PLA, which was under the theoretical control of the head of the PLO. Units of the PLA were stationed in Egypt, Jordan and Syria and in effect became auxiliaries of the armies of their respective host countries.

The proliferation of commando groups, many Arab journalists noted, caused several problems. There was competition in recruiting and, embarrassingly, multiple claims of credit for this or that operation in Israel. Lacking a central command that would hold them responsible for their actions, some of the commando groups were unruly. A Syrian paper commented that commando groups in 1968 in Jordan were taking advantage of their popularity. They refused to produce their identification cards to Jordanian authorities, they got drunk and shot their weapons in the air, scaring the citizenry, and many commandos spent their days in public cafes drinking coffee and showing customers how to operate their weapons.[145]

Perhaps an even more fundamental problem of the Palestinian resistance was its inability to find an Arab country with a border contiguous to Israel that was willing to turn itself into a north Vietnam. Egypt, as we have noted, argued its territory was not suitable for commando activity. Syria forbade operations, except *al-Ṣā'iqah*, which it controlled. This left only Jordan, where the Hashimites looked suspiciously at the rise of any armed group because of the known hostility of the Palestinians to the Hashimite rulers, and Lebanon, a country divided over the Palestinian question and plagued by economic and religious problems.

The tension that existed between the Lebanese authorities and the commando movement was the result of complex factors. In this confessional state, the Lebanese army had come to be identified amongst the Muslims as the army of the Christians. Thus, the Muslim press tended to view positively the Palestinian armed presence while the Christians, and their press, were hostile to "armed strangers" who threatened Lebanese sovereignty. As a result of the National Pact of 1943, the Christian element, consistently dominated by the Maronites, retained the upper hand in the political arena though their percentage of the population became smaller every year as a result of the higher Muslim birth rate. The Christians' political dominance gave them economic benefits. By the late 1960s, there was a serious and growing dichotomy in Lebanese society between the very rich, who tended to be Christians, and the very poor, who tended to be Muslims. The combination of political and economic impotence on the part of Muslim society, best epitomized by Shiites from the south, was leading Lebanon toward civil war. The Shiite population felt the government was unresponsive to its economic plight and prejudiced against its religion. The Palestinian, also poor and prejudiced against by Arab as well as Israeli, was thus a natural ally for his Lebanese counterpart. Though this explanation is undoubtedly an oversimplification, it still does serve to inform us that the presence of armed Palestinians in Lebanon complicated an already labyrinthine domestic situation. As early as the summer of 1968, there was tension between the Lebanese army and the commandos that resulted in fighting between the two sides. But what perhaps brought the smoldering hostility to the surface was the Israeli raid in late December 1968 on the Beirut International Airport, a response to a Palestinian attack on an El A1 plane in Athens a few days earlier. The warning was clear. Israel was demanding that the Lebanese make choices. It could choose to control the commandos and thus retain its traditional non-belligerence in the Arab-Israeli conflict or support the commandos and risk making of Lebanon the Vietnam the commandos desired.

Editorial comment on the Israeli raid was mixed. Many newspapers, both Christian and Muslim, lamented the absence of an adequate Lebanese defense against the raids. "Why was the brutal attack [allowed] and why was there no response to it?" was not an uncommon question.[146] But the real issue went beyond one raid. Lebanon, which largely had escaped the tragedies that had befallen other Arab states with borders touching Israel, now had come to that time which it had sought to avoid. *Al-ʿAmal*, spokesman of conservative, establishment, Christian opinion in Lebanon, wrote:

> The problem lays in the choice that Israel is trying to place before Lebanon; either to fight commando activity or enter an actual war with Israel.
>
> The choice is not difficult, and Lebanon is not hesitant in making it, because Lebanon is a partner in the great problem [...].
>
> This means that Lebanon is committed to commando action as long as this action is committed to the Palestine question.
>
> However, the meaning of partnership will be lost if Lebanon is not consulted on the operations of this partnership.

> This means that if we are to support commando action [...] we at least have the right to agree on the plan of action.
>
> Thus far, we do not know with whom to come to agreement, because the commando organizations are numerous, and this has led to the loss of a responsible organizational leadership. [...]
>
> If such a dialogue [between Lebanese authorities and the commandos] existed, then we could reach an understanding regarding the targets at which commando action should be aimed. We then could tell the commandos, the heroes, that inflicting damage on one Israeli plane is not equal to the destruction of the Lebanese commercial aviation fleet....
>
> We want to bear our responsibility for commando action. But this must be preceded by commando activity shouldering its own responsibility. [...] Those who are responsible for the [Palestinian] cause must understand the meaning of partnership.[147]

The Israeli strike against Beirut airport did have one beneficial aspect for the Arab cause since it resulted in the imposition of the French arms embargo of Israel. But if the Israeli attack was meant to cause a cleavage in Lebanese society over support or non-support for the Palestinians, then, according to Haykal, the raid was a success.[148]

Other editorials tried to calm anti-Palestinian sentiment resulting from the Israeli attack by pointing out that the Israeli desire for the waters of the Litani River were well known and had nothing to do with the commandos.[149] Still tensions continued to rise and clashes amongst the Lebanese occurred on April 23, 1969. Though it might be tempting, the Palestinians were warned not to divert their attention from the task of liberation in order to become embroiled in a domestic issue.[150] One day after the clashes, the government of Prime Minister Rashīd Karāmī resigned while suggesting that it was now time for the Lebanese to choose which course they desired to follow. This political crisis lasted seven months while the Lebanese debated and fought over the role of the Palestinian revolution on their soil.

Editorial opinion outside of Lebanon generally supported the idea that the Palestinians should have access to the Lebanese border with Israel. The Syrian press warned Lebanese authorities against striking the commando movement saying that such action would bring harm to Lebanon.[151] Egyptian editorials echoed the same theme.

> It is said in Lebanon, for example, that Palestinian commando action should take into consideration the sovereignty of the Lebanese state. This is reasonable.
>
> It is also said in Lebanon that Palestinian commando action should take into consideration the success of the coming tourist and summer season in Lebanon. This is not reasonable.[152]

Being lectured to by other Arab states did not sit well with those who opposed the unilateral use of Lebanese territory. There was something hypocritical about self-serving editorials while Syria, for example, prohibited virtually all activity from its soil and was arresting members of the Baghdad-backed ALF and deporting them to Iraq.

> We will not blame – and must not blame – Syria, Iraq, or Egypt for taking measures to protect their interests. [...]
>
> But we are allowed to blame Damascus, Baghdad, and other Arab capitals when they insist that there should be in Lebanon what they themselves refuse..., and when they insist that Lebanon should permit commando activity they themselves are banning....
>
> We also blame Damascus, for example, for using commando action in Lebanon as an excuse to spread subversive [socialist] ideology [...].[153]

The tense situation affecting the Lebanese gendarmes and army, on the one hand, and Palestinian commando units continued to deteriorate as 1969 progressed. Heavy fighting erupted on August 28 between Lebanese forces and Palestinians at the Nahr al-Bārid camp near Tripoli. Editorial opinion sympathetic to the Palestinian position in Lebanon warned the Lebanese not to clamp down on the commandos.[154] Papers that placed Lebanese sovereignty above the Palestinian cause demanded law and order.[155]

It was obvious that some agreement had to be reached between the two contending points of view. Egypt offered to mediate and on November 3, 1969 a secret "Cairo Agreement" was signed by representatives of both the PLO and the Lebanese government. *Al-Nahār* eventually published the text of the agreement[156] whose main points included Palestinian control of their camps, commando access to the ʿArqūb region in southeast Lebanon, and that all commando operations launched from that area had to occur in Israel, that is to say no firing from the Lebanese side of the border into Israel. By this agreement, the Palestinians gained control over their training sites and an area from which to operate while Lebanese sovereignty was recognized over the majority of its territory. It was a compromise hailed at that time by the press, no matter its bias toward the question of the Palestinians. [157] On the political level, the crisis now solved allowed the end of a seven-month ministerial hiatus with the formation of a new cabinet on November 25, 1969. The ability of the Lebanese and Palestinians to compromise was, in the Egyptian press, a sign of strength. Lebanon, with its religious and ideological diversity, had proven it could exist within its pluralism. Lebanon was "that which we seek in the future for Palestine where Muslims, Christians, and Jews would find a place to live together instead of the closed, racist, Zionist Israel that is exclusively for Jews."[158]

In the middle of May 1970, Israel attacked into the ʿArqūb. Commandos and elements of the Lebanese army, with Syrian air support, fought the Israelis in the largest attack ever launched up till then against Lebanon and the guerrillas. "We have been waiting for this for a quarter of a century,"[159] was one prideful statement. But perhaps more aware of what lay ahead for Lebanon and the Palestinian movement was the questioning editorial written in the Phalangist organ, *al-ʿAmal*:

> How will we face the enemy when he repeats his aggression in the near or distant future?
>
> Shall we leave it to others (and the others are the commandos and Israel) to decide for our army, and without its knowledge [...] the time and place of the battle [...]?

> Is it in Lebanon's interest and that of the Arabs that Lebanon should be afflicted with the disaster [of occupation] now suffered by three sister Arab countries?[160]

Jordan was the other Arab state with borders touching Israel from which commandos operated. That these raids caused Israel discomfort can be ascertained by the ferocity with which it attempted to end them and by the widespread speculation in Arab editorials that the United States was putting pressure on King Ḥusayn to stop giving sanctuary to the Palestinians.[161] The king would have liked to stop commando activity and said so in a letter to the London *Sunday Telegraph*. There he wrote that he had no intention of turning Jordan into a "guerrilla state" or a "chimpanzee state." Nor, in fact, did he have the least interest in any other form of "monkey business."[162]

Periodically the Jordanian army, with its backbone being the Bedouin forces who were fiercely loyal to their king descended from the Prophet, and to the family of his mother, led by the king's maternal uncle, Sharīf Nāṣir Ibn Jamīl, would try to force the king into taking action against the commandos. But the Hashimites were caught between two tendencies, that of preserving the Hashimite monarchy, which was threatened by radical Palestinians, and the popular feeling that the commando movement had engendered amongst the Arab masses. When in October 1968 it was reported that the Bedouin Corps had taken up positions in areas controlled by the commandos and that the government was going to apply restrictions on their movements, editorial reaction was hostile to the Hashimites.[163]

One month later, a hitherto unknown commando group, *Katā'ib al-Naṣr* (The Victory Phalangists), attempted to storm the US embassy in Amman and brought about the first commando-Jordanian armed confrontation. Just as in Lebanon, the question now presented itself as to how the Palestinians could carry on with what they perceived as their sacred duty in attacking Israel while at the same time respecting Jordanian sovereignty. In Jordanian eyes, the attack on an American embassy was not going to speed the liberation of occupied territory. Jordanian editorial opinion was hostile to the attack and called for the removal of "irresponsible elements" from the commando movement and establishing coordination of commando activities with the Jordanian regime.[164] While a compromise was possible in Lebanon, it probably was not in Jordan. The traditional enmity between the Hashimites and the Palestinians is well known and dates to the reign of Ḥusayn's grandfather, 'Abd Allāh, and his dealings with the Israelis. So, though an incident might be smoothed over, the eventual clash to determine the future course of the East Bank was perhaps inevitable. Commando operations from Jordan continued and Israeli attacks against Jordanian territory also escalated. In August 1969, Israeli fighter planes destroyed Jordan's East Ghor Canal which watered the citrus and banana groves in the north of the Jordan Valley. This was an essential irrigating project for Jordan, vital for a healthy economy. On January 21, 1970, the Israelis again attacked commando bases in Jordan. The Hashimite government reacted the following month by banning the carrying of arms in public and the stockpiling of explosives in Amman and other cities. The Jordanian press called for "the honest commando groups" to respect law and order.[165]

The situation between the two sides continued to deteriorate. Palestinians and their supporters stormed the US embassy and the US Information Agency offices in April to protest the impending arrival of American Undersecretary of State, Joseph Sisco. American Ambassador Harrison Symmes announced the cancellation of Sisco's trip, implying that King Ḥusayn did not have control of his country. The king was urged by his uncle to clamp down on the Palestinians. The commandos responded with an assassination attempt on the life of the king on June 9 and the PFLP captured the Intercontinental Hotel the following day demanding that Sharīf Nāṣir be removed as commander-in-chief of the Jordanian armed forces. The fighting that ensued resulted in more casualties than were suffered by Syria and Jordan in the 1967 war. A little over a month later a ceasefire was agreed to and the removal of Sharīf Nāṣir secured. But this was only a respite for both sides. The press of August 1970 warned that a crackdown on the commandos in Jordan was imminent.[166] They were correct. The precipitating event occurred on August 28 when members of the PDFLP tried to hang posters on the walls of Amman's central post office. They were challenged by Jordanian forces and in the ensuing melee, two were killed. Within days the Jordanian civil war engulfed the country and reached such intensity that the month was known as "Black September." The only paper that appeared as the civil war began was *Fatḥ*. As the paper of the central committee of the PLO, it was naturally condemnatory of the Jordanian military force, which was ranged against the commandos. In other Arab states, editorials also spoke of the "Amman massacres" and the "liquidation" of the commando movement in Jordan.[167] As if to further test the Jordanian authorities, on September 6 the PFLP, in what was certainly the most spectacular operation to date, hijacked four commercial planes, two of which landed at "Revolution Airport," an undisclosed location in Jordan.

Though we have mentioned the first hijacking in July 1968, it would be best now to reexamine editorial opinion of the subject and the relationship of hijacking to the civil war of 1970. Though editorial opinion was generally favorable to the first hijacking, one editorialist at the time noted that not one Arab government openly supported it.[168] This too was a problem for the journalists. In no one's mind was there doubt that hijacking was an escalation of the war against Israel. Was it worth the cost that Israel would extract? was one question asked. Another was the morality of killing innocent people. The response was mixed and not along lines that one might expect. For example, after the February 1969 hijacking, *al-Ḥayāt*, which had close ties to the more conservative regimes in the Arab world, dismissed criticism of hijacking by those who said that this kind of operation would give Israel the excuse to strike back. Israel attacked without excuses.[169] On the other hand, *al-Muḥarrir*, which ordinarily sided with the Palestinian commandos, commented some time later about hijackings and other commando activities carried on outside of Israel:

> The relative ease of carrying out some of these operations may allure the smaller groups to undertake such operations in order to attract attention to themselves; thus the spirit of adventure would seep in instead of the sense of responsibility. [...] Such a situation would

> provide our enemies with the opportunity of themselves carrying out sabotage and then blaming the commandos for them […].

Al-Muḥarrir concluded that "Revolutionary violence" was not an expression for its own sake, nor was it an expression of anger. It was violence that should serve the revolution and its goals.[170]

Arab editorial opinion was by no means united on the efficacy of hijacking operations. The fear of Israeli reprisals and world condemnation weighed heavily in criticisms by editorial writers. At least one of the aims of the Palestinian movement was to gain public sympathy for the Palestinian people. "It is certain that disturbing the stability of international civil air transport" would not help world opinion but "on the contrary stir a feeling of condemnation and indignation in the average uncommitted person […]."[171] Certainly the Hashimite monarchy was not uncommitted on the subject of hijackings. It opposed them and felt its sovereignty threatened, especially when Jordanian air space and territory were used in the spectacular operations of September 1970. When the commandos blew up the airplanes they had commandeered, this act was condemned, even by those who originally thought the operation was justifiable, because it deprived "the operation of its moral and persuasive force."[172]

A ceasefire between the Palestinians and Hashimite authorities, arranged on September 8, did not last through the day it was signed. One can imagine the humiliation the king, his relatives, and supporters felt in seeing the hijacking drama in Jordan being turned into an international media event. On September 17, 1970, the civil war increased in ferocity with the shelling of Palestinian camps and commando positions in Amman, al-Zarqā', al-Salṭ and Ṣwayliḥ. The presence of the guerrillas in Jordan was being challenged. Amongst the press that was sympathetic to the commando movement, the Hashimite moves were "genocide" and aimed at "exterminating" the Palestinian people. Editorial cartoons showed King Ḥusayn wearing an eye-patch; the archenemy, Moshe Dyan, was operating in Jordan.[173] Even the press that supported the Jordanian regime or tried to understand its point of view was shocked by the severity of its assaults on the Palestinians. "Everything in the Arab World needs reviewing and this includes the Arab man, the Arab ideologies, the Arab commando, and the Arab leaders themselves […]."[174]

Once again, as 'Abd al-Nāṣir had done a year earlier during the Lebanese-commando disturbances, Egypt offered to mediate. The situation was complicated by Israeli and US moves in support of the Hashimites and alleged Syrian intervention on the side of the Palestinians. Nonetheless, a ceasefire agreement was signed between Jordan and the commandos on September 27, 1970. 'Abd al-Nāṣir died the next day, a milestone event in the history of the Arab-Israeli conflict. Especially for the Soviets, they lost perhaps their closest ally in the Middle East, though some would argue that an even greater loss was Ḥāfiẓ al-'Asad's overthrow in 1970 of Syrian President Ṣalāḥ Jadīd.

Though we have examined the rise of the Palestinian movement and its effects on Lebanon and Jordan, we have largely neglected editorial comments at the same time in two major confrontation states, Syria and Egypt. In attempting to integrate opinion in those two countries with developments in the period after the 1967 war, the Egyptian press was far more important. The Syrian press devoted itself to educating the masses on the merits of socialism and the necessity to be steadfast in the face of adversity. On the other hand, the Egyptian press engaged in an often perceptive way in a discussion of what future Egypt and the Arab world had. Haykal's analysis of the defeat in 1967, which we have examined, was the best commentary in the press on that subject. Likewise, it was he who led the discussion in Egypt over the question, What future for the Arab cause? Perhaps it was natural that he should be the leading editorialist in the Arab world. His country was the largest Arab one, and Egypt's president was the recognized leader of the Arab people. That Egypt was unsure about the results of commando operations for the Arab cause, we have discussed. It should not be unexpected, when discussing the post-1967 period, that editorials in Egypt, and to a lesser extent Syria, should perceive the conflict differently than the Palestinians. Sinai was not going to be liberated by commandos. It was in this context that Egyptian editorial opinion, and responses in the press of the other Arab countries, operated.

Unlike the experience in 1956, it was apparent that the United States did not intend to compel Israel to withdraw from the territories that it occupied in 1967. Without American pressure, Israeli withdrawal was unlikely. It was in this atmosphere that the Arab Summit Conference in Khartoum was held from August 29 to September 1, 1967. Commenting on the decisions of the conference, Haykal wrote that the Arabs were committed to the position adopted at Khartoum of "no recognition of Israel, no negotiations with it, no peace, and no dealing with the Palestine question because that is the right of the Palestinian people."[175] Yet within a month Egypt's ambassador to the United Nations was negotiating over the form of what was to become 242, which Egypt accepted. Thus, though Egypt was committed by the Khartoum summit to no negotiations and no peace with Israel, it had implicitly accepted both when it acceded to 242. A Lebanese editorialist pointed out this contradiction in January 1968.[176] And added some months later that it was clear that the Arabs wanted peace but "no one knows how to achieve it. [...] [Thus] there is no war and no peace."[177]

That Egypt agreed to a peaceful settlement after its acceptance of 242 in 1967 seems unquestionable. But the problem then became, What type of peace? Immediately after its conquests in 1967, Israel began to change the demographic nature of the occupied territories paying special attention to the Old City of Jerusalem. One editorialist wrote that while the Arabs resorted to diplomacy, out of their commitment to a peaceful settlement, the Israelis adopted a policy of defiance of UN resolutions. The consequences of this policy for Israel, warned the writer, would be the outbreak of a new war in the Middle East.[178] In fact this last sentence summarizes Egyptian editorial opinion after the adoption of 242. It said that the Arab world accepted the resolution as the basis for peace. But, in the eyes of Egyptian writers, Israel wanted land not peace. If the Arabs, therefore, were to recover their lost territories, they had no choice but to fight for them. To think that Israel would unilaterally change its expansionist policy was to indulge in the most bizarre fantasy.

> As far as Israel is concerned, all Arabs are the same. [...] Israel would not pull out of Sinai [...] even if King Farūq, or the Khedive Ismāʿīl returned. [...] Israel would not give up its desire for Lebanese water [from the Litani River] even if [Pierre Gemayel and Kamīl Shamʿūn] were in power. Israel will not return Jerusalem even to al-Ḥājj Amīn al-Ḥusaynī.[179]

One Egyptian journal lamented that while the rest of the world debated the best way to obtain peace, the Israelis debated the best way to seize territory, mislead the world, and how to continue its aggression with the support of America.[180] Of special concern to all Arab editorialists was the annexation of Jerusalem and the attempts to plant Israeli settlers in the West Bank. The unification of the New and Old cities was widely criticized in the Arab press. Editorials focused on the religiously important Mosque of al-Aqsa and the Dome of the Rock. One Lebanese writer said that the Israelis wanted to destroy these structures in order to construct the Third Temple.[181] When a fire was deliberately started in al-Aqsa on August 21, 1969, it seemed that the worst Arab fears were coming true. Though Israel might claim it was not responsible for the fire, and had no intention of building another temple, still "there is a reality that, nonetheless, cannot be concealed by any propaganda. That is that the Aqsa Mosque, one of the holiest shrines of Islam, was burned under Israeli occupation and that many other Muslim and Christian sanctuaries have been desecrated before [...]."[182] The scene was a bleak one for Arab editorialists. The Arab sector of Jerusalem was annexed, a part of the Noble Sanctuary burned, Hebron was under covetous Israeli eyes, and new settlements were being built on captured territory. "Israel is exploiting the time during which a peace solution is being sought in order to complete its measures for establishing the *fait accompli* in the territories it is occupying [...]"[183] What was to be done? Even before the adoption of 242, the Syrian press noted that there were two trends in the Arab world, one that accepted diplomacy and one that advocated resistance. "The Arab masses know from their historical experience that dignity does not come by way of surrender but by resistance and heroism and that freedom is not given by compromises and concessions but is taken at the point of bayonets and through armed popular struggle [...]."[184] In not quite so dramatic terms, Haykal came to the same conclusion – war was inevitable. Though Egypt and the Arabs might like a political settlement, war could not be avoided. What the Arabs wanted Israel rejected and the Palestinian resistance would never be able to attain.

> [...] the popular war now being waged by the Palestinian resistance inside Palestine cannot be expected, not by anyone, to achieve a conclusive end to the struggle.[185]

> [...] as a result of the battles of the six days in June, Israel emerged in the stronger position vis-à-vis the Arab nation.
>
> This is where the situation stands now. Logically speaking, Israel will not give up this position of strength unless we remove her from it by force. There is no other logic.[186]

> The existing military situation suits the Israeli plan, and the enemy, therefore, wants to keep it that way. But his military situation does not suit the Egyptian plan ... and, therefore, our efforts will be directed, and must be directed, to change it. [...] Israel wants to maintain the present status quo, and we have no alternative but to change it [...].[187]

The goals of the Arabs in the next round, Haykal wrote in a series of columns spanning 1968 and 1969, will be limited ones. There will be no crematories for Jews à la Hitler, nor any talk of throwing the Jews into the sea. But one of the objectives will be to score a victory in battle over Israel, not necessarily win a large war. To be able to inflict 10,000 casualties on the Israelis will be success enough. This will destroy the myth of Israeli military invincibility, upset the Israeli army which portrays itself as the backbone of the nation and cast doubt upon the ability of the army to protect Israel. This will cause the fall of the Israeli military establishment and prove that the Israeli strategy of imposing peace through force will not work.[188]

The first step that had to be taken in order to achieve these goals was to rebuild the confidence of the Arabs in themselves. Here the press played an important role in showing that the losses in the 1967 war were not caused by genetic deficiencies. The Arabs received their first big boost on October 21, 1967 when the Israeli destroyer "Eilath" was sunk after it entered Egyptian waters. The Arab press called it a turning point in the Middle East. It proved that the Arabs knew how to use the weapons they possessed and that, though Israel was strong, it was not invincible.[189]

The Israelis responded with increasingly damaging raids against the cities along the Suez Canal with the result that some 200,000 Egyptians became refugees starting as early as 1967. The "War of Attrition," as it later became known, was underway. As it proceeded, the Arabs were told to be steadfast and not overconfident. When on July 20, 1969 Israel attempted to invade Green Island in the Gulf of Suez but had to withdraw, it was difficult not to boast. "It has been a violent shock for the invading forces and their schemes."[190] One week later in the first action of its kind in over two years, the Egyptian air force struck into Sinai on a punitive raid. Two days later, the Syrians did the same in the Golan.

> Yesterday's operation is more significant than a mere retaliation against the Israeli raid on our position two days ago. It indicates that the Arab forces in general are in a position to prove themselves in the field of battle [...].[191]

To Haykal, what was occurring after the 1967 defeat was ironic. Israel was now beginning to lose and this loss was the direct result of victory over the Arabs. The myth of Israeli invincibility was being destroyed.

> This myth must be eliminated [...] because the all-embracing battle cannot begin in the psychological atmosphere created by this myth. The all-embracing battle must begin in an atmosphere of reality and not an atmosphere of myth.

> Reality says that the Israeli army is strong. But to say that it is invincible is a myth produced by our illusions which were brought on by defeat which we inflicted on ourselves rather than it being inflicted on us by the Israeli army.[192]

The "War of Attrition" had a positive affect on Arab writers, if we may judge from their editorials. Dismayed after June 1967, they began to write more optimistically by 1970 in response to some positive news from the battlefront. Though Arab casualties were high in the renewed fighting, centered largely on the Egyptian front, it was certain that Israel also was being hurt. There could be some consolation in knowing the enemy was not the only one delivering blows. Even bombings of highly dense areas like Cairo could now be dismissed as being psychologically motivated.[193]

The air attacks were aimed at demoralizing the populace but editorialists argued they might have just the opposite effect. When one such raid hit a school, killing 31 students and one of their teachers, reaction was hostile but determined not to be capitulatory. "Israel cannot go on killing civilians and innocent children and claim to have world public opinion on its side [...]. What it is paying now in [the loss of] public opinion support, it will pay tomorrow on the battlefield."[194]

Whether it was the rise of the Palestinian commando movement or the heating up of the Egyptian-Israeli front, the United States in December 1969 began to move on the stalemated political situation with a new initiative we know as the Rogers' Plan, named after Secretary of State William Rogers. The plan was actually nothing new except for its call for a three-month ceasefire on the Egyptian front. It called in essence for the implementation of 242 or at least using the United Nations' resolution as the basis for negotiation. The editorial response to the Rogers' initiative was similar to the reception 242 had received 2 years earlier. Syrian newspapers charged that the United States only saw the Middle East conflict in terms of borders. It did not take into account the "Fascist ideology embodied in the Zionists" and it also forgot the rights of the Palestinians.[195] The official publication of the PLO, *Fatḥ*, also opposed the Rogers' initiative, just as it did 242, since neither spoke of the Palestinians as a people but either ignored them or said they were refugees.[196]

Of equal interest, since ʿAbd al-Nāṣir eventually accepted the Rogers' Plan, was the appearance of opposition to the plan within the Egyptian press. One editorial warned that a new ceasefire might be dangerous for Egypt and the Arabs since it would freeze the situation with Israel still occupying Arab territory. Another argued that the aim of American policy in the Middle East was to isolate the UAR and get it out of the Arab-Israeli conflict.[197]

When, in a speech commemorating the eighteenth anniversary of the Egyptian revolution, ʿAbd al-Nāṣir accepted a three-month ceasefire and the Rogers' Plan, opposition to the president was widespread. Some editorialists argued that the reason ʿAbd al-Nāṣir accepted the American initiative was because the war of attrition was being lost by Egypt. The Syrian press was the most hostile saying that acceptance of the Plan was "surrender" to Zionism and would result in large scale Jewish immigration into Israel, economic dominance of the area by Israel and its allies, and lead to open warfare between Arab states.[198]

Palestinian editorial opposition was equally strident seeing in the Rogers' initiative the neutralization of not only Egypt but of Jordan, which had also accepted the Plan. For the Palestinian press this was the beginning of the liquidation of the Palestinian movement. The "contradiction" amongst Arab regimes was now in the open. The incongruity existed between those who accepted a political solution and those who rejected it.[199] The theory, as expounded by those editorialists opposed to a political solution, was that once a settlement had been agreed to, the Palestinian resistance movement would be a stumbling block to capitulation. It would therefore have to be removed – by force if necessary. That the Jordanian civil war began shortly after ʿAbd al-Nāṣir accepted the American plan was not a coincidence in many Arab eyes.[200]

Support for the acceptance of the Rogers' Plan came from the press of Jordan, parts of the Lebanese, and from Egypt. Quite naturally the controlled press of Egypt was loudest in its support, though it began in a defensive mood by talking about what acceptance did not mean, not what it meant. It did not mean that commando operations would have to end, or even that other fronts could not be opened. The "War of Attrition" which was announced solely by Egypt could be ended by it when it wanted. Some editorialists pointed out, chidingly, that the Rogers' initiative made no mention of any front except the Egyptian because, presumably, the ceasefire had never ended on any other.[201] When criticism continued from other Arab states, Haykal wrote:

> The Iraqi regime says that its army is ready. The Syrian papers say that their army is ready, and the Algerian leadership says that it can send all its forces to the front in 24 hours … there is nothing to stop them, especially since the three armies together cannot be smaller than the Egyptian army – or at least this is what we have the right to assume […]. Those who do not fight do not have the right to teach others who do fight […].[202]

In a stinging interview with Fuʾād Maṭar of Beirut's *al-Nahār* on August 2, 1970, Haykal warned that the anti-Egyptian campaign could result in the withdrawal of the Egyptians from the Arab world:

> The Arab World must know that it has to help the supporters of Arabism inside Egypt who believe in the Arab character of Egypt. That is because no Arab country has as much potential for secession as Egypt does. The Egyptian people lived, during a certain period of their history, in isolation from the rest of the Arab world. More than any other Arab country, Egypt possesses the elements of a state in isolation from its surroundings. More pressure on Egypt, of the cheap variety which we see now, may result in a serious [Egyptian] backlash.

Eight days after ʿAbd al-Nāṣir's acceptance of a ceasefire, the Israeli government also agreed. This caused a minor crisis in the Jewish state since the Gahal Party, led by Menachem Begin, immediately resigned from the coalition, opposing 242 as the basis of negotiation because of its call for Israeli withdrawal from occupied territory. In late August, Israel, Jordan, and the UAR began indirect talks in New York City under the auspices of the United Nations, represented by Gunnar Jarring. That Israel came reluctantly soon became apparent. With the outbreak of the Jordanian civil war, the Israelis withdrew from the talks. In a strong criticism of the "Ḥabashiyīn," supporters of George Ḥabash, Mūsā Ṣabrī wrote:

> Israel was able in the shadow of the violent storm [caused by the hijacking] [...] to wreck the peace initiative without anyone sensing it [...] and to shatter the Jarring mission without the least reproach from anyone.[203]

The end of the Rogers' initiative, the scuttling of the Jarring mission, and the violent eruption of the Jordanian civil war all occurred in September 1970. But if we were to ask what the most important event was that occurred in Black September, surely the answer would be the passing of ʿAbd al-Nāṣir. The leader of the Arabs died while his people still looked to him for direction in escaping the dilemmas and humiliations that the Arab-Israeli conflict had caused. Though tainted by his acceptance of the Rogers' initiative, he had been the undisputed boss. His death signaled the end of an era.

The history of the Middle East between 1958 and 1970 was filled with momentous events. If one excludes the 1967 war, however, the important events often did not deal with the Arab-Israeli conflict. Arab editorial opinion frequently was focused outside Palestine, on the union of Egypt and Syria or the intra-Arab rivalry in Yemen, for example. Nonetheless, the period was important in our study of the Arab-Israeli conflict for a number of reasons. It was during this time that Haykal emerged unchallenged as the leading Arab editorialist. This position came not only from his writing but also because he became identified as the unofficial spokesman of President ʿAbd al-Nāṣir. He was also the first important Arab writer to call for the use of oil as a weapon in the struggle with Israel.

The period between 1958 and 1970 also witnessed the growth of the Palestinian resistance movement, led ultimately by the PLO. Editorialists were fascinated with the guerrillas, conjecturing about their leaders and about their chances of success. Undoubtedly the arming of the Palestinians struck a response cord in the press. Though Bourguiba of Tunisia might call for a negotiated settlement and Haykal warn that the guerrillas would not be able to liberate any territory, the last part of the 1960s belonged to the fedayeen.

This support for the guerrillas increased with the catastrophic losses the regular Arab forces suffered in 1967. In Lebanon there began to appear in the late 1960s a definable press that supported the Palestinians. Ghassān Kanafānī was the leading Palestinian editorialist. He, and those of like mind, called for continued armed struggle as the only solution to the conflict with the Jewish state. But the press of Egypt, and to a lesser extent Jordan, analyzed the reasons for the losses of 1967 and came to the conclusion that though the guerrilla movement was of value, it could not end in the victory of the Arabs. Therefore, the choice had to be made as to whether or not to continue the warfare, using regular forces, or whether to opt for a negotiated settlement. Papers sympathetic to the guerrillas argued that a peaceful settlement would be accomplished at the expense of the Palestinians. Still

ʿAbd al-Nāṣir agreed to negotiate, and some would argue the Jordanian civil war broke out as a result. In the midst of this tension-filled situation, with Arab fighting Arab, President ʿAbd al-Nāṣir died. Egypt's vice-president, Anwar al-Sādāt, assumed his position, though few thought he could take ʿAbd al-Nāṣir's place. Editorial opinion bemoaned the passing of the Arab leader and looked with trepidation toward the future. It is to a study of the post-ʿAbd al-Nāṣir era of the Arab-Israeli conflict that we next turn out attention.

Notes

1 *Al-Ahrām*, February 15, 1959. See also *al-Shaʿb* (Egypt), February 15, 1959 and *al-Akhbār* and *al-Ahrām* on February 16, 1959.
2 *Al-Naṣr* (Syria), February 17, 1959, which had in this one issue extensive coverage and commentary on Jewish immigration.
3 See for example *Bayrūt al-Masāʾ* throughout the middle of February 1959.
4 *Al-Nidāʾ*, February 18, 1959.
5 May 5, 1969.
6 *Al-ʿAmal*, April 21, 1959.
7 May 25, 1959.
8 *Al-Nidāʾ*, December 11, 1959.
9 See among others *L'Orient*, December 15, 1959.
10 *Al-Waḥdah*, July 20, 1959.
11 *Bayrūt al-Masāʾ*, July 20, 1959.
12 *Filasṭīn*, September 7, 1959.
13 *Al-Jumhūrīyah* (Egypt), March 10, 1960.
14 *Al-Naṣr*, February 6, 1963.
15 *Al-Jumhūrīyah* (Egypt), December 12, 1963. Also see Tūfīq al-Muqdasī, *al-Jarīdah* (Lebanon), December 13, 1963.
16 *Al-Baʿth*, December 7, 1963.
17 *Rūz al-Yūsuf*, December 16, 1963, as quoted in *L'Orient*, December 17, 1963.
18 Ghassān Kanafānī, *al-Muḥarrir*, December 19, 1963.
19 *Al-Baʿth*, January 3, 1964 and December 18, 1963.
20 *Al-Ahrām*, December 27, 1963. Kuwait's weekly, *al-Waṭan*, during the first week of January 1964, replied that oil should be kept out of the conflict with Israel. Palestine had already been lost. Let us not, the journal said, also lose the oil. *Al-Shaʿb* [Lebanon], January 9, 1964, wanted to know if oil was not a weapon against Israel, what was it to be used for, buying concubines?
21 *Al-Ahrām*, September 4, 1964.
22 Ibid., June 19, 1964.
23 Kāmil Murūwah, *al-Ḥayāt*, May 7, 1964.
24 *Al-Baʿth*, February 26, 1964.
25 See for example *Al-Thawrah* and *al-Ḥayāt* on November 21, 1964.

26 *Al-Anwār*, October 17, 1965.
27 Mishāl Abū Jawdah, *al-Nahār*, December 2, 1964.
28 *Al-Jarīdah*, April 15, 1965. For the interview with ʿAbd al-Nāṣir, see *Jeune Afrique* 228 (April 18, 1965): 16–17. For the resolutions adopted at Bandung, see *New York Times*, April 25, 1955.
29 *Al-Akhbār*, April 24, 1965.
30 *Al-Anwār*, April 24, 1965. See also *al-Jumhūrīyah* (Egypt) on April 24, 1965 and *al-Ahrām* on April 25, 1965.
31 *Al-Akhbār*, April 28, 1965. Also see *al-Ahrām*, April 23, 1968.
32 *Al-Ahrām*, June 14, 1966.
33 Ibid., May 21, 1966.
34 *Al-Thawrah*, May 24, 1966.
35 Abū Jawdah, *al-Nahār*, May 22, 1966.
36 *Al-Baʿth*, February 20, 1967. See also the same paper on February 13, 1967.
37 See, for example, *al-Thawrah* on June 2 and 20, 1966.
38 Ibid., May 21, 1966.
39 *Al-Baʿth*, July 11, 1966.
40 *Al-Muḥarrir*, June 20, 1966. Baʿth
41 Ibid., January 18, 1965.
42 David Hirst, *The Gun and the Olive Branch* (London, Futura Publications, 1977). *Al-ʿĀṣifah*'s "Military Communiqué No. 1 described a raid that never took place. The Lebanese security forces got wind of the planned operation and arrested the would-be raiders before they set out" (276–77).
43 *Al-Muḥarrir*, March 16, 1966.
44 *Al-Manār* (Jordan), June 14, 1966.
45 *Al-Baʿth*, November 17, 1966. Waṣfī al-Tal was Jordan's prime minister at the time and was viewed as the arch-enemy of the Palestinians who called him Waṣfī Tel Aviv.
46 See, for example, *al-Thawrah* on October 9 and 13, 1966.
47 *Al-Baʿth*, September 29, 1966. See also, for example, *al-Ahrām*, October 10, 1965.
48 *Al-Baʿth*, November 24, 1966.
49 See *al-Difāʾ*, and *Al-Manār* (Jordan) on November 14, 1966.
50 *Al-Baʿth*, November 17, 1966. See also *al-Ahrām*, November 21, 1966, *al-Akhbār* (Egypt), November 22, 1966, and *al-Baʿth*, December 7, 1966.
51 November 29, 1966.
52 See *al-Baʿth* and *al-Thawrah* on August 16, 1966.
53 Kanafānī, *al-Muḥarrir*, August 17, 1966. See also *al-Baʿth* and *al-Thawrah* on August 17, 1966 and *al-Muḥarrir* of September 21, 1966.
54 *Al-Ahrām*, May 20, 1967.
55 See for example, *al-Baʿth* and *al-Thawrah* on May 18, 1967.
56 *Al-Zamān*, May 15, 1967.
57 *Al-Shām*, May 24, 1967.
58 Bāsim al-Jisr, *al-Jarīdah*, May 25, 1967.
59 Abū Jawdah, *al-Nahār*, May 27, 1967.
60 *Al-ʿAmal*, May 31, 1967.

61 See, for example, *al-Nidā'* and *al-Thawrah* on May 30, 1967.
62 Taken respectively from *al-ʿAmal*, *L'Orient*, and *al-Nahār*, June 6, 1967.
63 *Al-Muḥarrir*, June 8, 1967.
64 *Al-Dustūr* (Jordan), June 9, 1967.
65 Abū Jawdah, *al-Nahār*, June 10, 1967. See also *Al-Anwār* and *al-Muḥarrir* on the same date.
66 Adil Malik, *al-Jarīdah*, June 13, 1967.
67 June 21, 1967.
68 Bāsim al-Jisr, June 30, 1967.
69 Saʿīd Frayḥah, June 30, 1967.
70 *Al-Anwār*, July 9, 1967, and *al-Muḥarrir*, July 10, 1967.
71 The Jordanian press had consisted of five dailies but just prior to the 1967 War, a new press law reduced the number to three. *Al-Dustūr* was the only one printed in Amman.
72 July 26, 1967. Also see the same paper of July 27, 1967. *Al-Muḥarrir*, July 28, 1967, argued that the Arabs should support the Blacks in their revolution. Just as the United States had supported the formation of a racist state in the midst of the Arabs, they should back the creation of one in America.
73 *Al-Ḥayāt*, July 9, 1967.
74 For an account of Syrian action, or lack of it, in defending the Golan, see Khalīl Muṣṭafā, *Suqūṭ al-Jūlān* (The Loss of the Golan) (Amman, Dār al-Yaqīn, 1969).
75 See for example *al-Thawrah* on June 12 and 22, 1967 and *al-Baʿth* on June 16 and 28, 1967.
76 That ʿĀmir's death may not have been self-inflicted is to recall a not uncommon Arab comment on the subject, "They suicided him."
77 *Al-Jumhūrīyah*, June 15, 1967.
78 Al-Sayyid Faraj, ibid., June 19, 1967.
79 *Al-Ahrām*, October 6, 1967.
80 Ibid., October 13, 1967. Anwar al-Sādāt visited Pyongyang in May, so the information probably came from North Korea.
81 Ibid., June 14, 1968.
82 Ibid., June 14, 1968.
83 Ibid., June 21, 1968.
84 Ibid., June 28, 1968.
85 Ibid., October 6, 1967.
86 Ibid., October 6, 1967.
87 Ibid., June 21, 1968.
88 Ibid., October 13, 1967.
89 Ibid., October 20, 1967.
90 Ibid., October 6, 1967.
91 Ibid., June 28, 1968.
92 Ibid., October 13, 1967 and June 28, 1968.
93 Ibid., October 20, 1967. The actual quote uses the words "Arab intelligence" which we interpret as "Egyptian intelligence" since Egyptians, while their country was named the United Arab Republic, often referred to themselves as "Arabs."
94 Ibid., October 20, 1967.

95 Ibid., October 6, 1967 and June 21, 1968.
96 Ibid., June 21, 1968.
97 Ibid., June 28, 1968.
98 Ibid., July 12, 1968.
99 In the West Bank thousands of Palestinians were forced into Jordan, thus becoming refugees twice in one life time. In the Golan Heights, approximately 93% of the population, more than 100,000, were driven out, leaving only a small remnant of Druze. (Janet Abu-Lughod, "Israeli Settlements in Occupied Arab Lands," *Journal of Palestine Studies* 11, no. 2 [Winter 1982] 18).
100 *Al-Ba'th*, September 28, 1967.
101 *Daily Star*, July 11, 1969. See also among others *Ṣawt al-'Urūbah* on the same date.
102 *Al-Ahrām*, August 4, 1967.
103 See for example Muḥammad al-Jundī, *al-Thawrah* on August 6 and October 18, 1967.
104 January 29, 1968. There had been earlier criticism of Haykal's allusion to the American bull in the Egyptian press. *Al-Jumhūrīyah*, August 8, 1967, carried an editorial that said that when the editor-in-chief of a UAR paper writes something, it expresses his own opinion and no one else's.
105 Abū Jawdah, *al-Nahār*, April 5, 1968. See also *al-Sha'b* (Lebanon) on the same date.
106 *Al-Jumhūrīyah* (Egypt), October 12, 1968. Also see *al-Difā'* on the same date.
107 Abū Jawdah, *al-Nahār*, April 5, 1968. See also *al-Sha'b* (Lebanon) on the same date.
108 Edouard Saab, *Le Jour*, December 13, 1968. Also see Abū Jawdah, *al-Nahār*, December 10, 1968.
109 *Al-Ba'th*, December 11, 1968. Also see the same paper of January 22, 1969.
110 See for example *Akhbār al-Yawm*, October 18, 1969, and *al-Ahrām*, October 21, 1969. United States policy is based on the 1967 Supreme Court decision, Afroyim vs Rusk, 3(387 U.S. 253 [1967]). Since that case it has been legal for Americans to hold citizenship in a second country as long as they did not seek it.
111 See, for example, *al-Akhbār* (Egypt) on October 22 and November 13, 1969 and *al-Ahrām*, November 13, 1969 for comment before the presidential letter. After the letter, see *al-Rā'y al-'Āmm*, January 27, 1970 and *al-Akhbār* (Egypt), January 27, 1970. Abū Jawdah, *al-Nahār*, February 1, 1970, said American foreign policy in the Middle East was the longest running comedy play in the world.
112 Fatḥī Ghānim *Al-Jumhūrīyah* (Egypt), September 16, 1969.
113 *Al-Anwār*, August 4, 1969.
114 Abū Jawdah, *al-Nahār*, February 13, 1970. Also see, for example, *al-Sha'b* (Lebanon), February 13, 1970; Haykal, *al-Ahrām*, February 20, 1970; and *al-Muḥarrir*, March 3, 1970.
115 Abū Jawdah, *al-Nahār*, July 7, 1970.
116 Haykal, *al-Ahrām*, September 11, 1970.
117 *Al-Thawrah*, September 13, 1970. Not a bad idea according to William F. Buckley who suggested that Israel become the 51st state. "A New Future for Israel," *Current* 144 (October 1972): 62–63.
118 *Akhbār al-Yawm*, June 10, 1967. See also, for example, *Al-Anwār*, June 11, 1967.
119 *Al-Jumhūrīyah* (Egypt), June 26, 1967.

120 Al-Jundī, *al-Thawrah*, August 1, 1967. See also, for example, *al-Ba'th*, August 15, 1967.
121 See, for example, *al-Thawra* and *Al-Ba'th*, both on October 18 and November 9, 1967.
122 *Al-Ahrām*, January 17, 1969.
123 *Al-Anwār*, January 11, 1969.
124 For the American response and Israeli Foreign Minister Abba Eban's exegesis of it, see *New York Times*, January 18, 1969.
125 January 19, 1969. See also Malik, *al-Jarīdah* (Lebanon), January 20, 1969.
126 See, for example, *al-Nahār*, December 15, 1967 and *al-Akhbār* (Egypt), May 20, 1969.
127 *Bayrūt al-Masā'*, October 18, 1967.
128 *Al-Thawrah*, May 21, 1969. Also see the same paper, November 30, 1967.
129 *Al-Ahrām*, February 2, 1968.
130 *Al-Anwār*, May 18 and 19, 1968.
131 *Al-Ahrām*, November 10, 1967.
132 Ibid., September 15, 1967.
133 *Al-Thawrah*, November 12, 1967.
134 *Al-Ahrām*, January 26, 1968.
135 Kanafānī, *Al-Anwār*, November 16, 1967.
136 *Al-Ahrām*, March 23, 1968. Also see *al-Dustūr* (Jordan), March 23 and 25, 1968; *al-Difā'*, March 27, 1968; and *al-Jarīdah*, March 28, 1968.
137 *Al-Akhbār* (Egypt), April 18, 1968.
138 Kanafānī, *Al-Anwār*, May 15, 1968.
139 *Bayrūt al-Masā'*, July 25, 1968.
140 Kanafānī, *Al-Anwār*, June 11, 1968. For criticism of Sirhan's act, see *al-Hadaf*, June 6, 1968; *al-Ahrām*, June 7, 1968; and *al-Dustūr* (Jordan), June 7, 1968.
141 Abū Jawdah, *al-Nahār*, February 21, 1969.
142 Kanafānī, *Al-Anwār*, August 31, 1969.
143 *Al-Akhbār* (Egypt), April 10, 1969, and *al-Ba'th*, September 9, 1969. Eighty-two planes were hijacked to Cuba in 1969.
144 *Al-Nahār*, June 4, 1968.
145 *Al-Thawrah*, October 2, 1968. See also *al-Ahrām*, October 21, 1968, and *al-Muḥarrir*, May 12, 1969.
146 Frayḥah, *Al-Anwār*, December 30, 1968. Also see *al-Sha'b* (Lebanon), *al-Muḥarrir*, and *al-Jarīdah* all on December 30, 1968.
147 December 31, 1968.
148 Haykal, *al-Ahrām*, January 24, 1969.
149 *Al-'Amal*, January 3, 1969.
150 Ghassān Twaynī, *al-Nahār*, April 24, 1969. See also *al-Muḥarrir* on the same date.
151 See *al-Thawrah* on August 20, August 28, September 4, and October 22, 1969.
152 Haykal, *al-Ahrām*, May 9, 1969. Also July 11, 1969.
153 *Al-'Amal*, July 23, 1969.
154 See for example, *al-Ahrām*, September 8 and October 28, 1969; and *al-Ba'th* and *al-Thawrah*, both on October 28, 1969.
155 *Nidā' al-Waṭan*, September 9, 1969. See also Twaynī, *al-Nahār*, October 27, 1969.

156 April 20, 1970.
157 See, for example, *al-Sha'b* (Lebanon), November 4, 1969, and *al-'Amal*, November 5, 1969.
158 *Al-Ahrām*, January 13, 1970.
159 Twaynī, *al-Nahār*, May 14, 1970. See also *L'Orient*, May 13, 1970 and *Le Jour*, May 14, 1970, for official Lebanese and PLO reaction which was also positive.
160 May 14, 1970.
161 See, for example, *al-Yawm* (Lebanon), June 27, 1968; *al-Ahrām*, April 21, 1970; and *al-Thawrah*, August 12, 1970.
162 October 13, 1968.
163 See, for example, *al-Muḥarrir*, October 15, 1968; *al-Thawrah*, October 16, 1968; and *al-Bayraq*, October 17, 1968.
164 *Al-Dustūr*, November 5, 1968. See also *al-Ahrām*, November 7, 1968.
165 *Al-Difā'*, February 11, 1970.
166 See, for example, *al-Ba'th*, August 9 and 20, 1970, and *Fatḥ*, August 18, 1970.
167 See, for example, *al-Ba'th*, September 1, 1970; *al-Thawrah*, September 2, 1970.
168 Abū Jawdah, *al-Nahār*, July 27, 1968.
169 February 20, 1969.
170 Aḥmad Bahā' al-Dīn, *al-Muḥarrir*, February 28, 1970. The *Daily Star* reacted more harshly after a Swissair plane was blown up by the PFLP-GC on February 21, 1970 killing 47 people. "It is the most irresponsible, unforgivable and outrageous act that has ever been committed in the name of Palestine" (February 22, 1970).
171 *al-Ahrām*, September 8, 1970. See also *al-Akhbār* (Egypt), September 9, 1970.
172 Jurj Skāf, *al-Jarīdah*, September 13, 1970. Compare this with his laudatory editorial of September 10, 1970. See also *al-Ahrām*, September 14, 1970.
173 *Al-Hadaf*, September 24, 1970. See also *al-Muḥarrir*, September 23, 1970; and *Al-Anwār* and *al-Thawrah* on September 24, 1970.
174 *Al-Jarīdah*, September 22, 1970.
175 *Al-Ahrām*, September 29, 1967.
176 Abū Jawdah, *al-Nahār*, January 24, 1968.
177 Ibid., October 5, 1968.
178 *Al-Akhbār* (Egypt), October 4, 1967.
179 Abū Jawdah, *al-Nahār*, March 23, 1968.
180 *Al-Jumhūrīyah* (Egypt), May 21, 1968.
181 *Al-Anwār*, July 16, 1968.
182 *Al-Akhbār* (Egypt), August 26, 1969. Also see *al-Ahrām* on the same date.
183 *Al-Jumhūrīyah* (Egypt), February 10, 1969. See also *al-Ahrām*, April 17, 1969; *al-Dustūr*, October 19, 1969; and *al-Ba'th*, August 6, 1970.
184 *Al-Ba'th*, August 31, 1967.
185 *Al-Ahrām*, January 19, 1968.
186 Ibid., January 26, 1968.
187 Ibid., September 20, 1968.
188 Ibid., August 23, 1968; March 7, March 28, April 11, December 5, 1969.

189 See, for example, *al-Difāʿ* and *al-Hadaf* on October 23, 1967 and *al-Jarīdah* (Lebanon), October 25, 1967.
190 *Al-Ahrām*, July 21, 1969. Also see the Egyptian *al-Akhbār* and *al-Jumhūrīyah* on the same date.
191 *Al-Baʿth*, August 1, 1969.
192 *Al-Ahrām*, August 8, 1969. Also see Haykal's article, ibid., October 10, 1969.
193 See Egypt's *al-Akhbār* on January 21 and March 16, 1970 and *al-Jumhūrīyah*, March 3, 1970.
194 *Al-Ahrām*, April 15, 1970. Also see *al-Thawrah*, *al-Akhbār* (Egypt), and *al-Ahrām* on April 9, 1970 and *al-Jumhūrīyah* (Egypt), April 10, 1970.
195 *Al-Baʿth*, December 15, 1969. Also see the same paper on December 23, 1969.
196 August 25, 1970.
197 *Al-Akhbār*, February 9 and *Al-Ahrām*, March 13, 1970.
198 *Al-Baʿth* of July 27–29, and August 17, 1970. *Al-Thawrah* of July 28 and August 4, 1970. See also *al-Hadaf*, August 22, 1970.
199 *Fatḥ*, July 24 and 27, 1970. The "Voice of *al-ʿĀṣifah*" and the "Voice of Palestine," two Palestinian radio stations operating out of Cairo, were so critical of ʿAbd al-Nāṣir's acceptance of the Rogers' Plan that they were shut down on July 28 by the Egyptian authorities.
200 See, for example, *al-Thawrah*, August 12, 1970, and *al-Rāʾy al-ʿĀmm*, September 2, 1970.
201 *Al-Ahrām*, July 27 and 31, 1970. For other editorials in support of Egypt's acceptance of the initiative see *Le Jour*, July 24 and August 4, 1970; *L'Orient*, July 24, 1970; and *al-Muḥarrir*, July 30, 1970.
202 *Al-Ahrām*, August 14, 1970.
203 *Al-Akhbār* (Egypt), September 14, 1970. Also see *al-Ahrām*, September 7, 1970.

Chapter 7

The Arabs Move to the Offensive: 1970-74

The multi-faceted drama of September 1970 was resolved at least in one area with the release of the airplane hostages in later September. In return, Layla Khālid and six others were freed from prisons in West Germany and Switzerland where they had been held for various guerrilla activities. Though this might have been the center of press attention at another time, the Arab world continued to focus on the death of ʿAbd al-Nāṣir. Even though he was castigated earlier by the segment of the press that supported the Palestinian cause, because of his acceptance of a political settlement, in death he was praised and recognized as the center of the lives of both friend and foe.[1]

A two-pronged attack on the Arabs, by Israel and the United States, quickly followed the death of ʿAbd al-Nāṣir. The assault was largely psychological but Arab journalists wrote that it was no coincidence that Israel and the United States should become more strident in their negotiating positions just when the Arabs were leaderless. "Hardly had the tears of the Arab peoples dried, when Israeli-American diplomacy and intelligence began their maneuvers and political and psychological pressure."[2]

Israel's hardened position against Egypt was because it accused Cairo of violating the ceasefire that had gone into effect on the night of August 7–8, 1970 by moving SAMs to the Suez Canal. Israel said it would not return to the talks until the situation on the Canal was "rectified." In support of "rectification," the United States called for the suspension of the Big Four talks that included Britain, France, and the Soviet Union. In a December press conference, Nixon pressed for congressional passage of legislation giving Israel more arms. At the same conference, he said that UN Security Council Resolution 242 was negotiable, implying that Israeli withdrawal from occupied territories was not a certainty. Haykal wrote that all these acts and statements were deliberate provocations to test the Arab will in the post-ʿAbd al-Nāṣir era. The Arabs "will be exposed to a fierce offensive which will try to measure our strength [...]." The Arab enemies were trying to find out how solid the Egyptian front was under its new president, Anwar al-Sādāt, how far the Soviet Union would go to support the Arabs, and what kind of support the Arabs could gather in the rest of the world.[3]

In light of this hostile activity, the Egyptian press asked the international community to force Israel back to the negotiating table. Editorial opinion said Israel was "procrastinating and stalling" in order to solidify its control of Arab territory.[4] When Israel agreed on December 28 to return to the peace talks under the auspices of Gunnar Jarring, the reaction was mixed. The Egyptian press said that Israel's return was not as important as whether or not progress was made. The Syrian press said war was inevitable; the Lebanese press urged

Egypt to persevere; while the press that supported the Palestinian cause said Israel would sabotage the talks, and then conclude a separate agreement with Jordan.[5]

The first 90-day ceasefire, which had been arranged as part of the Rogers' initiative, expired in early November 1970 and was extended for another 90 days. As February approached, the Egyptian press, for example *al-Akhbār* of January 31, was pessimistic about the chances for a negotiated settlement. Nonetheless, President al-Sādāt, on February 4, consented to a final 30-day extension of the ceasefire. Headlined *al-Muḥarrir* the next day, "Al-Sādāt Places Israel Before the Final Choice: Either Begin Withdrawal in 30 Days … Or Resumption of Fighting to Liberate the Land by Force." The Egyptian agreement to extend the ceasefire was then followed by two dramatic Arab announcements. UAR ambassador to the United Nations, Muḥammad Ḥasan al-Zayyāt, said in an interview that Egypt was ready to recognize the "legal existence" of Israel.[6] He was the first Arab official to openly state his country would recognize Israel. On February 23, the Jordanian foreign minister also agreed to recognize the Jewish state if it would withdraw from territory occupied in 1967. Though at least one paper questioned Arab willingness to recognize the Jewish state,[7] opposition to the Jordanian and Egyptian moves was muted.

When Israeli Foreign Minister Abba Eban stated that his country would never go back to its 1967 borders, Arab editorials were quite angry. By making this statement, Eban, in Arab eyes, was rejecting the Rogers' Plan. "What Israel wants is both peace and Arab territory," was a typical response.[8] The hopeful atmosphere of six months earlier, with its ceasefire along the Suez, was dissipating. Along with Eban's declaration, there was another Israeli action that angered Arab editorialists. Gunnar Jarring had submitted a series of questions to Israel and Egypt asking what each side perceived as the final acceptable solution of the Arab-Israeli conflict. Egypt gave its answers to the Swedish ambassador. Israel, however, instead of answering the questions, submitted a critique of Egypt's responses. An exasperated Haykal wrote:

> Egypt has done all it can politically beginning with her acceptance of the Security Council resolution of November 1967 [and ending with] the positive response to Jarring's detailed proposals based on the resolution. No one can ask Egypt to give more than she has. In fact, I can say more than that: Egypt cannot give more than she already has.[9]

President al-Sādāt, in a hardline speech on March 7, declared that the ceasefire would not be extended.

The question was, Now what shall be done? The Middle East's leading journalist was almost never without an answer. Beginning March 5, 1971, Haykal wrote a series of columns dealing with the future of the area. The first of the articles was the most controversial and the questions he raised caused a furor in the Arab press. In it, Haykal analyzed the Arab-Israeli conflict and dealt especially with the role of the United States in the strife. As long as the United States supported Israel, the chance of Arab victory, political or military, was minimal. Haykal, perhaps recalling his column of the American bull, suggested again that in order for the Arabs to win, they would first have to neutralize the United States. In fact, Haykal's article appeared at a time when there was considerable debate within the Arab world about which means would realize Arab goals. Arguments evolved around three possible scenarios. One of them advocated abandoning the United States, attacking its interests in the Middle East, and drawing closer to the Soviet Union. The leading spokesman of this point of view in Egypt was 'Alī Ṣabrī, in 1971 a vice-president of the UAR. The opposite pole advocated embracing the United States, thereby weaning it from Israel. The conservative Christian press in Lebanon advocated this avenue as did the more conservative monarchies of the region. The third approach, and the one Haykal championed, suggested a compromise between the two extremes. Arab political pressure in the future should be aimed at persuading America that its policy was wrong while at the same time maintaining close ties with the Soviet Union. Haykal suggested, in his article of March 5, that the United States be made aware that its policy would eventually threaten its interests in the Arab world, would lead to a decline in its prestige in the region, would bring it into conflict with the USSR, and most importantly, America would wind up supporting the side that would eventually lose. Even assuming the ploy was successful and the United States could be persuaded to stay out of the warfare, Haykal wrote that Egypt's task still would be formidable. He argued that in the next round Egypt would fight alone, and would face what no other country had ever had to face in battle, a natural barrier, the Suez Canal, with a defense line immediately on its edge manned by the Israelis. It would be a difficult task to liberate the Sinai, especially since the other Arab states would not fight but only issue statements and declarations.[10]

Al-Jumhūrīyah, the paper of Egypt's Arab Socialist Union and loyal to 'Alī Ṣabrī, characterized Haykal as a prophet of doom, and this opinion was supported elsewhere. Particularly galling, to those who advocated a military solution to the Middle East conflict, was the attempt to rehabilitate the United States.[11]

Though the debate on what path the Arabs ought to take was important, the more immediate concern was the conflict in Jordan. In spite of an agreement reached in September 1970 to end hostilities, continued tension erupted periodically into fighting. The following month, for example, a man handing out *Fatḥ* pamphlets was killed by Jordanian police. Despite editorial warnings that persistent brawling would drain Arab energies and thus benefit Israel,[12] large scale fighting erupted on January 8, 1971. Practically all editorials outside of Jordan were condemnatory of the Hashimite action and said that their respective governments would not tolerate the liquidation of the commando movement.[13] As the warfare continued to accelerate throughout March, and particularly during the last week of that month, it was clear that the Jordanian forces were going to succeed and that no Arab state was prepared to intervene on behalf of the Palestinians. In February, an official Jordanian spokesman said that of the 10,000 commandos in Jordan in September 1970 only 3000 remained. Two months later, another spokesman announced that between April 7 and 14, 2000 commandos had left Amman.

The commandos found the area under their control gradually diminishing so that by the summer large scale Jordanian attacks were concentrated in the Jarash-Ajlun area. By July 20,

1971, Prime Minister Waṣfī al-Tal could proclaim that there were no more commando bases in Jordan. Throughout the Jordanian crackdown on the guerrillas, editorial opinion was extremely hostile toward the Hashimites. "It is now certain that the Jordanian regime stands against the Palestinian question, the resistance movement and the Arab nation. Therefore in order to reach Palestine, we must pass through a liberated `Amman [...]."[14] *Fatḥ* began calling Ḥusayn the "Butcher of Amman" and Haykal wrote a column describing the rape of a Palestinian woman by Jordan's Bedouin Corps.[15] The Syrian press was somewhat less critical, only because its government was trying to mediate. After the mediation failed in July, criticism became more strident.[16]

Lebanese editorial opinion was also hostile. But of the editorials that appeared as the year-long civil war in Jordan progressed, Ghassān Twaynī wrote one of the more insightful. In it he asked what the implications were for Lebanon of the suppression of the commandos and their flight out of Jordan. Syria was not allowing independent guerrilla operations from its territory. Nor was Egypt. Now the only country that did was Lebanon.

> [...] Our [national] interest is also to stop Lebanese political and ideological hostility toward the Palestinian revolution from becoming a military one. In other words, to stop Lebanon's southern territory from becoming the last, and perhaps the desperate, base for scuttling a peaceful settlement and it [south Lebanon] from becoming the only – and perhaps the last – front.[17]

That Lebanon was becoming more involved, perhaps against its wishes, was disclosed dramatically when Prime Minister Waṣfī al-Tal was assassinated on November 28, 1971 by a new commando group called "Black September." One of the four Palestinians who took part in the killing said that "Black September" had its headquarters in the pine woods of ʿAramūn, south of Beirut. A new front in Lebanon had indeed been opened by the guerrilla movement.

The murder of the man held responsible for the Palestinian defeat in Jordan brought editorial condemnation from all sides. What was most deplored was that Arabs were killing each other rather than focusing on their common enemy. "At the zero hour, which requires careful moves, maximum alertness, and burying grievances [...] an Arab assassinates an Arab official [...]. In whose interest was Waṣfī al-Tal murdered? Does his murder achieve one step in retrieving our lost dignity?"[18] Jordanian editorial opinion, even before the death of al-Tal, was bitter toward the commandos. Papers called Ḥabash and Nāyif Ḥawātmah, leader of the PDFLP, agents of the enemy.[19] As for the head of the PLO, Yāsir ʿArafāt:

> We do not know the name of your father nor that of your mother. We only know you as a masked man. You even hide your eyes. Your nose, ears, and the features of your face are those of a Jew.[20]

The suppression of the commando movement in Jordan, and its expulsion to Lebanon, led to a several-month period of quiet insofar as their activities against Israel were concerned.

The only major strike carried out by a Palestinian group occurred in June 1971 when the PFLP attacked an oil liner flying a Liberian flag but leased to an Israeli firm. The assault took place at Bab al-Mandab at the entrance to the Red Sea. The avowed purpose was to show that even if Israel held part of the Sinai, to ensure shipping through the Strait of Tiran, that shipping still would not be safe since the Red Sea was essentially an Arab lake. Editorial opinion noted this and pointed out how impotent the notion of "secure borders" was for Israel.[21]

As 1972 began, however, the commandos steadily increased their activities, launching raids from their last sanctuary, Lebanon. The Israelis were not long in bringing pressure to bear on Lebanon, as it had done on Jordan. On January 10, in the largest action in a year, Israel attacked into Lebanon. An Egyptian editorial said that the primary purpose of the raid was not to kill or destroy but to drive a wedge between the Palestinians and Lebanese thereby weakening the resistance movement.[22] If editorial opinion in Lebanon was a way of judging whether Egyptian fears were correct, then the raid succeeded. Though some papers, like *al-Muḥarrir,* wondered where the Lebanese army was to help defend the country against attack, the majority of Lebanese editorials were mildly critical of Palestinian abuse of Lebanon's sovereignty. They decried the continued violation of the Cairo Agreement,[23] which called, among other things, for no firing from the Lebanese side of the border and the restriction of commando presence to certain areas within Lebanon.

> None of the Lebanese wants a conflict with the Palestinian resistance [...]. Lebanon, in all of its factions and confessions [...] stands with the Palestine question and with those who fight for it [...].
>
> There is no doubt that the privileges the movement has taken from us so far are far beyond our ability to give [...]. The movement, in fact, has imposed on us things that it should not have insisted upon.
>
> Therefore it has become necessary to reach a new understanding with the resistance movement [...].[24]

As 1972 unfolded, the consequences of the commando defeat in Jordan became apparent. They were heating up the Lebanese border with Israel, to the hostility of a sizeable group of Lebanese. Meanwhile, having driven them from Jordan, the king sought to reassert his claim to the West Bank, a claim that had been diminished by the growth of the PLO. Having suppressed their military capability, King Ḥusayn announced on March 15 his plans for a United Arab Kingdom composed of two states, one Palestinian with its capital in Jerusalem and one Jordanian with its capital in ʿAmman. The reaction to the plan was along predictable lines. The Jordanian press was loud in its praise and the press in Lebanon that traditionally supported the conservative monarchies, for example *al-Ḥayāt* and *L'Orient-Le Jour*, said that the plan was worthy of study, though the French-language paper did publish a column by Samīr Franjīyah on March 16, which was critical of the plan.

Although the reaction in Egypt was slow in appearing, it too was ultimately critical. *Al-Jumhūrīyah* predicted relations between Egypt and Jordan would be broken and called the Hashimite king a traitor.[25]

In *al-Ahrām* Haykal argued that Ḥusayn's plan was aimed at something the Israelis were never able to achieve, the liquidation of the Palestinian cause. Haykal went so far as to write an accusatory column in which he said that Ḥusayn and Israel's Deputy Premier Yigal Allon had met in October 1970 to discuss the implementation of the king's United Arab Kingdom. According to Haykal, after annexing part of the West Bank to Israel, the rest would be demilitarized and the Palestinians would be given some self-rule in consultation with Israel and Jordan. Israel would maintain fortified Israeli settlements along the Jordan River and have military access to them. The Palestinian flag of the United Arab Kingdom would be flown over holy places under Muslim control and over some administrative buildings, but control of Jerusalem would be Israel's. In fact, the Arab administration of parts of Jerusalem would operate under a status similar to that which the Vatican had in Rome. Eventually, wrote Haykal, the plan called for the transfer of populations, Jews from the West Bank to Israel and Christian and Muslim Arabs in Israel to the West Bank.[26]

The Syrian and pro-Palestinian press were obviously quite worried about the possibility that other Arabs might approve of the plan. Shafīq al-Ḥūt, a spokesman for the PLO writing editorially, argued that the Palestinians had said no to Ḥusayn's plan but wondered what the rest of the Arabs thought.[27]

As if to impress the world that they alone would determine their own fate, Palestinian commandos, aided by some new allies, began a series of exploits that culminated in the storming of the Israeli residence at the 1972 Olympics held in Munich. Prior to that, however, there was in May the hijacking of a Sabena Airliner to Tel Aviv. While negotiations were allegedly proceeding for the release of imprisoned guerrillas, Israeli commandos, posing as members of the International Red Cross (IRC), stormed the plane, released the passengers and killed three of the four Arab commandos. Editorials that appeared in the Arab press criticized Israel for using the IRC for its own ends, thus compromising the international organization.

> The world, or at least the passengers of the plane, should understand a basic fact: the reason they are alive today […] is not because of the adventure by the Israelis […] but the hope of the four heroes that Israel would be convinced and release the commando prisoners.[28]

> At the beginning, the operation appeared as though it might succeed. It was more than courage. The Israeli nose appeared under foot.
>
> Arab courage emerged. However, the hijackers contented themselves with warnings and extending deadlines. The Israelis [on the other hand] acted swiftly.
>
> Such has been Arab courage for over a quarter of a century. This is the way they have always treated Israel. They waited. The Israelis have benefited from the time element, and

> heroism ended in tragedy. What happened at Tel Aviv airport yesterday summarizes the Palestine tragedy.[29]

This hijacking was followed on May 30 by an attack by members of the Japanese Red Army on Lydda airport, as a reprisal, said the commandos, for the Israeli duplicity while negotiating over the Sabena airliner and the death of the guerrillas. Once again, Arab editorial opinion was largely in favor of the operation, though there was some question about the use of non-Arabs even if they did sympathize with the Palestinian cause. *Al-Ahrām* argued, however, that the use of foreign allies emphasized the international support that the commando had acquired. In a rare case where the same paper printed commentaries which disagreed with each other, Haykal declined to support the machine-gunning of passengers in a plane terminal.

> [...] [U]nfortunately, I do not consider the Lydda airport incident an ideal example of struggle. With all sincerity, I feel deep sympathy for the three Japanese young men who offered their lives at Lydda airport. [Two died and one was captured]. But I do not believe in struggle by proxy.
>
> Nor do I approve of indiscriminate shooting. I am afraid such action does more harm to us than good with our friends. If the three Japanese had been three Arabs, I would have been enthusiastic, not out of a sense of struggle but in vengeance for the trick played with the Red Cross to kill the three Arabs at Lydda airport.[30]

By far the most spectacular operation, from a media point of view, was the Munich operation, or massacre as it is known in Israel and amongst its supporters. On the morning of September 5, eight members of Black September captured nine Israeli athletes in Munich's Olympic Village, and killed two other Israeli athletes. The guerrillas demanded the release of 200 prisoners in Israel. The Israelis refused to comply. The following morning, after German authorities had agreed to allow the commandos and their captives to fly to Tunisia, German snipers, with Israeli aid, opened fire on the commandos whereupon the Palestinians exploded hand grenades in the midst of their captives. All nine Israelis were killed as were five of the commandos. An indignant world condemned the Palestinian operation, focusing particularly on the invasion of the world of sport and the transgression against the spirit of the Olympics.[31]

Of the tragic ending, the Arab press was uniformly supportive of the commando activity. Arab editorials spoke of the moral hypocrisy of those who tried to judge the Palestinians on the basis of a morality of which the biggest sinner was Israel. Furthermore, the Palestinians ought not to be judged at all since they were the victims and their violence was only a reaction to Israeli barbarity and duplicity, as the use of the Red Cross some months earlier had shown. Over and over it was emphasized that the commandos had no intention of killing their hostages, that it was those who opened fire on the guerrillas and their captives who were to blame.[32] When the Israelis retaliated over the next two weeks, in air strikes that killed over 200 people and in the occupation for over 40 hours of some 850 square kilometers of Lebanese territory, Arab editorial opinion remained defiant. Why did the Western press not condemn these raids as they had Munich? was a question often asked. The Lebanese press particularly was pleased with what it perceived as the fine defense against the attacks put up by the Lebanese army in alliance with the Palestinians. "[President] Franjīyah is not [King] Ḥusayn. [...] And the brave troops of [Lebanon's military commander-in-chief] General Ghānim are not thirsty for Palestinian blood."[33] "Hail to you my country. Hail to our heroic army. [...] Today all our heads are held high."[34]

The Israeli attacks into Lebanon continued into February 1973 when attention was drawn from them to the shooting by Israel of a Libyan civilian aircraft that had strayed over Sinai. In so doing, over 100 people lost their lives. Cries for revenge appeared in all Arab newspapers, no matter their philosophy. The attacks against Lebanon, the Palestinians, and the Libyan aircraft could not go unanswered.

> We used to do our best to draw the attention of the commandos to the seriousness of some of their desperate actions. [...]
>
> Now what can we tell them? Is it our right to advise restraint, or are we now forced to say: If the world is ready to be silent about the madness of force, no one will blame you if you carry out your vengeance in any place.
>
> Strike wherever you want and against any target you choose. If someone wants to turn the world into a jungle, the Israeli wolf will not be the strongest of the beasts.[35]

The Israeli offensive against the Palestinians in 1973 had additionally at least one spectacular success and one embarrassing failure. On April 10, Israeli commandos landed by boat at Ramlah al-Bayḍā, Beirut, got into waiting cars, and proceeded into town where they assassinated leaders of the PLO while they slept. In one night, the Palestinian organization lost its official spokesman and its unofficial foreign minister. The surgical precision with which the operation was carried out, the lack of a Lebanese army presence, the obvious fact that there had been help from inside Lebanon, sent traumatic waves through Arab society. Prime Minister Ṣā'ib Salām resigned in protest. The editorial response to the raid gave different interpretations for the assassins' motives. Some editorialists felt that the assault was designed to further divide Lebanese against Palestinian. Others felt that the raid was for psychological reasons, intended to refurbish the myth, slightly tarnished after the Libyan incident, of Israeli invincibility. Still others said that the whole operation was designed to rob the Palestinians of their leaders and that the American CIA was involved in the operation, aided by the American embassy in Beirut which served as an Israeli outpost and safe-house.[36]

Less successful was the Israeli hijacking of a Lebanese airliner on August 10 in an abortive attempt to capture George Ḥabash who was originally booked for the flight. Several newspapers begged the Palestinians not to retaliate since this would only serve to take the mind of the world off the Israeli crime. Another editorialist was more philosophical, noting that "despite its previous actions [...] Israel can still make mistakes like any other guerrilla organization."[37] On the lighter side, before the pilot of the hijacked plane was released, he was forced to sign an invoice for the "cost" of landing at an Israeli airport. Subsequently, the Israelis submitted the bill, for $1750, to Middle East Airlines, the Lebanese national carrier. Several Beirut newspapers reported the story on August 20 without comment.

We should note, however, that the assassination of a portion of the Palestinian leadership, if it was intended to renew animosity between the Palestinians and their supporters in Lebanon and those who opposed a Palestinian armed presence in Lebanon, it succeeded in its purpose. Perhaps as a prelude to the *guerre civile sanglant* that erupted in 1975, about 40 people were killed and many more injured in one day of fighting on May 2, 1973. After the Israeli attack, tension in Lebanon increased between the two sides. The Rightists, or isolationists as their detractors called them, saw the Israeli attack as being the natural result of an armed Palestinian presence on Lebanese territory. The other side condemned the unwillingness of many Lebanese to help defend the Palestinians and their cause. The conservative Lebanese nationalist press urged the Palestinians not to abuse their welcome and to understand how many Lebanese felt. If a civil war broke out, only Israel would benefit.[38] The papers sympathetic to the Palestinians urged both sides to work out their differences and not to fight. There was nothing contradictory between the desire for Lebanese sovereignty over its own land and support for the Palestinian commandos.

> It is assumed that the Lebanese authorities and the Palestinian resistance movement have come out with a clear conclusion following the long bloody day yesterday, namely that the problems between them cannot be settled by violence. This is because there are two goals complementary to each other that the two sides must see and act on accordingly. The goals are: securing Lebanon's independence and preserving the Palestinian resistance [movement] [...].[39]

Although Palestinian clashes with Lebanese, Jordanians, or Israelis was important, they were far from being the totality of the Arab-Israeli conflict. Thus, the battles in Lebanon between pro- and anti-Palestinian forces became less important as the October 1973 war grew closer. Especially for Syria, Jordan, and Egypt, which had lost territory in 1967, the Palestinian issue was often secondary. Rather, how best to regain occupied land was often the subject of editorial opinion. In the post-ʿAbd al-Nāṣir era, there was increasing talk of the role of oil in the next round with the enemy. This growing speculation on the use of the petroleum weapon had at least two bases: Arab oil was largely in the hands of non-Arabs, and as a result of a decline in their own petroleum resources, the West was becoming increasingly dependent on oil imported from the Middle East. Why not use the West's dependence to Arab advantage, was a frequently asked question.

The first attacks on foreign control came in 1971 when Algeria and Libya nationalized their foreign holdings. Quickly thereafter ARAMCO agreed to allow the Saudis to buy at least 20% of ARAMCO's concession. Iraq and Syria followed suit by nationalizing their oil in the spring of 1972. Flexing their muscles on May 15, 1973, Libya, Kuwait, Iraq, and Algeria stopped pumping for an hour or more in a hostile memorial to the 25th anniversary of the birth of Israel.

Editorial opinion hailed the nationalization of the oil and immediately began to put pressure on the other Arab oil producing states to withhold supplying petroleum to countries friendly toward Israel. The editorialists argued that it was no longer logical to contend that oil should be sold to any country so the income produced could be used to support the confrontation states and the PLO. The fact was, the papers argued, that the West was now quite dependent on Arab oil and in order to receive that oil, it should change its policy toward the Arab-Israeli conflict. "How long will Arab oil continue to pour into the United States while Phantom and Skyhawk planes and American funds pour into Israel?" was a common question.[40] The editorial campaign seemed to have positive results – as did, of course, the increasing Arab control over their own natural resources. Otto N. Miller, Chairman of the Board of Standard Oil of California, wrote an open letter to stockholders and employees asking for more understanding of the Arab point of view on peace in the Middle East.[41] The leader of Saudi Arabia, in a press conference in Brazilia in late May 1973, said that his country would stop shipping oil to countries that "help our enemy." King Fayṣal also made the same warning in an interview with the *Washington Post*.[42] He said Israel was a "burden" for the United States from which America gained nothing. As long as the United States continued its bias, added the King, it would be increasingly difficult for Saudi Arabia to maintain its friendship with this Western nation. President Nixon replied that if the Arabs continued their present course on the use of oil, they would lose their markets. Arab editorial opinion hooted in response.[43]

Besides oil, another area of discussion by Arab editorialists between the death of 'Abd al-Nāṣir and the 1973 war was the relationship of the United States with the Middle East. Two issues can be explored here as exemplary: American military aircraft sold or given to Israel and the role of the presidential elections in the Arab-Israeli conflict. Though there were earlier rumors of new sales of Phantoms to Israel, an announcement was not made until early January 1972. The Phantoms were as much a symbol of the defeat of 1967 as was Moshe Dyan's eye patch. That America would continue to sell them to Israel, though the Jewish state already had defeated the Arabs, showed that the United States was determined to continue Israeli military dominance in the area. Haykal urged his readers not to succumb to the "Phantom myth" but the impact of the announcement was widespread in the Arab press.[44]

That the declaration was made as the presidential election campaign began was also noted. In the eyes of the journalists, election years were never good for the Arabs because the Arab-Israeli conflict became a domestic issue in the United States.

> [...] [T]he intention to supply Israel with more Phantoms has always been there, but it was postponed until the time when Nixon could get the greatest benefit from it in gaining the Jewish vote in the forthcoming elections.[45]

Other papers called the competition for the Jewish-American vote contemptible and noted sarcastically that the path to the White House passed through Tel Aviv.[46]

When Nixon was victorious, there was no joy in Arab editorials. Haykal earlier, on December 1, 1972, had reproduced a White House campaign chart that showed that military aid to Israel during Nixon's first administration alone was over six times as much as that received by Israel under all administrations since 1949. What that implied for the Arabs was not hard to discern. So that when Nixon was inaugurated in January 1973, one paper commented:

> No one talks more about freedom and supporting the people than American officials. Although in point of fact the United States is the worst enemy of the people's freedom and the most ferocious and brutal empire ever known in history.[47]

But to reduce American support for Israel to only a domestic cause would be shallow thinking. Muḥammad Haykal rhetorically asked the question, "Why was the U.S. so supportive of Israel and so hostile toward the Arabs, especially Egypt?" Haykal operated from the premise that America did not want a settlement to the Arab-Israeli conflict. There were several reasons for this. By keeping Egypt busy with Israel, the former could not assume its natural role as leader of the Arab world. This was good for the West since this allowed it to dominate the Persian Gulf. Preoccupation with Israel also meant that the Suez Canal would remain closed, which America also wanted in order to keep the Soviet fleet out of the Indian Ocean. On this issue, there was some friction with America's European allies who did not like to have to pay for their goods to be shipped around the Horn of Africa. But the American desire to keep Soviet influence out of the Asian continent outweighed European needs.

These were international considerations. There were also domestic factors. Haykal did not mention votes from pro-Israeli citizens as a reason for maintaining a pro-Israeli policy. But he did note that Zionist influence in America was strong enough to defeat any issue harmful to Israel even if it was in the best interests of the United States. He also wrote that the Congress, the military, and the CIA were all pro-Israeli. Men like Senator William Fulbright were in a very small minority. The American media was also pro-Israeli so that in the face of all this, the State Department, which might be more even-handed, was powerless. Perhaps most devastating of all, the American public really did not care that much about the Middle East and so let others make decisions for them.[48]

The State Department's weakness was attributed to the strength of Henry Kissinger who was pulling the strings as Nixon's advisor for security affairs. That Kissinger was a Jewish-American of German origin was discussed, with the expected comments that since he was a Jew he would have natural sympathies for Israel, just as there might be some trepidation in Israel if an American of Palestinian origin held the same position. Thus in August when William Rogers resigned and Kissinger was named to replace him at the State Department, there was renewed editorial fear that American policy, which was already pro-Israel, would become more so.

> Kissinger's appointment is an Israeli victory over the Arabs not only in America but also in [this] region as well [...].
>
> His appointment is certainly embarrassing to those Arabs who have been betting on the American horse [...].[49]

In some ways, the other equine in this two-horse race for influence in the Middle East, the Soviet Union, was not doing any better. Since the famous Czech arms deal of 1955, Soviet influence in the Middle East had grown with Egypt as the center of the Russian presence in the area. ʿAbd al-Nāṣir was a good ally and even after his death, the ascension of al-Sādāt appeared to pose no real threat to Moscow's primacy. In fact it was al-Sādāt who signed the USSR-Egyptian treaty of friendship and cooperation in late May 1971. But there were problems in the relationship. First there was, even before the signing of the treaty, the removal of ʿAlī Ṣabrī as vice-president, three days before the arrival of Secretary of State William Rogers. Though the move was allegedly to head off an attempt to overthrow al-Sādāt, still the deposal of Russia's staunchest supporter did not bode well for the Soviets.[50] Then there was the question of a political settlement or a military settlement to the Middle East question. The Soviet Union had consistently favored a negotiated settlement with 242 as the basis. Egypt, too, concurred as we have discussed by supporting both 242 and the Rogers' Plan. But this strategy had ended in failure with the expiration of the ceasefire along the Suez Canal in March 1971. The Egyptians recognized that the maintenance of the status quo was unacceptable. The longer Israel continued to occupy Arab territories the greater claim it would have to them. In this atmosphere, President al-Sādāt announced 1971 as the "Year of Decision," and the phrase was used repeatedly by the Egyptian press.[51] By using it, however, Egypt's leader and its press raised Arab expectations. Haykal had to explain that the decision did not necessarily mean that Egypt would go to war in 1971. "No one imagined that decisiveness meant reaching a final result by peace or war. Decisiveness here meant reaching a decision [as to whether to pursue peace or pursue war]."[52] That Haykal had to write this shows how far into a corner al-Sādāt had painted himself. The common joke of the time was that soon the Egyptian president would issue a decree extending 1971 into 1972.

On November 20, 1971, al-Sādāt told his armed forces that the decision had been made. Egypt would fight. Reaction to the announcement was mixed. *Al-ʿAmal* noted that the condition of no war and no peace was intolerable for Egypt, but would not another war with Israel bring greater disaster for the Arabs?[53] Generally, however, editorial opinion was sympathetic. "In our modern age, the decision to fight has to be done with precision. [...] It would appear Cairo has mastered this technique."[54] Now that the decision was made it was time for careful planning.

Nonetheless, domestic Egyptian pressure for an immediate resumption of military activity grew. The new president did not help himself when on January 13, 1972 he made, in defense of Egypt not resuming military activity during 1971, his famous "Fog Speech." President al-Sādāt began the address by narrating a story about how 'Abd al-Nāṣir in July 1967 had ordered the Egyptian air force to intercept an Israeli party that appeared to be going to try to cross the Suez. However, the Egyptians were unable to attack because fog made visibility impossible. Likewise, continued the president, he had ordered the Egyptian military to prepare to attack Israel in December 1971 but the "fog" of the Indo-Pakistani war then going on made the international situation inauspicious for the Arab side. Student riots erupted the following week. They were due, at least in part, to al-Sādāt's attempt to defend his policy of quiescence after making 1971 a year of promised activity.

> Al-Sādāt's regime is already a prisoner of its own contradictions. It allies with the Soviet Union but counts only on the United States to liquidate the consequences of the Six-day War. [...] It calls for war [...] but opts for peace.[55]

It is in the context of the decision to go to war that we should examine, the course of Russo-Egyptian relations. Though the picture looked generally good for their bilateral relations, apparently the Soviets did not support the decision to return to war. In February 1972, al-Sādāt made a trip to Moscow searching for arms with which to carry out his announced plans. Upon his return, the Egyptian press was jubilant. But rumors circulated suggesting that the trip to Russia had been a failure. He was to get only defensive weapons, and not very new ones at that. "It has become clear that al-Sādāt has failed to obtain offensive weapons from Moscow."[56]

Equally important in analyzing the disintegration of relations were reports of friction between Soviet advisors and the Egyptian military because the latter were being treated condescendingly. Jokes were recounted in which Egyptian honor, and masculinity, were threatened. When the number two man in the Soviet mission to Egypt was deported, it was alleged that this was done because of a joke he told to Chief-of-Staff, Lt. General Sa'd al-Dīn al-Shathlī. According to the Russian, an Egyptian army officer is unable to service his girlfriend and so she asks: "Shall I call in a Soviet expert...?"[57] Defense Minister Muḥammad Ṣādiq also frequently complained to al-Sādāt about Russian slurs.[58] To attribute what followed only to hurt feelings because of an offensive joke would be absurd. But that reports of friction between Russians and Egyptians were wide-spread is perhaps significant. At any rate, on July 18, 1972, al-Sādāt ordered all Soviet advisors to leave Egypt. Three weeks later, the two countries recalled their respective ambassadors, although diplomatic relations between them were not broken. Apparently in order to placate the Soviets, Muḥammad Ṣādiq was removed as Defense Minister.

The machinations between the two countries, especially the deporting of the Soviet advisers, had journalists puzzled. Some Arab editorial opinion was hostile saying that the action left the Arabs "feeling naked" and that they changed strategies like others changed shirts.[59] But the majority of commentaries were supportive of the Egyptian decision suggesting that there was a contradiction between the two countries. The Soviets wanted

Egypt to focus on internal development and thus accept a political settlement so that energy and wealth would not be wasted on another war. Egypt and the rest of the Arab countries, however, wanted to recover the territory they had lost before embarking on national development.[60] A more harsh judgment came from Haykal:

> [...] [O]ur conduct during the [1967] battle was annoying [to the Russians]. [...]
> All peoples may be defeated but we caused [ourselves] more defeat than we caused the enemy. [...]
> Although we were defeated we were ready to correct things and to improve. But when we asked the Soviet Union for advanced and developed weapons, they hesitated and sometimes suggested [...] that the Arabs lacked combat ability. [...] This was unfair. The defeat had already tortured us. We did not need more torturing from the closest of our friends.[61]

Once the decision to fight had been made, the withdrawal of Russian advisors, and all it implied strategically, did not lessen the Egyptian resolve to keep to the military solution. If one examines the Egyptian press, and especially Haykal's columns, there is a continuing theme: If Arab territory is occupied, and if Israel refuses to withdraw in return for peace, then not to fight is an Arab crime. The idea that not fighting was a crime was explained by stating that with the continuation of the ceasefire, the Arabs and the Egyptians would despair. There would be an ever-increasing credibility gap between the rulers and the ruled. The lack of resolve to fight also would encourage Israel to occupy more territory, for example in south Lebanon![62] Haykal even discussed the tactics that should be used in the coming round. In what he described as the theory of the anvil and the sledge hammer, he said that Egypt should be the anvil while the Jordanian and Syrian fronts would be the sledge hammer that administered the heavy blows. The opening of more than one front was crucial because of Israel's ability to deal successfully with any unilateral Arab action.[63]

The march toward war seems fairly clear when one examines the newspapers of 1973. On March 27 and 28, a new Egyptian cabinet was unveiled with al-Sādāt as prime minister as well as president. He also proclaimed himself military governor of Egypt. In April, air raid signals were tested for the first time in a long period. Warned *al-Akhbār*, just because there was a ceasefire did not mean the war was over. In fact it was just the opposite,.[64] A Lebanese paper wrote that Egypt had intended to start the war in May but fighting between Palestinians and Lebanese, plus the urgings of Saudi King Fayṣal to put the fighting off for a short while till the Arabs were better prepared, forced it to postpone the action.[65] Fu'ād Maṭar, a respected journalist and Egyptologist, wrote that his interpretation of the situation in July was that the war would start soon. Egypt was not going to allow the Israelis to strike first since this could erase six years of preparation.[66] And finally a Lebanese newspaper announced on October 2 that it had learned that Syria was in a state of military alert. Syria's reservists and retired military personnel were being recalled to duty.[67]

The October War began on the sixth when hostilities erupted on the Syrian and Egyptian fronts. It officially lasted seventeen days until the United Nations' called for a ceasefire on

October 22. Though initially successful for the Arabs, in the end they lost several hundred additional square kilometers of territory to Israeli occupation besides that which had been lost in 1967. But such is the nature of modern warfare that it is the psychological impact of events, not the amount of territory gained or lost, that allowed the Arabs to lose territory and still claim a victory. For example, there was Arab conjecture that if the Soviet Union had re-supplied the Arab side the way the United States re-supplied Israel, the outcome of the war might have been different. The Arabs realized this and rejoiced at their own strength. They had remained in the field for more than six days, an important point for them. Their armies were not destroyed. They crossed the Suez Canal and destroyed the Bar-Lev line in the Sinai. They used the Soviet SAM missiles well. The view in the Middle East was that the Israelis, for the first time, did not win an undisputed victory, and so they lost. The Arabs, for the first time, did not lose, and so they won.

From the start, Arab editorialists were jubilant about the initiation of the war. They were most of all glad to see their armies reasserting claim to lost Arab territories.

> We can say that the outcome of the war does not interest us because we are overjoyed with the mere breaking out of the war in the way it did. [...]
>
> [...] [W]e can almost say we have won this war because we waged it.[68]

"Whether Israel was taken by surprise or whether it was prepared for fighting makes no difference. One fact remains – Egyptian forces crossed the Canal and Syrian troops marched on the Golan through force of arms and despite Israel."[69] And so the editorials continued throughout the course of the war. No matter that the United States introduced a resolution in the United Nations calling for the Arabs to return to the October 6 lines, in defiance of 242 which had for 6 years called for Israeli withdrawal to the lines of June 5, 1967. No matter that the Americans were landing their aircraft in the Sinai to re-supply the Israelis. The passing of every hour, with the Arabs still fighting, was itself a victory. The shame of 1967 was erased. "If I were passing through other countries, I would not be ashamed to admit I was an Arab."[70]

As the war continued, and even after it ended, there was pride in another area, and that was the performance of the Arab media when compared to 1967. "The pens of our writers this time are moving steadily and the voices of our announcers are calm, thanks to the Arab fighters."[71] Compare this to the Israeli writer, "We shall turn your days into nights, and show you the stars at high noon. We shall put your faces and noses in the mud. We shall make the enemy leaders pay heavily for this. We shall crush your bones."[72] The contrast with 1967 is quite remarkable. There was very little censorship of the press in 1973, even toward the end of the fighting when the military situation favored Israel. Once again, the psychological lift by the Arabs fighting and doing comparatively well gave the writers such a sense of euphoria that even bad news was not that bad. The Arab press also took note of the fact that it was the Israelis whose voices were shrieking on the air waves and whose press was more heavily censored.[73] The take away was that when you think that you are winning, you can afford to tell the truth.

The United Nations Security Council passed resolution 338 which called for a truce to go into effect on October 22. Egypt immediately accepted the resolution and with some hesitation so did Israel. Syria said it would study the matter, and responded favorably to UN Secretary General Kurt Waldheim on the 23rd. There was some initial hostile comment, especially in the Lebanese press. Writers wondered what was to be gained by agreeing to end the fighting. That non-combatant Lebanese should call on the fighting Syrians, Jordanians, Egyptians, and others to stop was incongruous and pointed out by the pro-Syrian press in Beirut:

> Many, be they those who sit behind their desks [...] or those who sit at sidewalk cafes on Ḥamrā' [then Beirut's most fashionable street] [...], have their own theories [about the war and the ceasefire]. [...] We firmly believe that only those who made the plans [...] and who fought so gallantly [...] have the right to say the final world.[74]

Despite the initiation of the ceasefire, Israel continued to fight on the Egyptian front, having succeeded in piercing the Egyptian lines and establishing itself in Africa. Their aim was to capture Suez City and to cut off Egypt's Third Army, which was trapped on the east side of the Suez Canal, before accepting the ceasefire. Unable to stop the Israelis, al-Sādāt on October 24 called on the United States and the Soviet Union to both send troops to Egypt to enforce the ceasefire. America refused and the USSR said it would intervene unilaterally to help Egypt if the United States would not get its client state to abide by the UN call for an end to hostilities. Nixon responded by putting American forces throughout the world on alert. The president was going to war because he could not make Israel accept peace. One editorial suggested that Nixon, for his actions, ought to be put in a straitjacket. Kinder comments on his creating "a day of world horror" said he did it to distract American minds from Watergate.[75]

The situation quickly cooled when Israel, succumbing to American pressure, agreed to stop the fighting. Now it was time for journalists to assess the results of the war. We have already discussed the impact the war had on the Arab mind while the battles were in progress. This may have been the most important aspect of the fighting; that it showed the Arab was not genetically inferior and that he could fight as well as an Israeli.

Haykal, in defending the acceptance of the ceasefire, said that it was acceptable because another aim of the Arabs had been achieved. That goal was to destroy the Israeli-imposed peace, a peace based on the occupation of Arab land. Also the continuation of the war threatened to bring the United States into direct conflict with Egypt. Haykal, in the same article, quoted al-Sādāt as saying:

> We have dealt a blow to Israel which it will never forget. Now we see the United States in the war against us.
>
> This is undoubtedly an honor for us. It is an honor that I did not seek and that I certainly do not desire.[76]

The war also had resulted in several other advantages for the Arab side, according to writers. There was the ending of the myth of the occupied territories being necessary for Israel's security, the most commonly expressed Israeli reason for keeping the land it gained in 1967. "In spite of all its propaganda attempts, Israel can no longer claim that its security is linked to the lie of secure borders, which she had used as a pretext for expansionism." Israel had its secure borders on which to establish strong defenses and the Arab armies had broken through them in hours. Security was not land, concluded editorialists.[77] Another gain, in the Arab view, was that the military victory had led to the "disintegration" of the Israeli economy and the fall of its leaders. The papers of November related in great detail the quarrel in Israel over who was at fault in the war. It also reported and commented on the new taxes and postal and telephone fees that were being imposed in order to pay for the war. Sweetest of all, however, was the resignation of Golda Meir as prime minister. When the announcement was made on April 10, 1974, Arab papers the next day said the resignation was another fruit of the October War. Journalists added: It was a sign of the imminent collapse of the Jewish state. It was time for the people of Israel to begin thinking of alternatives to the Zionist state. Jews and Arabs had never had any trouble living together in the past, only after the Israeli state was created. There was no reason why both people could not return to that past.[78]

For Arab journalists, equally important as the political and military "victories" of the October War was the economic one. There had been talk, from the first days of the war, that the Organization of Arab Petroleum Exporting Countries (OAPEC) would impose an oil embargo on nations friendly with Israel. Though the rumors were not believed, there was still the precedent of 1967 when an embargo had been imposed without much result. But since then, the nationalization of oil had proceeded apace and world dependence on oil imported from the Middle East had grown. Japan, for example, imported more than 99% of its oil. After one week of fighting, pressure grew steadily on OAPEC to take some action. And if it did, "The White House itself will be suffering a very cold winter."[79] OAPEC did act on October 17 to reduce by 5% per month, every month, oil shipments to states friendly to Israel. When this vague plan was followed on the 19th by an American call for $2.2 billion in aid for Israel, Arab reaction was swift. Between October 19 and 21, the Arab oil exporting countries banned all petroleum sales to the United States. The embargo also was accompanied by another blow, a quadrupling of the posted price of a barrel of oil. On October 15, the cost of a barrel of Iraqi crude oil was $2.98. On December 23 that same barrel was valued at $11.65. Though the decision was an OAPEC one, the Organization of Petroleum Exporting Countries (OPEC) was happy to go along with the decision.

Though world opinion strongly criticized both decisions, Arab journalists were unanimous in backing them. On January 8, 1974, American Vice-President Gerald Ford stated that for every oil valve that closed, a farming tractor also would shut down. If there was no oil, there would be no food for the Middle East.

> America does not send food free to the area but on the contrary receives the full price. Consequently, America is not doing us a favor. It is profiting economically from the sale of its surplus food.[80]

> The Arab people consider the oil battle a part of the battle of liberation [...] and not merely an opportunity to increase profit for the benefit of the [oil] producing countries at the expense of [those fighting for] liberation.[81]

> If the world, or at least parts of it, shiver with cold, or will shiver with cold, we, the Arabs, are not responsible for this cold.

> [...] [T]he cold is due not only to the loss of oil but also, and primarily, to the absence of justice, to oppression, aggression, and the occupation of peoples' land and the plundering of their resources.[82]

The embargo did achieve a large number of the changes for which it was designed. In early November, the European Economic Community (EEC) called for Israel to go back to its borders before June 5, 1967. It also supported the legitimate rights of the Palestinian people. Commented Mishāl Abū Jawdah,

> The "Old World" is more reasonable than the [American] "New World." In siding with the United Nations' resolutions regarding the Arab-Israeli conflict and the rights of the Palestinian people, Europe has not become Arab. [...] All it has done was to stand by the higher values for which it has fought many wars.[83]

Within three weeks, Japan followed the lead of the EEC by calling on Israel to withdraw from Arab territory and for the legal rights of the Palestinians to be restored.

The ceasefire called for negotiations. These took place between Egypt and Israel from November 1973 to January of the New Year at Kilometer 101 on the road from Suez City to Cairo. The talks were difficult, suspended once by Egypt, but ultimately successful. They were covered widely in the Arab press, and there was some hostility at what was viewed as Israeli stalling on article 2 of the 6-article ceasefire agreement signed between the two nations on November 11. The article called for Israeli withdrawal to the lines of October 22 when the UN-approved ceasefire was supposed to go into effect. The Israelis argued that since the fighting was going on, no one knew exactly where the lines were. The Egyptian press was skeptical of this line of reasoning, countering that both Super Powers had satellites that were photographing the course of the war and thus could tell precisely where the fighting was at the designated ceasefire time. Equally disappointing for the editorialists were the implications of Israeli procrastination. It meant that Israel was determined not to have a "just peace" in the Middle East.[84]

In defense of the Israelis, they were preoccupied with their war-postponed elections that were held the last day of December. With the victory of the Labor Party, the Arab press said there were no excuses left. The arrival of Kissinger to smooth the process was successful, and on January 18, 1974 Sinai I, a partial disengagement of Israeli and Egyptian forces as well as the withdrawal of Israel from the west bank of the Suez, resulted. The Egyptian press was quite pleased. Though it was recognized and emphasized that this was only a beginning, still the first step had been taken. The Lebanese writer, Mishāl Abū Jawdah, said that Kissinger deserved the Nobel Peace Prize for his efforts while headlining his column "Believe it or not, the trip to peace has begun."[85] The Syrian press opposed the disengagement, because it was a bilateral agreement that did not include their country. Likewise, *Filasṭīn al-Thawrah*, the official PLO organ, warned that the aim of the United States in Sinai I was to conquer the Arabs by dividing them. The paper was also concerned that an Egyptian disengagement would be followed by disengagement on the West Bank, in which Jordan would negotiate and freeze the PLO out of the settlement.[86] The Jordanian press, on the other hand, was careful not to mention the PLO and the latter's claim to any territory evacuated by the Israelis. Reflecting governmental desires to move into the vacuum created by any Israeli evacuation, *al-Dustūr* said: "The near future will judge the new agreement [...] as a step toward a just and permanent peace [...] or just another link in a long chain of maneuvers [...] that Israeli aggression is imposing on the Arab peoples."[87]

Almost immediately there was pressure on the Arabs to respond to the positive American role in the negotiations, specifically by ending the oil boycott on the United States. Generally, editorial opinion was cautious. "As far as we know, all that has happened is that the Israeli enemy has pulled back a few kilometers east of the Suez Canal."[88] Nonetheless, on March 18, 1974, OAPEC ended its five-month embargo of the States. In that period of time, it had confronted successfully the greatest power in the world, been largely responsible for a distinct change in the foreign policy of several economically powerful countries, and managed at the same time to increase by a factor of four the price of its product. But what OAPEC was unable to do was to get Israel to accept 242 or to get the United States to put pressure on the Zionist state to withdraw. Despite, then, the many positive aspects for OAPEC of the embargo, the crucial issue, that issue for which the boycott of oil shipments had been introduced was still unresolved and editorial opinion questioned the wisdom of ending the embargo before complete victory had been obtained.

> They [i.e., the members of OAPEC] have finally lifted the embargo against oil supplies to the United States. What is more, they have decided to increase production, and have declared [West] Germany and Italy friendly nations [and thus eligible for an increased quota of oil] – as if there are any unfriendly nations on the list now that they put the United States on top of the list of friends. Have we forgotten that the United States was and still is the main supplier of weapons to Israel? Have we forgotten that West Germany has paid millions of marks in compensation [for World War II] to world Jewry?[89]

The next move in the step-by-step process was not talks on the disputed West Bank but rather negotiations on the Golan Heights. The bargaining was more prolonged and it appeared that Syria was a more difficult negotiator than Egypt had been. The Syrians, for example, refused to give the number of prisoners they had nor their names, leading to rumors in the United States that the Syrians had killed their hostages. This kind of pro-Israeli propaganda ultimately proved to be untrue, but it did reflect the mistrust that permeated the negotiations. Eventually the Syrians did produce the names of some 68 captives. The Syrian aim in the ploy of the prisoners was to gain Israeli withdrawal from as much of Syria's occupied territory as possible. In the 1967 war, Israel occupied the Golan and in the 1973 war captured an additional 550 square kilometers.

Henry Kissinger returned to the Middle East at the end of February 1974 to resume his shuttle diplomacy, this time centering his activities on Damascus and Jerusalem. This attempt to gain a disengagement agreement did not bear fruit and was abandoned. In fact, the Egyptian press accused the United States and Israel of stalling in order to get the oil embargo lifted.[90] The day after it was lifted, a four-hour fight ensued in the Golan thus leading the pro-Syrian press to bemoan the isolation of Syria and re-emphasize how incorrect the decision to end the embargo was.[91] There appeared to be some hope, however, when Kissinger reappeared in the Middle East at the end of April to resume his shuttle. President Nixon, in need of help to shore up his embattled administration, was allowed to make the announcement for Syria and Israel – a Golan disengagement had been reached. Editorial reaction in Egypt was favorable, though it was emphasized once again that these agreements were only interim ones till 242 could be implemented.[92] Where else, argued the Jordanian press, should the next disengagement take place but on the "Jordanian front," carefully eschewing the words West Bank or Palestine because they might recall for its readers the claims of the PLO.[93]

In Lebanon, the press responded along the divisions that had begun to appear in 1973. Flush with new oil money, Iraq and Libya began to buy into the Beirut press. *Al-Muḥarrir*'s change was the most notable. One day it was pro-Egyptian and the next it was pro-Iraqi and attacking al-Sādāt for deviating from the Nāṣirite tradition. Thus, the pro-Libyan and pro-Iraqi press in Lebanon were against a political settlement with Israel, rejected the disengagement agreement involving Syria, just as they had opposed Sinai I. The editorials in the pro-Moscow (*al-Sha'b*), pro-Cairo (*al-Yawm*), and pro-Damascus (*al-Sharq*) supported Ḥāfiz al-'Asad.

The Syrian press, as one would expect, was the most aggressive in its support of the Golan disengagement. The press went into great detail about the disengagement, enumerating the square kilometers that would be returned to Syrian control, which included all of the territory lost in 1973 plus 112 square kilometers occupied in 1967, including the city of al-Qunayṭrah. The editorials also pointed out that this was, in 1974, the first retreat of Israel since 1948.

> The Israeli leadership has for a long time considered the Golan part of Israel [...] but then it had to withdraw from the city of al-Qunayṭrah. [...] This is a defeat of the enemy's will and destruction of its arrogance. [...] This would not have been possible without President al-'Asad's ability [...] and without the will of the fighters to be victorious.[94]

Syrian and Israeli prisoners were exchanged as part of the agreement.

Some four years after the death of ʿAbd al-Nāṣir, the Arab world had witnessed remarkable changes. The atmosphere in the fall of 1970 was filled with depression. No one seemed capable of replacing the Egyptian president. Yet Anwar al-Sādāt, though originally perceived as a transient, weak figure, had been able to establish himself as the Arab leader. There was, in the process, at least one *faux pas* – the year of decision. But editorialists felt al-Sādāt vindicated himself well after the decision to fight had been made by providing the leadership that allowed the 1973 war to become reality.

The period after the death of ʿAbd al-Nāṣir was also eventful for the Palestinians. Defeated in Jordan, they were forced to concentrate all of their activity in Lebanon. There they encountered editorial hostility from the Christian, nationalist press.[95] That the situation in Lebanon was tenuous for the Palestinians was shown by the April 1973 assassinations of three PLO leaders.

However, the problems of the resistance movement were overshadowed by the approaching 1973 war. As Arab editorials pointed out, the fighting was begun in order to improve the Arab's image of himself and to re-assert Arab claims to territory occupied in 1967. Well planned and initially successful, it also brought oil into play. Editorial opinion felt oil and war did mix and the result of both weapons was a psychological victory in the field and tangible benefits on the international level. The EEC called on Israel to withdraw from occupied territory. Henry Kissinger began his shuttle diplomacy. The era of Zionist expansion ended to be replaced by Israeli contraction. 1974, as the Jewish state reluctantly evacuated territory once considered part of Eretz Israel, was for the Arabs the apogee of the period since 1948. True, the press in Lebanon loyal to Libya and Iraq opposed the agreements that resulted in Israeli withdrawals arguing that they were incomplete and ominously silent on the future of the Palestinians. But these reservations could be ignored for the time being. The countries that fought had the right to determine when to negotiate. Thus the press of Egypt and Syria supported their respective disengagement agreements. Journalists wrote that the 1973 war showed that the Arabs were not to be trifled with. They were strong, united, wealthy, and had world public opinion on their side. If they remained that way, they could virtually dictate their terms, end the suffering of the Palestinians, and bring peace to the region. Everyone agreed that the next step should be one that dealt with all the issues that were still outstanding.

Notes

1 See, for example, *al-Hadaf*, October 1, 1970. Almost any Arab journal published at the time of the death of ʿAbd al-Nāṣir carried laudatory statements. For several days after the death of the president, the Egyptian press contained practically nothing but eulogies.

2 Bāsim al-Jisr, *al-Anwār*, October 4, 1970.

3 *Al-Ahrām*, October 30, 1970. Also see *al-Baʿth* of October 12 and 13, 1970 and *al-Ahrām* of December 12, 1970.

4 *Al-Ahrām* of October 28; December 17, 20, and 29, 1970; and *al-Akhbār* (Egypt), October 28, 1970.

5 *Al-Akhbār* (Egypt), January 4, 1971; *al-Ba'th*, February 15, 1971; and *al-Kifāḥ*, December 29, 1970.

6 *New York Post*, February 16, 1971.

7 *Al-Kifāḥ*, February 16, 1971.

8 Mishāl Abū Jawdah, *al-Nahār*, February 18, 1971. Also see *L'Orient* on the same date.

9 *Al-Ahrām*, February 19, 1971.

10 Ibid., March 5 and 12, 1971. The new strongman of Syria, Ḥāfiẓ al-'Asad, in an interview with 'Alya al-Ṣulḥ, said *al-Ahrām* (i.e. Haykal) was wrong since Syria would undertake fully its duties in any future war. *Al-Nahār*, March 17, 1971.

11 'Abd al-Hadī Nasif, *al-Jumhūrīyah* (Egypt), March 18, 1971. Also see *al-Hadaf*, *al-Akhbār* (Lebanon), and *al-Siyāsah* (Lebanon), all on March 20, 1971 for similar comments.

12 *Al-Akhbār* (Egypt), December 17, 1970. Also see *al-Jumhūrīyah* (Egypt), January 9, 1971.

13 *Al-Ba'th*, January 11, 1971, and *al-Thawrah*, January 12 and 13, 1971. For Egyptian comment see *al-Ahrām* and *al-Akhbār*, both on January 11, 1971. Also see *Le Jour*, January 12, 1971.

14 Shafiq al-Ḥūt, *al-Muḥarrir*, April 1, 1971.

15 *Fatḥ*, April 15 and 22, 1971. *Al-Ahrām*, April 16, 1971.

16 See for example the relatively mild editorial comment of July 18, 1971 in *al-Ba'th* while the mediation is still going on and then compare it to the same paper, August 4, 1971, after mediation had failed.

17 *Al-Nahār*, February 8, 1971.

18 *Al-Jarīdah* (Lebanon), November 29, 1971. Also see *al-Nahār* on the same date. Like George Ḥabash and Wadī' Ḥaddād, al-Tal was a graduate of the American University of Beirut.

19 *Al-'Aqṣā*, December 22, 1971.

20 Ibid., August 25, 1971. Also see an Agence France Presse report in *Le Soir*, December 2, 1971, saying that 'Arafāt's father was a Jewish Albanian.

21 *Al-Anwār*, June 15, 1971, and the newly merged *L'Orient-Le Jour* on the same date.

22 *Al-Akhbār* (Egypt), January 12, 1972.

23 See details of the Cairo Agreement on page 143.

24 *Al-'Amal*, March 2, 1972. For similar editorials also see *al-Nahār* and *L'Orient-Le Jour* both on January 12, 1972. *Al-Muḥarrir*'s criticism of the Lebanese military can be seen on the same date.

25 March 16, 1972.

26 *Al-Ahrām*, March 24, 1972. Also see the Egyptian *al-Jumhūrīyah*, March 20, 1972, and *al-Akhbār*, March 27, 1972.

27 *Al-Muḥarrir*, March 17, 1972. Also see *al-Ba'th*, March 21 and 22, 1972; and *Filasṭīn al-Thawrah*, August 30, 1972.

28 *Al-Nahār*, May 10, 1972. For similar comment also see *al-Yawm* and *al-Liwā'* on the same date.

29 *Al-'Amal*, May 10, 1972. Also see *al-Ba'th* on the same date.

30 June 9, 1972. For the editorial in the same paper in praise of the operation see June 1, 1972. Also see *al-Akhbār* (Egypt), *al-Yawm*, *al-'Amal* and *al-Ahrām* all on June 1, 1972 and *al-Nahār*, June 8, 1972.

31 See a series of venomous letters in *Time* magazine, October 2, 1972.

32 To show how Arab editorialists defended the commandos in the tragic ending see *al-Jumhūrīyah* (Egypt), September 6, 1972. On September 7, see Edouard Saab, *L'Orient-Le Jour*; *al-Akhbār* (Egypt); 'Alī Ḥamdī al-Jammāl, in *al-Ahrām*; René Aggiouri in *al-Safa'* and Sa'id Frayḥah in *al-Anwār*.

33 *L'Orient-Le Jour*, September 20, 1972. Also see *al-'Amal*, *al-Nahār*, and *al-Anwār*, September 9; and *al-Ba'th*, September 11, 1972.

34 Sa'īd Frayḥah, *al-Anwār*, September 17, 1972.

35 Haykal, *al-Ahrām*, February 23, 1973. Also see *al-Thawrah*, February 25, 1973; and René Aggiouri, *al-Safā'*, April 11, 1973.

36 See, for example, *al-Akhbār* (Egypt), April 11, 1973; *al-Ba'th*, April 23, 1973; and *al-Muḥarrir*, April 24, 1973.

37 Abū Jawdah, *al-Nahār*, August 12, 1973. Also see *al-Ahrām*, August 13, 1973, which urges that there be no retaliation since that would result in ending world condemnation of the Israeli action.

38 Aggiouri, *al-Safā'*, May 7, 1973.

39 *Al-Muḥarrir*, May 3, 1973.

40 *Al-Jumhūrīyah* (Egypt), April 1, 1973. For similar opinion see *al-Akhbār* (Egypt), December 30, 1971, February 6, 1973, and August 9, 1973. Also see *al-Ahrām*, December 6, 1972.

41 *New York Times*, August 3, 1973. For kudos supporting the letter, see for example, *al-Ahrām*, August 6, 1973.

42 July 6, 1973.

43 See, for example, *al-Sha'b* (Lebanon), and *al-Ḥayāt*, September 7, 1973; and *al-Jumhūrīyah* (Egypt), September 11, 1973.

44 *Al-Ahrām*, January 7, 1972. Also see *al-Ba'th*, January 3, 1972, and *al-Nahār*, January 4, 1972.

45 *Al-Ahrām*, January 4, 1972. Also see *al-Akhbār* (Egypt), on the same date.

46 *Al-Jarīdah* (Lebanon), August 25, 1972, and *al-Ahrām*, September 4, 1972.

47 *Al-Akhbār* (Egypt), January 22, 1973.

48 *Al-Ahrām*, June 18, 1971.

49 Abū Jawdah, *al-Nahār*, August 24, 1973. Also see *al-Muḥarrir* and *al-Bayraq* on August 23, 1973.

50 Al-Sādāt also replaced the Soviet Union's closest ally, Sha'ārī Jumā'a, as head of the Secret Police. These moves placed the Soviets on the horn of a dilemma – did they turn against the al-Sādāt government and lose a foothold in the Middle East, or agree to the sacrifice of a personal ally?

51 See, for example, *al-Akhbār*, June 9 and 24, 1971, and *al-Ahrām* on June 9 and 25, 1971.

52 *Al-Ahrām*, November 5, 1971.

53 November 25, 1971.

54 *Al-Muḥarrir*, December 30, 1971.

55 Edouard Saab, *L'Orient-Le Jour*, January 19, 1972.

56 Ibid., February 8, 1972. Also see Fu'ād Maṭar, *al-Nahār*, on the same date.

57 Maṭar, *al-Nahār*, March 23, 1972. Also see *Le Soir*, February 17, 1972.

58 Robert O. Freedman, "Soviet Policy toward Sadat's Egypt From the Death of Nasser to the Fall of General Sadek," *Naval War College Review* 26, no. 3 (1973): 63–79.
59 *L'Orient-Le Jour* and *al-Nahār*, both on July 19, 1972.
60 Amīn A'war, *al-Muḥarrir*, July 20, 1972, and Edouard Saab, *L'Orient-Le Jour*, July 21, 1972.
61 *Al-Ahrām*, August 11, 1972. The journalist Fu'ād Maṭar wrote a two-volume work on the deterioration of the Moscow-Cairo relationship with the thesis that it steadily declined from the day 'Abd al-Nāṣir died. The author argues that the Russians loved the president but the Egyptian military disliked the Russians. See particularly volume two, *'Ayna Aṣbaḥa 'Abd al-Nāṣir fī Jumhūrīyah al-Sādāt: Rusīya al-Nāṣirīyah wa Miṣr al-Miṣrīyah*, (What Has Become of 'Abd al-Nāṣir in al-Sādāt's Republic: Nāṣirite Russia and Egyptian Egypt), (Beirut: Khayats, 1972).
62 *Al-Ahrām*, June 16 and December 8, 1972.
63 Ibid., December 15, 1972.
64 Mūsā Ṣabrī, April 5, 1973.
65 Frayḥah, *al-Anwār*, June 7, 1973.
66 *Al-Nahār*, July 12, 1973.
67 *Al-Ḥayāt*.
68 Ghassān Twaynī, *Al-Nahār*, October 7, 1973.
69 Bāsim al-Jisr, *al-Anwār*, October 7, 1973. See also, for example, *al-'Amal*, October 9, 1973, or, literally, any other Arab paper on the same date.
70 *Al-'Amal*, October 10, 1973. Also see, for example, *al-Ḥayāt*, on the same date.
71 *Al-Ba'th*, October 16, 1973.
72 Quoted in *Newsweek*, October 22, 1973.
73 *Al-Ahrām*, October 10, 1973. For a discussion of some of the failures of the Israeli information media during the October War, see Elias Shoufani, "The October War and the Israeli Press," in *Middle East Crucible: Studies on the Arab-Israeli Was of October 1973*, ed. Naseer H. Aruri (Wilmette, Illinois: AAUG Press, 1975), 173–97. One of the more interesting statements in the article came from an Israeli who said that the Hebrew transmissions from Egypt and Jordan were more informative than the Israeli broadcasts. Even the *New York Times*, October 20, 1973, admitted war censorship was most severe in Israel.
74 *Al-Sharq*, October 23, 1973. Also see *al-Sha'b* (Lebanon) on the same date. For opinion adverse to the acceptance of the ceasefire, see *al-Muḥarrir*, October 25, and *al-Anbā'*, October 26, 1973.
75 See for example, *al-Anwār* and *al-Nahār*, both on October 26, 1973.
76 *Al-Ahrām*, October 26, 1973. A similar statement about not wanting to fight the United States may be found in al-Sādāt's autobiography, *In Search of Identity* (New York: Harper Collins, 1978), 290.
77 *Al-Akhbār* (Egypt), October 25, 1973. Also see the same paper on May 9, 1974.
78 *Al-Safīr*, *al-Ahrām*, and *al-Akhbār* (Egypt), all on April 11, 1974. Also see *al-Thawrah* on February 26, 1975.
79 'Alyā al-Ṣulḥ, *al-Muḥarrir*, October 15, 1973.
80 'Alī Ḥamdī al-Jammāl, *al-Ahrām*, January 10, 1974.
81 Ibid., January 7, 1974. Also see *al-Ba'th* and *L'Orient-Le Jour*, both on January 8, 1974.
82 Ḥanna Minah, *al-Ba'th*, November 13, 1973.

83 *Al-Nahār*, November 7, 1973.
84 *Al-Akhbār* (Egypt), December 3, 1973, and *al-Ahrām*, December 25, 1973.
85 *Al-Nahār*, January 18, 1974. Also see *al-Akhbār*, January 18, 1974, and *al-Ahrām*, January 19, 1974.
86 *Filasṭīn al-Thawrah*, January 23, 1974. Also see *al-Nidā'* and *al-Muḥarrir* both on January 20, 1974.
87 January 18, 1974.
88 *Al-Muḥarrir*, March 7, 1974. Also see *al-Sha'b* (Lebanon), on the same date.
89 *Al-Liwā'*, March 19, 1974. Also see *Lisān al-Ḥāl*, March 19, 1974.
90 See for example Egypt's *al-Jumhūrīyah*, March 11, 1974, or *al-Akhbār*, March 7, 1974.
91 See among others *al-Muḥarrir*, March 20, 1974.
92 See for example *al-Akhbār* (Egypt), May 30, 1974.
93 *Al-Dustūr* (Jordan), June 1, 1974. Also see the same paper of May 30, 1974.
94 Aḥmad Iskandar Aḥmad, *al-Thawrah*, June 1, 1974. Also see *al-Ba'th*, June 3, 1974.
95 Lebanese hostility toward the Palestinians extended beyond the pages of newspapers, and to be a Palestinian in any Arab country was not easy – witness what occurred to them in Kuwait in 1991 and 1992. Though dated, an example of what it was like to be a Palestinian during the 1960s and early 1970s can be found in the mildly anti-Arab, anti-Lebanese book by Fawaz Turki, *The Disinherited: Journal of a Palestinian Exile* (New York, NYU Press, 1972).

Chapter 8

Al-Salām or *Al-Istislām?* 1974-78

The events of 1973–74, from the October War through Sinai I, were remarkable, and some Arab countries, led by Egypt, wished to thank Washington for forcing Israel to retreat from its post-1967 borders, and did so by opening wider their doors to the West. While this policy developed, the Arabs appeared more assured of themselves, since, as a result of the 1973 war, they could negotiate without shame. The problem, as they saw it, was how to get Israel to go the next step and agree to implement Security Council Resolution 242. Russia had no influence over Israel and thus could not get Tel Aviv to the bargaining table. But America, with its massive military and economic ties to the Jewish state, did. When it came to fighting, the Arabs used Soviet SAM. When it came to a political settlement, they preferred Uncle Sam. Thus the need for an opening to the West, as it was called in the Arab press. It was, in a sense, a revolutionary idea. But it was one of the three options (opposition, neutralization, or befriending) that had long been debated when considering policy toward the United States. In Egypt, the major advocate of the principle of opposition to the United States was ʿAbd al-Nāṣir. Now that al-Sādāt had determined that befriending the United States was the best policy to gain Israeli concessions, the main supporter of neutralizing the United States, Muḥammad Haykal, was dismissed.

The removal of one of Egypt's great temples, for 17 years editor of *al-Ahrām*, was a result of the growing conflict between himself and al-Sādāt. Haykal wrote in his newspaper on January 11, 1974 that US policy in the Middle East had as its goal the removal of the Soviet Union from the area. Israeli moves were aimed at "completely isolating Egypt" from the other Arab states thereby allowing the enemy to freeze the situation as it now stood with the foe still occupying Arab land. One week later, he wrote that when Kissinger went to Israel to negotiate, he met not with one strong leader but with several groups. Haykal liked this since the search for peace "should be a common effort" taking into account differing opinions. Haykal said that this was the way Egypt should operate, taking into consideration various points of view. The implied criticism in both articles of al-Sādāt's policy was obvious. Then on February 1 he published in his weekly column a strong rebuke of the United States just as al-Sādāt was encouraging closer contacts with America. The editor of *al-Ahrām* argued that America had not changed, that it was still opposed to Arab goals, for example unity, and would use its power to protect Israel. Therefore, a policy of friendship with it was a mistake. On the same day his article appeared, he was fired.[1]

The Egyptian campaign of friendship with the West was now bannered in that nation's editorials.

> Our approaching the Soviet Union for arms was not at the beginning a matter of choice but was imposed on us. [...] [During the first years after the Egyptian revolution] the Soviet Union was the only state that agreed to provide Egypt with arms after the West had adopted an attitude of hostility toward the Egyptian revolution and refused to arm Egypt. [...]
>
> If the United States, in particular, and the west European states, in general, are really desirous of atoning for their mistakes and sins against the Arab nation over the past twenty years [...] then it would not be logical for us to shut the doors or refuse to have several sources of arms.[2]

The press, which opposed any political settlement, opposed al-Sādāt's policy. When President Nixon arrived in the Middle East in June 1974 on a triumphant tour and also to avert attention from his domestic problems, the anti-Western press called him "The American fox in the Arab chicken coop."[3] At the same time, the Egyptian press and the conservative Lebanese press praised and thanked him for his efforts for the cause of Middle East peace.[4] When Watergate forced the American president to resign, reaction was also divided toward him and his accomplishments. Wrote a supporter of the opening to the West,

> The Lebanese and Arabs are sorry for this not-so-great ending, as they see it, of a great American president. They are even more sorry because he leaves [office] in the middle of the road in respect to the Middle East crisis.[5]

Responded the editor of the pro-Libyan *al-Safīr*,

> Neither the millions of welcomers in Cairo and Alexandria, nor the welcome he was given by Arab kings and president in other capitals, nor the resumption of oil shipments to the Americans, nor the disengagement agreements in Sinai, the Golan, (and Jordan[!]) has done any good for Nixon. He started off a Zionist and ended as a fanatical Arab nationalist in the eyes of some of our Arab leaders. [...]
>
> Those who support [Nixon] are now left with only one of two choices; either prepare for war [...] or step down to save face, as he did.[6]

The coming of Nixon to the Arab world, the meetings at Kilometer 101, and the negotiations surrounding Israeli withdrawals were all part of what can be termed the euphoric atmosphere that enveloped most of the Arabs after the October War. Supporting this ethereal sense was the knowledge that Arab unity and military might had shaken Israel. The good fight had been waged, Arab masculinity restored, now even Israel could be accepted as a member of the Middle East community of nations. Resolution 338 reaffirmed 242 and the latter implicitly recognized the Jewish state. When Egypt and Syria approved 338, they accepted Israel. This was not a theme often heralded in the Arab press, but it was taken for granted. The opening to the West by Egypt was a natural corollary of this policy. The Arabs had trod this path once before, when Egypt and Jordan had acquiesced in the Rogers Plan, but that attempt had failed. The 1973 war changed the equation and now even Syria was willing to join the camp which agreed on a negotiated settlement. Where did this leave the Palestinians? *Al-Muḥarrir* reported that the PLO was debating the issue and felt that the inclination within the Palestinian movement was to participate in the peace talks to be held in Geneva. The PLO then would agree to establish a Palestinian national authority over any part of Palestine that was evacuated. Presumably this would be the Gaza Strip, the West Bank, and perhaps the Himmah region that Syria held before 1967. The newspaper emphasized that the Palestinians would accept this mini-state "not as a substitute for historical [Palestinian] rights [to all of Palestine] but rather as a step on the path of struggle leading to those rights."[7] Put in other terms, the PLO would go to Geneva if invited but would object to the agenda being 242 since 242 recognized the Israeli claim to part of Palestine, and referred to the Palestinians only as refugees.

To even consider going to Geneva meant the Palestinians were in a difficult position. There was covert opposition from Jordan which coveted the West Bank it had ruled for 19 years. Further, Syria and Egypt, now that they were formally committed to a negotiated settlement, probably would not aid nor look with favor upon Palestinian guerrilla activity that could scuttle their peace plans. Finally there was overt Israeli hostility toward the PLO, viewing it as a terrorist organization that had as its aim the destruction of the Jewish state.[8] In order to legitimize the PLO and thereby make it more palatable to the international community, the Arab heads-of-state, minus an angry King Ḥusayn of Jordan, met in Algeria and on November 27, 1973 recognized the PLO as the sole, legitimate representative of the Palestinian people. Editorial opinion was reserved but generally favorable to the resolution, except for the Jordanian press which was noticeably quiet, thereby reflecting official displeasure with the decision.[9] The question of the representation of the Palestinians at Geneva did not become a larger issue because there was only one meeting of the peace conference, and it was boycotted by Syria. Though it did not seem to be going any place at that moment, there was still the possibility that the conference would be resumed, if a negotiated settlement seemed likely, and so the question continued to be debated in the press, Should the PLO attend? As it seemed likely the PLO would go, the next question asked was what would the attendance of the PLO mean? It would mean that the PLO expected to negotiate with Israel, thus recognizing it, since the Jewish state would be there. By extrapolation, it would mean sharing historic Palestine, or put in other words accepting 242. The organ of the PLO, *Filasṭīn al-Thawrah*, recognized that, to some Palestinians, the recognition of the Jewish state was treasonous. But what would result if the PLO did not attend and negotiate for a mini-state? Jordan and Israel would work out an arrangement that would effectively exclude the Palestinians. Thus, no matter how loathsome, the Palestinians would have to negotiate.

> The exercise by the Palestinian people of its national rights on the territory that may be wrested from occupation [...] is the only national goal for which our people are fighting against Zionist occupation and Jordanian tutelage.[10]

This point of view was opposed by the Arab Liberation Front, the Popular Front for the Liberation of Palestine, the Popular Front for the Liberation of Palestine-General Command, Libya, Iraq, South Yemen, and Algeria. The problem with a negotiated settlement of the Palestine question was that in a settlement, Israel would probably keep over 75% of historic Palestine, leaving the remainder for the Palestinians who would thus be living in a non-viable state. For the press that felt this answer was no solution, the only alternative was to make sure the political avenue was closed by sabotaging it in Syria and Egypt if necessary, and returning to the battlefield.[11]

But the PLO, judging by its own paper's editorials, had decided to seek a political settlement. In order to further enhance Palestinian claims and to enhance the PLO's status, the League of Arab States decided to gain world-wide recognition of the Palestinian nation by bringing the issue before the United Nations. In advance of New York, the Arabs met at the Rabat Summit where the league, this time including reluctant Jordan, reaffirmed the PLO as the "sole legitimate" representative of the Palestinian people and gave to it the right to establish a Palestinian national authority over any part of Palestine that could be liberated. On November 13, 1974, Yāsir 'Arafāt received a tumultuous welcome as he rose to address the United Nations General Assembly where he delivered his famous and controversial "gun and olive branch" speech. Undeterred by dogs sniffing his bags at John F. Kennedy airport looking for hashish, President Sulaymān Franjīyah of Lebanon acted as the official representative of the Arab League in escorting 'Arafāt.

The Arab press was aglow. The ultimate humiliation had been handed to the Israeli enemy. "Israel is now witnessing the collapse of all that it built on the ruins of the Palestinian homeland."[12] Even that portion of the Lebanese press which was worried about the presence of the commandos in its country had warm praise for 'Arafāt, calling him a statesman.[13]

Almost simultaneous with the November 1974 appearance of the head of the PLO in New York, Kissinger returned to the Middle East. His step-by-step policy having earlier stalled, he came to encourage momentum. Editorials were filled with warnings, both to the United States and to the people of the Middle East. Could America be trusted? Why was Kissinger coming at the same time President Ford was threatening Arab oil producers? What was to be done about Israeli intransigence over the PLO when the latter had been given a mandate by the Arab League and the United Nations?

> America's history of harming the Arabs could fill volumes. Some of the harm is irreparable. Just the same the Arabs have given America an historic opportunity to change its stand in the area. […] Thus far the Arabs have received nothing from America […] and whatever they have gained, they won through thousands of martyrs.[14]

Outside of the Egyptian press, which consistently denied the possibility, Arab editorial fear was that with Kissinger's appearance, Egypt would agree to a separate peace with Israel. This specter had appeared briefly with Sinai I which Syria and the PLO opposed if it did not lead to other results.[15] Though the Kissinger trip in November 1974 was apparently unsuccessful, he flew back to the Middle East during the second week of February 1975. A few days before he returned, the Egyptian press wrote editorially that it did not consider the Geneva conference the only way to a Middle East settlement.[16] This statement confirmed the worst fears of Syria and the PLO: the Egyptian aim was a unilateral settlement with Israel. Egypt's journals, reflecting governmental thinking, was suggesting that there were other alternatives to negotiations. From the point of view of those opposed to Egypt making its own separate peace, the suggestion to bypass Geneva actually meant that Cairo intended to exclude the Soviet Union, which was co-chairman at Geneva, as well as the PLO and Syria, which were more intransigent then Egypt in dealing with Israel and America. Warned the Syrian press and a PLO journal:

> The participation of the Soviet Union in the [Geneva] conference deprives America of imposing its own solution. This [USSR participation] is a hindrance to the plans which aim at decreasing Soviet weight in the Middle East question [...]. So Geneva must be held immediately [...] because the alternative is the retrieval of land and rights by the only other option we have [war] which Israel knows very well.[17]

> The Palestinian revolution does not object to any partial withdrawal that will be a step on the road to liberating occupied territory. The revolution, however, rejects such partial withdrawal if it is meant to be a poisonous bait for breaking up Arab strength and striking at the Palestinian revolution.[18]

> Attempts to fragment the problem and circumvent a just solution by advancing incomplete and unilateral proposals are continuing [...]. These attempts are aimed at destroying Arab solidarity.[19]

Dramatically, Kissinger ended his shuttle in late March having failed to gain concessions from Israel. The day after the Secretary of State returned home, Egyptian editorial opinion blamed the United States, not Israel, for the lack of success:

> Arab logic refuses to believe that Kissinger's failure to move another step toward peace is due to Israeli rejection or intransigence. It is basically due to a lack of determination by America to carry out this step. Arab logic goes so far as to assume that America knew in advance of the [Israeli] rejection, and diplomatically set out to attribute this failure to Israel so the United States might continue to appear as the angel of peace safeguarding its interests in the Arab World.
>
> Therefore, Kissinger did not fail, but fulfilled his mission.[20]

However, when President Ford announced that the failure of the shuttle diplomacy was Israel's fault, and that as a result the United States was reassessing its policy toward the Jewish state, and suspending arms shipments there, the Egyptian press changed its tune. "The reason for the failure [of Kissinger] is the unreasonable and unacceptable Israeli conditions. Even in America itself officials blame Israel for obstructing the mission of the Secretary of State."[21]

Presidents Ford and al-Sādāt met in June 1975 in Salzburg to consider alternatives thereby giving rise to further speculation that another Sinai agreement was in the offing. Syria's President Ḥāfiẓ al-'Asad went to Jordan, apparently to bring the two countries closer together to face the possibility of being left out of another round of Israeli withdrawals. The Palestinians, through their journal, were apprehensive.

> [...] American imperialism is attempting to arrange conditions in the region while ignoring or denying the national and independent entity of the Palestinian people [...]. But peace in the Middle East will have to be a Palestinian peace in its essence and foundation or there will be no peace at all. [22]

Still Egypt seemed determined to proceed with another withdrawal from the Sinai while its press maintained that such an act was not an end in itself but merely a step on the way to complete peace. Editorials reassured the other Arab states that Egypt was not abandoning them.[23] On August 14, Egypt announced that the differences between itself and Israel over another Sinai withdrawal had narrowed and that Kissinger would soon resume his shuttle. When the text of Sinai II was produced on September 1, besides calling for further Israeli withdrawals into the Sinai, it contained two interesting articles. Article One renounced the use of force between the two sides and Article Nine said the agreement had no time limit. Outside of Egypt, Arab editorial opinion was highly critical. For the Syrian press, Israel's avowed purpose was to conquer the Arabs by dividing them. Commentaries argued that no Arab state had the right to make peace with Israel. Peace was a common effort, just as the October War had been.[24] Elsewhere, disapproval was harsher. In Lebanon, which now had pro-Iraqi and pro-Libyan papers, editorials virtually accused al-Sādāt of treason. He had sold the Arab cause for a few kilometers of sand and the Abū Rudayyis oil fields in Sinai that would soon go dry. Furthermore, through his actions, he had consecrated an American presence in the area, recognized the state of Israel, and in fact completely capitulated without visible lasting reward.[25]

Sinai II was even more ominous for the Palestinians. They were not a party to the agreement and it seemed to them that their national interests would be sacrificed in a peace that Israel and the United States would engineer. Several papers stated that Sinai II meant the end of the Arab struggle for the liberation of Palestine, since the leading Arab state had been neutralized. They further argued that it would mean an end to the Palestinian movement. But the Palestinians were not likely to accept their relegation to the Arab scrap heap without a battle. They would fight to preserve their claim to national rights. The atmosphere was reminiscent of 1970 when 'Abd al-Nāṣir accepted the Rogers' Plan that resulted in a ceasefire between Israel and Egypt but brought out Arab differences, or contradictions, which culminated in the Jordanian civil war of 1970–71. Though the result of Sinai II would be a truce between Israel and Egypt, in the rest of the Middle East it would create uneasiness and ultimately create an "internal war between those who accept and those who reject" Egypt's moves.[26]

Though Sinai II is a convenient focus for the beginning of the Palestinian problems that will come to a head in the Lebanese civil war, Israeli pressure against them became more intense at the time of the Golan disengagement. On May 16, 1974, Israeli air raids hit near Sidon causing considerable damage to Palestinian camps at Nabaṭīyah and 'Ayn al-Ḥilwah. The following day there were Israeli sea attacks on the Rashidīyah camp near Tyre. The following month, within hours of Nixon's departure from the area, a five-day aerial bombardment of Lebanon began in which scores were killed. By these attacks Israel was attempting to put pressure on the Lebanese government to end commando activity from its territory. The Palestinians, on the other hand, were trying to put pressure, not only on Israel, but on the Arab states so the latter would not abandon the resistance movement. Pro-commando papers stated again that the Sinai and Golan disengagement agreements meant that for all practical purposes the state of war between the Arabs and Israelis was over and the next step would be the suppression of the commando movement. "As for the war of Lebanon, it is the real Palestinian war [...] and it is the war [...] that will determine the destiny of the Palestinians [...]."[27]

The Israeli assaults were having their desired effect. Lebanese began to flee the south and criticism of the Palestinian armed presence in Lebanon grew. Nonetheless, some Lebanese rallied to the Palestinians, most notably the impoverished and the Muslims who saw Christians dominating the economy and political life of Lebanon. This is not the place to go into the causes that led to the civil war in Lebanon. But it is correct to express, at this point, the fact that it is more than a coincidence that the civil war erupted at the same time the majority of Arab states, including Jordan, Egypt, and Syria, had accepted a political settlement. Since Israel would not deal with the PLO, the latter was an obstacle to the implementation of 242. This is not to imply that the civil war did not have at its roots basic domestic Lebanese issues, largely economic. The civil war would eventually have happened even if there had been no Palestinian presence, but that presence hastened its advent. The Lebanese Left, largely Muslim, asked where the Christian-dominated government was when Israel attacked. The Lebanese Right, largely Christian, said there would be no attacks if the Palestinians were not in Lebanon and that Lebanon's strength lay in its military weakness.

The leader of the Katā'ib Party, defender of the Right, asked, in August 1974, for the removal of heavy weapons from Palestinian camps since this violated the Cairo Agreement of 1969. The Palestinians refused. As 1975 began, Israeli air raids increased against the 60-square-kilometer region of the 'Arqūb, recognized by the Cairo Agreement as the sanctuary of the commandos. The area was being turned into an uninhabited region by the bombing. Tension increased between the Palestinians and their Lebanese allies, on the one hand, and the Lebanese Right, on the other. The Palestinians viewed Lebanon as the last country from which their commandos could operate. The Lebanese Right viewed the Palestinians as purveyors of revolutionary ideologies and the principal reason for Israeli attacks. If the Palestinians would only go back to their camps and remain refugees, everything would be fine.

Tension between the two sides exploded on April 13, 1975. Trouble began on that morning in a Christian quarter of Beirut called ʿAyn al-Rammānah when residents quarreled with a commando, wounding him. Within a half hour some of his supporters, though their identities have not been established, came through the district and fired at a church killing a Katāʾib leader. Tension increased and later that afternoon a bus carrying Palestinians passed through the quarter. It was ambushed and all 26 of its passengers were killed. This event is now considered to be the starting point of the Lebanese civil war. Since it is a discrete event, it is something convenient on which to focus. Some might argue that a war was inevitable once the Arab states had agreed to a political settlement and the Palestinians resisted it. Others might say that when a company owned by former President Kamīl Shamʿūn received a license in February 1975 to fish and to open an automated fishing plant in Sidon, thus threatening the livelihood of the local fishermen, a showdown between the wealthy and poor, eventually involving the Palestinians, was inevitable. Still others might argue that the reluctance of the Christians to allow the Muslims, who were by the 1970s in the majority, a greater say in the government, commensurate with their numbers, was the real cause of the civil war. Undoubtedly, all of these factors were partly responsible. Since this study deals with the Arab-Israeli conflict, we can dismiss the domestic factors and deal, as much as possible, with the fighting in terms of its significance to the Middle East conflict.

Though the Lebanese Left and the Palestinians viewed the war which ensued as a just one in part to correct the social imbalance and to force the Lebanese government to actively support an increasingly isolated liberation movement, for the Right it was a war against the Palestinian foreigners who had brought with them warfare and Bolshevik ideology. The organ of the Katāʾib Party, stung by criticism of its attack on the bus, printed a list of 81 Lebanese soldiers and officers killed, it said, by Palestinians between 1969 and 1974.[28] On the other side, the attack was simply part of the Israeli plan to eliminate the Palestinian resistance:

> But the question that remains unanswered is, since Israel is behind these clashes, what is the role of the Phalangist gangs [...]?
>
> The Lebanese nationalist and progressive forces have become absolutely convinced that these incidents are not improvised but are pre-planned in coordination with imperialism and Zionism, and are aimed at gradually liquidating the Palestinians.[29]

The first round of the war did not last long and it looked as though a showdown between the contending sides might be averted. But even as military clashes declined in late April, editorial warfare continued in the press. *Al-Nahār*, on May 4, 1975, printed an article by a PLO member, Nabīl Shaʿth, in which he expounded the benefits that had accrued to Lebanon as a result of the Palestinian presence. Four days later *al-ʿAmal* responded, point by point. The PLO member said that Palestinians had aided the development of Lebanese agriculture in the south. The only thing planted in the south as a result of the Palestinians, *al-ʿAmal* wrote, were Israeli land mines. The Palestinians had protected Lebanese territory from

Israeli invasion. Not so, retorted the Kata'ib organ. Palestine been lost as well as territory in Jordan, Egypt, and Syria. Nothing of Lebanon was touched until the Palestinians started mounting commando operations from Lebanese territory.

The PLO representative went on to argue that the Palestinians were guests in Lebanon and resented being treated like foreigners. The Armenians were equally non-Lebanese yet they were not discriminated against. The Lebanese should change their ways. *Al-'Amal* responded that Lebanon's doors were open to all refugees and that the Palestinians had been welcomed. But the attitude of the Lebanese changed when the Palestinians began,

> [...] the arming of the [refugee] camps, and the erection of check-points, and the independence of the camps from all Lebanese authority. Armed men began to walk about as they wished, and every outlaw began to find a hiding place in the camps out of the reach of justice and the life and property of every Lebanese became threatened [...].
>
> The Armenians were and still are good examples of a guest. They did not set up armed camps and they did not attack the sovereignty of the state and they still abide by Lebanese law.[30]

The situation gradually deteriorated, though there appeared to be some hope of averting warfare in April. A ceasefire broke down in the middle of May as the government of Prime Minister Rashīd al-Ṣulḥ was unable to govern. Over and over again it was pointed out in editorials that the only beneficiary of fighting in Lebanon was Israel.[31] That Israel was determined to keep the pressure on Lebanon was also clear, with perhaps the aim of further dividing Lebanese society and encouraging the Lebanese Right to attack the commandos. Israeli agents were responsible for an explosion at the offices of the PDFLP.[32]

Throughout July and August, the Israelis assaulted the south. *Al-'Amal* asked the Palestinians to stop their activity, which the Rightists felt was responsible for Israeli attacks.[33] At the same time, the Palestinians felt more and more isolated as Egypt and Israel negotiated over Sinai II.

Though all the events of 1975 were ominous, still the fighting showed signs of dissipating as no one seemed to want total warfare. Yet tension was often high and accusations were common. The Egyptians perceived the activity in Lebanon as a plot on the part of the Israelis to exploit differences between the Left and Right. The Zionist aim was to force the Syrians to intervene thus giving Israel an excuse to invade the south up to the Litani River which it had long coveted.[34] Papers of the Lebanese Left charged the Right with wanting to stir up trouble in Lebanon in order to prevent the redistribution of political power. The Right was also trying to tempt the Palestinians into entering the fray more openly so the Lebanese could bring before the Arab League the whole question of a Palestinian armed presence. The ultimate aim was to tame the commando groups. Reports filled the Leftist press that Israel was the source of Rightist arms.[35] The titular head of the Leftist movement was Kamāl Junblāṭ, a Druze feudal leader from the Shuf. His weekly publication, *al-Anbā'*, throughout the large majority of its editorials during the civil war, maintained the real issue in Lebanon was not between Lebanese and Palestinians but between Lebanese and Lebanese. The Palestinians were simply an auxiliary question. No doubt this analysis has some validity. If one assumes that the fighting was ideological, not national, then one would expect the Palestinians, as the fighting progressed, to have taken opposing sides, just as the Lebanese did. This was in fact the case. *Al-Ṣāʿiqah* and elements of the Palestine Liberation Army fought with the Rightists while the ALF, PFLP, and PFLP-GC fought with the Lebanese Leftists.

The war took a turn for the worse toward the end of November, about the 22nd, Lebanon's national day. The Israelis kept up their pressure by bombing the Badawī and Nahr al-Bārid camps in the north of Lebanon and the Nabatīyah camp in the south. The raids came on the heels of the United Nations General Assembly adoption on November 10, 1975 of a resolution which defined Zionism as "a form of racism." Editorial opinion strongly supported the resolution,[36] but comment on it was not as widespread nor as ebullient as condemnation of it was in the United States. The Arabs were too occupied with the Lebanese situation. The December fighting was particularly vicious and the British, Australian, and West German embassies advised their nationals to leave the country. By the middle of December the security situation in Lebanon had deteriorated completely. Explosions were averaging one every six seconds, sniping was so bad medical teams could not reach people wounded in the streets nor could the fire department get to fires. President Franjīyah, who had declined to make a speech to commemorate Lebanon's birthday, spoke out on December 10 only to inflame the situation. He said that the Lebanese Left and Zionism were plotting to destroy the multi-religious state and to set up small religious enclaves. The Israeli motive was to prove that people of different religions could not live together, thus justifying a religious state in Israel.

Franjīyah's interpretation was farfetched. Generally the Christian Right viewed the enemy as the Palestinians, not the Israelis. This is clear if one examines *al-ʿAmal*, the organ of the Phalangist Party. Its editorials often focused on the important role Christians had played in the defense of the Palestinian cause, citing presidents Shamʿūn, Charles Helou, and Franjīyah as eloquent Arab spokesmen. In return for this support, and the hospitality extended when the Palestinians were thrown from their own country, the Lebanese received bombs. The Right felt that the Palestinians would destroy Lebanon if they could get Palestine back. Could Lebanese be blamed if they felt their own country was more important?

> Presidents Shamʿūn, al-Ḥilū, and Franjīyah, and Prof. Charles Malik, have explained the Palestinian question and defined it in the United Nations and in international forums [...].[37]

> Lebanon gave the Palestinians what no other country gave them [...] and bore, because of them, losses in lives and property that no other Arab country did.[38]

> The identity of the fighters on the other side was known in spite of phony names and imaginary [Lebanese] "national" organizations. The Palestinian resistance "with its countless groups" was the enemy in all battles and on all fronts.[39]

> When the troubles became serious and Beirut burned and factories were destroyed [...] and green Lebanon became red Lebanon, as the brother refugees wanted it, they then wanted Lebanon to assume its responsibility [...].[40]

> To Abū ʿAmmār [*nom de guerre* of Yāsir ʿArafāt] and his brothers: I advise you to know the truth about the Lebanese Christian [...] that he is different [from Christians in other Arab and Muslim countries], he is not tolerant and he refuses what they accept and he rejects those who want to infringe on his dignity, sovereignty, freedom, and rights.[41]

The fighting in 1976, as the PLO committed more of its forces to the side of the Lebanese Left, turned in favor of what were called the progressive forces. Just as victory seemed within the grasp of the leftist alliance, Damascus threatened to intervene against it. Syrian policy was motivated largely by a desire to prevent the establishment in Lebanon of a radical regime that would allow the country to be turned into the North Vietnam for which the Palestinians yearned. If the Left was victorious, the Arab-Israeli conflict might then heat up and Syria could be dragged into a conflict with Israel for which it was not prepared and which it did not want. For the Syrian press and that of Jordan, which had drawn closer to Damascus after Sinai II, the Israelis were waiting for the situation in Lebanon to deteriorate to such an extent that they could invade the south. In this scheme, Egypt the traitor was goading the Syrians into a trap.[42]

The Egyptian press, on its part, tried to redeem its fallen image with the PLO. It became their champion and warned Syria against intervening in Lebanon. How, the Egyptian press wanted to know, could Syria think of invading another country when part of its own territory was under Israeli occupation? It also asked the PLO to be rid of elements in its ranks, apparently the pro-Damascus *al-Ṣāʿiqah*, that were in the pay of "foreigners."[43]

The Syrian threat to intervene in Lebanon had become so great that it began to dictate the terms of what it perceived to be a settlement, the most important elements of which were the ending of the fighting and the return of the Palestinians to their camps and to the ʿArqūb region, allotted to them in the Cairo Agreement. That the Syrians were going to impose this just as the Leftist-Palestinian alliance was about to triumph was fiercely condemned in the press loyal to the Left.

> We have to make clear in these critical circumstances that the conflict between the [Leftist] National Movement and Syria does not serve the interests of either but it only serves the interests of the isolationists [i.e., the Right] who are trying to benefit.[44]

> With all the love we hold for Damascus we wish to raise our voice with that of the [Palestine] Resistance and the National Movement by warning about the American trap that is being laid to push Syria into more involvement in Lebanon. In a direction that contradicts its interests and our interests.[45]

> We have become for the Syrian Ba'th [leaders] a commodity that is sold, mortgaged, or bartered in the market of political bargains and diplomatic barter. They consider Lebanon a card in their hands which is a winner especially for the Americans and Europe. They think that they can gain something internationally concerning the Golan or they can become guardians of the Syrian-Jordanian confederation that will include, according to Syrian-American planning, blessed by Israel, the partially recovered West Bank [...]. In other words they return to the project of the Kingdom of Jordan and Syria [...].
>
> They are also bargaining with the Palestinian people [i.e., using the Palestinians as a bargaining chip] for a few kilometers of the Golan.[46]

Another manifestation of Syrian power was the way they could virtually dictate the election in May of Ilyās Sarkīs, or Sarkīs the Damascene as his detractors called him, as president of Lebanon to replace Sulaymān Franjīyah whose 6-year term would end in September 1976.

The worst fear of the Palestinians was realized when Syria invaded Lebanon on the evening of May 31–June 1, 1976. The Syrian press was very defensive about the move, undoubtedly because of the negative implications involved with one Arab country invading another. And even worse, in order to end the bloodshed, they were forced to move against the Palestinians. But, said Damascus' editorials, Syria was determined to do what it felt right.[47] For allies of the Left, Syria had committed a terrible act.

> [...] [T]he Syrian invasion has been carried out in agreement with Israel [...]. [Israel] welcomed the Syrian invasion as a way of destroying the Palestinian resistance and of repeating the Black September massacres [of the Palestinians in Jordan] about which no one should be silent.[48]
>
> They continue.
>
> They continue raiding, bombing, exterminating, and invading land and people.[49]

With the entry of the Syrian forces, the position of the Lebanese Left and the PLO changed from victor to vanquished. The Palestinian commandos began to return to the south, a move the Syrians did not hinder. Though there still remained some areas where the Palestinians had to be destroyed, in the eyes of the Lebanese Right the cause of the war was being subdued. But at least one Lebanese writer wrote reflectively of the situation:

> [...] [T]o say that the Palestinians are the cause of the conflict may look alright in an over-simplified analysis [...] but the deeper reality is that we [Lebanese] were divided in our outlook toward the Palestinian question since it was raised [...].
>
> Just as the Palestinian question attracted the Muslims, the Christians were afraid of a Palestinian presence in Lebanon [...].
>
> So the Christians exaggerated their support of the question in order to cover their reservations on the [Palestinian] presence [...] and the Muslims welcomed the Palestinian presence because it increased their shares in the Lebanese [confessional] formula.[50]

Neither the assassination of American Ambassador Francis Meloy nor the hijacking of an Air France plane to Entebbe, Uganda, could take the eyes of the Arab press from the unfolding drama in Lebanon. The Lebanese Right, increasingly symbolized by President Sulaymān Franjīyah, affectionately called Abū Tony in Damascus, was being saved from defeat by the intervention of those very Syrians who had been the Palestinians' staunchest ally throughout the history of the Arab-Israeli conflict.

The PLO and the Syrian government reached an understanding in late July 1976 whereby the Palestinians agreed to withdraw from the civil war, return to the south and to their camps, and for good measure, in the communiqué attached to the agreement, denounce the Sinai II accord. The agreement was to take effect during the first few days of August, but the Syrians moved slowly in enforcing it while the Lebanese Right continued the siege, which had begun in June, of the Tal al-Zaʿtar refugee camp. To the Right it was a center of crime in which the Japanese Red Army, the Italian Red Brigades, and the German Baader-Meinhof gang trained for international terror. It also had to be captured because of its strategic location. Tal al-Zaʿtar in Palestinian hands could "paralyze Christian Beirut and deprive it of its lungs, the mountains."[51] But to the fighters of the Left, Tal al-Zaʿtar was a symbol of their struggle. It had been originally a camp of some 6000 people but had swelled during the fighting to figures that ran as high as 50,000. The hated symbol of the Palestinians, to the Christian Right, it ironically had been located where it was at the urging of Christian industrialists in the nearby Makallis district who wanted to exploit cheap Palestinian labor.

Wrote the pro-Libyan *al-Safīr*,

> What is happening on the east side of Beirut should make all nationalists proud and give them something to think about.... The vicious attack on Tal al-Zaʿtar...illustrates a new reality that came into being with the Syrian intervention on the side of the isolationist forces.[52]

As the siege of Tal al-Zaʿtar continued, pro-Palestinian and pro-Leftist comment in the press became more hostile. What had happened to President Ḥāfẓ al-'Asad, champion of progressive Arab causes? Look at who his two principal allies were, Franjīyah and King Ḥusayn. How could he still claim to be a friend of the Palestinians?[53] That Syria was the focus of inverted love and hate was illustrated on July 11 when there was firing of arms in the air in the Muslim-held districts of Beirut. A rumor had spread that the Syrian president had been overthrown. The same day there was firing in the Christian districts when it was discovered that al-'Asad was still in power.

The fall of Tal al-Zaʿtar was assured when Syria intervened on the side of the Right. The latter had offered to allow the camp to be evacuated, but apparently for political considerations having to do with the negative impact surrender would have on the movement and the great amount of positive media comment that was being generated throughout the world over the undoubtedly brave defense of the camp, the PLO leadership decided to have their people fight on.[54] *Ṣawt al-Aḥrār*, the new illegal publication of Shamʿūn's National Liberal (NLP), announced on August 10 that it was "Tal al-Zaʿtar week." Two days later the 52-day siege was over and the camp fell, thanks, said the Left, to the treasonous activities of Syria and the Right.[55] For the Phalangists, however, it was a noble triumph befitting their cause. In a reflective essay on the fall of the camp, *al-'Amal* wrote:

> Will the Palestinians become our "historical enemy"?
>
> As though the Palestinians are the "historical enemy" which the Lebanese need to discover their national entity.
>
> Years ago, who would have believed it? Who would have believed that a people who claimed itself a brother would become what Germany was to France or Israel to the Arabs?[56]

The fall of Tal al-Za'tar was followed by the end of the Franjīyah regime. The man who had been elected 6 years earlier with the votes of parliament members friendly to the Palestinians, and with the blessing of the PLO, now departed, vilified by those who supported the Left. *Al-Nidā'* summed up the occasion with the headline, "The Butcher Departs [...] but the [Syrian] Invaders Stay."[57]

As the civil war slowed in 1976, the Syrians seemed determined to extend their control over Lebanon west of the Lebanon mountains and south of Beirut. Undoubtedly they would have liked this control of southwest Lebanon to have included the area up to the Israeli border where the Palestinians had retreated. But the Israelis made it clear that they would react militarily if Syrian troops crossed the Litani River. On October 1, the "Battle of Alay" began, the mountain top town on the main east-west road was a Leftist stronghold. Inexorably the Syrians widened their control over Lebanon. Barely noticed, however, was the fact that while the major action was going on on the Beirut-Damascus road, Christian forces with Israeli aid were attacking the Palestinians and the Leftists from the latter's rear in the south. On October 19, 1976, the Leftist press noted that the town of Marj`ayūn had been occupied by the Israeli-backed Christian forces. The papers blamed the Leftists and their allies for allowing this to happen since it meant another, perhaps more serious, setback for the commando movement.[58]

The purpose of the activity on the Israeli border, commented one Leftist paper, was to establish a six-kilometer-wide security belt stretching from al-Naqurah on the Mediterranean to the 'Arqūb region in the east along the Syrian border. The function of the *cordon sanitaire* was to stop the Palestinians from using the area militarily as they attempted to re-implement the Cairo Agreement.[59]

Except for the situation south of the Litani River, Syria had succeeded in virtually bringing the civil war to an end by November 1976. The League of Arab States called for the stationing of Arab Deterrent Forces (ADF) in Lebanon to separate the belligerents until a political settlement could be reached. The ADF was dominated by the Syrian military though technically responsible to the Lebanese president. Syrian editorials tried to argue that since the ADF was under Lebanese control, and while Lebanon had no army (it had disintegrated into its disparate ideological and religious parts during the war), the ADF ought to be allowed to cross the Litani.[60] Israel would have none of it. Though Syria brought a temporary halt to the fighting, it could not contain the civil war that continued for more than a dozen years.

As 1976 ended and one looked reflectively back at the Middle East scene since 1973, the years were filled with tumultuous events that indirectly influenced the Arab-Israeli conflict. 1974 was the year the Sinai disengagements, but also of Watergate. The fall-out from the latter precluded any further American initiated momentum in the Middle East. Many Arabs felt the scandal was robbing them of the only time the United States was even-handed in the region: during the second term of a non-reelectable Republican president. The Lebanese civil war occupied 1975 and 1976. Many people welcomed the Syrian intervention simply as a way to end the carnage that eventually claimed the lives of perhaps 100,000 people. Though its population was seventy times larger, the United States suffered half as many deaths in Vietnam. Then there was the closely contested presidential election in America. The Arabs thought they might be dealing with a Democratic president in 1977 after Ford, in the third debate with Jimmy Carter, stated there was no Soviet domination of Eastern Europe.

Of equal interest to the Arab press was another election campaign, that in Israel in the spring of 1977. Most writers argued that there was really no difference between Israeli parties. They only differed "on how to eat the Arabs: roasted, fried, or cooked [by boiling]."[61] After the election, which one paper called an electoral coup d'état,[62] editorial reaction to Menachem Begin reflected the cleavage between Egypt and the remainder of the confrontation states. The Egyptian press, following their government's commitment to a peaceful settlement as embodied in Sinai II, said that the only difference between Israeli political parties was in tactics. All of their goals were the same. Presumably if one could renounce the use of force with the Labor Party of Israel and seek peace in that way, so too could one pursue the same line with the Likud.

> Before the Israeli election took place, the point of view of Egypt, which has not changed after the results showed the success of the Likud Bloc, is that there is no difference between [Shimon] Peres, [Menachem] Begin, or any other Israeli. There will never be any conflict between one Israeli and another inside Israel. At any rate the difference between them inside Israel will not show that one is a dove and the other a hawk [...]. On the Egyptian side, the Egyptian standpoint does not change and is not influenced by persons or by the classification of doves and hawks.
>
> The standpoint of Egypt is that the question must not be frozen and the road to peace goes through Geneva and peace is achieved through the withdrawal from all territory occupied [by Israel] after June 1967 and the Palestinians attaining their legitimate and just rights.[63]

The press which reflected a more hard-line attitude toward Israel after Sinai II was harsher in its criticism. "Mr. Begin promised [immediately after his election] to consider Arab occupied territories as liberated Israeli territory and that he will continue to persevere in the establishment of colonies [in those territories]." Thus, the editorial continued, he has thwarted the United States and has no intention of evacuating any land or "recognizing the rights of the Palestinian people."[64]

> In reaffirming, yesterday, the alleged Biblical right of Israel to all of Cisjordan, and excluding any form of PLO participation in the negotiations (but if Cisjordan is not

> negotiable, then what is the use of Geneva?), the head of the "Likud" has broken the last strings to which the unconditional [Arab] optimists could have attached themselves.[65]

The election of a new leader in Israel in 1977 was also accompanied by a change in administration in the United States. One of Jimmy Carter's first acts was to send his new Secretary of State, Cyrus Vance, to the area to test the political waters. Though comment was guarded about his coming in February, one could not characterize it as hostile. The Arab governments, with Egypt in the lead, were committed to a political solution. It was time for movement along that path.

> America knows the realities of the region better than anyone else because some of these realities are of its own making [...].
>
> Kissinger's step-by-step approach was movement in the unknown where no one knew what the next step, nor the last step, was going to be except the lead player. Vance's approach is to reach agreement on where the end of the road is going to be and set up stations on the way.[66]

The same paper theorized, in a more negative way, on what the outgoing secretary might have said to the incoming one:

> Do not get to the heart of the problem, but rather keep moving on its fringes. Do not speak of any Palestinian role and do not think of a place for the Palestinians in Geneva before they recognize Israel. Do not offer a comprehensive settlement but try to get a disengagement agreement in the Golan first and then in the Sinai.[67]

But movement there was, if it was only politicians jockeying for position. King Ḥusayn and Yāsir ʿArafāt met for the first time in 7 years in Cairo in March. Anwar al-Sādāt made a trip to Europe in the same month and in April went to the United States. He was followed the same month by Ḥusayn. In May, Carter and al-'Asad met in Geneva. Between February and May there was also the important announcement by Carter that the core of the Middle East conflict was the Palestinians and he called for a "homeland" for them. Though this was a breakthrough for the Arabs, the fact that he did not mention where the homeland was to be raised fears in the Jordanian press. The United States, it wrote, "wants to make Jordan a substitute homeland for the Palestinians."[68]

Editorial comment about the meeting between the American and Syrian presidents was interesting in that it clearly showed that Syria, Jordan, and Egypt were committed to a peaceful settlement. The Syrian journal *al-Thawrah* commented:

> Certainly the Middle East problem will remain complicated and will benefit from cooperation and [...] [whatever reservations we have] does not hide our desire for a just and durable peace.[69]

Added the Egyptian *al-Ahrām*:

> The Geneva meeting between al-'Asad and Carter emphasized once more the Arab realities that President al-Sādāt brought up in the meeting with the American president. The purpose is one and only one, that is complete Israeli withdrawal from all occupied Arab territory and the establishment of an independent Palestinian state.[70]

But the determination of the new Israeli government to consolidate its hold over occupied territories through the establishment of new settlements and the bolstering of old ones was also apparent, much to the chagrin of the United States and the Arabs. Even as al-'Asad and Carter were in session, the Israeli authorities announced the establishment of new settlements in the Sinai. More than one paper wondered about the timing and suggested that it was done to embarrass the two sides meeting in Geneva and to make the Syrians angry with the United States.[71]

Begin's victory in the May elections was disappointing for the United States. The relationship that followed was tenuous at best so that when the new prime minister went to Washington in July there was open concern in the Carter administration. The Arabs viewed him as a terrorist for his activities as head of the illegal Irgun, during the mandatory period, for his role in Dayr Yāsīn, and for all his government's hard line over the future of the occupied territories, especially the West Bank which Begin insisted on calling Judea and Samaria.

> A few hours before the Washington talks between American President Carter and Menachem Begin, and in the midst of the maneuvers that Israel is spreading to confuse public opinion about a peaceful settlement of the Middle East question, the standpoint of Egypt was clearly announced by President al-Sādāt. We are ready to sign a permanent and just peace agreement that will legally and politically end the state of war so that Israel – if it abides by international law – will become one of the countries of the Middle East. This means for the first time in history that Israel will have its own safe borders and existence [...] this is the price of peace.[72]

> The countries of the [Arab] region do not want from the Washington government complete partiality toward Arab rights. The people do not want from President Carter–they refuse totally–a complete American partiality toward Israel. All that the people of the countries of the region want from [the United States is] [...] American justice that recognizes human rights and the illegitimacy of occupying someone's land by force.[73]

Within a few days of Begin's departure from the States, the Israeli government legalized more settlements in the area occupied in the June war. This time the United States called the act a violation of international law and an obstruction to peace. How can anyone, be he Arab or not, asked Arab editorials, deal with the Likud and hope for peace?

> [...] [T]he American Secretary of State Cyrus Vance accused the last decision of Menachem Begin of legitimizing the three Jewish settlements in the West Band as being a violation of international law and an obstruction to peace efforts in the Middle East. The importance of this accusation.. .is the fact that it expresses an official American attitude.[74]

> The American response to the Israeli government decision to legitimize the new settlements in the West Bank...has disclosed the attitude Menachem Begin has chosen toward the present stage of the efforts aimed at convening the Geneva conference and achieving peace in the region. It seemed clear that Begin intended – in his last meeting with President Carter – to postpone discussing the major issues in the problem, such as occupied territory and the right of the Palestinian people to decide their own destiny [...]. Begin also intended to avoid confrontation with the Americans with the excuse that "each side has its own point of view." The attempt to avoid confrontation has failed.[75]

> The enemy did not only ignore...international displeasure but also insisted on defying international opinion when the Zionist Minister of Agriculture [Ariel Sharon] announced three days ago that the policy of settlement and building additional settlements in Arab occupied territory was and will be the cornerstone of the government of the terrorist Menachem Begin. [...]
>
> President Ḥāfiẓ al-'Asad expressed in a talk to the American magazine [*Newsweek*] that Israel does not want peace and is only maneuvering and is attempting to put more obstacles [in the way] and evade public opinion in the world and especially in the United States.[76]

Almost immediately after the Begin visit, Vance began his second tour of the Middle East, this time in August, and brought with him several proposals including one that had first been offered by Egypt. This called for the convening of a "working group" of selected invitees, notably excluding the Soviet Union and the PLO. It was another way of getting around the problem of Geneva where little progress could be made, at least Egypt, the United States, and Israel felt, as long as rancor might break out amongst the participants and the USSR would serve to veto any settlement, acting as the protectors on an absent PLO.

The Egyptian response to Vance was positive, saying that a preliminary meeting would be necessary if there was any hope of returning to Geneva by the end of 1977. But the Syrian response was negative.

> The Arabs know for sure that Israel continues to play the waiting game that so far has helped the 10-year de facto occupation [of Arab territory] and because of that, it wants the American mediation role to continue. Because it [America's role] achieves its [Israel's] aim by putting off the Arab and international confrontation with it [Israel].[77]

> In spite of all the attempts by Israel to give the impression that it seeks peace, the aggressive and expansionist tendency remains prevalent and still dominates the Israeli mentality. And while Vance is on his tour of the area looking for a means of establishing peace, Begin makes a provocative tour of the Syrian and Lebanese borders. What Begin announced during this tour is sufficient to show Israel does not want to establish peace but the thinking of its leaders is centered on aggression and expansion. Begin said, "The Golan is for Israel a security belt." And he pointed out, in an indirect way, that Israel will continue in its efforts to keep the situation in Lebanon critical.[78]

The situation in Lebanon was the scene of tension even at the "end" of the civil war as the commandos began returning south of the Litani River. After Damascus intervened in Lebanon, the Israelis made it clear that the Syrian-dominated ADF could not extend its control over that area. In order to deny the commandos access to the border with Israel, the Israelis had trained and armed Lebanese Christians to fight the Palestinians in the south. In keeping with this policy of weaning the Lebanese away from the Arab struggle against Israel, the Jewish state had established the "Good Fence" whereby Lebanese produce and people could move between Lebanese territory and Israel in search of markets and jobs. Many southern Lebanese responded positively to this, having been increasingly disillusioned by the Palestinian presence that seemed to bring them no visible good. But the Palestinians were determined to regain their former, and now their last, stronghold. In the fighting that continued throughout 1976 and after, but which was rarely reported in the Lebanese press because of censorship, the Israelis provided air, artillery, and men to aid their Christian allies. In the spring of 1977, the situation grew increasingly bloody and this was interpreted by the press as a prelude to an Israeli invasion to put an end forever to the Palestinian presence in the south. That Lebanon was split itself over the issue, that various Arab regimes aided different commando groups, that the Palestinians themselves were divided over a political or military solution, that Syria was caught in the dilemma of being blamed for the war in the south but was not allowed to send troops there to quell the fighting, all this added to the terrible confusion that threatened to destroy the territorial entity of Lebanon, its political and economic bases having long since disappeared. "Lebanon remains the site of the abscess of the Arab-Israeli conflict. The laboratory where the apprentice sorcerers of peace persist in trying to implement their most complicated formulas."[79]

Lebanon became a temporarily minor problem when attention shifted to the 11-day visit of Vance to the Middle East in August 1977. But the Secretary of State seemed not too optimistic about the future. This was a matter of grave concern for those Arabs who were counting on the Americans to pressure Israel and to take positive steps to include the Palestinians in the peace process since this had even been acknowledged as necessary by Washington.

> Four wars have taken place in the region in support of the Palestinian people and the whole world recognizes the fact that the base of the problem is the Palestinian people. [...] In spite

> of this Israel alone sees nothing in the world which is called Palestine or the Palestinian people.
>
> We believe that the declaration of Vance himself in occupied Palestine that he could not get any concessions from Israel concerning its recognition of the rights of the Palestinians and [concerning] the West Bank should be enough for the American administration to reconsider its policy toward Israel. [...]
>
> In any case the responsibility for the failure of the peace effort falls first on Israel and then on Washington, since it is the only international force that can impose on Israel what it [the United States] wants.[80]

After Vance left the Middle East, Israel extended public services to the West Bank and the Gaza Strip. These services previously had been under Arab control. The next day it announced three new settlements in the occupied territories. The Egyptian press, the most moderate national press under study, responded in disbelief.

> It is clear now that the Begin government has vowed to do everything it can to undermine peace opportunities in the region and everything any sane or insane government could do to demonstrate its arrogance and its defiance at all efforts aimed at a just peace. [...] The Begin government has shocked the world be deciding to implement Israeli law in the West Bank and Gaza, followed – 24 hours later – by a new decision approving the establishment of three new settlements in Arab occupied territory.[81]

As 1977 approached an end, the feverish diplomatic activity continued, providing ample subjects on which the editorialists could comment. Besides the continued fighting in the south of Lebanon, there were the first tenuous steps taken by the new governments in Israel and the United States. Every day seemed to bring something new. On October 1, the United States and the USSR issued a declaration, as co-chairmen of the Geneva Peace Conference, that called for Palestinian participation in the peace process and for Palestinian "rights", a word that was consistently used in Arab editorials to mean a state and was therefore anathema to the Israelis. The Arab press was overjoyed.[82] But within a week when Carter spoke at the United Nations, he did not mention the need for Israel to withdraw from Arab territory. When an official US source, quoted in the Arab press, said that a Palestinian homeland did not have any "political" implications, Arab editorials lamented the weakness of the Carter administration which would give in so quickly, after the US-Soviet declaration, to Zionist pressures.[83]

In Israel itself, the government, in the perception of Arab writers, was daily becoming more intransigent. The Begin regime called for a return to the Geneva talks but said, through Foreign Minister Moshe Dayan, that the Israelis would not negotiate with the PLO nor allow a Palestinian state in the West Bank.

> The Israelis want "peace" but they are not willing to withdraw from the West Bank, Sinai, or the Syrian Heights. Jerusalem will remain the unified capital [i.e., it will not be divided

again between Arab and Israeli]. The rights of the Palestinians must not be discussed, even deciding their own destiny is rejected. Settlements [in occupied territory] are not an issue at any Geneva meeting. And the settlements may be established anywhere in the "historical [Biblical Israeli] land." The United Nations resolutions concerning the return of the Palestinians to their land are not only rejected but they must not be considered at all.[84]

> The real dilemma that faces Israel now is that the Begin government does not want to make practical decisions which would help all parties to the conflict go to the negotiating table in Geneva.
>
> Dayan announces: No Palestinian state, no Palestinian entity, no Palestinian homeland, the PLO should not be a discussion topic in the conference. [...] Then he announces that Israel wants a Geneva Conference without preconditions. What a contradiction![85]

Frustration with Israel increased when the United Nations General Assembly passed a resolution condemning Israeli settlements in the occupied territories. The vote was 131 to 1. Israel, isolated in the world body, cast the lone opposing vote. Asked one paper, "How long is the policy of ignoring the international community going to continue?"[86]

Even before Israel could answer, the Middle East conflict took a turn that one week earlier would have been termed unimaginable. President al-Sādāt said that he was willing to go to the Israeli Knesset in Jerusalem to present the Arab case in the enemy's own house. It was a colossal gesture; an attempt to break the chain of hatred that had enslaved the minds of both sides for decades. Before carrying out his decision, al-Sādāt made a trip to Syria where he tried to convince al-'Asad to support his initiative. Their final press conference was moving. There was sorrow but no rancor. In fairness to al-Sādāt it was a courageous decision. But it seems not to have been well planned and the Arabs were not consulted except on a perfunctory level. The resignation of Ismā'īl Fahmī as Egypt's Foreign Minister in protest to al-Sādāt's trip to Jerusalem only confirmed the general uneasiness. Even Egyptian papers, when writing about the historic trip and the results it might bring, often qualified their editorials with the phrase, "if successful."[87] A reading of the headlines of the papers of the two major antagonists, Egypt and Syria, reveals how each press perceived the trip to Jerusalem. *Al-Ba'th* wrote, "Syria Rejects al-Sādāt's Visit to Israel." *Al-Ahrām* tried to accentuate the positive: "Al-Sādāt Will Pray the Feast [of al-Aḍḥā] with the Palestinians in the Mosque of al-Aqsa."[88]

The surprising decision of al-Sādāt to go to Israel captured the imagination of the world and was a media event in the States when a leading television commentator got the famous enemies to talk to each other, via satellite, and agree on the visit. Eventually the Egyptian president was, because of his "heroic vision," *Time* magazine's Man of the Year in their issue of January 3, 1978. Kissinger nominated him for the Nobel Prize, the privilege of nominating others being one of the rights of past winners. In the Gallup polls and in the Egyptian press, al-Sādāt's trip was a success. But in the rest of the Arab press, he did not fare so well. First let us look at how the Egyptian writers perceived the event.

> [Everyone should understand the following about the president's trip:]
> 1. When al-Sādāt announced that he was ready to go to the end of the world or even to the Knesset for peace, he meant peace based on justice.
> 2. That he is not going for a separate or a partial agreement.
> 3. Al-Sādāt wants to prove [that it is the Arabs who want peace] in front of the people [of Israel] and before the whole world.[89]

> Al-Sādāt, the leader, goes to Jerusalem to place before the Israelis the realities of a just peace.
> It is an historical moment. It is the hour of courage.... Without any attempt at personal gain, the fighter, Anwar al-Sādāt, goes on the peace trip with all its difficulties.[90]

Responded the Syrian editorials:

> Al-Sādāt has finally turned his back on the Arab nation and decided to do something he secretly has been thinking of since the years following the October War.
> The decision of the Egyptian president and his insistence on visiting Israel is a painful blow to the Arab nation. [...]
> This step of al-Sādāt's, besides being contemptuous of the Arab nation and the will of the Arab people, especially in Egypt, has as its objective the undermining of Arab solidarity that was achieved in October [1973].[91]

> It was obvious from the speeches given in the "historical session" in the Israeli Knesset that President al-Sādāt has given free to Israel what it could not get through all of its aggressive wars against the Arabs and what the expansionist and terrorist generals never dreamt [i.e., Jerusalem and recognition].[92]

Editorial comment in Jordan and Lebanon was equally severe since the press of both countries rejected a unilateral settlement, which is the way al-Sādāt's trip appeared to them. In Jordan a separate peace would mean no West Bank while in Lebanon an Egyptian-Israeli settlement would mean thousands of refugees would have no chance of returning to their homeland, and would be permanently settled in Lebanon. A unilateral agreement would also leave Israel free to concentrate its forces on subduing the Palestinians and thus bring about another round of war as the Palestinians fought back. The Jordanian and Lebanese journals, however, agreed that the area would never be the same. How could it be with pictures flashing across the wire services showing the president taking a gift from Golda Meir after kissing her and seeming to get along famously with Menachem Begin? Al-Sādāt had entered history, but next to Herzl, Balfour, Weizmann, and Ben-Gurion. Papers also commented on the apparent lack of results. The president had taken great risks but his gamble of the century had brought no benefits. It was also noted that even the United States was swept away by the events. American foreign policy in the Middle East consisted only of Carter urging everyone to pray for peace.[93]

Upon al-Sādāt's return to Egypt after his November 19 flight to Israel, he called for the convening of a Cairo Conference of Arabs and Israelis to prepare for Geneva. In the press which opposed his initiative this was seen as another attempt to get around Geneva and the Soviet presence there. The United States was invited, and eventually did accept an invitation along with the United Nations and Israel. Not one Arab state accepted even though the Egyptian leader said he would pursue his enterprise alone if necessary, thereby warning the other Arab states. Headlined Syria's *al-Ba'th*, "Al-Sādāt Attacks Syria, Insults the Palestinians, and Praises Israel." Continued the same edition's editorial:

> We wonder if anyone can imagine that a question which has existed for thirty years, led to four wars, and could have caused a third world war, can be solved in 15 days…?
>
> […] furthermore we have to say that al-Sādāt's attack on Syria and the Palestine Liberation Organization […] makes us say that such conduct indicates that al-Sādāt is trying be all means possible to arrive at a complete peace agreement with Israel. Undoubtedly all indications show that the agreement has already been prepared and what is happening now is only a charade. [94]

> President al-Sādāt is the man who initiates individual solutions […] starting with the ceasefire in the October War, to the acceptance of the step- by-step policy, to the Sinai [II] Agreement, and the visit to Israel.
>
> When he stopped the fighting in the October War he said: Wait! The land will return if the Arabs agree to go to Geneva…
>
> [He said "Wait" when he had the rapprochement with the United States, when he accepted Kissinger's policy of step-by-step, and Sinai II].
>
> The strange thing about President al-Sādāt is that after he closed all the doors that lead to a just peace, i.e., the option of war, the option of Arab solidarity, the option of preparing for war while continuing diplomatic efforts…, he took the impossible option and insisted on a wrong and irresponsible attitude. So the distance between him and peace has increased and so has the distance between him and the ability to return to the option of war.
>
> I can say that President al-Sādāt is no longer capable of peace and no longer capable of confrontation.[95]

The editorial war pitting Syria and its Arab allies against Egypt continued steadily after the trip to Jerusalem. The implications for the Palestinians were, by their standards, terrible. Assassination rumors were rife and some commando groups threatened to kill all the Egyptians who went to Jerusalem with al-Sādāt. The Egyptian press tried to defend its president's act saying that he, and Egypt, would never abandon the Palestinians. "Nevertheless the dogged attack on Egypt continues without reason."[96]

Those who rejected al-Sādāt's proposed Cairo Conference with Israel gathered at Tripoli in Africa during the first week of December where they held a Steadfastness Summit.

Though they were careful not to burn all their bridges with Egypt, they did say they would freeze their relations with it. Al-Sādāt responded on December 5 by breaking relations with Syria, Iraq, Algeria, Libya, and South Yemen. It was another "new bomb" which the president of Egypt seemed capable of exploding almost daily. The following day the United States, slowly coming around to supporting what they originally perceived to be Egypt's impetuous behavior, announced, and did so reluctantly since they knew it would alienate Syria and the Russians, that it *was* possible to have peace without reconvening the Geneva peace conference. Egypt had thrown all its eggs into the American basket. The United States grudgingly accepted the new burden.[97]

As a result of al-Sādāt's trip, it was agreed that Begin should come to Egypt and a meeting was planned in the city of Ismā'īlīyah. Before going to Egypt, however, the Israeli prime minister went to the United States to discuss the next stages of negotiations. The Cairo press was filled with warnings for the Israelis not to maneuver for time but to accept their responsibility.

> The Israeli government must now make difficult decisions. Those decisions are related first and foremost to two basic questions: withdrawal and security. Cairo's point of view is frank and firm, and it has been recognized by the international community. And that is the illegitimacy of occupying other people's land by force and the return of their legitimate rights to their owners [the Palestinians] [...].
>
> Israel demands security and talks a lot about the lack of security in the region and forgets that real security and stability cannot be obtained while Arab territories are occupied.
>
> The government of Israel is facing a difficult choice. The foundations of peace will be established in the region [according to how well] it understands the dimensions of the historic [al-Sādāt] peace trip and responds to Justice and Right.[98]

But while in the United States, Begin announced that Israeli forces would be kept in the West Bank even after a peace treaty. There would be some autonomy for the Arabs of Gaza and the West Bank but no self-determination. Even for the most moderate Arab, the Israeli proposals were unacceptable. Several papers noted that there was no mention of the Palestinian right to return though the Israelis were to be allowed to settle in Arab territory. Further, the Arabs would never accept armed tutelage in areas allegedly returned to them. In summary, Israel wanted more than the Arabs could give and to give less than it was able.[99]

Thus within a month of al-Sādāt's trip to Israel, the hope for peace, never strong in anti-Sādāt papers, was beginning to fade. When Begin traveled to Egypt on Christmas day with an entourage that included ministers Ezer Weizmann and Moshe Dayan, expectations in the press were not high. When no statement of principles resulted from the meeting, only the decision to form two committees, one political and one military, the Syrian press immediately said the conclave at Ismā'īlīyah was unsuccessful. Headlined *al-Thawrah*, "A New Failure for al-Sādāt and His Submissive Program in His Meeting with the Zionist Terrorist Trio in Ismā'īlīyah."[100] Upon returning home, Begin reported to the Knesset and said that the Israeli position remained no self-determination for the Palestinians.

The Egyptian press looking for someone to blame criticized not Begin but Carter for allowing the Israeli prime minister during his US trip to have such an anti-Palestinian position.

> [...] He [President Carter] always talks about the legitimate rights of the Palestinians, then he says that the Palestinians should have a homeland in which they can live in peace. But he also expresses his support of Israel in rejecting the establishment of an independent Palestinian state. [...]
>
> How can the United States talk about the necessity of responding to Palestinian claims while the Palestinians have no right to their own destiny?[101]

The Syrian press directed its anger not at the United States or Israel but at al-Sādāt, calling for his overthrow. The time had come to admit the initiative was wrong, a failure, and therefore the person responsible for it had to be removed.[102]

If the Arab press was hostile, the Begin government did not help by announcing on January 4, 1978 that new Israeli settlements were being established in the Sinai, an obvious embarrassment to the Egyptians as well as being provocative. President al-Sādāt's peace initiative seemed to be unraveling.

> It seems that sending up test balloons has become one of the outstanding features of Israeli politics. After the balloon of autonomous rule that was meant to confirm the Israeli occupation of the West Bank, the leaders of Israel sent up the balloon of the Sinai settlements at a time when Begin knows more than anyone else that this question is non-negotiable.
>
> Last Friday the Israeli prime minister's office announced that the government has officially approved of new settlements in the Sinai, and it claimed that these settlements will continue to exist even in the case of a peace agreement with Egypt. Begin repeated yesterday [...] that if Egypt insists on removing the Israeli settlements in Sinai, Israel will demand the modification of the borders.
>
> So the Israeli maneuverings return. And so Israel imagines that the balloon of the settlements and keeping them on land in Egyptian Sinai may be [used for] pressure and a bargaining card.[103]

President al-Sādāt said in a January 12, 1978 interview that he was despondent over his peace initiative since the Israelis acted like "cunning merchants" who consistently refused to compromise. The hard-line Israeli position reached near disastrous proportions when on January 17, Menachem Begin lectured Foreign Minister Muḥammad Ibrāhīm Kāmil at a dinner in honor of the Egyptian minister and Secretary of State Cyrus Vance. Begin said Kāmil was too young to know how the concept of self-determination, which the Palestinians desired, had been misused (by Hitler) during the Second World War. Al-Sādāt recalled the Egyptian head of the political committee negotiating Sinai II the following day.

Muṣṭafā Amīn, writing in his column "A Thought," compared Begin to Shakespeare's Shylock. The Israeli prime minister had forgotten about his role in Dayr Yāsīn and that not long ago he was anathema to American Jewry. Now apparently rehabilitated, he was squeezing the Arabs the same way the merciless character from *The Merchant of Venice* extorted those in his debt. In this atmosphere, Egypt had no choice but to suspend the negotiations:

> Egypt broke off the negotiations with Israel after it became clear that the government of Israel does not want peace but wants surrender. It does not want to live amongst the Arab countries but to rule over the Arab countries. It does not want to make friends of Egyptians. It wants to make fools of Egyptians.[104]

The Israelis not only kept the pressure on but seriously upped the stakes in the peace game when in March they announced that 242's call for Israeli withdrawal from Arab territory did not apply to every occupied area. Israel agreed it would have to withdraw from Sinai, for example, but this did not mean withdrawal was necessary from the West Bank. The Begin government was the first Israeli administration to interpret 242 in this manner and Jimmy Carter called this interpretation of 242 a serious blow to the prospects for peace. By March the peace initiative appeared dead. The political committee formed after Ismāʿilīyah had been terminated and the military committee was getting nowhere. The euphoria, never strong except in Egypt, was turning to melancholy.

> [...] The great game, whose last chapter was President al-Sādāt's visit to Jerusalem, has ended in an Israeli victory, a Soviet victory, an American victory, and an Arab defeat.
>
> Israel is now stronger than ever. The Soviet presence in the area is wider and deeper than before ... America has become stronger in the Gulf, in Morocco, in Israel but not on Israel. It is even stronger in the confrontation states.
>
> As for the Arabs, they have lost the war card, oil card, and the road to peace.[105]

The negative implications of that quote weighed most heavily on the Palestinians. If al-Sādāt would not give up his initiative and went for a separate agreement, it would mean that the largest Arab state would be removed from the struggle. Palestinian intellectuals and the Palestinian press often asserted that the best way for the Palestinians to hinder that possibility was to make the cost of a separate agreement too great – through increased guerrilla activity. Yet the commando groups were themselves not convinced over the efficacy of that option. What if Egypt invited the PLO to participate in peace talks? Would it not be better to take half a loaf than to get nothing? Had not 30 years of rejecting compromise resulted in nothing for the Palestinians? Fighting in Sidon between rival commando groups on January 27, 1978 seemed to reflect the tension over what future for the Palestinians. ʿĀdil ʿUsayrān, a former Speaker of the Chamber of Deputies and a leader of the Shiite community in the south, called for the removal of all Palestinians groups from Sidon and the townspeople went on strike against the guerrillas on February 2. The Lebanese city that had had the closest identification with the Palestinians was abandoning the movement.

Attention focused on the Arab-Israeli conflict shifted briefly from Lebanon to Cyprus where on February 18, 1978 Palestinians assassinated Yūsuf al-Sibā'ī the Editor of *al-Ahrām*, apparently for accompanying al-Sādāt to Jerusalem. The following day in Cairo, the funeral of the fallen writer turned into an ugly demonstration against the Palestinian people. The Egyptian press called 'Arafāt a merchant who sold the Palestinian cause.[106]

> If it is true that those who committed this crime belong to extremist terrorist organizations, claiming to work in the name of Palestine, we condemn those who abuse the struggle of the Palestinian people and who make terrorism a means of killing the Palestinian revolution and its objectives.[107]

Further, the Egyptian people were resolute in their search for peace. An incident like al-Sibā'ī's murder would not deter them.

> Egyptian policy has never been and cannot be the captive of unforeseen events. It is not controlled by feelings [...] no matter what the justification [...]. If some Palestinian leaders [...] have fallen into the trap made for them, Egypt [...] can discard persons but cannot [discard] its strategic goals and causes.[108]

Al-Sādāt was not going to be deterred by the events in Cyprus. Once having made the trip to Jerusalem there was no turning aside, no matter the provocation. But that policy did not sit well with all Egyptians. We have noted the resignation of Foreign Minister Fahmī when al-Sādāt announced his determination to fly to Israel. Opposition also came from a newly organized leftist alliance, the National Unionist Progressive Party, headed by Khālid Muḥyī al-Dīn. The party published an anti-establishment newspaper, *al-Ahālī*, and the issue of March 1, 1978 criticized the government's reaction to the Sibā'ī affair. The paper said that the Sādāt administration had to take some responsibility for the violent anti-Palestinian mood of the country and also for the death of Egyptian commandos in the bungled attempt in Cyprus to free captured members of al-Sibā'ī's entourage. *Al-Ahālī* was quickly suspended for its *lèse-majesté*.

Opinion outside of Egypt was harsher. The press of Jordan and Lebanon pointed out that Egypt had brought most of its problems on itself by pursuing an unsuccessful, ill-timed, unplanned peace foray that actually had resulted in a greater chance for war. The press of Syria ignored the Cyprus events, barely mentioning al-Sibā'ī's death and its aftermath.[109]

Though the guerrilla attack in Cyprus was not successful in deterring al-Sādāt from his self-proclaimed venture for peace, the situation grew more dangerous when Palestinians on March 11 attacked into Israel 25 kilometers south of Haifa. They commandeered two buses and went on a rampage that ultimately brought death to over forty persons. For a change the Syrian and Egyptian press agreed on the meaning of the assault.

> Just executing the operation must mean to those concerned that the revolution of the Palestinian Arab people lives. It also proves this people are connected to the fatherland.[110]

> Establishing the Palestinian state and returning the legitimate rights to the Palestinian people is the only way for Menachem Begin to secure for his people their security and stability. Without that solution, the security of Israel will be a dream [...] and Israel and its people will remain the captives of fear.[111]

Fear was not limited to Israel as the Lebanese waited for the inevitable retaliation. Bad weather probably delayed it but by March 15 the skies had cleared enough to allow the bombing of Beirut and the long-awaited invasion from the south. The Israelis moved slowly northward toward the Litani River, an historic goal of theirs. Perhaps in 1967 they could have occupied south Lebanon for an indefinite period, but times had changed. The United Nations Security Council on March 19 called for Israel to withdraw forthwith. Later, talks between Jimmy Carter and Begin began in a strained atmosphere.

Lebanese interpretations in the press were divided along lines that appeared during the civil war that is along pro- and anti-Palestinian lines. For the papers of the Left, the reasons for the Israeli invasion were multifaceted. At least one motivation was a desire to create social and economic problems in Lebanon by pushing the people of the south out of their homes and into Beirut. This would keep the Palestinians and their leftist allies busy with other things than raiding into Israel. A second factor was a desire to create a buffer zone extending from the Litani to the Lebano-Israeli border that would be under Israeli influence and off limits to Palestinians.[112] Another goal was to add more territory to the Israeli empire. Despite threats from Iran to cut off its oil and censure from the United States, Israel was expansionist:

> Many say "Do not bother [to waste energy telling Israel to withdraw from Lebanon]." Israel wants both land and peace. And if it is forced to choose, it will choose land.
>
> This is true and it is also true that Begin looked around and saw Arab weakness, Arab division, and Arab inability. He also looked at President Carter and saw him the same way the Russians and Europeans see him. That is he talks forcefully and acts weakly.[113]

For the Lebanese Right, however, the cause of the Israeli invasion was the Palestinians:

> The Palestinians will not discover the horror of what they have done till it is too late. They have removed [in our eyes] any difference between themselves and their enemies [...] [Israel]. If it is true that there is a "national relationship" between the Palestinians and the Lebanese, what happened [in the south] has uprooted it.[114]

A publication that appeared as a result of the civil war and enjoyed picturing Yāsir ʿArafāt as a *shaitan* began an editorial by quoting the Lebanese penal code which defined treason and the penalties for it. The journal continued: "'Anti-Lebanese activity' has been going on since the arrival on our territory of the first commando [...] [their coming resulted in] the Palestinian occupation of the south which caused the Israeli invasion."[115]

Another Rightist editorial continued:

> The unification of Lebanon, with the Palestinians present, is an impossible task [...].
>
> Whether Israel withdraws totally or partially from the south, or does not withdraw, whether international forces can separate the "Israeli Defense Army" and "'Arafāt's Army" or not, a part of Lebanon and its people will remain under Palestinian control [as long as Palestinians remain in Lebanon].[116]

Perhaps the immediate concern for all was the presence of Israeli forces in Lebanon. The Israelis announced their willingness to withdraw but said they would do so at their own pace. The meaning was clear – they were going to perform certain "tasks" to make sure they might never have to return. One was the arming, training, and putting in control of the border area a member of the Lebanese army, Maj. Sa'id Ḥaddād. The major had established his own militia during the civil war and its avowed aim was to make sure there were no Palestinians in areas which it controlled. Ḥaddād openly collaborated with the Israelis and was a considerable embarrassment to the Christian population in Lebanon. The son of President Franjīyah called for his court-martial. Kamīl Sham'ūn, however, openly supported him. Newspaper reports carried stories that Ḥaddād was being put in control of villages from which Israel withdrew.[117] That Ḥaddād was finding a responsive chord in the hearts of many Lebanese was not dwelled upon in the press, though perhaps from the time the people of Sidon demanded that the Palestinians pull out of their city, there was no need to write about the problem. One paper attempted to interpret, in an extraordinary editorial, what was happening in Lebanon.

> The psychological invasion, dubbed "the good-fence policy" in Israel, preceded the armed assault [of 1978], starting almost simultaneously with Lebanon's two-year war [of 1975–76].
>
> It took the form of a wide range of Israeli services for the south Lebanese population: Israeli clinics for South Lebanese patients, Israeli jobs for south Lebanese labor, Israeli markets for south Lebanese farmers. [...]
>
> The results of the mental onslaught can be seen in south Lebanon today. Local opposition to the Israeli invaders, while it exists, is less pronounced than local opposition would normally be to invaders whose expansionist intentions have been common knowledge for 30 years.
>
> The brainwashing operation that paved the way for the 15 March invasion is now being resumed. The Israelis are offering the south Lebanese food, medical aid, and shelter.... Israeli soldiers have strict instructions to play the role of the good fairy with every South Lebanese villager they encounter.
>
> The 1975–78 "good fence policy" was the overture of the 15 March incursion. The current good fairy policy could be the overture of an immediate or future takeover of the South.

> The Zionist state, unable in the face of international opposition to stay in the south by force, is angling for an invitation to stay (or return) from the people of the south.[118]

For the two most important Arab confrontation states, Egypt and Syria, the implications of the Israeli invasion reached far beyond south Lebanon. President al-Sādāt was still committed to a peaceful settlement and the press under his control saw the attack of March 15 as an Israeli attempt to gain a better position at the bargaining table.

> Begin announced, after finishing the invasion of south Lebanon, Israel will keep the invading forces in an area of 1000 square kilometers that belong to no one until an agreement is reached whereby no Palestinian forces will enter the area again.
>
> Irrespective of the fact this declaration discloses that the Israeli aggression on Lebanon was planned, …it shows that Israel is going to add new cards as it is bargaining [the price] for establishing peace in the area….[119]

Undoubtedly the Egyptian leader was in a difficult position as a result of the Israeli action. His November peace initiative was all but dead. Menachem Begin had made a tough speech to the Knesset on March 29 opposing both a Palestinian state and 242. Al-Sādāt's options were already limited after having closed the door to Soviet participation in the peace process. He now seemed trapped in an Israeli-American web and, as a result, he would have to negotiate on an unacceptable basis or admit that his peace initiative had failed. Muḥammad Haykal commented on the apparently hopeless position in which al-Sādāt found himself. Writing a column in Lebanon that appeared simultaneously in Jordan and Kuwait, Haykal argued that the Egyptian position was unnecessary and counterproductive. The primary assumption that had motivated al-Sādāt's impetuous behavior – Russia was not interested in peace – was wrong. The Soviet Union wanted a negotiated peace but Egypt had "humiliated" the USSR by using its weapons to fight wars and then kicking the Russians out when they were considered superfluous. The Soviets were desirous of a peaceful settlement since they perceived it to be in their best interests. Peace would bring about social changes delayed by warfare and give rise to a new generation of Arab leaders who would find their interests more closely aligned with Russia than the United States. It was time to abandon the policy of alliance with the West.[120]

Yet it was Syria that found itself in the most difficult position as a result of the invasion. From the Sādāt initiative onward, perhaps even as early as Sinai II, its most valuable ally had been effectively neutralized. Al-'Asad could not stop the Israeli invasion though its press argued lamely that the Syrian air force was protecting 5/6ths of Lebanon. In reality it could only "protect" what Israel did not invade. Israel was laying a trap in south Lebanon for Syria, the Damascus press argued. At the same time, Egypt collaborated with the Jewish state by taunting Syria with the charge that it was not doing enough to protect the Lebanese and Palestinians, though Syria had over 25,000 soldiers in Lebanon and had seriously weakened its own defense capability on the Golan.[121]

> [...] [T]he Arab situation has reached unprecedented levels of deterioration, confusion, and lack of national responsibility, all of which are caused by the practices of President al-Sādāt's regime. [...] Sometimes one feels that the Arabs are not Arabs any more, especially since they know better than anyone that Israel does not want peace. [...]
>
> It is [also] time to be aware that America cannot give us a just peace.[122]

Syria correctly deduced that the initiative was dead if the United States did not attempt to resuscitate it. But by 1978, the United States began to theorize that al-Sādāt's initiative might serve American interests. If Egypt and Israel made a separate peace, this would insure military quiet for some time since Syria was in no position to fight alone. If the Saudis could be persuaded to join the group, on the argument that it was either America or the communists, then a second goal, continued access to oil, also could be obtained. The Carter administration thus belatedly began to exert exceptional effort to save the beleaguered peace process. A crucial sign of Western support for the Arabs had been access to technology, especially military. Hitherto the almost exclusive domain of Israel, the American government announced during the middle of February that it would sell planes to Israel, Egypt, and Saudi Arabia. The gesture was clear, the United States intended to support the country that was willing to make peace with Israel and to sell modern weaponry to another "moderate," read pro-American, Arab state.

For the Syrian press this move was just another sign that a separate treaty between Egypt and Israel was imminent. The former editor of *al-Thawrah*, Information Minister Aḥmad Iskandar Aḥmad, said the F-5E's that were to go to Egypt were outdated and had been called flying coffins in West Germany because so many of them crashed. On the other hand, said Syrian editorials, Israel was to receive the more advanced F-16. It was all part of a plot to prepare American and world public opinion for even more extensive sales of arms to the Jewish state.[123]

For Egypt the arms sale had a different meaning. It was a test of strength between the Israeli lobby and the White House over which should control American foreign policy in the Middle East.[124] When the Senate approved the sale of planes, the Egyptian press bannered it as "the first victory achieved by the peace initiative."[125]

In Syria, Lebanon, and Jordan, the approval of the plane sales was viewed with suspicion and hostility. In obtaining the planes, Egypt committed itself not to use them against Israel. This probably meant that its role in the future would be to act as the American policeman in Africa.[126] The Syrian press continued that while this might ultimately be in Egypt's interests in Africa, to claim that it was a great victory for the Arabs in their conflict with Israel was a mockery. Israel received better planes, more would be sold to it than Saudi Arabia and Egypt purchased together, and Israel would probably receive its aircraft before the Arabs.

> So Israel is arming itself, expanding, and preparing for aggression, while some Arabs are insisting on making peace with the enemy [...]. Let us ask this question, Has the West Bank become the price of American planes given to the Arabs?[127]

Dissent in Egypt to the course of events was noticeable. President al-Sādāt seemed to some to have abandoned his friends to embrace his enemies. Muḥammad Haykal called al-Sādāt's initiative a failure in an April interview in *al-Ahālī*. The small weekly paper increasingly was becoming the focus of malcontent within Egypt, having demanded in several issues between February and May closer ties with the Soviet Union. It was in this context that the Egyptian president called on May 21 for a referendum that would give him the power to crack down on his leftist opponents.

> Mr. Sādāt is having to crack down on the dissident left in Egypt.
>
> It is safe to assume that the move was prompted by evidence of the Egyptian left's growing strength.
>
> The Egyptian left is developing from a mild nuisance into a potential threat, and it is not drawing its strength from any innate ideological virtue. It is drawing it from a combination of two factors:
>
> 1. Mr. Sādāt's refusal to abandon his solo peace initiative despite Israel's increasing intransigence, which many feel has turned him into an unabashed beggar for peace who should not be allowed to go on tearing down the prized dignity of the Arabs.
> 2. Mr. Sādāt's identification with Washington, the cornerstone of Israel.
>
> The left is returning to Egypt through the same gateway it used to enter the Arab world in the first place. The gateway was built and is being maintained by Washington's foreign policy architects.
>
> Had Mr. Sādāt's visit to Jerusalem succeeded in realizing the Arab moderates' demands, Cairo would have become the Middle East's major fortress against communism.
>
> Had Mr. Sādāt's refusal to drop his initiative persuaded the United States to squeeze the Jewish state [...] Lebanon, the Arabian Gulf and North Africa would not be as vulnerable to the communist tide as they are today.
>
> What Washington is refusing to recognize is that intransigent Zionism is the steed which communism has consistently used and will continue to use to ride into the Arab world.
>
> Blind U.S. allegiance to Israel at the expense of the Arabs is incompatible with any effort to keep communism at bay in this region, regardless of the temporary advantages that can be offered by individual Arab rulers.
>
> Even the United States cannot fight fire with a bellows.[128]

Less than 5 years after the October 1973 war, the Arab world seemed to have fallen on more difficult times than it had known even after the defeat of 1967. The unilateral decision of President al-Sādāt to go to Jerusalem and make peace with the enemy was the culmination of the disintegrative Arab process. Though one could make a strong case for the Egyptian decision, citing the waste of war and the desire of the Egyptian people for peace and for some material benefits that might accrue as a result, still in June 1978 peace seemed far away. What did seem close was the possibility of an Egyptian-Israeli alliance against the more radical countries in the area. To have voiced that possibility, a Zionist-Egyptian alliance against Arabs, 30 years ago would have been reason to be incarcerated in a place for the mentally insane. Yet, by the summer of 1978, its likelihood was openly discussed and written about.

All of this should come as no surprise, argued the journals of Syria, since the whole scheme had been apparent since Sinai I and pellucidly clear since Sinai II. When Egypt agreed to renounce the use of force, the Arab-Israeli conflict entered a new era. But did Egypt have the right to do so? The Egyptian press, with the exception of *al-'Ahālī*, felt that this was in Egypt's and the Arab's best interest. There would be no unilateral settlement, no selling out of the Palestinians' rights, but the Middle East was tired of war and so other avenues had to be pursued.

The Palestinians, licking their wounds from the defeat suffered in Lebanon and inflicted partially by allies of Israel and the United States, knew they were a weak pawn to be sacrificed. Also for the Lebanese, who might be stuck with tens of thousands of Palestinians on their soil, for the Jordanians who might forfeit the West Bank, and for the Syrians who might lose the ally who would help regain the Golan Heights, the Egyptian moves were a sellout. Al-Sādāt's trip to Jerusalem therefore was not so much something new as a part of the whole deal that began, according to the Syrians, when Egypt unilaterally accepted the 1973 ceasefire.

Promoted as the first great step toward peace, the trip to Jerusalem quickly turned to tragedy with the assassination of the director of *al-Ahrām*. The mood was further soured by Prime Minister Begin's interpretation of 242 as not including the necessity to withdraw even partially from all the regions occupied in 1967. As if to emphasize this point, the leader of Israel authorized new settlements in the occupied territories.

Neither Begin nor his policies could deter al-Sādāt. He gained the backing of the United States, the commitment that America would be a full partner in the search for peace. Jets for Egypt were a sign of Carter's desire to see the process through. But in the press of the Arab world, there was unease. If al-Sādāt could negotiate a settlement with which the Arabs could live, then good. But if he could not and then decided to take the Sinai and forget about the rest, this would not be peace but surrender. Half way through 1978, one could not be sure whether the Middle East was closer to peace or closer to war.

Notes

1 Haykal remained close to power even after his dismissal. He was a confident of the powerful for thirty years and a prolific journalist and writer for five decades. Haykal died in February 2016.

2 *Al-Jumhūrīyah* (Egypt), April 24, 1974.

3 *Al-Muḥarrir*, June 11, 1974. Also see *Filasṭīn al-Thawrah*, May 22, 1974.

4 See for example *al-Bayraq*, June 10, 1964; and *al-Akhbār* (Egypt) and the *Daily Star*, both of June 12, 1964.

5 Abū Jawdah, *al-Nahār*, August 9, 1974.

6 Ṭalāl Salmān, August 9, 1974.
7 October 31, 1973.
8 The issue of terrorism reminds one of the saying that where you stand depends on where you sit. Israel has consistently identified the PLO as a terrorist organization. On the other side, Robin Wright's book, *Sacred Rage,* has as a major theme that the continuous humiliation and degradation inflicted by Israel on the Palestinians and Arab society in general, is a major reason for their Islamization and radicalization (Touchstone: New York, 2001).
9 *Al-Ahrām*, November 29, 1973; *al-Ba'th*, December 4, 1973; and *al-Ḥayāt*, November 29, 1973.
10 *Filasṭīn al-Thawrah*, February 6, 1974. Also see the same paper of February 20, March 20, and March 27, 1974.
11 Mīshāl 'Aflaq, *al-Nahār*, April 16, 1974. Also see *Filasṭīn al-Thawrah*, April 17, 1974.
12 *Al-Akhbār* (Egypt), November 12, 1974. Also see *al-Ahrām* of the same date.
13 *Al-'Amal*, November 13, 1974. Also see, for example, *al-Nahār*, *al-Ahrām*, *al-Ba'th*, or *al-Nidā'*, all of November 14, 1974.
14 Aḥmad Bahā' al-Dīn, *al-Ahrām*, October 11, 1974. Also see *al-Nahār* of November 4, 1974.
15 See any Syrian paper of January 19, 1974 and *Filasṭīn al-Thawrah*, January 16 and February 6, 1974.
16 *Al-Akhbār*, January 16, 1975; and *al-Ahrām*, January 16 and February 3, 1975.
17 Bashīr al-Jallād, *al-Thawrah*, February 7, 1975. Also see *al-Ba'th*, February 4, 1975.
18 *Filasṭīn al-Thawrah*, February 16, 1975.
19 Muḥammad Manṣūr, *al-Ba'th*, February 20, 1975.
20 Ihsān 'Abd al-Quddūs, *al-Ahrām*, March 24, 1975.
21 *Al-Ahrām*, April 1, 1975.
22 *Filasṭīn al-Thawrah*, June 14, 1975.
23 *Al-Ahrām*, August 12 and 13, and September 3, 1975.
24 For example see, *al-Thawrah*, September 6 and 7, 1975, and *al-Ba'th*, September 6, 1975.
25 *Al-Safīr*, *Bayrūt*, and *al-Sharq*, all of September 2, 1975.
26 Abū Jawdah, *Al-Nahār*, August 21, 1975 and September 2, 1975.
27 Ghassān Twaynī, *al-Nahār*, August 21, 1975. Also see *al-Muḥarrir*, May 20 and June 21, 1974; and *Bayrūt*, May 30, 1974. In an interview with UN Secretary-General Kurt Waldheim, Abū Jawdah raised the question of Lebanese fear that their country might be turned into an inferno if the commandos were suppressed. Replied Waldheim, "I understand the reason for your concern. […] You see international forces in Egypt and [United Nations] observer forces in Syria, and you feel that Lebanon has been left alone. […] The matter is completely different and there is no need for fear [!!]" (*Al-Nahār*, June 4, 1974). Also see an interview in the same journal with Prime Minister Rashīd al-Ṣulḥ who says it is no coincidence that attacks on the Palestinians occurred at the same time there was lots of talk about a political solution to the Arab-Israeli conflict (April 28, 1975).
28 *Al-'Amal*, April 15, 1975.
29 *Al-Ba'th*, April 16, 1975.
30 *Al-'Amal*, May 8, 1975.
31 See among others *al-Thawrah*, May 27, 1975; *al-Akhbār* (Egypt), June 25 and 26, 1975; and *al-Ba'th*, September 10, 1975.

32 *Time* magazine, July 14, 1975.
33 August 8, 1975.
34 *Akhbār al-Yawm*, September 13, 1975.
35 See for example, *Bayrūt*, October 8, 1975; and *al-Muḥarrir*, November 24, 1975.
36 For example see *al-Muḥarrir* and *al-Ba'th*, November 11, 1975; and *al-Thawrah*, November 12, 1975. That even in the United States there was felt to be a connection between the United Nations resolution condemning Zionism as a form of racism and the bombing of Palestinian camps, see the political cartoon by Oliphant, *Time* magazine, December 15, 1975. The cartoon shows two Palestinians hiding behind a building in a camp as Israeli planes strafe. The one Palestinian says to the second, "They must have had a hard day at the U.N."
37 *Al-'Amal*, January 3, 1976. Almost a year earlier, ironically enough, *Filasṭīn al-Thawrah* also had high praise for Franjīyah saying he was responsible for diffusing the tension in Lebanon as the civil war started (April 19, 1975).
38 *Al-'Amal*, January 14, 1976.
39 Ibid., March 21, 1976
40 Ibid., January 6, 1976.
41 Ibid., January 17, 1976.
42 *Al-Thawrah*, January 22, 1976; *al-Rā'y*, January 23, 1976; and *al-Ba'th*, January 26, 1976.
43 *Al-Ahrām*, January 10 and February 9, 1976. The Syrian press responded that Egypt was always criticizing others to cover its own political deviation (*Al-Thawrah*, February 13, 1976).
44 Samīr Franjīyah, nephew of the president and a leading spokesman of the Left (!), *al-Safīr*, March 18, 1976.
45 Ibid., April 12, 1976.
46 Kamāl Junblāṭ, *al-Anbā'*, May 15, 1976. For a defense of the Syrian action see the Jordanian, *al-Rā'y*, April 24, 1976.
47 See for example, *al-Thawrah*, May 30, 1976; *al-Ba'th*, May 31 and June 7, 1976; and *Tishrīn*, June 9, 1976.
48 Aḥmad Zayn, *al-Akhbār* (Egypt), June 7, 1976.
49 *Al-Safīr*, June 9, 1976.
50 Twaynī, *al-Nahār*, June 15, 1976.
51 *L'Orient-Le Jour*, January 12, 1976. On Tal al-Za'tar as a center of crime, see *al-'Amal*, August 14, 1976.
52 Yūsuf Samāḥah, July 1, 1976. Also see Kamāl Junblāṭ, *al-Anbā'*, July 3 and August 1, 1976.
53 See among others, *al-Nidā'*, *al-Safīr*, and *al-Muḥarrir*, all of July 21, 1976.
54 John Bulloch, *Death of a Country: The Civil War in Lebanon* (London: Weidenfeld & Nicolson, 1977), 178–82.
55 See among many, *al-Kifāḥ al-'Arabī* and *al-Safīr*, August 13, 1976.
56 August 3, 1976.
57 September 23, 1976. Also see *Bayrūt*, *al-Kifāḥ al-'Arabī* , and *al-Muḥarrir* of the same date.
58 See for example *al-Safīr* and *al-Muḥarrir*, both of October 19, 1976. The extent of Israeli backing for the Christians and those Sunni Muslims who were opposed to a Palestinian military presence in Lebanon was revealed in *Time* magazine, September 13, 1976. Also see

a critique of Kissinger's foreign policy and the CIA in Lebanon in Roger Morris, *Uncertain Greatness: Henry Kissinger and American Foreign Policy* (New York: Harper and Row, 1977), 261. The author says that while the American ambassador was trying to arrange a cease-fire, the CIA was encouraging the Right with arms and other aid.

59 *Al-Safīr*, October 22, 1976.

60 See for example *Tishrīn*, January 28, 1977; or *al-Ba'th*, January 31, 1977.

61 Abū Jawdah, *al-Nahār*, January 2, 1974. Also see *al-Ba'th*, May 17, 1977, and *al-Akhbār* (Egypt), April 11, 1977.

62 *Al-Safīr*, May 19, 1977.

63 *Al-Ahrām*, May 25, 1977. Also see ibid., May 19 and 22, 1977.

64 *Al-Dustūr* (Jordan), June 21, 1977.

65 *L'Orient-Le Jour*, May 23, 1977. The hostility on the part of *L'Orient-Le Jour* to Begin reflects perhaps two realities, one of which was related to the Syrian occupation of East Beirut during the civil war. The first is to say that the editors of the paper honestly believed that Begin's government was harmful to Arab interests though the Egyptian press might argue there was no difference between Israeli parties. The second reality was that *L'Orient-Le Jour* was published in that section of Beirut which the Syrian-dominated ADF controlled. To publish an editorial not hewing to the Syrian government position was dangerous. For Syrian and Jordanian editorials along the same line see *Tishrīn*, *al-Sha'b* (Jordan), and *al-Dustūr* (Jordan), all of May 19, 1977. Also see *al-Ba'th*, June 1, 1977; and *Tishrīn*, June 5, 1977.

66 *Al-Anwār*, February 15, 1977. Also see *al-Bayraq* of the same date.

67 Rafīq Khūrī, *al-Anwār*, February 18, 1977.

68 *Al-Akhbār* (Jordan), April 5, 1977. See also *al-Sha'b* (Jordan), April 14, 1977.

69 *Al-Thawrah*, May 10, 1977, as quoted in *L'Orient-Le Jour*, May 11, 1977. Also see *Tishrīn*, *al-Sha'b* (Jordan), and *al-Ba'th* all of May 10, 1977.

70 May 11, 1977.

71 *Le Reveil*, May 11, 1977.

72 *Al-Ahrām*, July 18, 1977.

73 Ibid., August 1, 1977.

74 Ibid., July 29, 1977.

75 Ibid., July 30, 1977.

76 *Al-Ba'th*, July 31, 1977.

77 Ibid., August 7, 1977. Also see the same paper of August 2, 1977 in which the editorialist wrote, "In any case the visit of the American Secretary of State Cyrus Vance must not be given more importance than it deserves. [...] The visit, naturally, has a political limit beyond which the Americans do not want to go, though they can."

78 Muḥammad Manṣūr, *al-Ba'th*, August 8, 1977. For an Egyptian editorial arguing that a working group was necessary see *al-Ahrām*, August 4, 1977.

79 Issa Goraieb, *L' Orient-Le Jour*, April 24, 1977. Also see *al-Ba'th*, April 4 and 26 and June 1, 1977; and *al-Anwar*, July 13, 1977.

80 *Al-Ba'th*, August 12, 1977. Also see *al-Nahār* and *al-Safīr* also of August 12, 1977.

81 *Al-Ahrām*, August 12, 1977. Also see *al-Dustūr* (Jordan), August 15, 1977.

82 See, among many others, *al-Nahār*, October 4, 1977.

83 See for example *al-Anwār*, October 7, 1977; *al-Ba'th*, October 10 and 19, 1977; and *al-Thawrah*, October 16, 1977.
84 *Al-Ba'th*, October 13, 1977.
85 *Al-Ahrām*, October 16, 1977.
86 Ibid., October 30, 1977.
87 Ibid., November 16, 1977. *Al-'Ahālī*, a new opposition paper in Egypt, was harsher. It said the trip was wrong (February 1, 1978).
88 Both of November 18, 1977.
89 *Al-Ahrām*, November 18, 1977.
90 Ibid., November 19, 1977.
91 *Al-Ba'th*, November 18, 1977.
92 Maḥmūd Kāmil, ibid., November 20, 1977.
93 See for example *L'Orient-Le Jour* and *al-Safīr*, November 20, 1977; *al-Liwā'*, *L'Orient-Le Jour*, and *al-Nahār*, November 22, 1977; *al-Anwār*, November 25, 1977; and *al-Dustūr* (Jordan), November 27, 1977.
94 Manṣūr, *al-Ba'th*, November 27, 1977.
95 'Alī Sulaymān, *al-Thawrah*, December 8, 1977. On the role of the United States in abetting the Egyptian position, see Muḥammad al-Miṣrī, *al-Thawrah*, December 9, 1977. "It is now apparent that the contradictory declarations of the American president during the past year were planned to throw ashes in their [i.e. the Arabs'] eyes and to prepare for al-Sādāt's move. [These gave] him all the justification to continue in the plan (which America has which aims first and foremost at serving racialist Zionism) that could not be [otherwise] obtained in 30 years."
96 *Al-Ahrām*, November 28, 1977. Also see *al-Akhbār*, December 14, 1977.
97 For those editorials sympathetic to the Syrian-led point of view see *al-Safīr*, December 2, 1977; *al-Ba'th*, December 3, 1977; *al-Thawrah*, and *al-Nahār*, December 6, 1977; and *IKE*, December 7, 1977. For the opposite, Egyptian, viewpoint, see among others, *al-Ahrām*, November 30 and December 3, 1977.
98 *Al-Ahrām*, December 17, 1977. Also see *al-Akhbār*, December 14, 1977.
99 *Al-Anwār*, December 18, 1977. Also see *al-Jumhūrīyah* (Egypt) *and al-Anwār* of December 20, 1977.
100 December 27, 1977. Also see *al-Rā'y* (Jordan), *Tishrin,* and *al-Ba'th* all of December 27.
101 *Al-Ahrām*, December 31, 1977. Also *al-Rā'y* (Jordan), January 3, 1978.
102 *Al-Thawrah*, January 5, 1978. PLO displeasure with al-Sādāt's initiative was also widespread, leading *al-Ahrām* to comment: "The Palestine revolution eats its own children. The Palestine Liberation Organization, by following the rejectionist forces, takes the first step on the road to political oblivion" (January 6, 1978).
103 *Al-Ahrām*, January 10, 1978. Also see ibid., January 14, 1978.
104 *Al-Akhbār* (Egypt), January 19, 1978. The reference to Shylock immediately raised the specter of anti-Semitism. The frustration of the Egyptians since the conference at al-Ismā`ilīyah had given rise to increasingly offensive Egyptian editorials. The most deplorable of the commentaries were written by Anīs Manṣūr for *al-Ahrām*. He took pleasure in making fun of Jews through rather pitiful stories. See for example his columns December 25, 27, 30, and 31,

1977 and January 3, 5, and 6, 1978. When Prime Minister Begin rightfully called the attention of the media to these demeaning articles, the Egyptian press stopped its flirtation with anti-Semitism. See *al-Ahrām*, January 19, 1978, for a calmer discussion of the reason for the recall of Egypt's negotiators. For an interesting discourse on the whole episode, see Bernard Lewis, "Is Peace Still Possible in the Middle East?", *Commentary* 66 no. 1 (July 1978): 37–45. Lewis brings to the attention of his readers the Israeli disappointment over the Egyptian editorials. He goes on to say that (presumably during the same period) there was not one derogatory line in the Jewish press about Egypt or its president. The implication, untrue, was that the Israeli press had never said a nasty word about its enemy. Lewis argues that the lack of negative comment in the Israeli press was amazing since that press is not controlled. If censorship is control, then certainly the Israeli press, as was discussed earlier, was partially controlled.

105 *Al-Anwār*, February 8, 1978.

106 *Al-Akhbār*, February 20, 1978.

107 *Al-Ahrām*, February 19, 1978.

108 Ibid., February 27, 1978.

109 For example see *al-Ba'th* of February 1978, which published ten days late a small piece about the fallen editor. Also see the Jordanian *al-Rā'y* of the same date for condemnation of Egyptian excesses.

110 *Al-Ba'th*, March 13, 1978.

111 *Al-Ahrām*, March 14, 1978.

112 *Al-Sayyad*, March 22, 1978.

113 *Al-Anwār*, March 24, 1978.

114 *Al-'Amal*, March 23, 1978.

115 *Le Reveil*, March 29, 1978.

116 *Al-'Amal*, April 11, 1978.

117 See *al-Safīr*, March 30 and April 7, 1978.

118 *IKE*, April 6, 1978.

119 *Al-Ahrām*, March 17, 1978. A pro-Libyan paper, *al-Safīr*, March 24, 1978, felt that the most dangerous aspect of the Lebanese invasion was not that Israel would use it to demand more at the bargaining table. Rather the real danger was that the Israelis would promise to withdraw in return for the resurrection of al-Sādāt's peace initiative.

120 *Al-Anwār*, April 5, 1978.

121 *Al-Ba'th*, April 3, 1978; and *Tishrīn*, April 5 and 21, 1978.

122 *Al-Ba'th*, March 29, 1978.

123 See for example ibid., May 14, 1978.

124 Representative editorials may be seen in *al-Ahrām*, May 7 and 14, 1978.

125 'Alī Ḥamdī al-Jammāl, *al-Ahrām*, May 17, 1978. Mishāl Abū Jawdah was less enthusiastic. He called the approval a consolation prize for al-Sādāt for "not realizing any progress in his peace initiative" (*Al-Nahār*, May 18, 1978).

126 *Al-Ba'th*, May 22, 1978. For similar editorials see *al-Thawrah*, May 17, and *al-Ba'th*, May 19 and 21, 1978.

127 Ibid., May 24, 1978.

128 *IKE*, May 20, 1978.

Chapter 9

Conclusion

Arab editorials on the Middle East conflict may be summarized in any number of ways. Since we have discussed control and censorship at some length, perhaps we may best review the editorials by dividing them into two eras, those written in relative freedom up to 1958 and those written after that date.

As for those commentaries written in the earlier period, they can be further divided along two broad divisions. First, there is the question of Palestine and Israel and its relationship to the remainder of the Middle East, especially the Arab Middle East. Second, there is the role of Palestine and Israel in the World.

In its narrower context, that is, as an Arab problem, the issue of Palestine and Israel produced diverging responses in the Arab newspapers. It can be said unequivocally that from the beginning the loss of Palestine and the threat of Israel were not the great unifiers of the Arab world. The third chapter of this study showed that prior to the Arab intervention of May 1948, the Arabs were unified editorially before the Zionists. But this unity may have been more illusory than real. The Arabs' unity had not been tested in battle and, with a victory unquestionably before them, the editorials may have been only mouthing unity without a real understanding of the centrifugal forces in the area. On the other hand, there may be some validity to the argument that the Arabs were united prior to their defeat in 1948, but this defeat caused dissension. This line, however, upon closer scrutiny is not very convincing. The Arabs, in their contemporary history, have not been noted for their unanimity. It seems more likely that the failure of 1948 served as a catalyst to increase Arab fissures.

This is not to imply that Arab writers were not agreed upon a majority of points on Palestine. They repeatedly emphasized that Palestine was Arab and, by implication, that the State of Israel because it was not – ought not to exist. They wrote that Israel was a colonial, expansionist state with designs of enlarging itself till it reached from the Euphrates to the Nile. But even these pronouncements did not improve inter-Arab harmony. The writing dealing with those factors upon which all Arabs agreed was largely ignored. What was noticed by one writer, one paper, or one country was the hostile comment that emanated from contending newspapers.

At the commencement of the conflict, the Egyptians were criticized by the papers of Jordan, Syria, and Lebanon for their role in the prosecution of the 1948 war. The Egyptians were felt to have been less occupied with Palestinian considerations than with domestic problems. Even with the overthrow of Farūq, Arab editorials chastised the Egyptians for being more concerned with the Suez Canal and the British than with the problems facing the other Arabs. The Egyptians, themselves, were willing to concede that the problem of being rid of the British was their paramount concern.

Likewise in the 1940s and 1950s, Lebanon was attacked editorially for its position vis-à-vis Israel and the Arabs. It was accused of sacrificing Arab desires to nationalistic interests. Undoubtedly underlying these editorial attacks was some suspicion of the role of a Christian Arab nation in the midst of a Muslim Arab world. Lebanon was felt to be more interested in trade, in avoiding fighting, and in protecting its Jewish population than in redeeming the land lost in Palestine.

Jordan was attacked the most consistently and the most violently. Perhaps the greatest focus for Arab dissension was the Jordanian annexation of the West Bank of the Jordan River after 1948. The Jordanian pledge not to invade that portion of Palestine that was assigned to the Jewish state was harshly criticized. The disclosure of the meetings between Jordanian and Israeli leaders also was heavily castigated in the press. The special Hashimite relationship with the British was noted as another debit in the Palestinian question.

In the deluge of criticism that followed the defeats of 1948, only Syria escaped relatively unscathed.

The editorial comments of the writers of one country which attacked a second country were not always unfounded. The allegation that Lebanon was more interested in a sound economy than righting the wrongs committed in Palestine has some verity. The same may be said of all the Arab nations involved in this study. The reason for this may lie in the fact that each country that surrounded Palestine viewed the problem less often from an Arab viewpoint than from a narrower national aspect. The Arab leaders were thus criticized for pursuing limited national interest. This same condemnation may be applied to the Arab editorialist who defended his country's policies.

Undoubtedly, Lebanon had unique interests in the Middle East. It was a nation possessing a population approximately one-half Christian. There was no denial that many of that number feared Muslim rule. This apprehension was shown in a limited number of Lebanese editorials. The writers, almost unanimously, wanted to preserve the Lebanese entity and so often viewed the Palestine problem from the angle of their own security. Survival included the protection of all minority groups as well as the protection of Lebanese borders. The editorials of Lebanon said that the people were willing to aid the other Arabs, but on Lebanese terms. For this reason, nationalistic Lebanese editorial opinion was never an outspoken critic of the lack of Arab unity. In the back of these nationalists' minds was the fear that if the Arab armies did unite, Christian Lebanon would not survive. "For Palestine and not for the King of Prussia."[1]

Although the Syrians were not widely criticized, they did not escape the temptation to view Palestine from a nationalistic aspect. Certainly the uproar over the diversion of the Jordan River south of Lake Hulah and the draining of the marshes of the area evoked more editorial reaction within Syria than from any other Arab country. This parochial view was also manifest in the anti-Hashimite feeling of many Syrian writers. They remembered the desire of the Hashimites to center their kingdom in Damascus. The writers often viewed with equal alarm the activities of the Israelis and the Hashimites. There were numerous editorials that said that the Jordanians and Israelis were in allegiance against Syria. There was also a nationalistic tendency to believe that Syria was the main target of expansionist Israel. This fear of Israeli expansion, however, was not exclusively Syrian. The papers of each of the Arab countries tended to see their homeland as the next Zionist target.

Palestine and Jordan were also afflicted with narrow interests in their approach to Palestine and Israel. The monarchical designs of the Hashimites had to be considered. The pro-Western stance of 'Abd Allāh and his successors was also a factor in editorial opinion. If a paper wanted to continue to publish, even in the period before 1958 which we have characterized as being relatively free, it had to take into consideration the wishers of the regime. Equally important was the policy of Jordan and its related monarchy in Iraq. The possibility of leadership of the Arab world was important in molding editorial opinion in Jordan.

The Egyptian aloofness in the initial period, excusable as it may have been, demonstrates, however, that the leading nation in the Arab world has not always taken a leading position in the struggle against Israel. Editorially, the Egyptian press was removed from the problem of Palestine. It was more concerned with the British and the Suez Canal. *Al-Ahrām*, which quickly supported the RCC, reflected the official view that for the Egyptians, Britain was the major problem. This feeling was echoed in a significant number of Egyptian journals.

The Arab press, in the intertwining of national and regional interests with the Palestine question, seemed to have failed in two respects. First, the newspapers reflected growing nationalism in the Middle East. One may call this regional interests or religious interests, but it is indisputable that those who lived in Syria were beginning to think of themselves as Syrians, in Egypt as Egyptian, and so forth. And each was more worried about his own land. The editorial writer thus viewed the problems of Palestine from a very narrow base. Instead of being concerned with the broad implications for the Arab world of Israel, he was often only interested in what would be the local consequences of Israel.

Further, while writing from a narrow base, the editorialists accused each other of having narrow, nationalistic interests. While claiming that the danger from Israel was imminent for Jerusalem, the Jordanian writers would criticize the Lebanese for indifference. The Syrian would accuse the Egyptians of caring more for Suez than for the Jordan River. Everywhere unity was the clarion, but unity for limited nationalistic reasons. It seems that in calling for unity, while they were not themselves able to unify, the journalists were unrealistic. The writers were incapable of seeing that complaining about Palestine and Israel from a limited aspect and criticizing other correspondents for doing the same thing was incompatible with unity. The Arab writers pursued doggedly the myth of Arab unity while adding to the disunity. In fact, the call for Arab unity against the Zionists was enough to anger one writer or another. Who was to unify and be the leader of this unity were occasions for argument. In relentlessly pursuing this figment, the editorialists left the realm of probability for that of the ephemeral and thus hindered the Palestine cause by tapping energies to argue the pros and cons of a myth when those energies were needed for Palestine. It would have been better had they stuck to the realm of the possible and encouraged their readers along those lines.

If the editorialists are criticized for their flights of fancy in desiring Arab unity as a prerequisite to the successful defeat of Israel, they were less flighty in other areas dealing with inter-Arab alternatives in facing Israel. The Arab editorials were fairly militant in their calls for a solution to the Arab-Zionist question. In this respect, undoubtedly they mobilized Arab public opinion and may well have influenced their governments' views. Prior to the fighting of 1948, the writers rejected the United Nations' resolution and called the partition of Palestine immoral. To a large degree, the West was held responsible for this immorality – from the Balfour Declaration to the partition resolution. But the West was not the only segment criticized. Perhaps the original sin rested with the western European countries and the United States, but the Arab leaders were also held responsible for any adverse results in Palestine. In their militant call, the Arab writers, while willing to concede that the West was culpable, felt that the Arab leaders should arouse the people to fight the West and its representative, Israel. It was this feeling that allowed the journalists, prior to May 1948, to call for an armed solution to the Palestine question. When this satisfactory solution was not forthcoming, the Arab writers condemned, along with the West, the Arab League, King 'Abd Allāh, and any other Arab leader felt to be responsible for the debacle.

This militancy also led to the rejection of the first truce and, to a lesser extent, the second truce of 1948. The reasons for the rejection of the 1948 truces were overlapping. The editorialists were convinced of the justice of their cause. Often, they could not understand why others would not vouchsafe that justice was on their side. They were thus frustrated that right and justice, in this world, were not enough. They recognized that for justice to succeed, might was necessary. Perhaps this was a rationalization on their part for the use of force. Undoubtedly, every conqueror or would-be conqueror, including Arab and Israeli, has felt that right was on his side. Be that as it may, the Arab writers, impelled certainly be a deep sense of frustration, urged the use of force to gain their rights. They felt that the Arabs were superior in force and thus rejected the first truce. They often commented that the truce was only accepted under pressure. But since they viewed the partition resolution as immoral, they concluded that to submit to it was immorality itself.

The defeat of the Arabs, following the end of the first truce, and the imposition of the second truce tempered the Arab writers' militancy. They were not so bound to justice as an abstract point that they could not see the realities around them. Starting toward the end of 1948, over a prolonged period, the Arab writers' militancy slowly cooled. By the beginning of the 1950s, they were willing to accept peace. This same pattern was observable before and after the Suez War of 1956. Immediately prior to the war, Arab editorial opinion was forceful. When the war was lost, this militancy slowly died. War imposed its realities on the Arabs.

The realities that the editorialists accepted were that Israel was a strong power capable of defeating the Arab forces and that the Arabs had been defeated in war. These realities forced a startling reversal of opinion toward the acceptance of the United Nations' resolutions, especially the resolution dealing with the acceptance of Palestinian partition. But this acceptance was not wholehearted. Undoubtedly, the Arab writers hoped for better terms. Nonetheless, the armistice, negotiated in 1949, was accepted, and editorial opinion supported the three UN resolutions dealing with Palestine. It should be emphasized, however, that these resolutions were not accepted out of love, but out of many fears. Justice was still the same but political realities had changed. There was a fear of further Israeli expansion, a fear of Jewish immigration into Palestine, and a fear that if the resolutions were not accepted, a worse fate might befall the Arabs.

In being fearful and accepting of the resolutions, the editorialists felt that if only the Arabs could fight, editorial opinion would reject any peace with Israel. Conjecture may be made over the results had the Arab governments accepted the editorial advice and not negotiated a settlement. An argument may be made that had the Arabs and Israelis accepted a peace based upon the United Nations' resolutions, they might have refused to honor the peace settlement once the Arabs became militarily stronger. This type of argument results in a *reductio ad absurdum*. War is better than peace in the Middle East. A better argument would be that had they accepted a negotiated peace and had their boundaries been internationally guaranteed, the Arabs and Israelis would have respected their obligations.

One point should be noted concerning the armistices of 1949. When the Arabs began to accept the UN resolutions, they viewed the separate ceasefire resolutions as a prelude to peace. However, this differed sharply from the Israelis, and in some instances from Western opinion. The Arab editorialists viewed the cease-fire agreements as a stoppage in the fighting in order to implement previous United Nations' resolutions. The Israelis and their allies, however, viewed the cease-fires as preliminaries to a negotiated peace with concessions likely concerning the UN resolutions. For the Arab editorialists, the resolutions were the minimum acceptable. For the Israelis, the resolutions were maximum grants never envisaged as a possibility. In the minds of Arab journalists, there was no further reason to negotiate. The broad lines of a permanent peace had already been established. All that was needed was Israeli compliance. This attitude held true for 1956 as well as for 1948. As a concession for their defeat in both wars, the Arabs were willing to accept UN resolutions. However, the Israelis, because of their victories, viewed the resolutions as being outdated and denying them the fruits of victory.

As far as Arab opinion toward Israel in its world context was concerned, the Zionist state was seen as a foreign invention established to harm the Arabs. This editorial view was reinforced by the belief that it was not the massacres of Hitler that had led to the establishment of Israel; it was Jewish pressure in the Diaspora on world governments. Editorialists felt that this Western, Jewish pressure was instrumental in the establishment of Israel and had sinister motivations. There even developed the feeling that the Jews wanted to use Palestine as the center for some future empire. They were also accused of being the agents of the West who were intent on keeping the Arabs from progressing, from founding strong nation-states, and from choosing friends as they liked in the world community. These beliefs resulted in an increase in anti-Semitism. This feeling, although never widespread, was perceptible and appeared to grow stronger from 1947 to 1958. Early in the period covered in this study, some Arab writers could defend the Jewish Arabs. This was no longer possible in the late 1950s.

The major belief about Israel in its world context, that it was designed to be a disturbing influence in the Arab world, must be understood to fathom Arab editorial opinion. Once it is comprehended that the Arabs viewed Israel as a Western appendage inserted into the Arab East, editorial intransigence toward the West is better understood. All programs, no matter their shape or goal, were seen in the context of Arabs versus the colonial agent of the West, Israel.

As a Western agent in an Eastern area, Israel was invariably branded with the titles of imperialist and colonialist. Friendship with the Arab countries, wrote the editorialists, was incompatible with support for Israel. It was thus not surprising to discover the decline of editorial sympathy for the West.

It is in this light that American attempts at economic and defensive plans should be seen. The Tripartite Declaration was either a reaffirmation of old influences, an affirmation of the right to intervene in the affairs of the Arab states, or a guarantee of Israel's borders when UN resolutions had established different borders.

The Johnston Plan for regional development of natural resources was also seen in the light of the Arab-Israeli conflict, with the West acting as the major supporter of Israel. The Johnston Plan came too close on the heels of the beginning of the diversion of the Jordan River and the massacre in the Jordanian village of Qubīyah. It was announced while Ben-Gurion held both the portfolio of prime minister and that of Defense Minister. This latter point was thought to be another Western attempt to scare the Arabs into accepting the Johnston Plan.

The Baghdad Pact, besides antagonizing those Arab states opposed to Iraqi predominance, was viewed with suspicion because it included Turkey and Iran. Slyly the West was going to have peace by allying Muslim countries, two of which recognized Israel.

The Eisenhower Doctrine was issued at a time when the Israelis were still occupying portions of the Sinai Peninsula and the Gaza Strip. No further editorial comment was necessary.

In each of the five instances mentioned above, the Arab writers felt the West, and here especially the United States, was attempting to force an Israeli peace upon the Arabs. The question was repeatedly asked, Why did the Tripartite Declaration guarantee Israel's borders when a just settlement of borders could be established within the framework of United Nations resolutions? The answer which the writers announced was that Israel, being a client of the West, received privileged treatment. Why had the West chosen such a disturbed time to announce the Johnston Plan? The answer for the Arab writers was that Israel and the West were attempting once again to find an economic solution to a political problem already solved by the United Nations. The Arab editorialists repeatedly pointed out the lack of recognition of international borders in the planning. How else could one explain a plan by a group of engineers who had never surveyed the area about which they wrote? The activities of the Israelis and Prime Minister Ben-Gurion were aimed at showing the Arabs that if they did not accept the Johnston Plan they might expect the worst, including the seizure of their rivers and subsequent exploitation without Arab benefits.

The Baghdad Pact was another link in the chain of Western and Israeli conspiracies. While the Arabs were worried about the danger of Israel, the West wanted an alliance against communism, an alliance that would include, interestingly enough, Israel. Whether what they wrote was true or not is irrelevant. That it was written about and believed are critical points. Sometimes what is believed is more important than what is true. In this respect, the Eisenhower Doctrine was no different from the Baghdad Pact except that as blackmail, the Arab editorialists wrote, the United States would give no aid to Arab countries unless they subscribed to the Doctrine. A second difference between the Doctrine and the Baghdad Pact was the overt acceptance by Israel of the Eisenhower Plan.

The pattern was unmistakable. Every American and Western attempt to draw closer, to initiate dialogue, to aid, and to unite with the Arabs led to violent opposition in at least one segment of the Arab press – all this while Russian influence grew unabated. Arab editorial opinion, at the beginning of this study, was strongly pro-Western. By 1958, the best that can be said is that editorial opinion was about equally divided in support of East and West.

The conclusions are quite clear. As far as it may be judged from editorial opinion, there was no great love for the Soviets. But American blunders in the Middle East led to the rise of Russian influence. This is what the writers felt. The West backed Israel and so the Russians backed the remainder of the Middle East. The West proposed an unpopular plan and so the Russians opposed it. America and Britain withdrew support for the High Dam and Russia agreed to build it. This analogy extends to other areas. The West committed mistakes of major proportions by tying the Tripartite Declaration, the Johnston Plan, the Baghdad Pact, and the Eisenhower Doctrine to Israel. In all of them there was a link that would somehow bring the two belligerents together. There were no major Western plans for the area that did not include Israel. What this was at best was neutrality: a Western neutrality toward Israel and the Arab states. But neutrality was a sin, as Secretary Dulles had said. The Arab writers felt it was a question of either the Arabs or Israel. When the West insisted upon including Israel in all of its plans, the Arab writers could only infer that since the West was not with them, it must be against them. Perhaps the Arab editorialists may be chastised for caring more for their area than for the rest of the world. On the other hand, the West, as the editorialists pointed out, often cared more for itself than for justice in the Middle East.

The union of Egypt and Syria in 1958 marked a watershed in the history of the contemporary Middle East. Besides the obvious political implications of the foundation of the UAR, that year also saw the decline of a free press in much of the area under study. Greater control of the press, however, did not change the tone of editorials so much as signal, for a time, the shifting of major attention away from the conflict to other issues. We have discussed the fact that after 1958, focus was centered on intra-Arab questions, for example, the problem of Arab unity. What opinion was written about the Middle East conflict was generally sterile, often merely reflecting governmental dictates on a given matter. Journals of one country rarely disagreed over attitudes toward another country. But they had differed amongst themselves on domestic issues. After 1958 this too stopped. Gone were the days when a paper within a country reflected a certain constituency and debated a subject with other journals in the same country. Generally all papers in a given country voiced the same line. The one notable exception to that was in Lebanon where an unfettered press remained after 1958 till a significant portion was brought under Syrian control in December 1976. In the 1960s, Beirut became the center of Palestinian publications. In the 1970s, several oil rich countries, most notably Iraq and Libya, bought into the press, thereby introducing new options in the quest for influence in the Arab world. What the other Arab countries lacked in diversity was compensated for in Lebanon.

Besides Lebanon, another source of color in an otherwise gray era was the emergence of Muḥammad Ḥasanayn Haykal as the *eminence grise* in Egypt and the alter ego of Jamāl ʻAbd al-Nāṣir. His insightful columns, perhaps a natural result of his closeness with the president of Egypt, made *al-Ahrām* the most widely read Arabic newspaper. Though Mishāl Abū Jawdah was acclaimed as Haykal's successor, it was inconceivable that the leading editorialist for the Arab world could come from one of the smallest Arab countries. One should point out that with the removal of Haykal in 1974, *al-Ahrām*'s reputation also suffered.

With the exceptions we have mentioned, editorial comment on the Middle East conflict for the decade after 1958 was not of great interest. However, there was renewed attention toward the middle of the 1960s with the materialization of an organized guerrilla movement. But opinion about the efficacy of the Palestinian movement was not of great concern until after the disastrous defeat of 1967. Certainly, however, the war influenced the way Arabs thought about themselves. The military collapse had negative implications about Arab society and its ability to come to grips with the twentieth century. Though the initial inclination of the press was to reflect the depression of Arab society, papers ultimately served the state by seeking to improve the morale of the populous. This task was made easier when the Arab military began to make punitive raids on Israeli-held territory in 1969.

Another positive alternative that emerged after the 1967 war was the hope that commandos' action might be a way out of the dire circumstances. Undoubtedly, the success of the Vietnamese had an impact on how the Arabs thought. Though writers like Haykal might argue that popular war could not be fought in unpopulated areas like the Sinai, still guerrilla successes caught the imagination of Arab writers.[2] There were some problems, however. One was the moral question of attacking targets of third parties, for example French commercial aircraft. There was also the proliferation of guerrilla groups as ideologies and governments contended for recruits and iunfluence.

As if these problems were not enough for the newly emerging Palestinian nationalists, there was the beginning of Israeli raids against Arab host countries that allowed guerrillas to operate from their countries. The earliest spectacular attack was against the Beirut airport in December 1968. There were also increased assaults against Jordan. Editorial opinion in both countries began to question whether Jordan and Lebanon wanted to sacrifice themselves for the Palestinians.[3] Pro-Palestinian papers felt that the guerrilla movement did not threaten Lebanese sovereignty, that Jordan had an obligation to support the Palestinians, and that if either country tried to suppress the commandos, they would have to answer to the other Arab states.

Yet, each Arab country pursued its own interests, regardless of the Palestinians. When 'Abd al-Nāṣir accepted a political solution to the Middle East conflict by accepting the Rogers' Plan in 1970, pro-Palestinian writers felt the stage was set to suppress the guerrilla movement. Just when Lebanese Christians and Jordanians were questioning guerilla activity, Egypt apparently deserted the homeless Palestinians. Many writers felt that the Jordanian civil war was a natural outcome.

Perhaps with the Egyptian acceptance of the Rogers' Plan one can begin to speak of the internationalization of the Arab-Israeli conflict. The Soviet Union traditionally had been interested in a negotiated peace but lacked the influence in the area needed to produce one. The coming of America, though sanctioned by 'Abd al-Nāṣir, was met with editorial suspicion. Haykal had urged this course since the 1967 war as a way of neutralizing United States' influence with Israel. But this appeal for the Arabs to be more even-handed in its dealings with the outside world was met with derision by most editorial writers. Little did anyone imagine that after the death of 'Abd al-Nāṣir, his successor would go to even greater lengths to embrace the United States.

The death of 'Abd al-Nāṣir seemed to add to the Arabs' problems. His successor lacked domestic support and was viewed as weak. He unnecessarily brought derision on himself by proclaiming 1971 as a year of decision in the history of the Arab-Israeli conflict. He chased the Soviets from Egypt without obtaining concessions from America. Though scorned, he persevered and was successful in October 1973 in restoring Arab pride.

The 1973 war and the oil embargo were glorious according to editorials. The despair following 1967 vanished. But it was in the aftermath of the Arabs' greatest contemporary victory that their unity, never strong, dissolved. After the 1973 war, al-Sādāt wholeheartedly embraced the West and fired Haykal who called for neutrality between the two sides. These acts clearly signaled that al-Sādāt wanted a peaceful settlement. This was not necessarily anathema to Lebanon, Jordan, Syria, or the Palestinians. All sides, in their editorials, were willing to negotiate. Only the rejectionists, Libya and Iraq, who had bought into the Lebanese press, refused this path through their editorials. The majority of editorials, however, agreed with a negotiated settlement but urged the Egyptians to stand united with the Arabs in the quest for peace as they had in time of war. But Egypt seemed determined to travel alone witness the acceptance of the ceasefire, Sinai II, and the trip to Jerusalem. So it was, ironically, that following the Arabs' first military success, we see the greatest break in editorial ranks as writers scrambled to support the positions of their governments. Perhaps this best epitomizes the history of the Arab press' view of the Arab-Israeli conflict. One may write of the demise of a free press in the Arab world beginning in 1958, but as lamentable as that may be, it had little effect on newspapers' commentaries of Middle

East hostilities. Egypt was accused by the press of the other Arab states in the 1950s of being more interested in the Suez Canal than Palestine. In the 1970s substitute the Sinai Peninsula for the Suez.

National and regional feelings as well as governmental policy traditionally have been more important in determining the tone of deliberations on the Arab-Israeli conflict than the presence or absence of a free press. Perhaps they should be, but when editorials are dictated by any government, one cannot say categorically they represent popular will. In al-Sādāt's decision to have a unilateral peace treaty with Israel, the Egyptian press played no decision-making role. Its function was to publicize the decision and to encourage popular acceptance. One wonders then how the will of the people is made known in the Arab world?

The pretext given for the nationalization of the press in the Middle East was that it was intended to end the monopoly by small groups and individuals of the distribution of news. The owners of papers only published what benefited themselves not what was in the best interests of society at large. To stop this abuse, the governmental argument proceeded, papers should be owned by the people or, as in Egypt, the ASU, the party of the people. But both the ASU and the Egyptian writers' syndicate, to which you must belong in order to be able to write, are dominated by the president of Egypt. He uses both to further his goals. That there is no censorship in Egypt today is true because there is no need. Writers who criticize the regime are not allowed to write. The right of expression in Egypt is not free, nor is it in Jordan or Syria. In Lebanon, historically one bought the privilege. In none of the countries does it represent the expressed will of the people.

The examination of Arab editorials becomes difficult after the 1973 war. We have mentioned that editorials served after the 1967 war to build up the people's morale. After 1973, editorials served to further the interests of the state in which they were printed. As one looks back and interprets what occurred in Egypt after 1973, it seems easy to build a case that al-Sādāt wanted peace with Israel, no matter the cost to Egypt's relationships with the other Arab states. For him, perhaps, communism, threats from radical Arab countries, and rebuilding Egypt's war-torn economy were reasons enough to make peace with Israel. Egyptian editorials said that there would not be a unilateral peace with Israel, that the rights of the Palestinians would not be bartered, that the West Bank was Arab, and that not an inch of Arab territory would be given away. But, tellingly, the Egyptian writers warned that those who did not follow al-Sādāt's lead did so at their own peril.

Although we could have dismissed Jordanian and Syrian editorials after 1973, which warned of an Egyptian sellout of the Arab cause, in retrospect they may have been correct. Thus, the Lebanese civil war, even with its very real domestic causes, became part of an anti-Palestinian plot. It was an attempt by the United States, Egypt, and Israel to crush the Palestinians, thereby smoothing the way for a settlement acceptable to those who defeated the guerrillas.[4] This conspiratorial view of history is highly popular in the Arab world. It was voiced in the Arab press.

Whatever the reasons, a civil war did break out in Lebanon. It was a highly complex struggle that virtually defied analysis. For the Syrian press, it was the natural outcome of Egypt's treasonous flirtations with the United States and Israel. For the Lebanese Right, it was the result of foreigners bearing arms. For the Palestinians, it was a trap in which they were to be lured and destroyed. Fortunes, alliances, and editorial opinion shifted with the tide of battle. At one time or another all the newspapers outside of Egypt opposed al-Sādāt. The Lebanese press feared a separate settlement, which would leave the Palestinians in Lebanon. The Jordanians wanted the West Bank, which they could not obtain without Egyptian help. The Syrians dreaded isolation facing Israel. At another time, the pro-Palestinian press accused the Lebanese Right of being in collusion with Israel in trying to destroy the guerrillas. The Lebanese Right denied the connection and welcomed aid from Syria when it was losing. The Left said the Syrians were traitors and called on Egypt for aid. The Syrian press justified the action against the Palestinian-Leftist alliance and 2 years later in 1978 defended a crack-down on their erstwhile allies, the Right. The United States overtly tried to bring the fighting under control and clandestinely fueled the conflict with money and material. The Egyptian press, reflecting governmental thinking, said a plague on all your houses and proceeded to support a unilateral settlement with Israel.

The course of the Middle East conflict between 1973 and 1978, as described in Arab press editorials, challenges one's ability to comprehend. It is not so much a failing on the part of the commentators to present their positions clearly as the dizzying changes that occurred in the Middle East after 1973. Alliances shifted so quickly that what was true one day was no longer so the following. This was compounded by seemingly irrational realities. Could anyone have believed that one of the results of the Arab-Israeli conflict would be the destruction of Lebanon by Arabs? To suggest an Egyptian-Israeli alliance facing the Arab world would have been viewed as lunacy a decade earlier. If al-Sādāt and Begin could win the Nobel Peace Prize, then perhaps nothing should come as a surprise for editorialists. Did the awarding of the Nobel Peace Prize to two former terrorists mean that the Middle East was closer to peace, or closer to war? Forty years later, would anyone recall? Arab writers could be forgiven for asking, Who remembers Ralph Bunche?

Notes

1 Kesrouan Labaki, *L'Orient*, September 8, 1948.

2 In a serialization of 'Abd al-Nāṣir's life, Haykal wrote that guerrilla activity not only captured the Arabs' imagination but also that of the People's Republic of China. The Egyptian writer related that Mao Tse-Tung and Chou En-Lai both urged 'Abd al-Nāṣir to continue fighting in 1967 by forming guerrilla units in the Sinai. The Egyptian president responded by saying that the Sinai was an unpopulated desert and that one could not wage a people's war of liberation without people. The Chinese were not impressed (*Al-Nahār*, October 31, 1971).

3 The question of national sacrifice for the Palestinian cause was a recurring one. While agreeing that the Palestinians should sacrifice for their cause, Pierre Gemayel was the most outspoken critic of others sacrificing their nation for the Palestinians. See an interview of him on this topic, *al-Ḥawādith*, February 6, 1975.

4 We have already mentioned CIA connections with the anti-Palestinian Lebanese Right. The most unyielding member of this alliance was former president Kamīl Sham'ūn. He is alleged to have made a secret trip to Israel seeking aid against the Palestinians (*Chicago Tribune*, August 24, 1978). His ties with the CIA are much older – it helped fix an election for him when he was president (see Charles Yost, *The Conduct and Misconduct of Foreign Affairs* [New York: Random House, 1972], 95).

Bibliography

I. Books

Arabic

'Abd al-Raḥmān, Awātif. *Humūm al-Ṣihḥāfah wa al-Ṣiḥāfiyīn fi Miṣr* (Concerns of the Press and Journalists in Egypt). Cairo: Dār al-Fikr al-'Arabi, 1995.

'Abduh, Ibrāhīm. *Jarīdat al-Ahrām* (The Newspaper al-Ahrām). Cairo: Dār al-Mu'āraf, 1951.

al-'Alamī, Mūsā. *'Ibrat Filasṭīn* (The Lesson of Palestine). Beirut: Dār al-Kashshāf, 1949.

al-'Aqqād, Aḥmad Khalīl. *Al-Ṣiḥāfah al-'Arabīyah fī Filasṭīn, 1876–1948* (The Arabic Press in Palestine 1876–1949). Damascus: Maṭba'at al-Wafā', 1966.

al-'Ārif, 'Ārif. *Al-Nakbah* (The Calamity), Vol. III. Ṣaydā, Lebanon: al-Ṭab'ah al-'Aṣrīyah, 1956.

Bayhum, Muḥammad Jamīl. *Al-'Urūbah wa al-Shu'ūbīyah al-Ḥadīthah* (Pan-Arabism and Contemporary Populism). Beirut: Maṭābi' Dār al-Kashshāf, 1957.

Darwazah, Muḥammad. *Ḥawl al-Ḥarakah al-'Arabīyah al-Ḥadīthah* (About the Modern Arab Movement), Vol. III. Ṣaydā: al-Ṭab'ah al-'Aṣrīyah, 1951.

———. *Al-Qaḍīyah al-Filasṭīnīyah fī Muktalif Marāḥilihā* (The Palestinian Problem in its Various Phases). Beirut: al-Maktabah al-'Aṣrīyah, 1960.

Farrūkh, 'Umar. *Difā'an 'an al-Waṭan* (In Defense of the Homeland). Beirut: Maṭba'at al-Najmah, 1946.

Ibrāhīm, Muḥammad Sa'ad. *Ḥurrīyah al-Ṣiḥāfah* (Freedom of the Press). Cairo: Dār al-Kutub, 1999.

al-Khūrī, Bishārah Khalīl. *Ḥaqā'iq Lubnānīyah* (Lebanese Truths), Vol. III. Beirut: Awrāq Lubnānīyah, 1961.

Maṭar, Fu'ād. *Ayna Aṣbaṣa 'Abd al-Nāṣir fi Jumhūrīyah al-Sādāt: Rusīyah al-Nāṣirīyah wa Miṣr al-Miṣrīyah* (What Has become of *'Abd al-Nāṣir* in al-Sadāt's Republic: Naṣirite Russia and Egyptian Egypt), Vol. II. Beirut: Khayats, 1972.

Murūwah, Adīb. *Al-Ṣiḥāfah al-'Arabīyah* (The Arab Press). Beirut: Dār Maktabat al-*Ḥayyāh*, 1961.

Sa'ādah, Anṭūn. *Marāṭil Al-Mas'alah al-Filasṭīnīyah* (The Stages of the Palestine Problem). Beirut: Maṭba'at al-Jihād, 1957 (?).

al-Tal, ʿAbd Allāh. *Kārithat Filasṭīn* (The Catastrophe of Palestine). Cairo: Maṭbaʿat Miṣr, 1959.

Ṭarrāzī, Fīlib. *Tārīkh al-Ṣiḥafah al-ʿArabīyah* (History of the Arab Press). Beirut: al-Maṭbaʿat al-Adabīyah, 1948.

English

Abdallah of Jordan, King. *My Memoirs Completed*. Translated by Harold W. Glidden. Washington: American Council of Learned Societies, 1954.

Abdul Nasser, Gamal. *Egypt's Liberation, The Philosophy of the Revolution*. Washington: Public Affairs Press, 1955.

Abidi, Aqil Hyder Hasan. *Jordan: A Political Study*. London: Asia Publishing House, 1965.

Abouchdid, Eugenie Elie. *Thirty Years of Lebanon and Syria*. Bayūt: Sader-Rihani, 1948.

Al-Obeidi, Jabbar. *Censorship in the Middle East*. Lewiston: Edwin Mellon Press, 2007.

Antonious, George. *The Arab Awakening*. Philadelphia: J.B. Lippincott Company, 1939.

Ayalon, Ami. *The Press in the Arab Middle East*. New York: Oxford University Press, 1995.

———. *Reading Palestine: Printing and Literacy, 1900–1948*. Austin: University of Texas Press, 2004.

———. *The Arabic Print Revolution*. Cambridge: Cambridge University Press, 2016.

Bar-Zohar, Michael. *Ben-Gurion, the Armed Prophet*. Translated from the French by Len Ortzen. Edgewood Cliffs: Prentice-Hall, 1968.

Binder, Leonard, editor. *Politics in Lebanon*. New York: Wiley, 1966.

Eytan, Walter. *The First Ten Years, a Diplomatic History of Israel*. London: Weidenfeld and Nicolson, 1958.

Fisher, Carol, and Fred Krinsky. *Middle East in Crisis: A Historical Documentary Review*. Syracuse: Syracuse University Press, 1959.

Glubb, John. *A Soldier With the Arabs*. New York: Hodder and Stoughton, 1957.

Green, Stephen, *Taking Sides: America's Secret Relations with a Militant Israel*. New York: William Morrow and Co., 1984.

Gunter, Barrie, and Roger Dickinson. *News Media in the Arab World: A Study of 10 Arab and Muslim Countries*. New York: Bloomsbury Press, 2013.

Hirst, David. *The Gun and the Olive Branch*. London: Harcourt Brace Jovanovich, 1977.

Hudson, Michael C. *The Struggle for Palestine*. New York: W. W. Norton, 1950.

———. *The Precarious Republic*. New York: Random House, 1968.

Hurewitz, J.C. *Middle East Dilemmas*. New York: Harper and Brothers, 1953.

International Press Institute. *The News from the Middle East*. Zurich: International Press Institute, 1954.

Kimche, Jon, and David Kimche. *Both Sides of the Hill*. London: Secker and Warburg, 1960.

Kirk, George E. *The Middle East, 1945–1950*. London: Oxford University Press, 1954.

Kirkbride, Alec. *A Crackle of Thorns*. London: J. Murray, 1956.

Laqueur, Walter Z. *Communism and Nationalism in the Middle East*. New York: Fredrick A. Praeger, 1956.

———. *The Israel-Arab Reader*. New York: The Citadel Press, 1969.

Lenczowski, George. *The Middle East in World Affairs*. Ithaca: Cornell University Press, 1962.

Mandel, Neville. *The Arabs and Zionism Before World War I.* Berkeley: University of California Press, 1976.
Marlowe, John. *Anglo-Egyptian Relations, 1800–1953.* London: The Cresset Press, 1954.
McDonald, James G. *My Mission in Israel, 1948–1951.* London: Victor Gollancz, 1951.
McFadden, Tom J. *Daily Journalism in the Arab States.* Columbus: Ohio State University Press, 1953.
Mellor, Noha. *Modern Arab Journalism.* Edinburgh: Edinburgh University Press, 2007.
Merrill, John C., Carter R. Bryan, and Marvin Alisky. *The Foreign Press.* New Orleans: Louisiana State University Press, 1964.
Mosten, Trevor. *Censorship in Islamic Societies.* London: Saqi Books, 2002.
Pappe, Ilan. *The Ethnic Cleansing of Palestine.* Oxford: Oxford University Press, 2006.
Patai, Raphael. *Jordon, Lebanon, and Syria: An Annotated Bibliography.* New Haven: Hraf Press, 1957.
Polk, William R. *The United States and the Arab World.* Cambridge: Harvard University Press, 1969.
Qubain, Fahim I. *Crisis in Lebanon.* Washington: Middle East Institute, 1961.
Rodinson, Maxime. *Israel and the Arabs.* Middlesex: Penguin Books, 1968.
Rugh, William. *Arab Perceptions of American Foreign Policy During the October War.* Washington: Middle East Institute, 1976.
———. *The Arab Press.* Syracuse: Syracuse University Press, 1979 and 1987.
———. *Arab Mass Media: Newspapers, Radio and Television in Arab Politics.* Westport: Praeger, 2004.
al-Sadat, Anwar. *Revolt on the Nile.* Translated by Thomas Graham. London: Allan Wingate, 1957.
Seale, Patrick. *The Struggle for Syria, a Study of Post-War Arab Politics, 1945–1958.* London: Oxford University Press, 1965.
Shwadran, Banjamin. *Jordon, State of Tension.* New York: Middle Eastern Affairs Press, 1959.
Stevens, Georgiana G. *Jordan River Partition.* Palo Alto, California: Stanford University Press, 1967.
Talhami, Ghada. *Palestine in the Egyptian Press.* New York: Lexington Books, 2007.
Torrey, Gordon H. *Syrian Politics and the Military, 1945–1958.* Columbus: Ohio State University, 1964.
Wint, Guy. *Middle East Crisis.* London: Penguin Books, 1957.
Wright, Robin. *Sacred Rage.* New York: Touchstone Press, 2001.
Yost, Charles. *The Conduct and Misconduct of Foreign Affairs.* New York: Randon House, 1972.
Ziadeh, Nicola A. *Syria and Lebanon.* London: Ernest Benn Limited, 1957.
Zurayk, Constantine K. *The Meaning of the Disaster.* Translated from the Arabic by R. Bayley Winder. Beirut: Khayats, 1956.

French

Gemayel, Pierre. *Connaissance des Kataeb.* Beirut: Kataeb Party, Studies Department, 1948.
Majzoub, Mohamed. *Le Liban et L'Orient Arabe.* Aix-en-Provence: La Pensée Universitaire, 1956.

II. Articles and Pamphlets

Arabic

Murūwah, 'Adīb. "Dawr Lubnān al-Ṣiḥāfī fī al-Majāl al-'Arabī" ("The Journalistic Role of Lebanon in the Arab Sphere"). *al-Thaqāfah al-'Arabīyah* (*Arab Culture*) V (January 1962): 10–15.

English

Abdel Gawad, Mohamed. "Attempts of the Arab World to Participate in Balancing the Flow of Information." In *The Third World and Press Freedom,* edited by Philip C. Horton. New York: Praeger Publishers, 1978.

Alan, Ray. "Lebanon: Israel's Friendliest Neighbor." *Commentary* XIII (June 1952): 551–559.

Anonymous. "S.O.S The Lebanon, The 'Christian National Home of the Near East.'" (Early 1945). Distributed in the streets of Beirut.

Ben-Hanania, J. "The Arab Press in Palestine." *Palestine Affairs* III, no. 2 (February 1948): 19–20.

Benyacov, Itzhak. "The Egyptian Press Today." *Middle Eastern Affairs* I, no. 1 (January 1950): 13–17.

Berger, Miriam. "Palestine's Occupied Fourth Estate: An Inside Look at the Work Lives of Palestinian Print Journalists." *Arab Media and Society*, no. 17 (Winter 2013).

Cattan, Henry. "Plunder in the Holy Land." *Al-Kulliyah* XXX, no. 2 (February 1955): 10–12.

Childers, Erskine. "The Other Exodus." *The Spectator* CCVI, no. 6933 (May 12, 1961): 672–75.

Cioeta, Donald J. "Ottoman Censorship in Lebanon and Syria, 1876-1909," *International Journal of Middle East Studies*, no. 10 (1979).

Cohen, Yeruham. "The Secret Negev Talks, Full Story of Allon's Conversations with Colonel Nasser." *Jewish Observer and Middle East Review* (February 13, 1953): 6–8.

Dajani, Nabil. "The Myth of Media Freedom in Lebanon." *Arab Media and Society*, no. 18 (Summer 2013).

Dulles, John Foster. "Report on the Near and Middle East by Secretary of State John Foster Dulles." *Department of State Bulletin*, no. 28 (June 15, 1953): 831–35.

Ebon, Martin. "Communist Tactics in Palestine." *The Middle East Journal* II, no. 3 (July 1948): 255–69.

Freedman, Robert O. "Soviet Policy toward Sadat's Egypt from the Death of Nasser to the Fall of General Sadek." *Naval War College Review* 26, no. 3 (1973): 63–79.

Hottinger, Arnold. "Zu'amā' and Parties in the Lebanese Crisis of 1958." *Middle East Journal* XV (Spring 1961): 127–40.

Khuri, Zahi N. "The Lebanese Press." *Middle East Forum* XXXVIII (February 1962): 11–15.

Kitchen, Helen A. "*al-Ahram* - The Times of the Arab World." *Middle East Journal* IV, no. 2 (April 1950): 155–69.

Lewis, Bernard. "Is Peace Still Possible in the Middle East?" *Commentary* 66, no. 1 (July 1978): 37–45.

Martin, Robert. "The Arab Press." *Nieman Reports* III, no. 2 (April 1949): 6–7.

Musallam, Adnan. "Arab Press, Society and Politics at the End of the Ottoman Era," 2013. http://bethlehem-holy-land.net/Adnan/publications/EndofTheOttomanEra.htm.

———. "Turbulent Times in the Life of the Palestinian Arab Press: The British Era, 1917–1948", 2013. http://bethlehem-holy-land.net/Adnan/publications/Turbulent_Times.htm.

Nolte, Richard H., and William R. Polk. "Toward a Policy for the Middle East." *Foreign Affairs* XXXVI, no. 4 (July 1958): 646–58.

Perlmann, M. "The Egyptian Press." *Middle Eastern Affairs* I, no. 1 (January 1950): 11–13.

Shoufani, Elias. "The October War and the Israeli Press." In *Middle East Crucible: Studies on the Arab-Israeli War of October 1973*, edited by Naseer H. Arurui. Wilmette, IL: AAUG Press, 1975.

Smith, Henry Ladd. "The Egyptian Press and Its Current Problems." *Journalism Quarterly* XXXI (Summer 1954): 331–36.

Stevens, Georgiana G. "Arab Refugees: 1948–1952." *Middle East Journal* VI, no. 3 (Summer 1952): 281–98.

Torrey, Gordon. "The Role of the Military in Society and Government in Syria and the formation of the U.A.R." In *The Military in the Middle East*, edited by S.N. Fisher. Columbus: Ohio State University Press, 1963.

Van Alstyne, Richard W. "Whither Palestine?" *Current History* XIV, no. 78 (February 1948): 76–83.

Weigert, Gideon. "Arab Writers Look at Israel." *The World Today* XV, no. 12 (December 1959): 501–08.

Williams, Francis. "The Press in Israel." *New Statesman* LVI, no. 1426 (July 12, 1958): 36–37.

Yaari, Samuel. "The Lebanese Press." *Palestine Affairs* II, no. 11 (November 1947): 114–16.

———. "The Syrian Press." *Palestine Affairs* III, no. 6 (June 1948): 73–74.

French

"Note sur la Presse du Proche-Orient en 1946". *Cahiers de L'Orient Contemporain*, no. 4 (1946): 809–17.

Newspapers

Arabic

Al-Ahrām (The Pyramids). Cairo.
Al-Aḥrār (The Liberal). Beirut.
Al-Akhbār (The News). Cairo.
Al-Akhbār (The News). Damascus.
Ākhir Sā'ah (The Last Hour). Cairo.
Alif Bā' (A. B.). Damascus.
Al-'Amal (In the Service [of Lebanon]). Beirut.
Al-Anbā' (The News). Beirut.
Al-Anbā' (The News). Damascus.
Al-Anwār (Lights). Beirut.
Al-Ayyām (The Days). Damascus.
Al-Ba'th (The Renaissance). Damascus.
Al-Balad (The Country). Damascus.
Al-Balāgh (The Report). Cairo.
Baradā (The Baradā River). Damascus.
Al-Bayraq (The Gleam). Beirut.
Bayrūt (Beirut). Beirut.
Bayrūt Al-Masā' (The Evening Beirut). Beirut.
Al-Bilād (The Country). Latakia.
Al-Binā' (The Structure). Damascus.
Al-Difā' (Defense). Yāfā and Jerusalem.
Al-Diyār (The Country). Beirut.
Al-Dustūr (The Constitution). Amman.
Al-Fayḥā' (Fragrant, Vast, Green – epithet of Damascus). Damascus.
Filasṭīn (Palestine). Jaffa and Jerusalem.
Al-Hadaf (The Goal). Beirut.
Al-Haḍārah (Civilization). Damascus.
Al-Ḥayāt (Life). Beirut.
Al-Inshā' (The Construction). Damascus.
Al-Iṣlāḥ (The Restoration). Aleppo.
Al-Jabal (The Mountain). Al-Suwaydā', Jabal al-Durūz.
Al-Jarīdah (The Newspaper). Beirut.

Al-Jīl Al-Jadīd (The New Era). Damascus.
Al-Jumhūrīyah (The Republic). Cairo.
Al-Kifāḥ (The Struggle). Damascus.
Al-Manār (The Lighthouse). Damascus.
Al-Masā' (Evening). Cairo.
Al-Miṣrī (The Egyptian). Cairo.
Al-Nahār (Daytime). Beirut.
Al-Nās (The People). Damascus.
Al-Nidā' (The Appeal). Beirut.
Al-Niḍāl (The Struggle). Damascus.
Al-Qabas (The Flash). Damascus.
Al-Qāhirah (Cairo). Cairo.
Al-Rā'y (The Opinion). Amman.
Al-Rā'y Al-ʿĀmm (Public Opinion). Damascus.
Ṣadā Lubnān (The Echo of Lebanon). Beirut.
Ṣawt Al-Ummah (The Voice of the Nation). Cairo.
Al-Shaʿb (The People). Cairo.
Al-Shaʿb (The People). Damascus.
Al-Shabāb (The Young Men). Aleppo.
Al-Shām (Damascus). Damascus.
Al-Sharq (The East). Beirut.
Al-Shirāʿ (The Sail). Beirut.
Al-Siyāsah (Politics). Beirut.
Al-Siyāsah (Politics). Cairo.
Al-Thawrah (The Revolution). Damascus.
Al-Tilighrāf (The Telegraph). Beirut.
Al-Yawn (Today). Damascus.
Al-Zamān (The Times). Beirut.
Al-Zamān (The Times). Cairo.
Al-Zamān (The Times). Damascus.

English

Daily Star. Beirut.
IKE. Beirut.

French

Le Jour. Beirut.
L'Orient. Beirut.
L'Orient/Le Jour. Beirut. Joined together in 1970.
Le Réveil. Beirut.

Index

Numbers in bold refer to pages of particular importance.